PRIVATE BANKING IN EUROPE

Private Banking in Europe

Rise, Retreat, and Resurgence

YOUSSEF CASSIS AND
PHILIP L. COTTRELL

OXFORD
UNIVERSITY PRESS

OXFORD
UNIVERSITY PRESS

Great Clarendon Street, Oxford, OX2 6DP,
United Kingdom

Oxford University Press is a department of the University of Oxford.
It furthers the University's objective of excellence in research, scholarship,
and education by publishing worldwide. Oxford is a registered trade mark of
Oxford University Press in the UK and in certain other countries

First Edition published in 2015

Published in the United States of America by Oxford University Press
198 Madison Avenue, New York, NY 10016, United States of America

British Library Cataloguing in Publication Data
Data available

Library of Congress Control Number: 2015930099

ISBN 978–0–19–873575–5

This book has been published with the support of the "European Association for Banking and Financial History (EABH)".

Preface

This book has had a long and ultimately sad history. Philip Cottrell and myself had agreed with the EABH (European Association for Banking and Financial History) to write a commissioned history of private banking from the early modern period to the present. The project was exciting in view of the apparently inexhaustible capacity of private bankers to rise from the ashes and reinvent themselves. With the triumph of finance and the assertion of a new financial elite at the turn of the twenty-first century, this was an ideal moment to step back and take a long-term view of these transformations. We were further motivated by the fact that the topic had never been dealt with, as such, in the financial history literature. Our project was to write a creative synthesis, relying on our combined research experience as banking and financial historians, complemented by the secondary literature.

The journey has been longer and more tortuous than originally planned, because of the vastness of the subject, and because of Phil Cottrell's ill health. Phil passed away before he could edit all the chapters he had drafted. He gave me all his notes a few months before his death. Working on this material was at once very rewarding intellectually—because of Phil's immense knowledge and acute understanding of banking history—and very painful emotionally—because of being so vividly reminded of the loss of a dear friend. I have done my best to complete the book we had originally planned and I am responsible for any errors that it may contain.

It has only been possible to write such a book because of the innumerable debts we have contracted over the years towards our many fellow financial historians. It would be impossible to name them all, but they will hopefully all recognize that they have not been forgotten. We would like to thank the EABH heartily for giving us the opportunity to write this book.

My last thoughts and words go to Philip Cottrell. It has been a privilege to work so closely with him. This book is published in honour and in the memory of one of the finest banking historians of his generation.

Youssef Cassis

July 2014

Contents

Introduction 1

1. Instruments, Institutions, Centres, and Networks: Developing the Structural Framework, *c.*1300–1700 7
2. Public and Private Markets for Capital and Credit, 1688–1793 39
3. War and Economic Transformation, 1793–1815 79
4. Golden Age, 1815–1870 113
5. The Onset of the Corporate Economy, 1870–1914 165
6. Indian Summer, 1914–1931 217
7. Decline and Renaissance, 1931–2015 247

Conclusion 285

Index 289

Introduction

What is a private banker? Behind the cachet, the glamour, and the discreet charm of the *haute bourgeoisie*, there has been much confusion in recent years about the function of private banking and those who undertake it.

The traditional definition of a private banker—and the one used in this book—is a banker who owns and manages his (or more rarely her) own bank—a private bank. As a rule, private banks have been family firms and included several partners—usually though not invariably members of the family circle. Their legal form has generally been that of a partnership and general partnership, with partners bearing unlimited liability. However, limited partnerships and even joint-stock companies, whose directors have remained major shareholders, can be considered private banks—in the sense of being owned and managed by the same people. This legal approach clearly distinguishes the private bank from the joint-stock bank and the public bank. It is an important differentiation to make since in current, early twenty-first-century usage 'private bank' is sometimes confusingly taken to mean all other banks apart from a nation's central bank, as well as state-owned banks. Although the term 'private bank' only became current in English from the late seventeenth century, there were private bankers and 'proto-private bankers' at work centuries before.

Private bankers' activities—in other words private banking—have been, for most of their history, very varied. Private banks could be merchant banks (they all started as an adjunct to mercantile activities); they could be commercial banks, taking deposits and granting loans; they could be investment banks; and they could be universal banks—a combination of all these activities. Private bankers have tended to deal with a fairly wealthy and exclusive clientele, mainly in the major capital cities, less so in the provinces, and some have, from an early stage, specialized in wealth management. However, it is only in the last two decades of the twentieth century that 'private banking' has come to designate a specific banking activity: wealth management on behalf of high net worth individuals. This is another important difference in current terminology. Throughout this study, we will use the term 'private banking' in the traditional sense of the word and specifically refer to wealth management when using the more recent definition.

This book analyses the experiences of European private bankers from the early modern period to the early twenty-first century. It examines, first, the slow emergence of specialist private bankers, largely from amongst those who provided commercial credit. This initial consideration culminates in a focus upon the roles that they variously played both during the onset of the continent's industrialization, and in orchestrating the finances of the emerging world economy. Its second theme is private banking's waning importance with the rise of joint-stock competitors, which became increasingly apparent in Britain during the mid-nineteenth century, and elsewhere within Europe some decades later. Lastly, attention is paid to the decline of private bankers in the twentieth century—a protracted and uneven decline, combined with the persistence and even the enduring success of some segments of the profession. It concludes with the revival of private banking in the late twentieth century as a response to the development of a new market—the management of personal wealth.

Studying private bankers in Europe over seven centuries is another way of looking at banking history. The very *longue durée* raises the question of continuity and change in the profession—in terms of both business activity and business organization. Private bankers in early modern Europe were engaged in the provision of commercial credit and foreign exchange, and they continued to do so well into the twentieth century. This close relationship between trade and finance has clearly been one of the long-term, if not permanent characteristics of private banking. The same can be said, for the most prominent amongst them, about lending to the state, which also remained one of their prerogatives for several centuries.

At the same time, the business of banking has changed considerably over the centuries. The bills of exchange introduced in Genoa in the thirteenth century were improved in Antwerp in the fifteenth century, in Amsterdam in the sixteenth and seventeenth centuries, and in London in the nineteenth century. The modalities of state borrowing also improved dramatically—to the benefit of both lenders and borrowers. In this respect, and despite an impressive long-term continuity, the history of private banking is also that of permanent adaptation to changing market conditions, and of incremental and sometimes radical innovations.

This can be seen in the role played by private bankers in the emergence and development of banking as an independent profession, no longer subservient to another one—whether commerce, law, or state finances. This was a slow process. In the eighteenth century, private bankers were also merchants in Amsterdam, state financiers or notaries in France, court bankers in Germany. A separate profession of *private banker* first emerged in the course of the eighteenth century, though it took a different route in Britain and Continental

Europe. The process was most original in Britain, where private bankers specialized in issuing notes and discounting bills of exchange—the credit side of the profession. In Amsterdam, and to a lesser extent in Frankfurt, private bankers remained closer to their mercantile origins, specializing in financing trade and issuing foreign loans. Likewise, private bankers reshaped the banking landscape in the nineteenth century through their decisive contribution to the emergence of joint-stock banks—before being devoured by these new giants.

Concentrating on private bankers inevitably leads to paying some attention to individual banks, because of the power and prestige of the greatest houses—from the Medici to the Rothschilds—and because of the prominent position of private bankers in the economy and in society—another long-term characteristic of this business group. In all periods, private bankers have been able to make a great deal of money, because of the opportunities offered by financial activities, but also because of the rewards deriving from risking one's own capital. While the latter was a common feature of the banking profession before the growth of joint-stock banks, it became the major distinction between private bankers and joint-stock banks' executives in the modern era, with implications for the conduct of business. This takes us back to the role of private bankers as innovators and indeed as entrepreneurs.

This also raises the question of private banks as family firms, with their specific characteristics, not least in terms of networks: family networks, but also religious networks, often superimposed on family ones, especially those formed by the Protestant and Jewish minorities, as well as social networks. Interestingly, family-owned banks have not been able to prosper in all fields of the banking industry. While some small to medium-sized firms remained global players in investment banking and international finance well into the twentieth century, none managed to do so in commercial and especially retail banking, a field dominated from the start by giant managerial companies.

The continuity of private banks is particularly striking from a legal point of view. Partnerships as a form of business organization did not change radically over the centuries and private banks remained family firms. What changed was the environment within which private banks operated. Put another way, until the nineteenth century, the world of private banking coincided almost entirely with the world of banking. From the mid-nineteenth century, with the rise of the big banks, private banking became an ever decreasing part of the banking world. Family partnerships were the norm in the former period, the exception in the latter. Private bankers' economic significance thus changed in the course of the nineteenth century, as did the challenges with which they were confronted, in terms of competition, adaptation, and survival. This explains the, at times, different approach adopted in the book, with a greater emphasis on *banking* for the early modern period, and on *banks* for the modern one.

While some emphasis is placed throughout the book on the elite amongst European private bankers—those who became substantially involved in high finance—the study is concerned with the gamut of private banking. Consequently, attention is also paid to, for example, English country bankers and French provincial bankers, including *escompteurs*. The overall aim is to provide a balanced discussion and analysis of the history of private banking's wide constituency by studying developments in the major financial centres alongside those beyond the principal cities and towns. This broad purview is particularly important for comprehending the importance of private banking during the inception of Europe's economic modernization.

The book is divided into seven chapters, organized in chronological order. In Chapter one, the modern origins of private banking are considered by examining the sequential financial development of increasingly formalized marts at which the primary products of northern Europe were traded for Mediterranean manufactures and luxuries. The timeframe of the chapter is set by, on one hand, the rise of Italian banking in the late thirteenth and early fourteenth century, and, on the other, Amsterdam's decline as a commercial centre during the early eighteenth century. This is a period when private banks, with some notable exceptions, had not yet gained a distinct identity. The focus is thus on Venice and Florence, Bruges, Antwerp, and Amsterdam—each being, in turn, the continent's leading mercantile and financial centre for a discrete period—and the networks of which they were the central nodes. Greater attention is paid to private banking, and indeed banking *tout court*, than to private banks: in other words, to the evolution of the instruments of mercantile credit, in particular the bill of exchange, and the emergence during the seventeenth century of a fully-fledged, formalized capital market at Amsterdam.

Chapter two considers the greater formalization, and concurrent growth, of private banking, aided by the establishment of the first quasi-central banks, such as the Bank of England, and the development of capital markets with completer articulation. Its timeframe is set by the so-called English financial revolution on the one hand, and, on the other, the end of Amsterdam as a major international capital market, brought out by the invasion of French revolutionary forces. Formalized private banking developed in depth and width first within the British Isles, initially in London during the late seventeenth century, and thereafter within the provinces. This major financial advance, which had a multifaceted relationship with the onset of industrialization, is contrasted with the roles played by lawyer-bankers and financiers during the last century of the *Ancien Régime* in France, and those of court bankers in the German states.

More than twenty years of almost continuous warfare had a very substantial impact, affecting bankers and financiers throughout Europe. The third chapter analyses its wide-ranging effects: by examining the consequences for the continent's most important mercantile and financial centres, which were negative for Amsterdam, Hamburg, and Frankfurt, but accelerated London's rise to a dominant position; by reviewing how the war with revolutionary and Napoleonic France was financed; and by assessing the effect of long-lasting wartime inflation upon private banking, particularly in England and France.

The period from 1815 to 1870 was the private bankers' golden age and is discussed in Chapter four. Banking activities expanded while competition from the nascent joint stock banks was very limited. The leading houses, above all Rothschild and Baring, established themselves, starting with the financial requirements of the peace settlement negotiated in Vienna and the precocious wave of lending to new South American republics. The houses that raised loans for European states and Latin America, primarily in London, also played a part, along with other private bankers, in providing the liquidity that enabled international trade to recover. The mid-nineteenth century was a period of accelerating economic growth throughout Europe and attention is paid to the contrasting experiences of private banking in the Rhineland, France, and England, on one hand, and to the role played by London merchant banks and the Parisian *haute banque* in international finance on the other. It was during this 'golden age' that the 'financial revolution' of the mid-nineteenth century took place, with the expansion of metropolitan-based, branching joint stock banks in England and the creation of the Crédit Mobilier in France, though its effects would not really be felt for another twenty years.

From 1870 onwards, private bankers were confronted with the rise of increasingly large and powerful joint stock banks, in a fast expanding and internationally open economy. How successful were they in facing these challenges and did they still represent a significant component of the world of banking on the eve of the First World War? Answers to these questions are provided in Chapter five. Private banking remained a key component of the banking world at three levels. The first is the world of the *haute banque*, above all the London merchant banks; the second is the less glamorous world of the local and regional private banks, which continued to provide essential banking and financial services to many areas of continental Europe; and the third level is the enduring persistence of private bankers who were often able to retain a commanding position in the financial world, especially in international finance, where the game continued to be played according to the unwritten rules and code of conduct of the banking aristocracy.

Chapter six suggests that the First World War did not mark a turning point in the history of private bankers. Private banks were unevenly affected by wartime conditions, some suffered heavy losses while a few made handsome profits. In all countries, private bankers continued to enjoy a competitive edge in international finance. The economic and financial problems inherited from the war and early post-war years (inflation, suspension and restoration of the gold standard, Reparations, Allied Debts) ultimately required political decisions, but were often of a high degree of technical complexity. For the last time, private bankers were in a position to play a central role in international affairs, as advisers to the government, as ambassadors, or as actors on the capital markets. This unique role was to end with the definitive collapse of the Gold Standard and the old international monetary order in September 1931.

The book's final chapter considers the accelerated decline of private banks from the 1930s on. Private country banks, which had retained some significance in France and Germany, were (nearly) wiped out by the Great Depression. In their case, there was to be no revival in the post-war years. The *haute banque*, on the other hand, managed to survive the banking crises, the slump and the war years—except in Germany, where the leading Jewish private banking houses were eliminated by the anti-Semitic policy of the Nazi regime. The London merchant banks enjoyed a remarkable revival in the 1960s—thanks to the emergence of the Euromarkets and their specialization in corporate finance. However, as they regained power and influence, most of them converted into public companies. Paradoxically, private banking enjoyed a revival at the very time when the last surviving private banks in London and Paris were disappearing. The renewal of private banking from the 1980s has primarily been the remarkable growth of a banking activity (wealth management), which has come to be known as *private banking*. Today's 'private' banks mostly consist of subsidiaries of the world's largest banks—private banking has become divorced from the old-established private banks.

1

Instruments, Institutions, Centres, and Networks

Developing the Structural Framework, c.1300–1700

Economists consider that banks discharge two essential functions: supplying money, and intermediating between savers and borrowers. With the major exception of British developments from the mid-seventeenth century, European private banks seldom undertook the direct circulation of banknotes. Substantially, that prerogative remained with the state, which was always jealous of independent money powers. It was only passed *in extremis* to private interests from whom the state obtained financial resources. Such occasions were usually to support warfare, while their suppliers, in turn, received corporate privileges, sometimes including the right to issue banknotes. As a result, European private bankers were primarily financial intermediaries, taking deposits on the one hand and, on the other, lending such funds (together with their own capital), and thereby creating 'bank money'. Banking in these terms during the late seventeenth century in either Amsterdam or London was essentially little different to that undertaken by a twelfth-century Genoese, who might have described himself as a *bancherius*.

THE EMERGENCE OF PRIVATE BANKING IN LATE MEDIEVAL AND EARLY MODERN EUROPE

From the late twelfth century, some payments within Genoa and its immediate region were made by transfers between bank accounts and not only amongst those held by one banker but also between accounts at different banks.[1]

[1] R. de Roover, 'New Interpretations of the History of Banking', *Journal of World History*, 2 (1954).

However, this was an exceptional, precocious development. In other major commercial centres, such as Barcelona, Bruges, Lerida, Valencia, or Venice, payments through inter-account movements were not to have any significance until the late thirteenth century or the early fourteenth century.[2] Nonetheless, the banking habit, indicated by the holding of an account, was spreading over the course of the fourteenth century to the cities and towns of north-western Europe and to Constantinople.[3] The consequent growing importance of bank deposits led to a differentiation in their nature—between what would later be called current and term accounts. Furthermore, such deposits were increasingly mobilized through bankers pursuing fractional reserve policies, which meant that 'bank money' had come into existence. The employment of deposits by bankers for lending resulted in the expansion of the money supply, as in Venice by the first quarter of the fourteenth century.[4] Similarly, the writing of what would now be called 'cheques' grew from the mid-fourteenth century, first to substantiate oral instructions given by account holders to their bankers and then as transfer documents in their own right. Such a basic instrument of deposit banking was developed in Barcelona, Florence, Genoa, and Pisa but its use in Venice was resisted by that city's bankers.[5]

However, it would be wrong to take a late twentieth-century perspective and place too much emphasis on bank accounts and cheques. A twelfth-century Genoese banker was primarily a merchant who, along with accepting deposits and making loans, had considerably greater business interests. These comprised investments in trade and dealings in goods, especially textiles. Indeed, banking generally remained for centuries a secondary and informal activity and, consequently, the businesses of the 'pure' exchange bankers of thirteenth-century Asti, Piacenza, and Siena were very much the exceptions rather than the rule.[6] Furthermore, holding a bank account was unusual during the Middle Ages, the Renaissance, and for centuries thereafter. For instance, by the early sixteenth century, Venice had become the forcing house for the development of banking practices. Yet, even here, only at most 10 per cent of the city's residents had bank accounts and they came predominantly from the nobility.[7] Nonetheless, the rise

[2] A. P. Usher, *The Early History of Deposit Banking in Mediterranean Europe*, 1 (Cambridge, Mass., 1934), pp. 239, 256–7; and R. de Roover, *Money, Banking and Credit in Medieval Bruges* (Cambridge, Mass., 1948), pp. 171 ff.

[3] R. de Roover, *L'évolution de lettre de change (XIVe–XVIIIe siècles)* (Paris, 1953), pp. 24 ff.

[4] R. C. Mueller, 'The Role of Bank Money in Venice 1300–1500', *Studi Veneziani*, new ser. 3 (1979).

[5] M. Spallanzani, 'A Note on Florentine Banking in the Renaissance, Orders of Payment and Cheques', *Journal of European Economic History*, 7 (1978).

[6] For a survey, see D. Abulafia, 'The Impact of Italian Banking in the late Middle Ages and the Renaissance, 1300–1500', in A. Teichova, G. Kurgan-van Hentenryk, and D. Ziegler (eds), *Banking,Trade and Industry* (Cambridge, 1997).

[7] F. C. Lane, 'Venetian Bankers 1496–1533', *Journal of Political Economy*, 45 (1937).

of formal banking during the Middle Ages was sufficient to cause its regulation by the authorities. Venice introduced minimum capitalization requirements for exchange bankers in 1270, whereas other protective provisions for account holders were put in place in Barcelona in 1300 and 1321.[8]

Much, if not most, private banking during the late Middle Ages and the Early Modern Period was concerned with exchanging different moneys and establishing exchange rates. This grew directly out of proto-bankers' substantial merchanting interests coupled with the widening development of international trade from the thirteenth century, and the consequent difficulties posed by varieties of coin, their fineness, and physical condition. Except in a few major commercial cities, coin constituted *the* form of monetary exchange, as it was to do throughout most of western Europe until the late nineteenth century, if not the early twentieth century. The wider international transfer of coins over the Middle Ages led to an alteration in the nature of exchange banking. Transactions, comprising taking travellers' silver bars or pouches of gold dust for local coinage, were increasingly replaced by bankers establishing exchange rates between currencies. By the beginning of the thirteenth century, with coins replacing bullion to a significant extent as an international medium of exchange, bankers came to set local rates of exchange directly between different coinages. This development first became marked in towns and cities within southern and western France, the central Rhineland, and Tuscany.[9]

Banking development in Europe has been the result of an ever-accumulating inheritance of innovations, passed from one generation to another—with the emergence of instruments and institutions, and the further rise of commercial and financial centres linked by both personal and impersonal networks. Like the diffusion of industrial techniques, there was a spatial transfer, beginning in the twelfth century, of evolving banking and financial practices. Nonetheless, this was neither a linear, nor an ever-widening, evolving process. Rather, dissemination and further innovation took place through a series of 'jumps' and 'leaps'. These were sometimes the consequences of positive responses to new opportunities; in other instances, they arose from turmoil and dislocation, especially that produced by the Reformation and Counter-Reformation. European private banking was always cosmopolitan, especially at an international level. However, waves of forced intra-continental migration arising from religious schism and persecution, which began in 1492, and were generated again in the 1520s and 1530s, during the 1580s, and, once more, a century later, all played substantial parts in giving European private banking its enduring character.

Banking and financial innovations largely arose as positive reactions to the expansion of economic activity, especially the growth of trade during the

[8] Mueller, 'Bank Money in Venice'; and Usher, *Deposit Banking*, p. 73.

[9] P. Spufford, *Handbook of Medieval Exchange* (London, 1986), pp. xix–xx; and see also Spufford, *Money and its Use in Medieval Europe* (Cambridge, 1986).

thirteenth century, and, again, during the sixteenth century. However, they were also devised to meet the financial needs of sovereigns and states, especially those arising from waging war. The bank account, cheque, and bill of exchange had their origins in northern Italy from where their use spread. Later, the transmission of practices and techniques involved transfers from the southern Netherlands, especially sixteenth-century Antwerp, to Amsterdam and Hamburg. Similarly, the progenitors of the major public banks, beginning with the Amsterdam Wisselbank of 1609, were the systems of inter-bank transfers—giro—that developed from the twelfth century in northern Italy. Subsequent dissemination operated at a number of levels and, during the sixteenth century, took place through personal transmission, carried by Lutheran, Calvinist, and Jewish refugees from Antwerp, France, Portugal, and Spain. The mobilization of the bill as a powerful credit instrument first became fully established in sixteenth-century Antwerp but was to play its most important role in the transformation of the English economy some two centuries later. Likewise, the necessary techniques for the secure establishment of public borrowing in England—the 'financial revolution' of the late seventeenth and early eighteenth centuries—were first developed during the fourteenth-century in the cities and towns of the Netherlands.[10]

Practitioners of banking in particular financial centres were linked by continent-wide networks, first constituted by the trading connections of merchants and merchant bankers. From the sixteenth century, these structures became increasingly global through the Old World's growing engagement with the New and the development of oceanic trade routes to the Orient. In all this, the most remarkable changes in the 'system' were not so much those connected with Mediterranean Europe's relative economic decline but with the rapid and near total ascendancy of Amsterdam and the Dutch Republic over Europe's increasingly world connections from the late sixteenth century.[11] One consequence was that multi-centred financial networks that spanned Europe during the Middle Ages and the Renaissance became progressively replaced by single financial centres wielding hegemonies. Amsterdam developed as the financial centre of Europe from the early seventeenth century, but its paramount position was ultimately taken by London, a changing global order that had clearly got underway by 1730. However, within London's rise to be the prime financial centre, the early emergence of domestic deposit banking was the result almost solely of local developments. This involved innovative financial reactions to the growth of remittances between the English

[10] See A. Carter, 'Comment' to H. C. Johansen, 'Contribution to the Discussion about the Structure of the Public Banks', and H. van der Wee, 'Anvers et les innovations techno-financières des XVIe et XVIIe siècles', both in *Troisième conférence internationale d'histoire économique, Munich 1965*, 5, Deuxième groupe, 'La structure de la banque'.

[11] J. I. Israel, *Dutch Primacy in World Trade, 1585–1740* (Oxford, 1989), pp. 1–6.

countryside and metropolis as well as the transformation of the goldsmith's craft. The city economies of Antwerp and Amsterdam had had close, supportive connections with their immediate hinterlands, but they were nonetheless primarily international centres of commerce and finance.

The rise of formal market structures and the development of new techniques assisted banking's maturation as a profession. However, as private bankers have continually restated, the essence of their services was to be found in the confidential relationships maintained with their clienteles. Similarly, while commercial and financial markets came to be more integrated as a result of improved communications, private bankers continued to rely heavily on their personal networks, constituted by filial and business connections, and those arising from a shared faith or belief. Moreover, confidentiality and personal relations were to be as important in private banking during the mid-twentieth century as they had been in the late thirteenth century.

ITALIAN PRIVATE BANKERS

As its very name implies, modern banking had its origins in medieval Italy. Italian bankers, both local and those whose businesses had a wider range, established not only the necessary book-keeping methods but also evolved the bill of exchange, the basis of merchant banking.[12] This mercantile/banking instrument emerged during the thirteenth century in Genoa,[13] being particularly used for transactions arising from the Champagne fairs, then Europe's principal bullion and money market. By the early fourteenth century, the bill had become the normal commercial transfer instrument for payments between a substantial number of cities and major towns. However, these bill-using centres remained largely clustered within northern Italy, especially Tuscany and Mediterranean Europe. Elsewhere, in western Europe, bills could only be regularly obtained in Bruges, London, and Paris, and at the fairs of Champagne. Beyond commerce and finance, the creation of bills was related to the business and administration of the Roman Catholic Church. They could be obtained at the Pope's current residence and were also employed by travelling bishops and papal collectors. The latter were primarily drawn from the major banking houses of Asti, Florence, and Siena (such as the Medici).[14]

[12] See de Roover, *L'évolution de la lettre de change*.

[13] See C. Marsilio, 'Genoese Finance, 1348—1700', in G. Caprio (ed.), *Handbook of Key Global Financial Markets, Institutions, and Infrastructure* (London, 2013), vol. 1, pp. 123–32.

[14] See R. de Roover, *The Rise and Decline of the Medici Bank, 1397–1494* (Cambridge, Mass., 1963).

The bill also became an international transfer instrument with growing attributes. The extant record of evidence for the employment of bills—to make funds available at another distant place and obviate the risky carriage of bullion—begins in 1161.[15] By 1300, it could involve a transaction embracing three commercial centres, such as the Champagne fairs, Florence, and Naples. The market negotiation of bills, undertaken by exchange brokers, followed from Florentine bankers' establishment of branches at Bruges during the early fourteenth century. This further continental expansion of their business interests resulted in Bruges becoming the money market for north-western Europe.[16] Exchange brokers, who brought buyers and sellers of bills together, had possibly first emerged as financial specialists in early fourteenth-century Pisa. At Bruges, such intermediaries and other members of the city's international merchant banking community met regularly at what came to be called the Place de la Bourse. This was probably the loggia of the Florentine consul's house, with the name of its financial market stemming from that of the Beurze family. Here, rates of exchange for bills were regularly established and noted in a written form for clients to consult. Comparable, increasingly impersonal, markets were also developed in Barcelona, London, and Paris at similar precise locations, such as Lombard Street. This ever more formalized international exchange banking went hand-in-hand with local banking. Bills were acquired by payment from a bank account and their recipients would pay bills into their own accounts, as in Barcelona, Bruges, Genoa, and Venice.[17] Nonetheless, net balances between commercial and financial centres continued to be met in gold and silver, the intra-continental transfers of which grew in volume, and these forms of final settlement became ever more important with the development of the sea-borne trade to the Orient.

Furthermore, Italian bankers and merchants systemized the collection of information. Beginning in the twelfth century, data were collected about depositors, borrowers, and the general business climate. Indeed, 'news on the mart', such as events that could affect the movement of prices and exchange rates, were regularly compiled and disseminated by those involved in commerce and banking. The consequences of such innovative developments were very evident some 200 years later in the *listini dei prezzi* drawn up by Italian merchants' agents throughout continental Europe and its economic extensions, as in Damascus and London. Price data were standardized in forms regularly used in the Italian city states and the market-price

[15] E. Ashtor, 'Banking Instruments between the Muslim East and the Christian West', *Journal of European Economic History*, 1 (1972).

[16] J. Schneider, 'The Significance of Large Fairs, Money Markets and Precious Metals in the Evolution of a World Market from the Middle Ages to the First Half of the Nineteenth Century', in W. Fischer, R. M. McInnis, and J. Schneider (eds), *The Emergence of a World Economy*, Part 1, *1500–1850* (Wiesbaden, 1986), pp. 16–17. See also de Roover, *Medieval Bruges*.

[17] Spufford, *Handbook*, pp. xxx–xxvii, xlvi–xlvii.

listings were, in turn, the forebears of the printed price currents of the Early Modern Period.[18]

Printed information allowed a considerably wider dissemination and reduced market imperfections. The publication of market prices first occurred in major international commercial and financial centres, such as Antwerp and Venice, from the second quarter of the sixteenth century. Extant copies of printed price currents point to their use in Frankfurt from 1581 and in Amsterdam and Hamburg less than a decade later. Their appearance was soon accompanied by the publication of exchange rate currents. These most likely were a formalization of the previous reporting of exchange-banking business conducted at the major fairs. The Lyons Fair, the most important in Europe during the century after 1450, was controlled by Florentine bankers, who were responsible for the introduction of practices previously established at Italian exchange fairs. The earliest published exchange rate current to have survived is for Antwerp in 1550, the format of which is clearly modelled on the procedures that had been developed in Lyons, and later Besançon—and it was published in Italian.[19] From the mid-sixteenth century, merchants, some of whom conducted banking, had given birth to financial journalism by linking their own information networks to the power of the printing press. The resulting printed price and exchange currents mark an important stage in the development of international trade and its associated finance, the realms within which most private bankers undertook the majority of their business before the late seventeenth century.

Italian financial pre-eminence was embodied in powerful private banking dynasties, above all in Florence. While Venice was the world's leading financial centre in the fourteenth and fifteenth century, Florentine merchant bankers were clearly the dominant players: the Bardi, the Perzuzzi, and the Acciaiuli around 1300; the Frescobaldi, the Medici, and the Strozzi after 1350. Rather than banks, it has been suggested that these firms should be called 'super companies', on account of both the geographical spread and the wide range of their activities.[20] The Peruzzi, for example, were indeed bankers, but also commodity traders, wool merchants, general merchants, and manufacturers—depending on the part of the world where their business affairs were conducted. Moreover, several Florentine banks invested in real estate, both as a buffer against hard times and as a mark of respectability.[21]

[18] J. J. McCusker and C. Gravesteijn, *The Beginnings of Commercial and Financial Journalism. The Commodity Price Currents, Exchange Rate Currents and Money Currents Of Early Modern Europe* (Amsterdam, 1991), pp. 22–3.

[19] See C. Gravesteijn, 'Amsterdam and the Origins of Financial Journalism', in M. North (Hg.), *Kommunikationsrevolutionen. Die neuen Medien des 16. und 19. Jahrhunderts* (Cologne/Weimar/Vienna, 1995).

[20] See E. S. Hunt, *The Medieval Super-companies. A Study of the Peruzzi Company of Florence* (Cambridge, 1994).

[21] Abulafia, 'Impact of Italian Banking', p. 22.

Merchant banks operated as family enterprises—though only to a limited extent. In fifteenth century Florence, a firm was usually divided following its head's death, with his sons each engaging in separate business ventures. Partnerships were established on a short-term basis and periodically renewed.[22] In addition to contributing to part of the firm's capital, partners were required, if necessary, to provide extra funds yielding a fixed income (between 6 and 10 per cent). Firms also relied on managers, who were asked to expand liquidities by opening deposit accounts, on which interest was paid. Deposits were also collected from the public and could earn as much as 12 per cent per year. Such practices were considered usurious by the Church—yet cardinals, as well as the papacy's Treasury, deposited their funds in such a way at the Medici Bank.[23] Put together, capital, long-term loans, and deposits provided the largest companies with ample resources, enabling them to play a major role in international trade and its financing through bills of exchange. The scale of their operations was also made possible by the, at least, partial use of double-entry accounting.

There were probably as many as eighty large banks in Florence in the mid-fourteenth century, with a total of some 500 to 800 partners. The Peruzzi Company employed around ninety managers in 1336 while, in 1641, the Acciaiuli Company had sixteen independent branches, eleven partners, thirty-two managers and an unknown number of employees. Yet even the largest banks could face serious difficulties, as witnessed by the failure of the Bardi and the Peruzzi in 1345, as a result of over-extension, lack of flexibility in their relationships with their branches, and excessive lending to Edward III of England, who defaulted on part of his debt.

The best-known of all Italian merchant banks, the Medici Bank, was officially opened in Florence in 1397, though members of the family had been involved in banking since the early fourteenth century. Vieri di Cambio, in particular, had established a bank in Rome to do business with the curia; he was joined in 1385 by a nephew, Giovanni di Bicci, the father of Cosimo di Medici—the creator of the great Florentine bank. Its success was in large part due to their privileged relationships with the popes and the Vatican's administration. During the councils of Constance (1414–18) and Basle (1431), for example, the Medici acted as the papacy's main bankers. The bank expanded rapidly, with branches in Rome and Venice, and in Geneva outside Italy. Following a major reorganization in 1435, it expanded to Pisa, Milan, and Naples, and, outside Italy, to Bruges, London, Avignon, and Lyons. Under Cosimo, it adopted a more decentralized structure, with each branch forming as it were an independent company, with its own capital. Agents became

[22] R. A. Goldthwaite, 'The Medici Bank and the World of Florentine Capitalism', *Past and Present*, 114 (February 1987), pp. 9–17.

[23] H. Van der Wee et al., *La banque en occident* (Antwerp, 1991), pp. 101–2.

partners in their branch—though the Medici retained a 50 per cent share of the capital and thus full control over the entire company. Nevertheless, Rome remained at the very heart of the Medici Bank's affairs throughout its existence, contributing 52 per cent of the bank's profits between 1397 and 1420 (as against 17 per cent for Florence and 15 per cent for Venice) and 62 per cent between 1420 and 1435 (as against 13 per cent for Venice and 9.5 per cent for Florence). It remained at about 30 per cent after 1435, ahead of Venice (21 per cent). By then, Florence's share had fallen to under 8 per cent, less than Geneva (15 per cent) and Avignon (14 per cent).[24]

The Medici Bank was indeed the largest bank of its time, but not by a very wide margin—Capponi or Strozzi were not far behind—and in no way did it enjoy a dominant economic position. Competition with other banks was stiff, whether in Florence or in the other cities where it operated. In Lyons, for example, almost 140 other Florentine firms were active at the time.[25] To its economic power, the family added great political prominence, especially under Lorenzo 'the Magnificent', Cosimo's grandson, who had little interest in business. As well as increasingly adverse economic conditions, the firm suffered from typical third generation entrepreneurial decline. In the end, it was political upheaval and the family's expulsion from Florence in 1494, two years after Lorenzo's death, which sealed its fate.

THE RISE AND FALL OF ANTWERP

During the Early Modern Period, the continent's economic epicentre was moving, albeit with faltering steps, north-westwards from the Mediterranean world to the littorals of the North Sea. This shift in the continent's economic centre of gravity was partly produced by the great central European silver-mining boom. It had got underway during the mid-fifteenth century and reached an apogee over the first four decades of the sixteenth century. The mining ventures were financed by the major south-German merchant banking houses: the Fugger, Welser, Höchstetter, and Imhof.[26] These undertakings, following the previous practice of Italian banking companies, established continental networks of branch houses, not only in Bruges, Milan, and Venice, but also in Eastern Europe in Krakow and Buda. The extraction of silver in

[24] De Roover, *Rise and Decline of the Medici Bank*; Goldthwaite, 'The Medici Bank'; Van der Wee, *La banque en Occident*.

[25] Goldthwaite, 'The Medici Bank', p. 16.

[26] For an introductory overview, see, M. North, 'The Great German Banking Houses and International Merchants, Sixteenth to Nineteenth Century', in Teichova et al., *Banking, Trade and Industry*, pp. 35–8.

central Europe played a substantial part in the continent's prime financial locus being transferred from the Rialto in Venice to, in the first instance, cities and towns such as Augsburg, Nuremberg, and Prague.

This development went in parallel with the growth in exports of Anglo-Netherlands textiles to southern and Eastern Europe, which grew to such an extent that the business of Bruges was eclipsed. During the early sixteenth century Antwerp became linked not only to Venice but also to Cologne and Frankfurt-am-Main and, thereby, to central Europe. Alongside new banks, agencies of the great south German merchant houses were established in Antwerp, joining representatives of the leading Italian and Iberian bankers, and all benefited from the further fall in interest rates that came with the considerable expansion of silver mining in central Europe.[27]

As a result, the Antwerp market grew to be the commercial and financial centre of north-western Europe, building upon the successful competition with Bruges over the city's fairs from the early fifteenth century. A strictly regulated Bourse was established in 1485 to house, under one roof, the gamut of commerce and finance that had developed over the previous century by Antwerp merchants progressively extending the period of the city's fairs to bring about continuous trading. Antwerp's financial stature was marked from 1531 by money-changing dealings on the Nieuwe Beurs setting daily exchange rates. During the 1540s, commodity prices and exchange rates determined on Antwerp's formalized markets came to be regularly published in a printed form.[28] This innovation went along with other developments, for example, the growth of mercantile commission trades and the publication of commercial text books, the latter constituting a further step in the standardization of dealing practices.[29]

International finance was further developed in Antwerp by the completion of the bill of exchange's evolution as a negotiable security, which had first got underway in fourteenth-century Tuscany.[30] This transformation was due to the growth at Antwerp of the practice of serial endorsement. It involved the backs of bills coming to contain lists of signatures of the merchants and bankers through whose hands they passed. Endorsement allowed collection by a third party and replaced previous entries in bankers' bills registries. Thereby, such bills became fully developed, totally impersonal, instruments by which foreign payments could be made through enabling the transfer of

[27] For the development of Antwerp, see H. van der Wee, *Growth of the Antwerp Market*, 3 vols. (Antwerp, 1963).

[28] McCusker and Gravesteijn, *The Beginnings of Commercial and Financial Journalism*, p. 86.

[29] Schneider, 'The Significance of Large Fairs', pp. 18–19.

[30] R. de Roover, 'Le marché monétaire au moyen âge et au début des temps modernes', *Revue Historique*, 94 (1970).

claims on individuals' balances at other trading centres.[31] This creation of a readily transferable and marketable financial instrument, the standing of which was attested by the names that signed it, obviated to a significant degree the need for the costly transmission of specie. Consequently, exchange banking was substantially transformed from assaying bullion and weighing coin to requiring knowledge of the wealth and probity of those who added their names to bills. The most reliable information arose from personal connections between the various major international trading and financial centres in Europe. Furthermore, the endorsement of bills at Antwerp went along with a growing practice of bill discounting, which provided a form of short-term lending that, critically, did not run counter to the usury laws. Such provision of credit constituted another major financial innovation.[32]

Over the course of the sixteenth century, the Antwerp market was transformed from a subsidiary centre, where dealings were largely conducted by agents of merchants resident elsewhere (in Lisbon, London, or Germany and Italy), to a prime centre of trade in its own right. The shift from a passive to an active role involved an increasing interaction with its local industrial hinterland, coupled with developing as an entrepôt for Asiatic and American goods. It resulted, by the mid-century, in the city having its own resident mercantile élite, a melding of those groups, local and otherwise, previously engaged in commerce, banking, and finance.

However, the crisis of the 1550s, and especially Habsburg intervention on the Antwerp Bourse, crippled the city's money market, leading to London gaining a greater importance.[33] Subsequently, during the Spanish repression of the Dutch revolt from 1572, Antwerp was sacked in 1576, captured by the Duke of Parma in 1585, and the city's ultimate demise as a major centre of overseas trade finally came when Dutch troops closed the mouth of the River Scheldt. Thereafter, Antwerp was only a node of regional trade, although its merchants collectively remained a force in European finance, with the city's Bourse continuing to be important for bill dealings until the 1670s. However, Antwerp's decline from the closing decades of the sixteenth century was more than counterbalanced in the Low Countries by the almost meteoric rise of Amsterdam to be *the* European trading and financial centre.

[31] H. Van der Wee, 'Monetary, Credit and Banking Systems', in E. E. Rich and C. Wilson (eds), *Cambridge Economic History of Europe*, 5, *The Economic Organisation of Early Modern Europe* (Cambridge, 1977).

[32] J. Schnieder and O. Schwarzer, 'International Rates of Exchange: Structure and Trends of Payment Mechanism in Europe, Seventeenth to the Nineteenth Centuries', in Fischer et al., *Emergence of a World Economy*, pp. 144–5.

[33] See I. Blanchard, 'Credit and Commerce: From the Mediterranean to the Atlantic in the Sixteenth Century', in H. Diederiks and D. Reeder (eds), *Cities of Finance* (Amsterdam/Oxford/New York/Tokyo, 1996).

AMSTERDAM'S SUPREMACY

Amsterdam had some wider significance as a commercial market by 1550,[34] but four decades later its mercantile community swiftly achieved European prominence amidst the subsistence crisis of the early 1590s. This growing dominance in commerce and finance came with the re-establishment of Dutch control over trade with the Baltic. It was made plain during the ten-year rise in demand from 1589 for northern grain caused by population growth, especially in the Mediterranean region. Baltic rye and wheat were freighted in Dutch-owned ships along with iron, timber, and naval stores. These basic and bulky but necessary products were acquired by Amsterdam and other Dutch merchants in exchange for beer, cloth, and herrings, the specialities of Holland and Zealand, together with salt, Rhine wine, and non-European luxuries. Dutch mercantile houses established permanently-based factors in Baltic ports, usually family members to give a secure, filial basis for the conduct of business over a distance.[35] In all this, Amsterdam became the great warehouse for Baltic goods—the products of agriculture, forestry, and mining—and for those that were used to acquiring them: fine Anglo-Dutch woollens, Iberian salt, Mediterranean produce and, from the early seventeenth century, Javanese spices.

The city's growing strength in these international dealings—the *moederhandel* (mother trade)—which linked northern and southern Europe, was augmented as a result of an inflow of refugee merchants from Brabant and Flanders, provinces that remained under Spanish rule. The formal agreement regarding their movement from Antwerp allowed them to bring not only their personally acquired expertise in bill dealings but also sizeable amounts of their wealth. Furthermore, Amsterdam's commercial and financial position within Europe was buttressed by continuing private links between the city's own new commercial community and those merchants who had fled from the southern provinces of the Low Countries but chose to go to Danzig, Frankfurt, Hamburg, Leghorn, London, or Stockholm.[36] Forced transfers of sections of Europe's mercantile communities caused by religious persecution also included

[34] J. D. Tracy, *A Financial Revolution in the Habsburg Netherlands* (Berkeley/London, 1985), pp. 48–9; and J. A. Houte, *An Economic History of the Low Countries* (New York, 1977), pp. 182–7.

[35] M. Bogucka, 'Dutch Merchants' Activities in Gdansk in the First Half of the 17th Century', in J. P. S. Lemmink and J. S. A. M. van Koingsbrugge (eds), *Relations between the Netherlands and North-eastern Europe 1500–1800* (Nijmegen, 1990). See also M. Bogucka, 'Amsterdam and the Baltic in the First Half of the 17th Century', *Economic History Review*, 2nd ser., 26 (1973); and M. Bogucka, 'The Role of Baltic Trade in European Development from the 16th to the 18th Centuries', *Journal of European Economic History*, 9 (1980).

[36] For an outline of the experience of one such family—the Tryons—who went to London, see F. T. Melton, *Sir Robert Clayton and the Origins of English Deposit Banking, 1658–1685* (Cambridge, 1986), pp. 42–3.

the movement of Spanish and Portuguese Jewish families, such as the Texeiras, as a result of the Inquisition.

Amsterdam's increasing prosperity was reflected in the expansion of its population, which rose from about 30,000 in 1550 to 105,000 in 1622, and to 120,000 by the mid-seventeenth century. Amongst these growing numbers were individuals possessing great wealth. Whereas, in 1585, a capital impost had led to declarations in which only seven Amsterdammers had admitted to having more than 70,000 guilders, in 1631 a comparable tax revealed that the city had a hundred residents with stated assets in excess of 100,000 guilders. Although inflation over this period has some tempering effect on nominal valuations, wealth within Amsterdam over the first half of the seventeenth century was rising in real terms and rising substantially.[37] The city's commercial rise was also marked by change in its built form that led to the emergence of one of the first modern business centres—expressed in the building of the Beurs, near Dam square, which was ready for use in 1613. Four years earlier, the Wisselbank (Exchange Bank) had opened its offices in the old town hall on Dam Square, and in 1614 the Municipal Loan Bank was founded. All these institutions were within walking distance of one another in the heart of the inner city.[38]

The building housing Amsterdam Beurs followed in style the earlier Antwerp Bourse and the London Exchange. In 1617, a separate grain exchange was established while dealings also took place in surrounding coffee houses and taverns, the haunts of burgeoning numbers of licensed brokers. They were solely intermediaries, forbidden to undertake transactions on their own account. From the mid-1610s, what were, to all intents and purposes, world prices for a wide range of both bulk and high-value goods were set by about 300 licensed brokers amongst whom ten Sephardic Jews were the specialists in eastern Mediterranean and Spanish-American produce and products. Within what was a spectrum of markets, futures trading developed as a hedge against marked oscillations in commodity prices, especially of grain and herring.[39]

Activity in these purpose-built and purpose-designated markets was recorded and disseminated through the publication of price currents. Their production was institutionalized in January 1613 by municipal regulations which gave them an important official standing.[40] The printing of the weekly Amsterdam price current continued until 1796, with soon a French translation being produced, an Italian rendering from the mid-seventeenth century and

[37] Tracy, *Financial Revolution*, pp. 198–9.

[38] H. Diederiks, 'Bankers, Banks, and other Financial Institutions in the Urban Landscape of Amsterdam, late 16th–20th Centuries', in Diederiks and Reeder, *Cities of Finance*.

[39] C. H. Wilson, *Anglo-Dutch Commerce and Finance in the Eighteenth Century* (Cambridge, 1941), p. 13; and Israel, *Dutch Primacy*, pp. 74–5.

[40] McCusker and Gravesteijn, *The Beginnings of Commercial and Financial Journalism*, pp. 43–50.

an English version from 1678. A gauge of Amsterdam's importance in European trade and finance is that in 1656 it gave exchange rates for thirteen cities and, in 1700, for twenty cities.[41] This development of the city's Beurs over the seventeenth century to become the pivot of the European exchanges was due in part to the successful foundation of the Wisselbank.

The Wisselbank, or the Bank of Amsterdam as it became colloquially known, was a public, municipally-owned, exchange bank, established after several years of discussion in order to give greater confidence to mercantile transfers. The rapid expansion of Amsterdam's commerce over the closing decade of the sixteenth century had led to near financial chaos by 1606 and the bank was created to give stability and order. It was designed to replace the activities of private money-exchangers, negotiators, and cashiers and, thereby, also to stop the export of full-weight coin from Holland. Although subsequently emulated in other Dutch and foreign towns and cities, its foundation in 1609 was not an innovation. It followed on from the creation of the Bank of Palermo in 1552, whereas the origins of such institutions in general can, in turn, be traced back to earlier progenitors, such as the Frankfurt Wessil of 1402 or the giro amongst Venetian bankers. Similarly, the bank's introduction in Amsterdam of standard account money—the florin banco—replicated the previous practices of the fairs at Geneva, Lyons, and Piacenza, and the Wechselzahlung of late sixteenth-century Frankfurt.[42]

With the foundation of the Wisselbank, all bearer bills in Holland having a value of more than 600 guilders had to be paid at its offices. As a result, major mercantile transfers became centralized at the bank, where accounts were conducted in its own monetary unit—the florin banco. This obviated the problems that arose from exchange rate fluctuations, evident from the printed price currents, coupled with those produced by debased coinage caused by both continuing inflation and disruption arising from warfare. Amsterdam's exchanges with towns and cities in the United Provinces and northern Europe were conducted in cash through the Wisselbank's ledgers, whereas bills arising from trade over greater distances were usually payable at the bank. Over its first year of operations, the bank attracted 731 accounts; by 1620 it had 1,202, and by 1651 1,875 accounts. This was all testimony to the speed with which the Wisselbank had achieved an established standing; and this rising confidence led it to rapidly become a bank of deposit. Many of its earliest depositors were refugees from the southern Netherlands who had settled in

[41] Gravesteijn, 'Amsterdam and the Origins of Financial Journalism'. See also N. W. Posthumus, *Inquiry into the History of Prices in Holland*, I, *Wholesale Prices at the Exchange of Amsterdam 1585–1914, Rates of Exchange at Amsterdam 1609–1914* (Leiden, 1914) and McCusker and Gravesteijn, *The Beginnings of Commercial and Financial Journalism*, pp. 66–9.

[42] On the development of money of account, see Spufford, *Handbook*, pp. xx–xxvi.

Amsterdam.[43] Although never formally a bank of issue, from 1688 its deposit receipts circulated in a money-like fashion.

The practice of the transfer of bills between merchants and private proto-bankers by endorsement grew in the Netherlands from the 1620s, with printed bill forms having been in use from at least 1597. This critical step in the development of the provision of international credit by the Amsterdam market probably happened through the transfer of practices from Antwerp. They were brought northwards as a result of the expulsion of Jews and Protestants from that Flanders city in 1585.[44] The settlement of bills at Amsterdam was given further standing by being undertaken through transfers—from foreign to Dutch merchants and vice versa—amongst their accounts at the Wisselbank. Moreover, the quality of such bills was in the process enhanced through being underwritten by the increasing reputations of the Wisselbank and its unit of account, the florin banco. Yet, the greater growth of the Amsterdam exchange market, and the development of practices that allowed credit thereby to be extended, led to the re-emergence of *kassiers* (cashiers), whose activities it had been intended to suppress through the Wisselbank's creation in 1609.[45] The growing use of bill transfers was belatedly accepted in law by a series of ordinances passed from 1651. Nonetheless, the legal recognition of discounting came up against the usury strictures and, in the Netherlands, only particular forms of bill transactions that involved the payment of interest came to receive the courts' blessing.

Following the lift of the ban on their activity in 1621, cashiers gradually became Amsterdam's leading private bankers in the seventeenth century.[46] Cashiers had not completely disappeared after 1609, and had continued to handle local transactions in florin current. From the 1630s onwards, they were able to take advantage of the greater stability of the florin current and its more or less fixed ratio with the florin banco; the latter increasingly lost its specific advantage as a stable currency, as the former offered the same guarantee of security and could be used in all types of settlement. Amsterdam merchants engaged in international trade increasingly turned to cashiers for payments and receipts in florin current, and were soon to use the accounts opened to that effect for transfers of funds. Moreover, it was through these accounts that

[43] Barbour, *Capitalism in Amsterdam*, ch. 2; Davis, *Rise of the Atlantic Economies*, pp. 179, 246–7; and Israel, *Dutch Primacy*, pp. 77–8; See also J. G. van Dillen, 'The Bank of Amsterdam' in J. G. van Dillen (ed.), *History of the Principal Public Banks* (The Hague, 1934); and J. G. van Dillen, 'La Banque de Change et les banquiers privés à Amsterdam aux XVIIe et XVIIIe siècles', in *Troisième Conférence internationale d'histoire économique, Munich 1965*, 5, Deuxième groupe 'La structure de la banque'.

[44] L. Neal, *The Rise of Financial Capitalism. International Capital Markets in the Age of Reason* (Cambridge, 1990), pp. 5–8.

[45] J. C. Riley, *International Government Finance and the Amsterdam Capital Market 1740–1815* (Cambridge, 1980), p. 28.

[46] The following paragraphs are based on Van der Wee, *La banque en Occident*, pp. 216–26.

cashiers granted their customers loans, overdrafts, and discount credits—an activity greatly enhanced by the fact that the Wisselbank was forbidden by law from making commercial loans.

Cashiers not only became important providers of commercial credit in florin current, they also became brokers in florin banco. This could for example be the case if a merchant was short of the funds he needed at the Wisselbank in order to make an international transfer: the cashier could use his own account at the Wisselbank to carry out the transfer, while at the same time debiting his customer's account. Merchants were not even required to open an account at the Wisselbank if a cashier could act on their behalf. On this basis, cashiers were able to develop their banking activities: lending vast sums of money to merchants, whether in florin current or in florin banco; buying and selling huge amounts of bills of exchange for these merchants; and discounting bills for customers, leading to the opening of current accounts. At the same time, some merchants started to engage in international finance through accepting and discounting bills of exchange—an activity which was to expand considerably in the eighteenth century.

Interestingly, as Hermann Van der Wee has pointed out, the major innovative force in seventeenth century Amsterdam was not the Wisselbank, but the private cashiers. The Wisselbank played a stabilizing role, not least by concentrating international settlements in a single institution, but its attitude was fundamentally conservative, especially as it did not extend credit to merchants. This opened the way for cashiers to become the main source of financing for Amsterdam's international trade. In the process, they developed banking facilities, above all for deposits, transfers, and discounts, and they started the practice of acceptance credits.

An 'open', public capital market on the Beurs further developed in Amsterdam following the creation in 1602 of the United East India Company (Veenigde Oostindische Compagnie/VOC), a corporation with a permanent share capital.[47] Dutch merchants had begun to trade with Java from 1595 and the VOC institutionalized and regularized this activity. The East Indies remained the focus of Dutch commercial interest in the Orient with, during the first half of the seventeenth century, the VOC having a near-monopoly of the European import by sea of the most valuable Indonesian spices. It was trade that nicely complemented that with the Baltic and so underwrote Dutch mercantile and financial supremacy within the continent until the 1660s.

More than half of the VOC's initial capital of 6.4m guilders came from the Amsterdam Chamber of the Company, its initial list containing 1,143 names, amongst whom eighty-four individually subscribed 10,000 guilders or more. Subsequent transactions in VOC shares were most active for those held by

[47] N. Steensgaard, 'The Dutch East India Company as an Institutional Innovation', in Aymard, *Dutch Capitalism*.

Amsterdammers, if only because a majority of the company's capital was held in the city and some concentration of holdings soon developed. The continuing participation of the Amsterdam mercantile community in the company's capital is indicated by the soon flourishing secondary share market on the Beurs, and speculation in the shares was not checked by a 1610 Company decree requiring transfers to take place within a month of a transaction. Amsterdammers' significant participations also arose because share transfers had to be registered with the VOC's bookkeepers, a somewhat cumbersome process, but the Company's head office was close to the Wisselbank and the Beurs.[48]

There were close ties between the VOC and the Wisselbank, whether at a personal level (individuals who had been either the cashier or the bookkeeper at the Wisselbank became VOC directors, including Hillebrand Schellinger, Hendrik Reynst, and Pieter Hasselaer, during the first half of the seventeenth century, and were all members of Amsterdam leading patrician families); or in business affairs, with attempts at the VOC to make the Wisselbank its sole supplier of bullion for exports—the Company's exports of precious metal rose from 5.18 million guilders in 1602–10 to 8.8 million guilders in 1640–50 and 19.72 million guilders in 1680–90.[49] Indeed, the supply of treasure that the VOC required for outward voyages to the East Indies was one aspect of Amsterdam's development to be Europe's key bullion market, a position it retained until the 1730s.

Amsterdam's pivotal role in European trade and its financial clearing was clearly evident by the last quarter of the seventeenth century. Whereas the only addition to the list of exchange quotations in 1656, compared with 1609, was the one on Paris, by 1676, a further eleven rates on other European centres were being quoted on the Amsterdam Beurs, including quotations for Cadiz, Madrid, and Seville, together with Genoa and Leghorn, as well as Lyons and, even more importantly, Breslau and Leipzig, with the Leipzig Fair being the great hub for trade with eastern and south-eastern Europe.[50]

Dealing in bills, bullion, and currency, together with mercantile and shipping advances, comprised much of mid-seventeenth-century banking. This range of financial assets in Amsterdam could be enlarged through transactions linked to shares in the VOC. Other possibilities arose, as they had earlier, for

[48] Wilson, *Anglo-Dutch Commerce*, pp. 13–14, 81–2.

[49] F. S. Gaastra, 'The Exports of Precious Metal from Europe to Asia by the Dutch East India Company, 1602–1795', in Richards, *Precious Metals*; F. S. Gaastra, 'The Dutch East India Company and its intra-Asiatic Trade in Precious Metals', in Fischer et al., *Emergence of a World Economy*, Part 1. See also I. Schöffer and F. S. Gaastra, 'The Import of Bullion and Coin into Asia by the Dutch East India Company in the Seventeenth and Eighteenth Centuries', in Aymard, *Dutch Capitalism*.

[50] Schnieder and Schwarzer, 'International Rates of Exchange', pp. 143, 145–6 and Table 1, p. 162.

lending to sovereign powers but 'high finance' was a treacherous business as the consequences of the bankruptcies of the major European rulers, and many members of their courts, had shown only too clearly during the late sixteenth century. Mighty German, Italian, and Spanish merchant banking houses had then either been brought low or collapsed entirely.[51] However, in many respects, the Dutch secular experience of sovereign lending was different. Towns in Holland had issued *renten* from the fourteenth century and had been but little affected by the late fifteenth-century financial crisis. Critical innovations, progenitors of the English 'Financial Revolution' of a century and a half later, were made in the mid-sixteenth century, with the issues of *renten* secured on excise and land taxes that were quickly amortized; and of redeemable *lijfrenten*, modelled in many respects upon the format of popular civic life annuities. They were largely acquired by magistrate families. By 1598, there were no significant arrears on past issues of *renten* arising from the turbulence of the first phase of the Dutch revolt and the initial period of outright warfare with Spain.

The cutting edge of Dutch commercial prowess remained keen until the early eighteenth century. Nonetheless, its vitality was increasingly sapped by growing English and French competition. This rivalry was increased by the introduction of navigation Acts designed to deny Dutch participation in their trades,[52] and by costly warfare, especially with France in 1672–8, 1689–97, and 1702–13. The relative decline of Amsterdam as an entrepôt for Oriental produce was clearly marked in the development of direct trades undertaken by the chartered companies of its western and south-western competitors. Moreover, the Dutch share of the 'mother' Baltic trade also fell from the 1720s, which was in part a consequence of the exhaustion of natural resources around the littorals of Scandinavia. Consequently, by 1740, Amsterdam was faced with a thorough-going rival in the shape of the City of London, whereas Hanseatic Hamburg, forever neutral in the rivalry of European powers, had also gained at the expense of Dutch commerce.[53] Nonetheless, Amsterdam's relative decline as Europe's premier mercantile centre did not go hand-in-hand with a diminution of the city's importance as a financial centre.[54] Indeed, Dutch bankers and financiers became major players in the European capital market of the eighteenth century.

[51] Davis, *Rise of the Atlantic Economies*, pp. 245–6; and North, 'The Great German Banking Houses', p. 37.

[52] Wilson, *Anglo-Dutch Commerce*, pp. 6–7.

[53] Davis, *Rise of the Atlantic Economies*, pp. 190–1.

[54] On the scholarly debate over the state of the Dutch economy during the eighteenth century, see M. North and F. Snapper, 'The Baltic Trade and the Decline of the Dutch Economy in the 18th Century', *Baltic Studies*, 1 (1990).

HAMBURG AND FRANKFURT

By the late seventeenth century, Hamburg, together with Amsterdam, were the prime western nodes within the overall pattern of the continent's trade and associated financial payments. The Leipzig Fair was the other major hub, drawing in business from Europe's core and eastern borders. The structure of connections, market-based and personal, within this 'system' was in marked contrast to that of the mid- and late sixteenth-century network by which Antwerp was then linked, via Cologne, Frankfurt, and Nuremberg, with Venice.

During the early seventeenth century, the conduct of Hamburg's commerce and its associated finance had been re-shaped by Flemish migrants and other émigrés. As in Amsterdam, they introduced the vital practices for mobilizing the bill of exchange—serial endorsement and discounting—that had been developed in sixteenth-century Antwerp. In the late sixteenth century, compared with Amsterdam and London, Hamburg had been less developed as a centre of European commerce. The opportunities for expansion were exploited successfully by waves of immigrants arriving in the city from as early as the 1550s. They included Italian Catholics, although their commercial force was spent by the 1630s, followed by Sephardic Jews, and Dutch Calvinists, and Lutherans. As in Amsterdam, these incomers brought wealth and, more importantly, commercial contacts. Their mercantile endeavours resulted in Hamburg's commerce not experiencing the decline that beset other Hanseactic ports during the late sixteenth century.

Migrants' business activities did not supersede those of the existing, resident commercial sector but, instead, complemented the city's established trades and industries. Indeed, like Amsterdam, Hamburg became a centre for both west European and Mediterranean trade, and intercourse with the New World. The initiation of the transformation of the city-port's importance was marked by the establishment of a Börse in 1558. This considerable change was coupled with the local development of textile production to enlarge the basis of both the city's economy and its wider dealings. The exceptional role played by Dutch migrants is clearly indicated in the Hamburg commodity price current, which first appeared during the 1590s. It was published in Dutch, with German not being adopted until 1736.[55] In 1600, Dutch migrants made up about a quarter of Hamburg's population of some 40,000, while, overall, incomers comprised half of the city-state's residents. Until the mid-seventeenth century, they continued to account for 50 per cent of Hamburg's growing numbers which reached about 55,000 during the 1650s. Thereafter, these 'foreigners', joined by French Huguenots from the 1680s, remained a

[55] McCusker and Gravesteijn, *The Beginnings of Commercial and Financial Journalism*, p. 224.

vital element in local wealth creation with their entrepreneurial successes, in turn, attracting substantial numbers of German migrants from Lower Saxony.[56]

The Hanse city's Sephardic Jewish community, which made the most disproportionate contribution to the development of its commerce over the seventeenth century, expanded from the 1580s as a result of an inflow of Portuguese migrants escaping the Inquisition. By 1610, it comprised 116 members but with many others claiming outwardly to be Catholics. Using their economic position and their continuing political links with Spain, they obtained a contract with the Hamburg Senate specifying their rights and privileges. The community had expanded to about 500 by 1646 and many of its members openly pursued an ostentatious mode of living—that of merchant princes—and established a synagogue. However, these heretical developments led to a confrontation during the late 1640s, resulting in the first Judenordnung of 1650. By this measure, the Hamburg Senate attempted to balance the necessary assuaging of Lutheran pastors' wrath against the obvious advantages that the city gained from the presence of Sephardic Jews.

The Portuguese community reached its peak in both numbers and wealth during the 1660s, the latter typified by the Texeira family's international power and influence. Decline came at the end of the century after the Jewish issue had come to the fore once more, in part the result of an inflow of Ashkenazi Jews from north Germany and Poland. A special levy of 20,000 Marks to fill the City of Hamburg's empty coffers, coupled with a new contract in 1697 that treated Sephardic and Ashkenazi alike, to the repugnance of the former, resulted in the departure of the Portuguese community's wealthiest members in 1688. By 1730, Hamburg's Sephardim only comprised forty-nine families and none had the character of the dynamic merchants and financiers who had played such a part in the city's transformation over the seventeenth century.[57]

However, during the mid-seventeenth century, the first roots had been established of what was to be one of Hamburg's most famous private banking houses. In 1647, Jacob Samuel Warburg settled in Altona and was joined in 1668 by his father, Juspa-Joseph. The family had been Court Jews in Warburg since 1559 but, following the Thirty Years War, migrated northwards to become moneychangers and pawnbrokers in the Hanse city. The Warburg firm continued to describe itself as moneychangers until 1863, when the description 'Bankiers' was adopted.[58]

56 J. Whaley, *Religious Toleration and Social Change in Hamburg 1529–1819* (Cambridge, 1985), pp. 9–10, 48–9.

57 Whaley, *Religious Toleration*, pp. 73–80.

58 R. Chernow, *The Warburgs. The Twentieth-Century Odyssey of a Remarkable Jewish Family* (New York, 1993), pp. 3–5, 13.

Hamburg's residents gave their greatest welcome to the Dutch Lutherans that arrived in the city from the late 1560s, and especially after 1585. Such a warm reception was assisted by an almost common tongue, a shared belief, and their arrival in a series of small groups. Although many of these migrants, Calvinists as well as Lutherans, were to intermarry with the local population—to form a major section of the mercantile élite—not all were rich and wealthy and many never settled permanently. Indeed, Hamburg's Dutch community experienced a continuous turnover in its membership, especially the Calvinist section, with some returning to the Netherlands to be replaced by fresh incomers, a feature which persisted into the eighteenth century. However, the Calvinists were regarded as heretics and were subject to the same degree of religious intolerance within Hamburg as the city's Sephardim, and this persisted even after the Peace of Westphalia.[59]

In 1619, an Exchange Bank, on the model of the Wisselbank, was established in the Hanseatic city-state, largely on the initiative of Dutch and Jewish migrants. Likewise, a Hamburg exchange rate current was first published on 26 April 1659 and subsequently, during the 1680s, was compiled by Herman Hermanssen, a Hamburg exchange broker. Like the commodity current, it first appeared in Dutch, with German not being substituted until the 1690s. Like Amsterdam, over the seventeenth century Hamburg became a trade clearing centre. This function was to have a special, continuing significance for northern and eastern Germany until the last quarter of the nineteenth century. A significant proportion of the port's international trade during the eighteenth century, as in the sixteenth century, was conducted with London to give the city an enduring English aspect to its character.[60]

By the 1670s, Frankfurt had slipped to second place, behind Hamburg, as a distribution centre for goods amongst the German states. Thereafter, the importance of the city's spring and autumn fairs further declined, despite some commercial revival from the beginning of the eighteenth century. However, the city's vitality as a financial market continued, building upon the commercial foundations that had been laid down first during the early fourteenth century, when its market had benefited from the decline of the Champagne fairs; and, subsequently, over the second half of the sixteenth century, when it benefited greatly from the decline of the businesses of Augsburg and Nuremberg merchant banking houses.

[59] Whaley, *Religious Toleration*, pp. 118–23.

[60] H. Siveking, 'Die Hamburger Bank', in van Dillen, *History of the Principal Public Banks*; W. Reiss, 'Historical Exchange Rates', in Fischer et al., *Emergence of a World Economy*, Part 1; North, 'The Great German Banking Houses', pp. 38–9; Whaley, *Religious Toleration*, p. 75; Davis, *Rise of the Atlantic Economies*, pp. 192–3, 235, 248; and K. Newman, 'Hamburg in the European Economy, 1660–1750', *Journal of European Economic History*, 14 (1985).

By 1620, Frankfurt had a population of about 20,200, an increase of 76 per cent over 1550, which was largely due to substantial immigration from the Low Countries. These Protestant migrants, such as Johann von Bodeck of Antwerp, reinvigorated the conduct of bill dealing and foreign exchange arbitrage. In 1585, the major merchant houses that controlled the fairs had received the city's permission to conduct foreign exchange transactions. A price current for the Frankfurt fairs was published from at least the autumn of 1581 and soon contained reports of exchange transactions. Protestants from the Spanish Netherlands also gave Frankfurt's market makers an increasingly important connection with Amsterdam, leading to the German city subsequently developing as a 'little Amsterdam'. Its growth as a financial centre further drew on the expertise of Jews expelled from Augsburg, Cologne, Mainz, Nuremberg, and Ulm.[61]

Exchange activity at Frankfurt rapidly surpassed that undertaken at Cologne and this mounting volume resulted in intra-European financial transfers occurring through the city's money markets, by-passing Antwerp or Genoa or Lyons. As a result, Frankfurt became once more the major node for trading and other payments between Italy and southern Germany on the one hand, and England, Hamburg, and the Low Countries on the other. Consequently, within Europe, the Frankfurt Börse, established in 1615, gained an importance second only to Amsterdam. A separate exchange rate current was produced from 1625, twice a year, to report financial activity at the city's spring and autumn fairs. It was compiled by exchange brokers under city authority and this official record was augmented from 1687 by private memoranda compiled by merchants. Initially, Frankfurt exchange currents listed twelve rates, thereafter expanding in content to indicate, within a century, an exchange network encompassing seventeen cities.[62]

This growth, largely arising from the activities of immigrants, was accompanied, as in Hamburg, by religious intolerance that led to persecution. Calvinists were prohibited from enjoying free public worship but the rising numbers of this community and, more importantly, the substantial merchants from France, the Low Countries, and Switzerland that it contained, led to their partial acceptance as denizens (resident aliens). The greatest strife developed with the Jewish community, who were forced to live in a crowded ghetto and were despised and feared. Religious intolerance, but more particularly agitation over money lending, resulted in the ghetto being plundered in 1614, while its occupants were expelled Yet, the Jewish community re-formed, being given imperial protection by the Stattigkeit of 1616, a measure which also

[61] G. L. Soliday, *A Community in Conflict. Frankfurt Society in the Seventeenth and Early Eighteenth Centuries* (Hanover, NH, 1974), pp. 1–3, 35.

[62] McCusker and Gravesteijn, *The Beginnings of Commercial and Financial Journalism*, pp. 206–7.

subsequently allowed its members to play off the city authorities and the Emperor's representatives against each other.[63]

Compared with other German cities, Frankfurt was less affected by the exactions of the Thirty Years War. The war led to the city's commercial and financial market developing into an important recruitment and military outfitting centre, so sustaining the role that it had already undertaken in the conflicts of the late sixteenth and early seventeenth centuries. From the 1660s, Frankfurt gained a new speciality in the distribution of increasingly fashionable French wares, especially cloths and clothing. This new trade attracted merchants not only from France but also Italy, the Palatinate, the United Provinces, the Spanish Netherlands, and Switzerland. These dealings, essentially wholesaling activity, were accompanied by the comparable trading of bullion, colonial produce including tobacco, English serges, jewels, wines, and silk. The major figures in the trading of these products—wholesale merchants—were the dominant force in Frankfurt's European commerce but they were surrounded in the market by those who undertook business on commission and provided banking services.

The commercial and financial importance that Frankfurt gained in the 1670s, in the aftermath of the Thirty Years War, continued for a century. Nonetheless, by the early eighteenth century, in terms of overall significance within the pattern of continental trade and payments, Frankfurt's fairs were gradually being eclipsed by those held at Leipzig. By 1700, the city's commerce mainly focused upon Dutch- and French-, as well as German-produced articles. During the first part of the eighteenth century, Frankfurt's most dynamic merchants combined commission business with the shipping of goods and with dealing in bills of exchange. From the 1750s, banking at Frankfurt developed to become a largely separate, specialized activity.

LONDON'S EARLY PRIVATE BANKERS

Unlike in either Amsterdam or Hamburg, no exchange bank was established in London. However, the Merchant Adventurers Company, which undertook the export of woollens to northern Europe, the staple English trade of the early seventeenth century, made use of the exchange banks at Amsterdam and Hamburg, and at Delft and Rotterdam. Other exchange business was totally concentrated within London's mercantile community, aided by Dutch and Italian 'remitters' who negotiated foreign bills of exchange. These merchants and bankers were located at the dominant hub of the economy's domestic and

[63] Soliday, *A Community in Conflict*, pp. 5, 43, 175.

international trades. London was the premier port, whilst the metropolitan region, whose share of the total population of England and Wales increased from about 5 per cent in 1600 to nearly 10 per cent by 1700, constituted the greatest centre of consumption and wealth within the economy.[64]

All English merchants and traders conducted their businesses within a web of credit so that prices for goods contained an interest element to the extent that price discounts were given when, unusually, a cash transaction was involved. This meant that at the commencement of a commercial career, following an apprenticeship, capital was required to gain creditworthiness. If the venture was to be undertaken on a sole basis, the necessary minimum stake was £500 before the 1650s. Yet, ten times that sum might be needed in some dealings with Europe, and all trading investments increased in their financial demands over the second half of the century. The newer trades with the Mediterranean and across the Atlantic required comparable amounts, as did private trade through the new joint-stock companies.[65] Such capital, in the form of money or physical assets, might be acquired from parents and relations and by a marriage dowry. Other sources were, possibly, a former master, or, as was the custom, through a short-lived partnership. However, every indication points to the subsequent use of credit in the pursuit of business. However, a new entrant without substantial backing normally lacked the necessary security to attract the provision of loans on bonds and, consequently, would be forced back upon usurious trade credit.[66]

The foreign bill of exchange had long been used in England, whereas the inland or domestic bill's importance grew, especially from 1666 when the custom of merchants was incorporated in the legal code. This order to pay was close in character to a promissory note (an unsealed, informal, bill of hand), but, despite mercantile pressure, they were not placed on the same legal footing until the late seventeenth century.[67] Such bills and notes were commercial creations, the products of mercantile banking, whereas paper banking instruments proper emerged from the mid-century. The use of cheques, then

[64] F. J. Fisher, 'The Development of London as a Centre of Conspicuous Consumption in the Sixteenth and Seventeenth Centuries', *Transactions of the Royal Historical Society*, 4th ser., 30 (1948); F. J. Fisher, 'London as an "Engine" of Economic Growth', in J. S. Bromley and E. H. Kossman (eds), *Britain and the Netherlands*, 4, *Metropolis, Dominion and Province* (London, 1971); E. A. Wrigley, 'A Simple Model of London's Importance in Changing English Society and Economy, 1650–1750', *Past and Present*, 37 (1967); E. Kerridge, *Trade and Banking in Early Modern England* (Manchester, 1988), chap. 1, 'The Rise of Metropolitan Markets'; and P. J. Corfield and N. B. Harte (eds), *London and the English economy* (London, 1990).

[65] For one analysis of the changing composition and pattern of English overseas trade, see R. Brenner, *Merchants and Revolution. Commercial Change, Political Conflict, and London's Overseas Trades, 1550–1653* (Cambridge, 1993), pp. 3–195.

[66] R. Grassby, *The Business Community of Seventeenth-Century England* (Cambridge, 1995), pp. 82–3, 84–5, 86–7, 241. On the Difference between usury and interest, see Kerridge, *Trade and Banking*, pp. 34–9.

[67] See Kerridge, *Trade and Banking*, chap. 4, 'The Rise of the Inland Bill of Exchange'.

termed 'a drawn note', upon London banking accounts—deposits held with money-scriveners or goldsmiths—grew from the 1660s, although their transmission through mails, like bankers' notes, could give rise to fraud.[68]

Credit was acquired through standing, connections, or business associations. Yet these informal and private networks were increasingly supported by professional intermediaries. Once more, the undertaking of banking functions grew out of other business activity, as was the case with the emergence of scriveners as loan-brokers from the mid-sixteenth century. Their financial intermediation developed from their previous primary service of drafting conveyances and money bonds. Performing these services provided knowledge and understanding of legal searches amongst the public enrolments haphazardly held in London depositories and, hence, also an appreciation of the value of the securities involved. However, from the early seventeenth century, the scrivener's major role within the legal world came to be superseded by that of the professional lawyer. Consequently, the money-dealing activities of a number of scriveners, like those of John Milton, the father of the poet, gained greater importance.

The interest of scriveners in transactions based upon land gave them a connection with the agrarian economy beyond London. Consequently, their business became an important financial conduit linking the metropolis with the provinces. Within the Elizabethan money market, London scriveners had taken money deposits from sheep drovers, arising from sales at the late-summer Smithfield market made on behalf of Midland graziers.[69] They acquired, directly, grander depositors in the lords and squires for whom they drafted documents. Such notables and country gentlemen required access to funds in London to meet the expenses of their political activities at Westminster and engagement in the 'Season'. These deposits were generated, as in Elizabethan England, by the seasonal agricultural production cycle and so tended to peak with the harvest, the slaughter, and the payment of rents at Michaelmas. Generally, scriveners did not give interest on deposits placed with them. Instead, they provided the services of London cashiers and loan brokers although their clients' requirements could go as far as requests to arrange marriages.

Strictly, the scriveners who took on banking functions became money brokers. Their rewards from the financial arrangements that they facilitated were a brokerage fee of a 0.25 per cent under the Usury Acts coupled with charges for drawing up conveyances and other legal instruments, such as penal bonds. However, it is clear that many took advantage of their clients' deposits, lending out a proportion on their own accounts over the periods when they

[68] F. Redlich, 'The Promissory Note as a Financial and Business Instrument', *Revue Internationale d'Histoire de la Banque*, 3 (1970); and Melton, *Sir Robert Clayton*, pp. 98–113.

[69] Grassby, *Business Community*, p. 265.

were idle. Indeed, the intimate personal links that developed between scriveners and their depositors provided knowledge of the seasonal timing of both the receipt of clients' incomes and expenditure habits. This could be turned to advantage, as was the case with Robert Abbott, who opened a scrivener's shop, the 'Flying Horse' in Cornhill, London, in 1635.

Abbott may well have taken up scrivening as a result of drafting the paperwork connected with the development of relations' country estates. Yet, his future prospects seem to have been only secured when, in 1637, he made a fortunate marriage to a daughter of a wealthy London grocer with interests in the East Indian trade. Abbot's royalist allegiances also proved ultimately to be profitable as he brokered loans for cavalier landowners for payment of the compounding fines required to protect their estates. These drew upon the £1.5 million that passed through his hands as deposits between 1646 and 1655, supplied during the first six years of this period by 186 clients. At the same time, a part of these client deposits, at least £6,600, was employed for the loans that he personally made within total advances of £19,271. Although Abbot's loans for his own account were usually for sums less than £500, during the late 1630s he was considered to be amongst the wealthiest occupants of Cornhill.

Abbott's lending business, both brokered for clients and on his own account, increasingly involved mortgages. He developed practices to ascertain the value of lands placed as security, searching the necessary records held in London and, ultimately, having parcels of estates surveyed. The rents swelled the deposits placed with him. When Abbott's business was taken over in 1658 by his former scribes, Robert Clayton and John Morris, it was developed into an enterprise that specialized in estate financing. They responded to the financial problems that arose from the 1650s with the growing importance of the strictly settled estate. This could only be made liquid through mortgages secured on the revenues that an estate generated as opposed to the land that comprised it. Indeed, Clayton and Morris established a substantial brokerage house that concentrated upon arranging mortgage loans, and undertook estate management and rent transfers, along with more general banking business. This sizeable and profitable business, demonstrated clearly by the grand premises in which it came to be housed, was no mere scrivener's shop. They employed a trained Chancery lawyer and an accountant, along with clerks rather than apprentices.[70]

Abbott's 'Flying Horse' and its successor establishment formed a link between the money-scriveners of the mid-sixteenth century and private finance in post-Restoration England. Money-scriveners developed some aspects of banking but

[70] The previous paragraphs have been drawn from Melton, *Sir Robert Clayton.* See also, D. C. Coleman, 'London Scriveners and the Estate Market in the Later Seventeenth Century', *Economic History Review*, 2nd ser., 4 (1951).

others arose through the transformation of the goldsmith's craft. Whereas the personal elements within most money-scrivener's banking activities generally involved small-scale lending, over the sixteenth century London goldsmiths gained a secure connection with the Royal Mint. Thereafter, during the next half century, some rose to prominence, to replace the Livery Companies as state financiers, a connection that persisted despite the turbulence of the Civil Wars. In parallel, goldsmiths traded in bullion, an activity legalized during Elizabeth's reign, and acted as pawnbrokers by advancing loans on the plate pledged to them. Typical of the inception of the initial phase of goldsmith banking was the business of the pawnshop of Thomas Vyner, opened in about 1623, following Vyner's apprenticeship as a goldsmith to his brother-in-law.[71]

Private banking came to be joined to the high finance conducted by some goldsmiths during the troubled decades of the mid-seventeenth century.[72] With the growing discord between king and parliament, lords and squires melted their holdings of plate and placed the bullion with goldsmiths, who, in turn, used the Mint as their established safe repository. Furthermore, because the mid-century civil strife turned their clerks into soldiers, London merchants turned to some goldsmiths to act as their cashiers and a portion of the deposits were mobilized as loans. Similarly, and somewhat in competition with some London money-scriveners, goldsmiths became recipients of the rural rents of the nobility and gentry, so further augmenting their potential banking deposits. Part of such sums was placed by goldsmiths with major individuals in their craft, such as Blackwell, a unique figure of considerable wealth, having expertise in the foreign exchanges and who acted as an agent for loans to Cromwell. Vyner, too, had achieved prominence by this time, being elected alderman for Billingsgate in 1647 and becoming sheriff for London in 1649 with the support of the Goldsmiths' Company. He received the same backing when he became Lord Mayor of London in 1653.

By the mid-century, Vyner was a merchant as well as a goldsmith and his successes in these affairs led him to have a deposit of £5,000 with Abbott's scrivener-bank, the 'Flying Horse'. He was a member of the East India Company, acting on its behalf in the receipt of Dutch compensation for damage done to the company's vessels during the Anglo-Dutch war that was brought to an end in 1654. Vyner's dealings in bullion enabled him to supply £1,700 of Spanish coin for the support of a voyage of an English fleet in 1650.

[71] Sir A. Heal, *The London Goldsmiths, 1200–1800* (Cambridge, 1935), p. 88; and D. K. Clark, 'A Restoration Goldsmith-Banking House: The Vine on Lombard Street', in C. Seymour et al., *Essays in Modern English History* (Port Washington/London, rep. 1971), pp. 6–7.

[72] A. V. Judges, 'The Origins of English Banking', *History*, 16 (1931); D. K. Clark, 'Edward Blackwell as a Royal Agent', *Economic History Review*, 9 (1939); and R. B. Outhwaite, 'Royal Borrowing in the Reign of Elizabeth I: The Aftermath of Antwerp', *English Historical Review*, 84 (1971).

These affairs went along with providing advice for the minting of the Commonwealth's coinage. Some of the new coins were struck from the treasure, amounting to £30,000, obtained by the capture of the Spanish fleet in 1656. Vyner, with Blackwell, bought the bullion on terms which involved a £50,000 advance to Cromwell and meeting the minting costs, while they transferred the surplus to the East India Company for export to the Orient.[73] By the Restoration, Vyner's shop, the Vine, now in Lombard Street as opposed to its original site in St Clement's Lane, was a place for the conduct of banking business. Its affairs involved other bankers, London's commercial community, and the state and, from 1662, these dealings were largely overseen by his nephew, Robert. The bank's clientele comprised the notables of the period but also embraced representatives of society's middling ranks and not just in the metropolis but also in the provinces.[74]

The immediate post-Restoration period was not untroubled: the Plague of 1665, the Great Fire of 1666, followed by the presence of Dutch warships at Chatham in 1667, led to runs on London goldsmith banks, including Blackwell's. Indeed, over the next century and for a variety of reasons, goldsmith banking, at the level of a particular enterprise, was frequently transitory. This was not simply due to bankruptcy or failure but also arose from an only partial personal commitment to providing banking services.

Goldsmiths, as a group, certainly became deposit bankers, yet a number went further and issued banknotes and so were fundamental innovators. It would appear that these notes first went into circulation in the mid-century, with Henry Futter, a goldsmith from 1633, being credited with this critical step—the circulation of paper money. The circulation of goldsmiths' notes began in the 1670s but in an uncertain fashion and amidst a myriad of proposals for the introduction of acceptable paper money. Distrust of goldsmiths' notes increased with the 'Stop of the Exchequer' in January 1672 so that they were not to be accepted by government departments as 'money' for nearly a decade thereafter.[75] As a consequence, London goldsmith bankers themselves ceased payments.[76] At least fourteen goldsmith banking firms were directly affected, with the list headed by those of Edward Blackwell, Sir Robert

[73] Clark, 'Restoration Goldsmith-Banking House', pp. 7–11.

[74] Clark, 'Restoration Goldsmith-Banking House', pp. 14–17.

[75] J. K. Horsefield, 'The Beginnings of Paper Money in England', *Journal of European Economic History*, 6 (1977).

[76] Some London goldsmith bankers, and their clients, had invested in assignable short-term government debt—Orders of Payment—but not all of it was secured upon specific taxes. However, the king's continuing need for funds to finance war, coupled with a refusal by the goldsmiths to make further advances, led to the prohibition of payments on certain kinds of this debt from 5 January 1672. This has come to be known as the Exchequer 'Stop'. See P. G. M. Dickson, *The Financial Revolution in England* (London, 1967), pp. 43–4, 51; and J. K. Horsefield, 'The "Stop of the Exchequer" Revisited', *Economic History Review*, 2nd ser., 35 (1982). See also Clark, 'Restoration Goldsmith-Banking House', pp. 36–47.

Vyner, and Gilbert Whitehall—Blackwell went bankrupt in 1682, Vyner failed in 1684 and, by 1685, Whitehall had been imprisoned for debt. The debt's settlement involved a protracted series of court cases and Treasury reactions to judicial decisions until the sum involved became a component—the 'Bankers' Annuities'—of the National Debt in December 1705.

One goldsmith bank that continued to be listed amongst the forty-four goldsmith banks of the late 1670s, was Hoares. This had been established by Richard Hoare in 1673, but his business was possibly the continuation of a family goldsmith undertaking dating back to at least 1597. Richard, the son of a London horse dealer, had been an apprentice in the Goldsmiths Company. Until the early eighteenth century, he was predominantly a goldsmith, immersed in work for the court and notables. His production of plate and jewels continued and, when the business was transferred to Fleet Street, it involved the acquisition of the trade of a retiring goldsmith. Initially, he had provided banking services for friends and relations but the move to Fleet Street, close to the fashionable West End, brought a wider, although still private, clientele.[77]

By the 1710s, Richard Hoare was more a banker than a goldsmith as he held commercial and institutional accounts. Furthermore, he no longer paid interest on deposits which had been his initial custom. Rather, the range of his services expanded to involve arrangements for his depositing customers to be able to draw funds in the provinces, sometimes using tradesmen at fairs as the transmitters. By correspondence, Richard kept some of his clientele apprised of business news—the movement of the exchanges—and events of political import, such as the king's health. This was coupled with investing clients' funds in land, mortgages, government loans, and the stock of the chartered companies. The solidity of the bank was guaranteed by the high cash ratio that Richard Hoare maintained—22.5 per cent of total assets, which amounted to £146,364 and included gold, silver, and jewels valued at £9,489 (6.5 per cent).[78] During the mid-1680s, Child's Bank had had an even higher cash proportion—57 per cent—within assets of about £0.1m, in which loans accounted for £29,000.[79]

In 1657, James Howell in *Londinopolis* had maintained that London aldermen could buy a hundred burghers of Amsterdam, a xenophobic jibe that had some basis in the few metropolitan plutocrats with assets greater than £100,000.[80] Nonetheless, within Restoration England, there was concern for expanding trade, seen as the indicator of the nation's prosperity, and an admiration for Dutch society, although the extent of this acknowledgement

[77] See P. Temin and H.-J. Voth, *Prometheus Shackled. Goldsmith Banks and England's Financial Revolution after 1700* (Oxford, 2013).

[78] [C. Hoare & Co.] *Hoare's Bank. A Record 1673–1932* (London, 1932), pp. 1–26.

[79] D. M. Joslin, 'London Private Bankers, 1720–1785', *Economic History Review*, 2nd ser., 7 (1954), p. 168, n. 4.

[80] Grassby, *Business Community*, p. 247.

varied according to political allegiances. These anxieties led to proposals to found banks. The success of the Wisselbank was put forward as a justification but many of the schemes were for land banks as opposed to exchange banks, some involving the introduction of land registries comparable with those in Holland.[81] Land banks, although having in contemporary eyes the most solid of bases for the circulation of notes, were not to be successfully established in England. Instead, over the eighteenth century, some London private banks and provincial attorneys replaced money-scriveners as facilitators of mortgage loans. More importantly, despite the continuation of metropolitan goldsmith banking, if not the survival of particular firms, the 'Stop' of 1672 remained in the public mind. This adversely affected the chances of the many proposals for large-scale banks that were put forward from 1676.[82]

Ultimately, it was the state's continuing need for resources to pursue warfare, rather than the needs of trade and commerce, that led to the foundation of the Bank of England in 1694. The state turned to the question of long-term borrowing for the first time in January 1692. William Paterson, a Scot, developed his proposals, with Michael Godfrey, during 1692–3 and discussed them with Charles Montague, who was to be Chancellor of the Exchequer from 1694. These preparations resulted in the incorporation of the Bank of England through the provision of a £1.2m loan to the state of which half had to be in the Exchequer by 1 August 1694. The necessary fund was raised within ten days by subscriptions to the Bank's shares, allowing the Bank's charter to be sealed on 27 July 1694. Its first governor, John Houblon, and its deputy governor, Michael Godfrey, came from the City's mercantile community, like other members of the Bank's Court of Directors.[83]

The Bank's management very rapidly made efforts to increase deposits upon which notes to bearer and cheques could be drawn. Paterson's first proposal had involved an issue of currency and the Bank of England, unlike other European public banks, was from its beginning a note-issuing institution. It took forward as a corporate body the banking practices that had been developed in London since the mid-seventeenth century. The Bank's note circulation amounted to £2.01m in 1696 but fluctuated markedly over the ensuing twenty years, with a high of £2.07m in 1703 and a low of £0.59m in 1710, the latter in part a reflection of its own then uncertain position.[84] Thereafter, there is a greater year-to-year constancy in the amount of its notes in circulation, which also have a rising underlying trend until the

[81] Dickson, *Financial Revolution in England*, pp. 4–7.

[82] J. K. Horsefield, *British Monetary Experiments, 1650–1710* (London, 1960), pt. IV and pp. 280–8.

[83] Sir J. H. Clapham, *The Bank of England. A History*, I, *1694–1797* (Cambridge, rep. 1970), pp. 14–20; and Dickson, *Financial Revolution*, pp. 50–7.

[84] Bank of England, *Bank of England Liabilities and Assets, 1696 to 1966* (London, 1967), p. 2.

1740s, all of which is testimony to the Bank's solidity following its difficult first two decades.

Although the Bank of England competed with the goldsmith banks, it did not come to replace them. Rather, the reaffirmation of the Bank's corporate privileges resulted in the London private banks not having to contend with further metropolitan joint-stock banking institutions for a further century and a quarter—until 1833. This was due to the Bank of England gaining a monopoly of joint-stock banking in England and Wales from 1707 as a result of providing the state with £1.5 million in the previous year to finance war with France. The further supply of £2.9 million to the government in 1711 went with a more closely framed definition of the Bank's exclusive privilege. Henceforth, 'no [other] corporation or partnership of more than six persons should "borrow owe or take up any Sum or Sums of Money on their bills or Notes payable at demand or at any less Time than Six Months".'[85] However, even with the exclusive privileges that it thereby acquired for undertaking joint-stock banking throughout England and Wales, the Bank of England remained until the mid-1820s, primarily and particularly a banker to the state and to the élite of society.

During 1694, the first year of the Bank's existence, it held many goldsmith accounts but most seem to have been for facilitating occasional transactions in the Bank's own notes and they were largely closed by May 1695. Alongside these were the active accounts of major goldsmiths, including those of Freame & Barclay, Henry Hankey, Richard Hoare, and Sir John Sweetaple, and which remained open after spring 1695. However, the Bank's management initially distrusted the standing of goldsmiths' notes and only gradually came to accept them, holding some £9,636 at the end of 1696.[86] The total note circulation of goldsmith banks, or London bankers as they were increasingly styled during the early eighteenth century, is not known. Hoares' amounted to £10,000 before 1720, whereas a decade later Martins, a 'City bank' in Lombard Street, had a circulation of £19,476. From the 1710s, only the notes of the most reputable private bank had the same status as those of the Bank of England. As a result, the onset of crisis, as in 1720 and 1745, could raise problems with respect to encashing goldsmith notes. Non-corporate, 'private' note issues were maintained but increasingly more important among the activities of goldsmith bankers were discounting and the provision of mortgages, with the latter element of their businesses aided by the legal maximum rate of interest being reduced to 5 per cent in 1714.

By 1700, there were thirty-nine goldsmith bankers in London, of which at least twelve had been in business in 1687, and so, prior to the Bank of England's foundation. Most continued to be relatively short-lived undertakings but, increasingly from the turn of the century, longevity was being enjoyed by a

[85] 7 Anne, C.30, Sect.66. See Clapham, *Bank of England*, 1, pp. 58–65.

[86] Clapham, *Bank of England* I, pp. 29–33.

few to the extent that they would either continue until the twentieth century or provide the basis for a subsequent major bank. The English 'financial revolution', of which the Bank of England was one institutional product, by structurally changing the London money market provided private bankers with a range of liquid securities in which they could invest or which the clienteles could offer as the collateral for loans. The supply of this well-founded state paper was augmented by securities of the chartered companies, especially those of the East India Company. Yet, it should be remembered that many goldsmith bankers either gave up their businesses or went bankrupt over the first decade of the eighteenth century. Furthermore, the South Sea Bubble led to the disappearance of one in three London goldsmith bankers. Thereafter, until the mid-century, there were at any one time about twenty-eight goldsmith bankers in London, with bankruptcy being the main reason for the disappearance of such firms over the period 1739–42 and, again, during the crisis year of 1745.

The addresses of goldsmith banks in 1700 might possibly indicate the beginnings of a specialization in their customer bases, with only one goldsmith bank still being in Cheapside. Six were located in Lombard Street while the premises of another five were beyond the City's western boundary, close to fashionable St James's. By 1725, the number of these 'West-end banks' had increased to thirteen and, although they had client connections with London's mercantile community and the East India Company, their major customers were drawn from the landed aristocracy. Hoares' deposits, totalling some £0.2m in 1725, were fed by the rent rolls of provincial estates and were mobilized in mortgage loans to the nobility and the gentry, coupled with short-term advances on negotiable securities. Child's Bank conducted a similar business but also had a strong connection with the East India Company through its partners being directors of this corporation from 1719. Personal links, arising from marriage, friendship, or a shared faith remained important in the further development of these banks' clienteles. Such intimate connections also played a role in the business of the houses in Lombard Street—the 'City' banks. Their distinguishing feature was an emphasis upon bill discounting, undertaken for members of the City's mercantile community. A further characteristic of 'City' banking were the provincial clienteles for whom the banks collected payment on London bills and accepted customers' own bills and notes.[87]

[87] The previous paragraphs have been drawn from Joslin, 'London Private Bankers, 1720–1785'.

2

Public and Private Markets for Capital and Credit, 1688–1793

Among north-western Europe's surviving private banks in 1914, a few could trace their origins to before 1793: one in Amsterdam;[1] at least two in France;[2] five in London;[3] and six in the English counties,[4] as well as eight in Germany.[5] The list may not be long, numbering only twenty-three houses, but it is a pointer to the longevity of banks (both private and corporate), that was to become increasingly one of their general characteristics during the nineteenth century. Another feature of this group of long-established houses is the continuing ambiguity of the word 'banking' during the eighteenth century.[6] Only one French house and ten of the English banking foundations were significantly concerned, from the commencement of their businesses, with taking deposits. The other twelve banks comprised private bankers who maintained a major stake in commerce to the extent that they would still, even in 1914, call themselves 'merchants' as opposed to 'bankers'. In this, they might have shared an attitude expressed in January 1802 by the mother of Henry Thornton (a partner in the London banking house of Down, Thornton & Free), 'that to cease being a Merchant in order to become a Banker was to descend in life'.[7]

[1] Hope & Co., 1732.

[2] Banque Adam, Boulogne-sur-Mer, 1784; and Société Torlades, Paris/Lisbonne, 1719.

[3] Baring Brothers, 1762; Drummonds, 1717; Forbes, Forbes, Campbell, 1790; Glyn, Mills, 1753; and Hoares, 1771.

[4] Beckett & Co., Leeds/Bradford, 1750; Fox, Fowler & Co., Wellington, 1787; Gillet & Co., Banbury, 1784; Harris, Bulteel & Co., Plymouth, 1774; Neville Reid & Co., Windsor, 1780; and Tubb & Co., Bicester, 1793.

[5] Lobbecke Brothers & Co., Brunswick, 1761; Sal. Oppenheim jr. & Cie, Cologne, 1789; J. H. Stein, Cologne, 1790; Von der Heydt-Kersten & Sohne, Elberfeld, 1754; Gebrüder Bethmann, 1 Frankfurt, 1748; Johan Berenberg, Gossler & Co., Hamburg, 1730; Frege & Co., Leipzig, 1739; P. J. Valckenberg, Worms, 1786.

[6] P. L. Cottrell, 'Aspects of Commercial Banking in Northern and Central Europe, 1880–1931', in S. Kinsey and L. Newton (eds), *International Banking in an Age of Transition* (Aldershot, 1998), pp. 100–1.

[7] Diary of Henry Thornton, January 1802, quoted by F. A. v. Hayek, 'Introduction' to F. A. v. Hayek (ed.), *H. Thornton, An Enquiry into the Nature and Effects of the Paper Credit of Great Britain* (London, 1802; London, 1939, and rep. 1962), p. 17.

Nonetheless, modern private banking, in terms of the varied origins of these houses, had its immediate roots in the eighteenth century. They were nourished from different sources, since, within the British Isles, there was a marked growth of private banking designed to serve significant swathes of society, whereas in continental Europe banking remained substantially an adjunct of merchanting. In turn, this produced a form of banking in England, Ireland, Scotland, and Wales that focused in large part upon issuing notes and discounting bills, while, and above all in Amsterdam and Frankfurt, those who came to be called 'bankers' were mercantile houses during the second half of the century that undertook the issue of loans on the part of European states. The contrasting emphasis upon credit and capital reflected to a significant degree the differences that emerged during the eighteenth century in the economic development of Britain, on the one hand, and continental Europe, on the other.

TRADE AND FINANCIAL NETWORKS

By the late seventeenth century there were very substantial trading connections between the United Provinces and England, through which knowledge of new business opportunities was disseminated. Furthermore, there was a well-established Dutch community in London whose roots went back over a century. It had re-coalesced after the 1560s, establishing its own church in the 'square mile' in 1571. A hundred years later, the commercial and financial milieus of Amsterdam and London were closely intermeshed through mutual dealings in the export of English woollens, the re-export of produce from the New World and Orient, and the English import of continental European linens bleached in Haarlem. By at least the 1670s, these trades involved a continuous flow of business correspondence, carried by packets across the North Sea between Harwich and Amsterdam. This commercial intercourse was frequently conducted in Dutch, with London merchants either writing in that language or employing Dutch clerks for the purpose. Such close connections were demonstrated, and reinforced, by part of the business training received by younger members of mercantile families being frequently carried out through residence abroad—in either Amsterdam or London. This was also done to gain experience as a commission agent or factor. Similarly, their fathers and their uncles stayed at the family houses of foreign correspondents, especially when London merchants attended Amsterdam's spring or autumn linen sales. Likewise, Dutch merchants developed direct connections with London wool exporters and with some in the English provinces such as West Country clothiers, while a few of the largest Amsterdam commercial undertakings established London branch houses.[8]

The interlinking of principals involved in North Sea commerce at a personal, family level became both wider and deeper from the mid-seventeenth century as a result of political action in England and France. Cromwell's readmission of Jews to England led to an inflow of the Sephardim from Amsterdam. A further inflow of Sephardi Jews into London was caused by the Portuguese Inquisition of the 1720s and 1730s, a part of a flight that took other co-religionists and family members to Amsterdam, Bordeaux, and Hamburg. Yet another strengthening of mercantile personal ties between London and continental Europe arose directly and indirectly from the consequences of the revocation of the Edict of Nantes. Links, constituted by a shared faith, filial relations, and business connections, were subsequently sustained between London's post-1685 Huguenot émigré community and other members of this particular diaspora, especially those that took up residence in Amsterdam, or Geneva, or Hamburg.[9] London's Huguenot community augmented the metropolis' European trading network while the business focus of some of its constituents gradually shifted from commerce into being primarily concerned with state finance, and they have consequently been regarded as City 'banking' houses.[10]

The Huguenot exodus from France over the four decades from 1680 involved the movement of probably 0.2m people, of whom about 40,000 departed between 1685 and 1688. The greater part of these forced migrants, and its wealthiest section, went to the United Provinces, which, by 1715, had received between 50,000 and 75,000 Huguenots. It is likely that a further 45,000 came to England, amongst whom were also some of the richest Huguenot émigrés. Others went to Ireland. Another significant flow, of the order of 25,000 refugees, moved to Switzerland, although for many of them this was but the first stage of a journey to the German states. Nonetheless, between 3,000 and 4,000 French Huguenots became permanent residents in Geneva to comprise about a quarter of the city's population.

The post-1685 Huguenot émigré community, dispersed across the continent and its western offshore islands, reinforced existing ties within Europe's Protestant trading networks. Furthermore, its members' migrations significantly altered the continent's spatial distribution of mercantile and financial wealth. The richest Huguenots possessed the most mobile assets and had investments abroad. Their flight from 1685, which had involved the greatest

[8] C. H. Wilson, *Anglo-Dutch Commerce and Finance in the Eighteenth Century* (Cambridge, 1941), pp. 6–7, 9–10, 28–32.

[9] S. Chapman, *Merchant Enterprise in Britain. From the Industrial Revolution to World War I* (Cambridge, 1992), p. 33.

[10] Chapman, *Merchant Enterprise in Britain*, p. 32.

feasible prior liquidation of their wealth in France, caused a decline in aggregate French bullion holdings. There is strong evidence that this involved a flow of specie to Amsterdam. Certainly, the Wisselbank experienced a rise in deposits and reserves after 1685, with the number of its depositors increasing by a third. Comparably, the extent of the influx of Huguenot wealth into London during the 1680s led the East India Company to accept it on short-term deposit. Moreover, this particular flow may have played a part in generating an active secondary market in shares of new English joint-stock companies during the first half of the 1690s, especially by off-setting the depressive effects of war upon investment sentiment.

PRIVATE BANKERS IN THE BRITISH ISLES

In England, the financial revolution of the eighteenth century affected the public sphere far more than the private sphere, and its causes lay in the need to finance the war effort rather than in the development of trade and industry.[11] The 'revolution' referred to the setting up of a modern system of government finance,[12] following William of Orange's accession to the throne in 1688, and to the founding of the Bank of England in 1694. As the government's banker, the latter was given responsibility for managing the public debt, even though it was a private institution whose profits also derived from commercial banking activities and from the privilege of issuing banknotes. The state's opportunities for borrowing were thus greatly increased, with the public debt, which had been £14.5 million in 1697, growing steadily after each war (the Spanish War of Succession, the Austrian War of Succession and the Seven Years' War) to reach £132 million in 1763 and £188 million in 1781 (the American War of Independence). The financial revolution also gave rise to a genuine capital market, capable of attracting available savings, and where not only government securities but also those of large joint-stock companies, first and foremost the Bank of England and the East India Company, were traded.

The eighteenth century was also a period of spectacular growth in British overseas trade, whose volume doubled between 1700 and 1780. This dynamism can be explained chiefly by three phenomena: the increase in domestic demand for American and Asian consumer goods (sugar, tobacco, tea, and coffee) and for raw materials from northern Europe (particularly timber); the

[11] See, in particular, P. G. M. Dickson, *The Financial Revolution in England. A Study in the Development of Public Credit, 1688–1756* (London, 1967); L. Neal, *The Rise of Financial Capitalism. International Capital Markets in the Age of Reason* (Cambridge, 1990).

[12] This system was based on the centralization of tax collection and, above all, on the institutionalization of the public debt, with official recognition and partial securitization of the debt, to which was added a redemption plan controlled by Parliament.

re-export of American and Asian consumer goods to Europe; and third, the growth of markets in the American and African colonies, reserved for British goods.[13] But this commercial expansion also arose from the British navy's ever-strengthening position and from the acquisition of colonies in Canada, the West Indies, and India, which would more than compensate for the loss of the American colonies, a loss that, moreover, barely affected trading relations between the two countries. London, far more than the other British ports (Bristol, Liverpool, and Glasgow), whose growth was, however, by no means insignificant, was at the heart of this 'commercial revolution', which brought about a remarkable development in auxiliary services—the commodity markets, insurance, and banking.

London Private Banks

Britain thus had a sizeable and growing commercial sector, whose members probably contributed about an eighth of national product.[14] A significant element were merchants, a term which by the mid-century denoted those involved in overseas trade.[15] While the importance of the Atlantic 'outports' was ever increasing, London remained the predominant British focus of colonial trade, both Occidental and Oriental, and also of dealings with Europe.[16] The metropolitan commercial community of the mid-eighteenth century was the seed bed of the subsequent development of British fully-fledged merchant banking in the nineteenth century—an essential component of the world of private banking. In the eighteenth century, however, the London private banks were the deposit banks that mainly grew out of the seventeenth century goldsmiths' profession.

The number of London banks would appear to have risen merely from twenty-seven in 1745 to thirty-two by 1763, despite the concurrent significant expansion of metropolitan commerce.[17] Although the businesses of both existing and newly-established banks may have expanded, the rapid growth

[13] J. M. Price, 'What did Merchants do? Reflections on British Overseas Trade, 1660–1790', *Journal of Economic History*, 49, 2 (1989), pp. 267–84.

[14] P. Dean and W. A. Cole, *British Economic Growth 1688–1959. Trends and Structure* (Cambridge, 1969), p. 156.

[15] D. Hancock, *Citizens of the World. London Merchants and the Integration of the British Atlantic Community, 1735–1785* (Cambridge, 1995), pp. 9–10.

[16] C. J. French, '"Crowded with Traders and a Great Commerce". London's Domination of English Overseas Trade, 1700–1775', *London Journal*, 17 (1992).

[17] D. M. Joslin, 'London Private Bankers, 1720–1785', *Economic History Review*, 2nd ser., 7 (1954), pp. 173–4; see also, D. M. Joslin, 'London Bankers in Wartime 1739–84', in L. S. Pressnell (ed.), *Studies in the Industrial Revolution* (London, 1960); Sir. J. H. Clapham, *The Bank of England. A History*, I, 1694–1797 (Cambridge, 1970), pp. 163–7; and F. T. Melton, 'Deposit Banking in London, 1700–90', *Business History*, 28 (1986).

over the mid-century of metropolitan foreign trade, especially colonial commerce, would not seem to have generated a substantial demand for increased banking facilities, particularly in Lombard Street, the location of the 'City' mercantile-oriented houses.

The number of London banks expanded during the 1770s and 1780s but the profession's growth was punctuated by the effects of war and financial crisis. Eighty metropolitan merchants went bankrupt between 1781 and 1783, but, by 1786, London had some fifty-two banking partnerships. This augmentation was sufficient to overcome the fatal effects of the 1772–3 crash upon the inexperienced or those that still combined banking with other, largely mercantile, ventures.[18] Some new, late eighteenth-century houses were formed by previous banking partners or clerks, but most reflected the formal entry into the profession of those who had already provided banking services—as financiers, merchants, or manufacturers—and had thereby amassed £20,000, regarded as the necessary equity for a specialist venture.[19]

This outline of developments can be fleshed out by considering the various experiences of a number of banks, new and old, within the City during the eighteenth century. Vere, Glyn & Hallifax, and Barclays both had metropolitan origins, whereas Smith, Payne & Smiths; Hanbury, Taylor, Lloyd & Bowman; and Jones Loyd were established in the 'square mile' by country bankers.

Vere, Glyn & Hallifax commenced business at the beginning of 1754. Its senior partner, Joseph Vere, had considerable experience, accumulated initially through an apprenticeship at Thomas Martin's goldsmith bank, leading to admittance to the Goldsmiths Company, before joining his uncle Samuel at the 'White Horse', Lombard Street and succeeding him in the partnership in 1734. Vere founded a new partnership at the 'White Horse' with Richard Glyn, a wealthy London drysalter and brought to the new undertaking not only £10,000, a stake equivalent to Vere's, but also a major connection with the silk trade that was subsequently to generate many banking customers.[20] Thomas Hallifax was very much the junior partner, contributing £4,000 to the bank's equity. He had grown up in south Yorkshire but, in the midst of a provincial apprenticeship, he decided to come to the City and during his twenties was chief clerk at Martin's Bank.

Initially, the new bank worked from the ground floor of Vere's house in Lombard Street but, in 1757, acquired a newly-erected building in nearby Birchin Lane. This had a layout similar to the premises of London merchants, with banking business taking place on the ground floor while Vere resided in

[18] L. S. Pressnell, *Country Banking in the Industrial Revolution* (Oxford, 1956), p. 21.

[19] Joslin, 'London Private Bankers', pp. 180–1.

[20] William Deacon's Bank Limited, 'Williams and Glyns and the Veres', in *Williams Deacon's 1771–1970* (Manchester, 1971), pp. 29–31.

the three upper storeys along with the clerks who lodged in. Customers, primarily commercial, seeking either facilities to support their trading ventures or assistance with investments in government stocks, were received in the bank's fine front room. The consequent paperwork was undertaken in two others at the rear, of which one, merely sixty-three square feet in area, was dominated by a newly-purchased mahogany desk at which three clerks worked.[21] The partnership was informally renewed in 1760, when the bank's equity was reduced to £16,000. Yet, this was more than counterbalanced by the growing social prestige that the bank gained through its partners' public activities. Glyn was Lord Mayor of London during 1758–9 and entered Parliament in 1759, initially sitting for the City and, subsequently, Coventry, a town linked to the bank and its partner by the silk trade. He was also a director of the Million Bank and one of the founders of Equitable Life Assurance. Hallifax followed in Glyn's wake, being elected a City Sheriff, with his standing assisted by the dowry of £20,000 that his first, short-lived wife, Penelope Thomson, had brought him. Glyn and Hallifax guided the bank's affairs, which required more of their time following Vere's death in 1766.[22]

During its first years, Vere, Glyn & Hallifax (Glyn & Hallifax from 1766) was well managed despite some accounting difficulties and so only accumulated bad debts of £450. While two major lines of credit totalling £6,500 became doubtful in 1765, a net profit of £3,700 was still generated. However, the bank was rocked by the crisis of 1772–3, caused by the failure of the Ayr Bank, a Scottish provincial banking company. Panic in the City was sparked by the collapse of a bank conducted by Alexander Fordyce, a Scot, and London agent for the recently established and forceful Ayr Bank.[23] Glyn & Hallifax was temporarily forced to stop payments, having been embarrassed by its own Scottish connections, and reopened in August 1772 with support provided by a range of parties. Some came from the Bank of England, part of the liquidity that the Bank supplied liberally to quell the crisis. These facilities from an early lender-of-last-resort operation were augmented by £20,000 from a customer, the third Lord Middleton, £8,500 provided by the father of Hallifax's second wife, and £10,000 offered by Charles Mills, an Indian merchant, who thereby became a partner in the bank.[24] From the 1772–3 crisis until 1790, the bank's affairs were shaped by Hallifax. He became the

[21] R. Fulford, *Glyn's 1753–1953. Six Generations in Lombard Street* (London, 1953), pp. 1–14.

[22] Fulford, *Glyn's*, pp. 15–23.

[23] On Fordyce, see J. Hoppit, *Risk and Failure in English Business 1700–1800* (Cambridge, 1987), pp. 134–7; on the Ayr Bank, see H. Hamilton, 'The failure of the Ayr Bank, 1772', *Economic History Review*, 8 (1955–6) and C. W. Munn, *The Scottish Provincial Banking Companies 1747–1864* (Edinburgh, 981), pp. 29–36; and on the 1772–3 crisis, see J. Hoppit, 'Financial Crises in Eighteenth-Century England', *Economic History Review*, 39 (1986).

[24] Fulford, *Glyn's*, pp. 14–16, 23–3; and Clapham, *Bank of England*, I, pp. 242–51.

senior partner in 1773, following the death of Sir Richard Glyn, whose place was taken by Richard Carr Glyn, his young second son. Mills had essentially a sleeping interest and, as a result of the exceptional circumstances of 1772–3, a clerk, Henry Mitton, was also made a partner. Hallifax gained new customers for the bank through his public activities: in the City, becoming Lord Mayor in 1776, and at Westminster, sitting for Aylesbury from 1784.[25] Glyns was to continue to evolve essentially as a family-based bank.

Barclays, another City family house, substantially developed not only through a sequence of filial relationships but also upon the basis of mutual Quaker beliefs, giving rise to very particular business connections. Barclays had late seventeenth-century origins: by the late 1690s it operated from a shop in Lombard Street, and in 1698 was styled Freame & Gould—John Freame having married Priscilla Gould the previous year. Initially a grocer, Freame was a goldsmith by 1694 and, forty years later, was known as a banker as well as being deputy-governor of the Lead Company. During the 1730s, the banking business was undertaken by his son, Joseph, and his son-in-law, James Barclay. These close family relationships were further tightened when James's father, David Barclay I, a London merchant, took as his second wife, Priscilla Freame, the daughter of his son's partner. Children of the marriage of David and Priscilla—David II and John—subsequently entered the bank as partners. The partnership was reconstituted several times in the course of the eighteenth century, with the Freame name disappearing and the Bevan and, in particular, Barclay names appearing in the 1770s.[26]

Other Quaker family connections in 1779 linked through marriage the 'Barclay' London bank with the Gurney bank in Norwich. Richard Gurney, a merchant and strict Friend, married the daughter and only child of David Barclay II. During the same year, Richard and his brother Joseph became partners with Barlett Gurney in the Norwich & Norfolk Bank, established by John and Henry Gurney four years earlier. It would seem that Richard assumed the direction of the Norwich bank and was certainly responsible during the early 1780s for opening connected banks elsewhere in East Anglia.[27] The Gurney's activities in the eastern countries were an important dimension of the remarkable rise of country banking over the second half of the eighteenth century throughout the British Isles, to be considered in greater detail in the following section. For the 'Barclay' London bank, the Gurneys' particular East Anglian banking developments brought a new type of business—acting as the metropolitan agent for country banks. Smith, Bevan & Bening, as the bank was known

[25] Fulford, *Glyn's*, pp. 38–41, 49, 57.

[26] P. W. Matthews (compiler) and A. W. Tuke (ed.), *History of Barclays Bank Limited* (London, 1926), pp. 30–9.

[27] Matthews and Tuke, *History of Barclays Bank*, pp. 104–7.

in the 1770s, had begun this, as agents for the Gurneys while also training John Gurney II as a banker.

Country agencies were largely taken up from the 1770s by 'City' banks, especially houses in Lombard Street or nearby. Older metropolitan banks, especially those in the West End, generally shunned the risks of this new business that developed rapidly over the last quarter of the century. Unfortunately, it is only possible to establish some quantitative indicators of the extent of country agencies in 1797, when forty-four London banks undertook this function but amongst which seven houses were dominant: Down (founded in 1782); Esdaile (created in 1781); Forster; Masterman (established in 1780); Robarts (formed in 1791); Sanderson (located in Southwark, across the Thames from the 'City'); and Barclays. They met bills drawn upon them by country banks, cashed their notes payable in London, supplied them with funds when required and undertook investments on their behalf in bills, stocks and shares. The basis for this multifaceted business was a deposit placed by a country bank with its London agent. This provided a further source of funds for the metropolitan house while, should the account go into debit, the London banker charged a commission for services rendered to the country bank.[28]

Such agency business was probably welcomed in Lombard Street since it provided opportunities that could offset the effects of greater competition from the Bank of England. The Bank not only came to the fore during liquidity shortages arising from the impact of either war (as during the early 1760s and the first half of the 1780s), or financial crises (when it acted as a lender of last resort (in 1763 and 1772–3),[29] but also as a commercial competitor. It has been estimated that, by the mid-1780s, the Bank of England was the single most important discounter in the City and, given its eligibility rules, it was probably taking up the best quality paper available on the market.[30]

A few of the new country banks made early direct connections with London by establishing their own associated City houses, such as: Smith, Payne & Smiths; Hanbury, Taylor, Lloyd & Bowman; and Jones Loyd.

The Smith bank had been founded in Nottingham during the mid-seventeenth century, an exceptional development, fostered in part by the business connections between Thomas Smith I, on one the hand, and Edward Backwell and Gilbert Whitehall, London goldsmith bankers, on the other. Further growth of the Nottingham bank came with the appointment of Thomas I as a sub-commissioner for the excise in 1671, related to his all-important ability

[28] Joslin, 'London Private Bankers', p. 183.

[29] M. C. Lowell, 'The Role of the Bank of England as Lender of Last Resort in the Crises of the Eighteenth Century', *Explorations in Entrepreneurial History*, 10 (1957).

[30] J. H. Clapham, 'The Private Business of the Bank of England, 1744–1800', *Economic History Review*, 11 (1941) and Joslin, 'London Private Bankers', p. 175.

to transmit funds to London. These tax receipts provided resources, albeit temporary, for Smith's activities as a mercer and an early provincial banker. The vital connection with the metropolis was institutionalized by Samuel Smith I, Thomas II's brother and a continuing partner in the Nottingham bank, establishing himself as a London goldsmith during the early eighteenth century. He acted as the London agent of the Nottingham bank while both houses had accounts with the Bank of England. On Samuel's death in 1751, the interlocking partnership ceased but the London house was maintained by Samuel's sons who remained agents for the Nottingham bank. However, a family quarrel led to a restructuring in 1758, with Abel Smith reconstituting the Nottingham house in partnership with John Payne, a London merchant and draper and chairman of the East India Company. Samuel's sons moved into the London silk trade while the Nottingham bank's London agency went to Abel's new bank, Smith & Payne, later Smith, Payne & Smiths.[31]

Abel Smith was prepared to put £40,000 into the new 'City' bank and play a direct part in its management since his political activities brought him regularly to the capital. Success seemed assured since Edward Payne, John's younger brother and mercantile partner, was a director of the Bank of England (and was to succeed to 'the chairs' during the troubled years of 1769–73). Although never having an equity stake in the bank, Edward acted as a consultant and thereby received half of the profits that the Paynes derived from it. Until 1769, Smith & Payne merely provided the metropolitan connection for the Nottingham Smith bank and in 1764 only had a capital of £16,963, probably the sum of the retained profits since 1758. The house's lack of development during its early years was due to John Payne's caution which at times exasperated Abel Smith.

René Payne inherited his father's banking interest in 1764 and was joined in 1773 by Robert Smith, Abel's son. Robert took the place of a cashier, William Bowman, who had been largely responsible for the house having incurred losses during the later 1760s. The bank was recapitalized, its equity amounting to £49,343 in 1773, and it was set upon a deliberate course of developing its own business. This strategy had some success, with profits of £10,282 during the mid-1770s, although these had required the support and assistance of the Nottingham bank. When Nottingham balances were run down during 1776–7, arising from Abel's investments in land and his activities within the East India Company, the City bank's situation became more difficult. Its partners were forced to rediscount commercial bills with the Bank of England—operations assisted by Edward Payne but, nonetheless, much frowned upon by the Bank's management. Family pressure was successfully applied and, by 1780, the London bank once more held £50,000 on the account of the Nottingham

[31] J. A. S. Leighton Boyce, *Smiths the Bankers 1658–1958* (London, 1958), pp. 1–19, 67–9.

bank. Profits rose from the late 1770s, which enabled the City bank to accumulate a reserve of £22,197 at the close of 1782. Although the mid-1780s proved less remunerative, Abel's conception of a London banking house was finally met during these years because it generated greater net revenues than its Nottingham counterpart.[32]

Despite leaving the Smith bank in 1770 under something of a cloud, William Bowman immediately became a partner in another Lombard Street house, Hanbury, Taylor, Lloyd & Bowman. This was an entirely new concern, established by the Birmingham bank of Taylor & Lloyd, itself of only eight years standing. Sampson Lloyd II was a Quaker ironmonger whereas John Taylor was a Unitarian maker of 'Birmingham toys' and they were joined in their original west-Midland banking venture by their sons, all four each taking stakes of £8,000. Initially, this bank had employed Smith & Payne as its London agents with a possibility that Abel Smith would become a Birmingham banking partner. Their own London house was set up by Lloyd's and Taylor's sons—Sampson III and John II—together with Osgood Hanbury, related to John II by marriage, and Bowman, all of whom individually contributed £5,000 to its equity. Bowman was the managing partner and resided at 14 Lombard Street, the bank's premises. As with the Smith bank, Hanbury, Taylor, Lloyd & Bowman benefited from the support of its provincial parent, in the shape of a deposit of £27,000 in 1771.[33]

The creation of London banks by provincial Nonconformist families continued, as with the establishment in 1778 of Joseph Jones & Co., the progenitor of Jones Loyd & Co. This was formed because Vere, Sapte & Co.,[34] metropolitan agents for the Manchester bank, Jones & Co., decided to give up its particular business due to what they regarded as its untoward, rapid expansion. Initially run by a son of the founder of the Manchester bank, the new London banking partnership went through a series of changes in 1791, 1794, and 1798 before assuming the style Jones Loyd in 1808 by which the bank was to become so well-known. In 1793, Lewis Loyd, a Unitarian Minister had married Sarah Jones, a relation of the founder of the Manchester bank, and immediately joined its associated London house. Their first child, Samuel Jones Loyd, (from 1850 Lord Overstone), was born in 1796 and was to manage the London bank from 1844 as one of the nineteenth century's most remarkable private bankers and monetary economists.[35]

[32] Leighton Boyce, *Smiths the Bankers*, pp. 75–85.

[33] R. S. Sayers, *Lloyds Bank in the History of English Banking* (Oxford, 1957), pp. 5–11, 26, 28.

[34] Vere, Sapte & Co. had its origins in Vere, Raymond, Williams & Lowe, formed in 1770 and in which Charles Vere, cousin of Joseph Vere, invested £10,000 from wealth accumulated through dealing in China. See William Deacon's Bank Limited, 'Williams and Glyns and the Veres', p. 32.

[35] T. E. Gregory, *The Westminster Bank through a Century* (London, 1936), I, pp. 320–1 and II, pp. 158–86.

'City' banks of the second half of the eighteenth century, whether of metropolitan or provincial origins, were constituted in a comparable manner to metropolitan mercantile partnerships. Senior members were frequently close relations, with the degree of family connections being almost intimate in the case of banks established by Nonconformists, especially Quakers, due to the limited social circles from which suitable marriage partners could be drawn. As over previous centuries, a shared faith gave further confidence in banking that was forced to rely largely upon mutual trust, since information sources were still limited and physical distance adversely affected communications. A common belief also assisted the development of business, as Nonconformists were important in not only the expansion of trade but also the growth of industry, especially brewing, coal, and iron. Nonetheless, adherence to a faith could vary. If family succession proved awkward due to the relative youth of the sons, then clerks were taken as partners, especially when banks had to be reconstituted as the result of either crisis or the sudden death of a partner. Restructuring could also take place because of family disagreements, with the Smith banks providing one example of this.

Like London mercantile undertakings, metropolitan banking partnerships were normally established for medium-term periods, such as seven years. But, if successful, they gained longevity through renewals of the underlying agreements, sometimes, as with Glyns in 1760, by informal acquiescence that could give rise to later legal complications when a partner died. Accounts were drawn up regularly at the year-end and profits frequently left to constitute a reserve. The major difference with metropolitan banking partnerships, if they were to be successful, was that they required considerably greater initial equity—about £20,000—than the £9,000 to 12,000 in the case of commercial concerns.

By the 1790s, most London private bankers had ceased to issue notes and largely worked on the basis of their capital and deposits.[36] Nevertheless, the full emergence of deposit banking in the metropolis by the end of the century went along in the case of most 'City' bankers with a rising volume of interbank payments originating from the earlier necessity to exchange notes. Both 'City' and 'West End' bankers had used clerks to undertake direct transfers between individual houses of notes and bills but the pressures of ever greater business, together with those exerted by the need to economize cash resources, led in 1773 to the establishment of the London Clearing House. However, this was solely a City institution: by 1777, thirty-one of the thirty-six banks comprising its membership were situated in, or near Lombard Street.

It has been argued that the institutionalization of clearing was particularly related to the growth of country agency business undertaken by 'City' banks.[37]

[36] Clapham, *Bank of England*, I, p. 162.
[37] Joslin, 'London Private Bankers', pp. 184–5.

Without doubt, agency work was rising during the early 1770s, yet the timing of the creation of the Clearing House does not chime with what is currently known about the full development of metropolitan-provincial banking links. They were only to come to the fore during the last decades of the century, some ten to twenty years after the formal establishment of the Clearing House. Initially, clearing practices had arisen simply from the daily routines of bankers' clerks who, during the early 1770s, found the 'Five Bells', Lombard Street, to be both a convenient lunchtime venue and an ideal place at which to undertake inter-bank business. By 1773, Lombard Street banks were contributing to the rent of a room at this public house. However, in 1784, premises for the Clearing House were jointly acquired by 'City' banks, a possible indication of the rate of growth of inter-bank transactions as well as of their search for a place of business with fewer distractions. Two decades later, the Clearing House occupied a room at the rear of the premises of Smith, Payne & Smiths, the bank that had come to be one of its most important members during the late 1770s. Net clearing balances came to be settled in Bank of England notes and, by 1793, about twenty-three London bankers had accounts with the Bank, including from among those who specialized in country agency business—Barclays, Esdaile, Robarts—and along with others, such as Jones and Smith, Payne & Smiths, that had direct provincial links.[38] The establishment of a formal Clearing House was to lead to a particular nomenclature for its subscribers—London clearing banks—and membership became monopolistic: it was used to confront the new London joint-stock banks of the 1830s and all new banks, with greater success, from the 1870s.

The Emergence of English Country Banking

The most remarkable European financial development of the eighteenth century was the growth in the provision of formal banking facilities throughout the British Isles. This took place within three distinct legal contexts, since Scottish law contained specific unique conditions regarding the formation of economic enterprises while Ireland was a separate country before the creation of the United Kingdom in 1801. Within England and Wales, the establishment of banks in the provinces was subject to the same legal constraints that affected their creation in London and which arose from the Bank of England's monopoly over joint-stock banking, granted in 1707 and 1711. This restricted the constitution of other English and Welsh banks to partnerships involving no

[38] G. Chandler, *Four Centuries of Banking*, (London, 1964) 1, pp. 151–3; Clapham, *Bank of England*, I, pp. 172, 222; Fulford, *Glyn's*, pp. 104–6; and Leighton Boyce, *Smiths the Bankers*, p. 122.

more than six individuals.[39] Given the relative sizes of the 'national' economies that comprised the British Isles, attention will be first directed to the development of provincial banking within England and Wales.

Country banking in England and Wales fully emerged as a formal, specialized service industry during the second half of the eighteenth century. Nonetheless, many country bankers, like their London counterparts, were not fully-fledged financial specialists during the late eighteenth century as they combined banking with other business activities. Indeed, the provision of wider banking services frequently emerged from, and then came to dominate, involvement in the supply of credit and the means of payment initially associated with a 'banker's' other business engagements. Industrialization has many facets, of which one was the further development of specialization. Within pre-industrial Europe, most economic actors undertook a range of activities if only to hedge against risk. However, as industrialization took hold, the number of individuals pursuing multiple occupations diminished as the economic rewards of specialization brought about a greater focus in their business affairs. The first stage in the formal emergence of country banking in England and Wales—from *c.*1750 to 1793—was characterized by this transition to specialization. Yet, it must be remembered that not all provincial bankers (and, likewise, those in London)[40] had become fully committed specialists by the outbreak of the French revolutionary wars in 1793.

Evidence from trade directories for country banking from 1750, although not totally reliable, is sufficient to indicate a remarkable expansion. Pressnell's careful corrections to the data indicate that there were some 128 country banks by 1784 (including at least one firm in Wales)[41] and about a further 157 provincial houses a decade later. However, as in London, this was far from being a smooth development. The establishment of provincial banking houses particularly took place during the early 1750s, the mid-1760s, and the opening years of both the 1770s and the 1790s. This temporal pattern has little relationship with the timing of metropolitan growth—only the early 1770s were a period of marked bank formation in both London and the provinces. The appearance of new country houses would appear to have been related to waves of credit expansion within the economy, especially its provincial components.[42] Specialist country bankers formally emerged if the demand for

[39] It would appear that only two early houses transgressed this: the Cornish Miners' Bank, Truro from 1771 and Davison-Bland & Co., Newcastle, established in 1788; Pressnell, *Country Banking*, pp. 106, 228.

[40] One example is Leslie Grove, 'Merchant, Banker, Dealer and Chapman', who failed in 1789 and for which, see Hoppit, *Risk and Failure*, pp. 154–6.

[41] For banking in Wales during the eighteenth century, see R. O. Roberts, 'Financial Developments in Early Modern Wales and the Emergence of the First Banks', *Welsh History Review*, 16 (1993).

[42] Pressnell, *Country Banking*, pp. 6–8.

borrowing could be readily met—though the business of country banking did not concentrate entirely upon providing credit, as it encompassed great variety, with individual banks performing particular functions, depending upon the articulated needs and demands of the local economies and communities that they were established to service.[43]

Within the heterogeneity of country banking, there was one common characteristic: most banks issued notes either against customers' deposits or through discounting bills of exchange. Indeed, the growing need for means of payment was one of the major demand factors that provoked the formal emergence of provincial banking. Its imperative was only tempered in areas, like southern Lancashire and parts of the west Midlands and the West Riding, where residents became prepared to take bills of exchange as close money substitutes.[44] This calls attention to another facet of industrialization, namely, the further expansion of the market economy and the consequent increased demand for means of payment. The growing general readiness to take up private bankers' notes within the provinces was due to the poor quality of the coinage coupled with a shortage of currency, with the former only being addressed by the state from 1797.

The lack of paper currency within England and Wales occurred despite the Bank of England's circulation increasing markedly from an annual average of £4.6 million (1753–62) to £8.2 million (1783–92)[45]—a rise occurring principally in the wake of the 1773 crisis, with the Bank's more commercial attitude towards discounting. Nevertheless, the circulation of the Bank's notes was largely restricted to London and the Home Counties, leading to its contemporary epithet of 'Bank of London' (although indirect evidence indicates that at the mid-century the Bank's notes were already known throughout southern England and, very occasionally, much further afield, in Berwick-upon-Tweed, Haverfordwest, Newcastle-under-Lyme, and Rotherham). In any case, despite a wider geographical use of Bank of England notes than is often acknowledged, two-thirds of their reported losses during the third quarter of the eighteenth century took place in London, the locus of the Bank's issuing.[46]

In coming to meet the undoubted growing void in provincial circulation, country bankers were little constrained by statute but, rather, out of pragmatic

[43] See H. V. Bowen and P. L. Cottrell, 'Banking and the Evolution of the British Economy 1694–1878', in A. Teichova, G. Kurgan-van Hentenryk, and D. Ziegler (eds), *Banking, Trade and Industry. Europe, America and Asia from the Thirteenth to the Twentieth Century* (Cambridge, 1997).

[44] T. S. Ashton, 'The Bill of Exchange and Private Banks in Lancashire, 1790–1830', *Economic History Review*, 15 (1945) and reprinted in T. S. Ashton and R. S. Sayers, *Papers in English Monetary History* (Oxford, 1964).

[45] Calculated from Bank of England, *Bank of England Liabilities and Assets 1696 to 1966* (London, 1967), pp. 2–4.

[46] Clapham, *Bank of England*, I, pp. 146–50.

necessity had to be prepared to redeem their notes when they were presented. Demand notes became common from the late 1780s, whereas country banks' earlier circulations had comprised paper hardly distinguishable from either bills of exchange or promissory notes. The issuing of small notes—under £1 and £5—was progressively forbidden by Acts passed during the mid-1770s and, in 1779, there was even the possibility of a measure requiring bankers to back their circulations with reserves comprising government stocks. By the late 1780s, country bank issues largely consisted of £5 and £10 notes (and their guinea variants, £5 5s and £10 10s, to enable holders to obtain gold coin), supported by others of larger denomination—£20, £50, and £100.[47]

The problems arising from the shortage of means of payment bore particularly upon industrialists and merchants, both in traditional trades, such as the Gurneys in wool, and, perhaps even more so, within the few but important branches of manufacturing that were being transformed structurally by new practices and techniques. The smelting of iron with coke, the development of coal mining, especially beyond the Great Northern coalfield, along with the production of cotton textiles during the water-powered phase of this particular industry's development, all tended to take place in rural locations, often remote and isolated. Consequently, entrepreneurs within these industrial branches were often confronted by a range of novel financial difficulties. Due to the national shortage of copper and other coinage, wage payments came to be made in trade tokens, their striking being relatively easy within the non-ferrous metals industries.[48] Other resorts that took industrialists into at least aspects of banking were the use of notes, rather than tokens, as substitutes for scarce coins in wage packets. These measures brought manufacturers into contact with shopkeepers, themselves not infrequently petty providers of credit, while another alternative was the enterprise's own 'tommy shop' and associated truck payments. Such monetary and quasi-monetary engagements went alongside customary involvements in the all-important, long-established web of credit—bill finance—that supported undertakings financially with respect to the provision of raw materials, sustaining inventories of goods being produced, and on-sales.

The resolution of these monetary and financial problems led industrialists to be one of the major groups that established country banks. An early house, Praed & Co. at Truro, had close connections with the Cornish copper industry. Three of its partners were directly involved in copper extraction, as also was the bank's first manager, and their mining ventures received special banking terms, such as interest-free overdrafts. At least four other Cornish banks were comparably involved in copper mining, which should cause no surprise, given

[47] Pressnell, *Country Banking*, pp. 138–9, 141–2, 501.

[48] See P. Mathias, *English Trade Tokens. The Industrial Revolution Illustrated* (London, 1962); and J. R. S. Whiting, *Trade Tokens. A Social and Economic History* (Newton Abbot, 1971).

this industry's growth over the eighteenth century and its consequent rising importance in south-west England.[49]

Nevertheless, it should not be assumed that all industrialists became bankers. Equally, despite Pressnell's seminal work and subsequent research, it remains difficult to discern with any precision, let alone quantify, the precise connections between the marked growth of formal country banking and the direct financial role that it played in the growth of manufacturing during the opening phases of the classic period of the Industrial Revolution—the decades from the 1760s.[50] Given the parochial nature of much provincial banking and its intimate basis, the creditworthiness of an industrialist was often assessed on personal grounds. Bankers were aware not only of an outline of the manufacturing dimensions of proposals placed before them but also, and more especially, the family and other connections of firms involved, all of which played a part in their calculations. Given this importance of the wider personal relationships, perhaps too much emphasis has been placed by scholars solely on whether banks and bankers granted either medium- or long-term facilities to those involved in manufacturing, let alone whether short-term credits to industrialists were rolled over to become, in practice, semi-permanent banking facilities. Rather, what does emerge is that being a new customer of a bank, as either an industrialist or a trader who lacked adequate personal guarantees, could mean that, if banking credits were provided, terms might be stiff until creditworthiness was proven. Generally, new bank clients of whatever background were accommodated if they either came from within the local community or had personal associations with it, but they were on more difficult grounds with bankers if they were total 'outsiders'. Accordingly, country banking can be regarded as a greater formalization of the existing web of credit based upon the bill of exchange—with the personal as well as the commercial relationships that this financial instrument expressed.

Industrialists might be regarded as forming a new contingent to the ranks of providers of banking services, although over the eighteenth century, in Britain at least, the merchant-manufacturer was increasingly being mutated into a specialist producer. The other major backgrounds of English and Welsh country bankers were more established, following somewhat in the footsteps

[49] Pressnell, *Country Banking*, pp. 14–19, 322–4; Matthews and Tuke, *History of Barclays Bank*, pp. 250–61, 264–8, 271–2; and, for context, J. Rowe, *Cornwall in the Age of the Industrial Revolution* (St Austell, 2nd ed., 1993).

[50] Pressnell himself concluded that 'the picture . . . is inevitably impressionistic'; Pressnell, *Country Banking*, p. 322. Later work by Cameron characterizes the evidence as 'circumstantial', albeit powerful: R. Cameron, 'England 1750–1844', in R. Cameron et al., *Banking in the Early Stages of Industrialisation* (New York, 1967), p. 23. For subsequent surveys, see P. Mathias, 'Capital, Credit and Entrepreneurs in the Industrial Revolution', *Journal of European Economic History*, 2 (1973); P. Mathias, 'Financing the Industrial Revolution', in P. Mathias and J. A. Davis (eds), *The First Industrial Revolution* (Oxford, 1990); and Bowen and Cottrell, 'Banking and the Evolution of the British Economy'.

of pre-1750 metropolitan developments, although without the seed germ of goldsmithing. Many provincial bankers emerged from the legal profession and its penumbra, especially those attorneys, money-scriveners, and scriveners already involved in financial transactions.[51] Engagement in the provision of capital, but more especially in the web of credit, also led to merchants, traders, and dealers becoming formal banking specialists. Indeed, many country bankers had previously been drapers or mercers while, alongside them, were those who had dealt in coal, or iron, or wine. The eighteenth-century London merchanting banker had his provincial counterpart, albeit that the latter was likely to have less capital and, perhaps, a more spatially restricted range of business and personal contacts.

Participation in the inland trades, or coastal shipments, or short sea movements often gave rise to metropolitan connections which enabled the ready remittance of funds to London, the continuing hub of the economy. The ability to undertake transfers to the metropolis was just as important in the emergence of specialist banking as either supplying means of payment or providing credit locally. Henry Burgess, the spokesman for country bankers, wrote in August 1835:

> Men, we believe, are still living who carried on business in parts of the country lying north of the mail-road from Liverpool to Hull, who kept their banking accounts in Nottingham; they resorted to a distance of more than seventy miles for supplies of cash and also, probably because they found it more convenient to pass their pecuniary transactions relating to their foreign trade through a bank at that place. Perhaps no bank at Liverpool and Manchester could so promptly and effectually manage such business—not having any resident partner in London.[52]

In this way, the Smith Bank at Nottingham, together with Gurneys of Norwich, had developed from the seventeenth century as provincial, quasi-bankers with metropolitan connections. By 1750, Smiths held the accounts of customers resident beyond the town and county of Nottingham in Cheshire, Derbyshire, Leicestershire, Lincolnshire, and Warwickshire, but only three of them lived in Yorkshire and only one possibly north of the 'mail-road'. This would have been the beginning of the type of business to which Burgess referred, yet to go further and examine in detail the decades after 1780 is not feasible with currently available material.[53] The sizeable business

[51] Pressnell, *Country Banking*, pp. 37–43. See also B. L. Anderson, 'The Attorney and the Early Capital Market in Lancashire', in J. R. Harris (ed.), *Liverpool and Merseyside. Essays in the Economic and Social History of the Port and its Hinterland* (London, 1969), reprinted in F. Crouzet, *Capital Formation in the Industrial Revolution* (London, 1972); B. L. Anderson, 'Provincial Aspects of the Financial Revolution of the Eighteenth Century', *Business History*, 11 (1969); and M. Miles, 'The Money Market in the Early Industrial Revolution: The Evidence from West Riding Attornies, c. 1750–1800', *Business History*, 23 (1981).

[52] *Circular to Bankers*, 370 (21 Aug. 1835).

[53] Leighton-Boyce, *Smiths* pp. 40–2.

hinterlands of some of the earliest country banks is graphically shown by the experience of Thomas & John Tipping, a major Manchester cotton merchanting firm. They were forced to discount regularly in 1760 with Smiths at Nottingham in order to obtain £2,000 in bullion at a time, brought back to south-east Lancashire by a carrier.

As has already been commented, Thomas Smith I's rise to be one of the earliest provincial bankers was assisted by his appointment as a sub-commissioner for the excise in 1671. Other such remitters likewise became country bankers over the following century, although they came to be solely responsible for the transfer of the land and assessed taxes and stamp duties because the collection of other imposts was reformed. While eighteenth-century provincial tax remitters were poorly remunerated for their services to the state, it was accepted that taxes could take time to reach the Treasury's coffers. During the interim, these sums might not only support the agent's business activities but also provide resources to fully engage in banking.[54]

Outside London, many, especially merchants, lawyers, tax remitters, and industrialists, became formal bankers, either through the further evolution of their existing businesses or by force of necessity. Qualifications have already been made to the precise nature of the relationships between the country banks and entrepreneurs in the developing industries that came to employ steam power and centralized production techniques. Further caveats need to be entered, despite the attractions of the apparent chronological parallelism, between the growth of formal country banking and the onset of the transforming 'spurt' of the Industrial Revolution from the 1760s. While provoking much debate, fresh scholarly attempts to establish the quantitative dimensions of the growth of the British economy during the eighteenth century have stressed 'evolution' rather than 'revolution'.[55] This chimes with other studies that, for instance, show that the further rise of the market economy from the 1670s, as expressed in the rising volume of traffic on roads and rivers, ultimately provoked transport improvements. Equally, the recent charting of the expansion of industrial production has highlighted the importance of traditional industries and trades before at least 1800 which, previously, had been left in the shadows by the spotlight that historians narrowly, although understandably, focused upon structural developments in cotton and iron.[56]

[54] Pressnell, *Country Banking*, pp. 45–58.

[55] N. F. R. Crafts, *British Economic Growth during the Industrial Revolution* (Oxford, 1985) and J. G. Williamson, 'Why was British Growth so Slow during the Industrial Rvolution', *Explorations in Economic History* (1987). For scholars' reaction, see M. Berg and P. Hudson, 'Rehabilitating the Industrial Revolution', *Economic History Review* (1992); J. Hoppit, 'Understanding the Industrial Revolution', *Historical Journal* (1987); and J. Hoppit, 'Counting the Industrial Revolution', *Economic History Review* (1990).

[56] C. K. Hartley, 'British Industrialisation before 1841: Evidence of Slower Growth during the Industrial Revolution', *Journal of Economic History* (1982); N. F. R. Crafts, S. G. Leybourne, and

A longer-term perspective for the Industrial Revolution is still debated but some scholarly consensus has been reached regarding the importance of divergent regional experiences. In all this, evolution has always been acknowledged in the emergence of country bankers as specialists. Furthermore, what is known of the earliest formal practitioners has pointed up the differences in the financial services that they provided, arising from the circumstances of the locality or region in which they were situated. The stagnation or decline of a region's manufacturing specialism was one factor possibly affecting the timing and extent of the emergence of specialist banking facilities. Another was relative eclipse, as indicated by population change. The two were related, since, until the late nineteenth century, town size only increased as a result of inward migration, the size of which was in turn related to the pulling force of urban magnetism. The waning vibrancy of a city's, or region's dominant trade might affect the advent of specialist banking in a variety of ways. Yet, the formal emergence of bankers could equally be crystallized by the influence of non-commercial and non-industrial factors, in particular, the further development of urban service and leisure functions.

In East Anglia, for example, partners in many early country banks had various connections with the traditional woollen trade.[57] One interpretation of their emergence as specialist bankers would stress the formalization of their roles within the ever evolving web of commercial and industrial credit. However, another equally valid generalization would be that the provision of banking services was a way to transfer the already acquired expertise in the provision of credit to a wider market, and, indeed, thereby hedging against the decline, if not the stagnation, of the traditional woollen industry of East Anglia. The general increase in economic activity over the eighteenth century required an expanded supply of circulating media—banknotes—while the changing natures of Bury St Edmunds, Colchester, King's Lynn, and Norwich brought in new banking customers amongst the rising middling groups of society which used these cities and towns as places of consumerism, culture, and leisure.[58] East Anglia had as much as one fifth of the total number of English and Welsh country banks during the mid-1780s. And proto-branch banking—a precocious indicator of English banking which was only to arrive generally in the last quarter of the nineteenth century—was developed by the

T. C. Mills, 'Trends and Cycles in British Industrial Production 1700–1913', *Journal of the Royal Statistical Society* (1991); R. V. Jackson, 'Rates of Industrial Growth during the Industrial Revolution', *Economic History Review* (1992); N. F. R. Crafts and C. K. Hartley, 'Output, Growth and the Industrial Revolution: A Restatement of the Crafts-Harley View', *Economic History Review* (1992); and N. F. R. Crafts and C. K. Hartley, 'Cotton Textiles and Industrial Output Growth during the Industrial Revolution', *Economic History Review* (1995).

[57] G. D. Ramsay, *The English Woollen Industry 1500–1750* (London and Basingstoke, 1982), p. 16.

[58] P. J. Corfield, *The Impact of English Towns 1700–1800* (Oxford, 1982), pp. 11–15, 20, 31; A. F. J. Brown, *Essex at Work 1700–1815* (Chelmsford, 1969), pp. 1–27, 111–12.

Gurneys, a family important not only for regional but, ultimately, national banking developments.

In Yorkshire, banking houses were very closely associated with the woollen and worsted trades in the West Riding, the dynamic regional centre of this manufacturing branch during the eighteenth century. By 1790 there were twenty banks within the three Yorkshire Ridings but only one came to have the involvement of an attorney: Lucas Nicholson, a partner in the Leeds Commercial Bank from 1792. In Yorkshire, attorneys as a group continued to be important financial intermediaries until the 1830s, attracting in particular the affairs of landowners, spinsters, and widows, but as part of a parallel financial market. Local members of the legal profession continued to arrange long-term loans whereas the new banks, formal and informal, provided means of payment, credits, and remittance facilities. The latter service was supplied through having an agent or trading partner in London. In many cases, West Riding country banks had industrial origins and emerged as quasi-formal institutions out of the local inter-personal credit market. Early examples of Yorkshire wool 'banks' are Ingram Kennet & Co. in Halifax during the mid-1770s and Leach, Pollard & Hardcastle over the late 1770s in Bradford. Early formal Yorkshire bankers frequently established a number of houses but, not as in East Anglia, on the basis of family connections. For example, William Pollard had been a founder of the first Bradford Bank in 1777 before becoming a junior partner in the Halifax Swain bank. These characteristics of Yorkshire country banking—industrial origins and interlocking partnerships—produced a tightly-knit banking community, intimately associated with the county's major, growing trade which it serviced through note issues, credits, and loans.[59]

Banking Crises

The first general, major wave of English country bank failures occurred during 1793, when sixteen houses closed between March and August. There were some regional clusterings amongst these banking fatalities—the lower Severn valley and the Lancashire and Cheshire cotton belt—but they took place throughout the country, with the only significant exceptions being the old and new districts of the woollen trade. However, the 1793 crisis was primarily a mercantile event, largely centred within England on the Atlantic ports of Bristol and Liverpool.[60] Country bankers were generally affected through their

[59] P. Hudson, *The Genesis of Industrial Capital. A Study of the West Riding Wool Textile Industry c.1750–1850* (Cambridge, 1986), pp. 215–23, 230; W. F. Crick and J. E. Wadsworth, *Hundred Years of Joint Stock Banking* (London, 1936, 3rd edn, 1958), p. 200; Chandler, *Northern Constituent Banks*, pp. 198, 200–7; and Pressnell, *Country Banking*, pp. 108, 110.

[60] F. E. Hyde, C. N. Parkinson, and S. Marriner, 'The Port of Liverpool and the Crisis of 1793', *Economica*, n.s., 18 (1951).

acquisition of cotton and West India bills as investments, assets which needed to be liquid in 1793 because of the financial strains generated by the national investment boom of the preceding three years in canals and enclosures. On this occasion, liquidity was provided by the state, through the issue of £5 million Exchequer bills, as opposed to ameliorative action by the Bank of England. Indeed, some contemporaries argued that the Bank had precipitated the crisis[61] but others maintained that the 'hurricane' of 1793 had been generated by those new nuisances—the country banks.[62]

The crises of 1772–3, 1788, and 1793 appeared to have arisen from within the business world, although, in 1788, the impact of war played a part by disrupting trade with the Americas. The central issue that came to the fore was the dynamics operating within the web of credit—credit creation and particularly its perverse mutation. By the late eighteenth century, the dynamism of industrialization had changed business expectations, which, in turn, affected attitudes towards the expansion of credit. Yet, with the emergence of country banking, especially its increasingly central role as the provider of credit, along with its developing links with metropolitan financial markets, credit upheavals were also seen as banking crises. Nonetheless, for a further century, contemporary commentators continually failed to agree about the nomenclature for these disruptive events, let alone their causes, since observers frequently characterized them as commercial crises as opposed to being either banking or monetary panics.[63]

The 1793 crisis also involved the collapse of two banks in Glasgow, triggered by runs caused by the outbreak of war with France, as opposed to the effects of mercantile problems as happened south of the border in England. Glasgow was the epicentre of the 1793 crisis in Scotland and the city's businessmen sought £320,000 Exchequer bills, an application only exceeded in amount by that of their counterparts in London. The provision of state relief did not prevent a further Scottish bank—A. G. & A. Thomson—from closing on 5 November 1793, although this may have been more due to particular reasons—inter-family loans to associated building and coal-mining interests. Other houses, such as the Dundee Banking Co. and the Perth Banking Co., were less affected, so that their managements were only forced to restrict accommodation to clients.[64] Subsequently, Englishmen, especially legislators at Westminster, solely retained in their memory the earlier failure of another Scottish banking company—the Ayr Bank in 1772–3—while being continually impressed by the stability displayed by Scotland's Edinburgh-based corporate, public banks: the Bank of Scotland founded in 1695; and the Royal Bank of Scotland established in 1727. Consequently, they overlooked the remarkable

[61] Clapham, *Bank of England*, 1, p. 261.
[62] Pressnell, *Country Banking*, pp. 455–9.
[63] Hoppit, *Risk and Failure*, pp. 132–3, 168.
[64] Munn, *Scottish Provincial Banking Companies*, pp. 49–51.

development from the mid-eighteenth century of the Scottish provincial banking companies of which the Ayr Bank was but one untypical representative.

A Scottish or an Irish Banking Model?

The Scottish provincial banking companies, such as the Arms Bank and the Ayr Bank, were partnerships, whose memberships were unaffected by the Bank of England's corporate privileges. These only applied within England, south of Hadrian's Wall, although this had not been realized by the founders of the Glasgow Arms Bank. As a result, some Scottish provincial banks had very many partners (109 in the case of the Aberdeen Banking Company of 1767) which led them to establish controlling committees of management, analogous to boards of directors. However, their shares were not freely transferable since the banking companies were based upon partnership contracts of finite duration, albeit that the achievement of success led to their renewal.

The evolution of private banking in Scotland, while having some distinctive features, generally followed what was to be the European path. Scottish merchants and industrialists during the early eighteenth century began to provide some banking services, although not to the extent of lending to the general public. Despite the towering presences of the Bank of Scotland and the Royal Bank of Scotland in Edinburgh (joined by the British Linen Company from the 1760s), the Scottish capital became a focus of private banking. Its roots went back to at least the mid-seventeenth century amongst Edinburgh's mercantile community clustered at the Cross in the High Street and the booths of goldsmiths in St Giles. Their successors became associated with the corporate, public banks whereas others emerged as fully-fledged private bankers by the 1740s, such as John Coutts, whose brother was a London private banker, William Alexander, James Mansfield, and Adam and Thomas Fairholme.[65] But the decision of the public banks not to establish permanent branch networks beyond Edinburgh, after some initial experimentation, left the provision of banking services beyond the Scottish capital almost completely open for others to exploit until 1774.[66]

By 1793, there were eighteen Scottish provincial banking companies. Although the first had been formed in Aberdeen in 1747, the Glasgow region became the prime centre of this private banking development. As in Edinburgh, Glasgow had something of a private banking community by the 1740s, although not so specialized. It members went by the general term 'exchangers',

[65] S. G. Checkland, *Scottish Banking. A History, 1695–1973* (Glasgow/London, 1975), pp. 6–7, 68–9.

[66] Munn, *Scottish Provincial Banking Companies*, pp. 2–6, 16.

with their financial activities being still largely embedded within their major business affairs: the tobacco and sugar trades, general merchanting, and the provision of marine insurance. Formal private banking only began with the establishment of the Glasgow Ship Bank in 1749 and, a year later, of the Arms Bank. These houses were initially supported by the public banks' managements, who hoped to replicate the pattern of banking that had emerged in Edinburgh since the beginning of the century. Edinburgh private bankers had developed the practice of borrowing from the public banks to augment their deposits, which they lent out to merchants and manufacturers.

Provincial banking companies were established in the 1760s in response to the rising demand for financial services not satisfied by the public banks' provincial agents. The underlying forces at work were the mounting needs for credit and currency—either coin or notes—and eleven new banking companies were note issuers with an aggregate circulation of about £700,000 by the close of the 1760s. The further development of banking came with the companies accepting one another's notes, following the model of the 1751 arrangement between the Bank of Scotland and the Royal Bank of Scotland. The failure of the Ayr Bank in 1772 did not impede the continuing creation of provincial banking companies in Scotland, with a further twelve entirely new houses being established between 1773 and 1793. However, these tended to have fewer partners than their mid-century predecessors—on average eight. The timing of the establishment of further banking companies was largely related to the pulse of the Scottish economy, which quickened from the mid-1780s following the end of the American War of Independence. More banks went along with their opening of branches, in emulation of the public banks' developments, and an increased emphasis upon the collection of deposits. The consequent thickening of the banking system involved the establishment of further local note exchanges while the Royal Bank, as well as opening a branch in Glasgow in 1783, became the Edinburgh agent for four provincial banking companies.[67]

The basis of the provincial banking companies' lending business was the cash credit system, which the public banks had introduced during the late 1720s. It involved the provision of advances solely against the security of personal bonds, each signed by the borrower and two guarantors. Under such an arrangement, the customer could take up bank credit at will, paying interest daily only on the amount by which the account was in debit. These facilities in many respects foreshadowed the overdraft. Customers' use of the cash credit system was carefully monitored by the senior managements of the provincial banking companies. They personally established these arrangements on behalf of their banks, supervising the drawing up of bonds and regularly reviewed the

[67] Munn, *Scottish Provincial Banking Companies*, pp. 40–9.

accounts. This was not only to oversee—quarterly, semi-annually or annually—their safe employment, but also to ensure that they were active (so as to maintain their banks' note issues) and to obtain thereby other banks' notes to meet inter-bank exchange requirements.[68]

The early emergence of formal banking in Scotland, both the private banking companies and the public corporate banks, has often been regarded by historians as precocious. This is because of its leading nature in relation to the timing of the Scottish economy's structural transformation. Furthermore, it heralded future, more general developments: systems of managerial control, joint-stock banking, branching, and the overdraft. Yet, in some respects, early Irish banking was in the vanguard. From its establishment in 1719, La Touche & Kane had a network of correspondents that covered nearly all of Ireland and, four decades later, Ireland had an embryonic national credit structure involving a substantial note circulation and a large number of banking offices. This built upon the foundation of a sizeable private note issue by the 1720s and the creation of banks in seven urban centres beyond Dublin by the mid-century. Nonetheless, secular growth was intermittent as Irish banking developments marked time during the second quarter of the century. This was due to a substantial contraction in the note issue in the 1730s, arising largely from the failure of Burton & Falkiner in 1733. Furthermore, fresh banking advances at the mid-century were not to achieve their full potential as they were subsequently impeded by growing tensions between mercantile and gentry bankers, together with those generated by religious divides and regional separatism.

PRIVATE BANKERS IN CONTINENTAL EUROPE

In the growing formalization of European banking facilities during the eighteenth century, developments within the countries of the British Isles were very much in the lead, especially because numerous formal banks were successfully established outside major metropolitan centres. This spatial spread of formal banking began in Ireland, then developed in England and Scotland from the mid-century with the growth of country banking and the emergence of the provincial banking companies. Elsewhere in Europe, formal banking remained essentially a metropolitan pursuit and financial services in the countryside, far less urbanized than England, were provided informally as an adjunct to trading and commerce.

Much banking remained in the hands of private bankers but in metropolitan centres like Dublin, Edinburgh, and London, they had to contend with the

[68] Munn, *Scottish Provincial Banking Companies*, pp. 3, 115–21; for the specific employment of cash credits, see pp. 194–216.

competition of corporate banks—the Bank of Ireland, the Bank of Scotland, the Royal Bank of Scotland, and the Bank of England. These were very different institutions to the municipal exchange banks that had been established throughout most of Europe and of which the most important was the Wisselbank in Amsterdam. Moreover, the Bank of Scotland's development of a branch network from the 1770s heralded the wider force of joint-stock competition that provincial private bankers were later to experience, as in France from the mid-nineteenth century. However, the interrelationships between Edinburgh's private bankers and the Scottish public banks also pointed to how, over the next century, European private banking would play a major role in the creation of joint-stock banks. In Landes' phrases, the 'old wealth' would substantially develop the 'new wealth'.

The sphere of the European private banker during the eighteenth century began to be encroached upon through the founding of joint-stock institutions. However, as in Scotland, some private bankers became involved in early corporate banks while the competition offered by joint-stock institutions was not to become serious until the 1820s within the British Isles and the Low Countries, and not for a further quarter of a century elsewhere in Europe. Yet, the first signs during the second half of the eighteenth century of a different banking world arose with the opportunities that led to the further development of bankers acting as intermediaries in the business of lending to states and sovereigns.

Amsterdam's Merchant Bankers

Amsterdam's position as the world's trading and financial centre originally derived from the Netherlands' economic prominence—with its higher level of urbanization than other European countries, its more productive agriculture, more advanced industry, and more developed international trade.[69] In 1700, the per capita income of the Dutch exceeded that of the English by 50 per cent, the next in line.[70] The Netherlands' commercial supremacy started to be undermined during the eighteenth century as the centre of gravity of world trade gradually shifted towards London. In around 1780, London certainly overtook Amsterdam as a trading centre, judged by the number of ships entering its port, not only in relation to goods traffic but also to auxiliary services, such as insurance or even the acceptance of bills.[71] However, Amsterdam asserted itself

[69] See J. de Vries and A. van der Woude, *The First Modern Economy. Success, Failure, and Perseverance of the Dutch Economy, 1500–1815* (Cambridge, 1997).

[70] A. Maddison, *Dynamic Forces in Economic Development* (Oxford, 1991), pp. 30–5.

[71] J. Jonker and K. Sluyterman, *At Home on the World Markets. Dutch International Trading Companies from the 16th Century until the Present* (The Hague, 2000), pp. 124–5.

as the world's financial centre even though its commercial leadership was crumbling. Its capital financed international trade or was invested in loans on behalf of foreign governments.

This was partly the result of strategic choices on the part of the city's merchants, on the lookout for new business opportunities. From the seventeenth century, the leading merchants accepted bills of exchange; in other words, they undertook to pay the respective amount upon the bills' maturity date on behalf of other merchants and businessmen. In the eighteenth century, trade financing gradually became dissociated from trade itself. First, an increasing number of merchants worked on commission rather than on their own account; or, put another way, they did not take the risk of purchasing and then reselling the goods but acted as brokers, putting purchasers and sellers in touch with each other and earning a commission on the price of their service. This solution enabled them to commit less capital, clear more stock, and use their surplus in credit transactions. Second, numerous merchant houses gave up physical trade in order to specialize in financing it by accepting bills of exchange. According to contemporaries, the volume of acceptances reached 200 million florins towards 1750. In both cases, these financial activities were linked less and less to the port of Amsterdam and more and more to international trade.

Amsterdam's rich merchants also turned to what would become the most prestigious activity of international financial centres: issuing foreign loans. From the middle of the seventeenth century, the Dutch had lent considerable sums to foreign states, including Austria, Sweden, and Britain, before investing heavily in the British public debt from 1688. But the development of a genuine capital market dates from 1713, when the Netherlands embarked on a policy of neutrality. From then until the end of the Seven Years' War in 1763, foreign loans amounted to an average of 4 million florins per year (i.e., a total of 200 million) and flowed almost exclusively to Britain and Austria. They then increased markedly (to an annual average of 8.3 million between 1763 and 1780) and flowed to the whole of Europe, notably with issues on behalf of Denmark, Sweden, Russia, and various German states. They reached a peak during the fifteen subsequent years, between 1780 and 1794, when issues on the Amsterdam market reached an annual average of 20 million florins.[72] In particular, Dutch commitment to French debt developed substantially during the 1780s. In 1800, seventy loans were listed on the Amsterdam Stock Exchange on behalf of fourteen different states, and the total Dutch foreign investment amounted, according to the most conservative estimates, to 500 to 600 million florins, representing twice

[72] J. C. Riley, *International Government Finance and the Amsterdam Capital Market, 1740–1815* (Cambridge, 1980).

the country's GDP. By way of comparison, foreign investment amounted to one and a half Britain's GDP on the eve of the First World War.[73]

In his survey of the international activity of the Amsterdam capital market, Riley has identified some fifteen firms which directly acted as principals for European states between the 1720s and the 1780s. In the case of Hope & Co., greater detail is known of the house's development and its shift into the finance of European states from 1768, initially on the part of Sweden.[74] Comparable with other Amsterdam financial principals for European monarchies during the second half of the eighteenth century, Hopes was a mercantile house and its eighteenth-century partners always regarded themselves as merchants rather than bankers. More distinctive was its Anglo-Scottish origins and these family links were sustained throughout the century and came to be augmented by the development of the house's business. For instance, an American nephew, Henry, was trained through an apprenticeship with Gurnell Hoare & Co., London, during the mid-1750s, which also replicated mercantile practice that had occurred within the economy of the southern basin of the North Sea since at least the late seventeenth century. Hopes retained a business connection with this Hoare London house throughout the eighteenth century.

These particular links, on occasion, could be very intimate, as with the employment during the mid-1780s of Robert Voûte, a commodity speculator, in conjunction with T. Littledale of Rotterdam and J. & F. Baring (with whom Hopes had had contacts since 1770). In turn, like the London 'City' bank of Glyns, Hopes through Hoares were affected by the Anglo-Scottish banking crisis of 1772, having mutually advanced £50,000 to Alexander Fordyce, the metropolitan agent for the Ayr Banking Co. In broader terms, Thomas Hope, effectively the senior partner from the early 1730s until his death in 1779, maintained an allegiance to his parent's Quaker belief. This barred him from holding Dutch public offices although, during the 1750s, he represented the stadholder in the Dutch West Indian Company while he acted as an adviser for the revival of the economy. Indeed, Thomas saw great advantages arising from his family origins which allowed him to pursue mercantile neutrality to the utmost within the increasingly politicized Dutch society of the late eighteenth century. By contrast, it was Thomas's son, John, who, through becoming a member of the English Presbyterian church in Amsterdam when nineteen, prepared himself, consciously or unconsciously, for entry into the Dutch regency, a social move subsequently assisted by marriage to a family with membership of the Rotterdam Vroedschap.

[73] De Vries and van der Woude, *The First Modern Economy*, p. 146.

[74] See M. G. Buist, *At Spes Non Fracta. Hope and Co. 1770–1815. Merchant Bankers and Diplomats at Work* (The Hague, 1974), and in particular the opening survey chapter 'The Family and the Firm', pp. 3–69.

While remaining mercantile traders, Hope & Co. began to move into European state finance during the Seven Years War (1756–63), a shift which greatly accelerated its growth as an enterprise. The house placed portions of British loans within Amsterdam and was responsible for the transfer of subsidies from London to Prussia.[75] Although conducting trade throughout Europe and North and Central America as general merchants during the second half of the eighteenth century and having undertaken its first state loan for Sweden in 1768, it would appear that the 1772 crisis was particularly responsible for propelling Hopes deeper into financing European monarchies. The house's 'money business' had a basis in exchange dealing and the provision of acceptance credits, activities which its partners' regarded as a proper part of a merchant's business whereas, equally, they saw no incongruence in both undertaking trade and issuing state loans. However, Dutch trade from the mid-eighteenth century lost its former dynamism as did bill broking in Amsterdam from 1772 due to rising competition from London, where it had the institutional backing of a quasi-central bank and a growing and deepening commercial banking system. This change in the business environment affected not only Hopes but also other leading Amsterdam mercantile houses.

Hopes undertook their international loan business over the last quarter of the eighteenth century through a complex of interrelated, tiered operations. The house itself was responsible for negotiating the underlying contracts, which involved taking loans at par (until 1794), for which it received commissions. Its issuing charge varied between 4 and 9.5 per cent, the precise amount on each occasion being determined by the urgency of the borrower for immediate funds and the liquidity of the Amsterdam market. Hopes obtained subsequent further commissions for servicing bonds once loans had been issued. The bonds were distributed through public subscriptions on which a discount of 0.25–0.5 per cent was given and by fulfilling direct orders via brokers from other houses, with those located in Austrian Brabant being particularly important in this respect. However, far more significant was the 'wholesaling' of loans through, in effect, 'underwriting syndicates', the assurance of which allowed Hopes to negotiate their loans 'firm' at par. These groups were organized by a special broker (Wed. W. Borksi from 1790 with respect to loans for Russia), who received a 0.25 per cent commission, and comprised other mercantile houses, some of which also issued sovereign loans on their own part but took on these occasions a commission of 1 to 1.5 per cent. Most of Hopes' 'underwriters' were located in Amsterdam although these syndicates also involved participation from across the three western provinces of The Netherlands. Between 1768 and 1794, the number of Hopes' direct backers in its international loan business became progressively larger.

[75] Buist, *At Spes Non Fracta. Hope and Co. 1770–1815*, p. 11.

The ultimate effect of all these arrangements was the distribution of bonds throughout Dutch society to the extent that some came into the hands of relatively small savers.[76]

After Thomas's death in 1779, Hopes experienced a series of further partnership changes in 1782, 1784, and 1790 but its capital increased from 8.7 million guilders, in 1782, to 13.4 million guilders in 1794. Foreign trade in Amsterdam during the late 1780s was adversely affected by domestic political discord and external—Prussian—intervention, although Hopes' purpose-built warehouses filled again with Russian produce and American orders during the early 1790s. However, extreme fluctuations in trade were more than offset for Hopes by the continuing growth of its international lending business. During the early 1790s, this was further aided by funds from Dutch disinvestment in French securities. Nevertheless, the safety of Hopes' capital, and that of the house's partners was increasingly threatened by Dutch and European politics. Hope's continuing political neutrality in Amsterdam was finally thrown off during October 1787, when its partners openly paraded their sympathies for the stadholder with orange cockades. These allegiances coupled with their continuing sizeable English connections and their wealth created further dangers for them from 1793, when the French Convention declared war against England and Holland. Henry, the American nephew but now senior partner, twice fled across the North Sea to remain in London from 1795 until 1802. During the interim, Hopes' affairs in Amsterdam were in the immediate hands of a trusted clerk supported by Voûte.[77]

There was diversity within Dutch eighteenth-century banking, as shown by the differences in developments between Amsterdam, on the one hand, and Rotterdam and The Hague, on the other. In Rotterdam, *kassiers* came to combine the provision of money transfer services with insurance broking, like Cordelois & De Vrijier during the early eighteenth century, and these firms had equal standing with the city's mercantile houses. With the decline of the exchange banks in both Amsterdam and Rotterdam over the last quarter of the eighteenth century, *kassiers'* paper became an important circulating medium once more, regulated by decisions of the magistrates. Some *kassiers* were regarded by the mid-1770s as banks, like Cordelois, De Vrijier & Mees. This was despite this particular firm's main function being broking, which completely overshadowed the provision of loans to its clientele and to the open market. Perhaps untypically, Cordelois, De Vrijier & Mees possessed by the late eighteenth century a sizeable capital of *c.*300,000 guilders—impressive for Rotterdam *kassiers*, although infinitesimal when compared to Hopes' own resources. Other features that distinguished this Rotterdam money-market

[76] Buist, *At Spes Non Fracta. Hope and Co. 1770–1815*, pp. 24–8.
[77] Buist, *At Spes Non Fracta. Hope and Co. 1770–1815*, pp. 41–56.

firm from its local peers were the deliberate limiting of its paper circulation and its long-standing interests in securities, thereby becoming a trustee of the ill-fated 1795 loan to the United States.[78]

Financiers, Foreign Bankers, and Notaries in Paris

In the eighteenth century, Paris's role as a financial centre primarily relied on the state's financial needs and on the opportunity to subscribe to its numerous loans. The pressures arising from unsound French state finance led to various experiments with formally constituted banking companies, beginning with the limited functions of the Caisse des Emprunts, 1702–15, and the Caisse Legendre, 1709–15, to be followed by John Law's ill-fated schemes. As memories of the 'Mississippi bubble' faded from immediate memory, others once more put forward ideas for a fully-fledged public bank. The Caisse d'Escompte was established in 1776 by Turgot and continued until 1793. This was founded by royal charter as a *société en commandite* with the powers to issue notes and to discount at 4 per cent. In practice, it acted as a bankers' bank, financing foreign trade and providing cheap credit, although its notes enjoyed a rising circulation over the first half of the 1780s. Furthermore and grievous for its future, it played an increasing role in lending to the crown from 1783. A state loan of 24 million livres in August 1783 to assist in financing the American war resulted in a rush to exchange its notes for specie. The Caisse survived, despite a growing subjection to government demands, but Necker was unable to transform it into a national bank in 1789.[79]

The complexity of French public finances in the eighteenth century, consisting of innumerable offices responsible for levying taxes, and of a growing debt made up of different forms of annuities, must be understood in the context of France's many wars and the huge financial burden imposed by these military efforts—France was engaged in the Wars of the Spanish Succession (1700–13), the Polish Succession (1733–8), and the Austrian Succession (1741–8), followed by the Seven Years War (1756–63) and the American War of Independence (1776–83). The French monarchy, just as modern states do, could raise taxation to enhance public finances during the

[78] J. B. Jonker, *Mees Pierson. The Link between the Past and Future. 275 years of Tradition and Innovation in Dutch Banking* (Mees Pierson, 1997), pp. 8–10, 23–6.

[79] J. F. Bosher, *French Finances 1770–1795. From Business to Bureaucracy* (Cambridge, 1970), pp. 92, 185, 186, 257–65, 273; F. Crouzet, 'Politics and Banking in Revolutionary and Napoleonic France', in R. Sylla, R. Tilly, and G. Tortella (eds), *The State, the Financial System and Economic Modernization* (Cambridge, 1999), pp. 27–30; and R. Bigo, *La Caisse d'escompte (1776–1793) et les origines de la Banque de France* (Paris, 1927).

war period or borrow the necessary funds on the market.[80] The type of 'private banker' active in the eighteenth century was in large part fashioned by these two functions—collecting taxes and providing funds to the state—and the way they were performed.

The French taxation system was itself extremely complex, with the coexistence, within the same realm, of different regional fiscal regimes, while local jurisdictions of towns and parishes could have different fiscal regimes within the same region. The nobility and the clergy were on the whole exempted from taxation, so the fiscal burden, composed of a variety of direct taxes (such as the *taille* or the *capitation*) and indirect taxes (such as the *gabelle* or the *aides*), rested on the shoulders of the third estate.[81] The monarchy conceded the right to collect taxes, both direct and indirect, to a company of tax farmers, the *Fermiers Généraux*. The concession from the Crown varied as regards duration, from six years to eight, and the sums due to the Crown ranged from 80 million livres in 1726 to 144 million in 1786. The appointment to the office of tax farmer was made directly by the king who generally followed suggestions made by members of his court, such as ministers, or favourites.

The majority of tax farmers belonged to the *noblesse de robe* (nobility of the robe) so they did not have any specific training in merchant activities or in trading in general. Together with the *régisseurs* (people in charge of the collection of royal rights due on royal lands), they constituted the group of *financiers* dealing with public finances and, more generally, having an interest in the management of royal wealth. Separate from this group were the *banquiers*, specialized in dealing with private money and discounting commercial bills. However, tax farmers were not mere tax collectors. They also fulfilled some of the functions usually ascribed to private bankers. In fact, these state office holders used their posts also to undertake general banking. Tax farmers most often bought their positions (which could cost between 622,000 and 1,560,000 livres) with loans raised on bearer notes and then turned their offices into quasi-banks by accepting peoples' savings and, in turn, investing in industry and commerce.[82]

[80] Nothing excludes also the combination of the two elements, taxation and borrowing, as a policy in times of war. For example, during the eighteenth century the British government issued numerous loans always backed by a specific tax that contributed to a fund to pay back interest on the loan. For the British way of dealing with war costs, see F. R. Velde, and D. R. Weir, 'The Financial Market and Government Debt Policy in France, 1746–1793' *Journal of Economic History* 52, 1 (March 1992), pp. 478–80.

[81] For a synthetic view of the fiscal system of Ancien Régime France, see P. T. Hoffman 'Early Modern France, 1450–1700', in P. T. Hoffman and K. Norberg, *Fiscal Crises, Lliberty, and Representative Government, 1450–1789* (Stanford, 1994). A more detailed analysis of the French fiscal system is offered by R. Mousnier, *Les institutions de la France sous la monarchie absolue, 1598–1789* (Paris, 1974), vol. II, pp. 37–41, 431–52.

[82] Bosher, *French Finances*, pp. 8–9, 75.

The specific French Royal Treasury was largely in the hands of the Court Banker until 1767 but the conduct of those who held this post led to reaction: a down-grading of its functions during the second half of the century. Consequently, Jean-Joseph de Laborde, who had married the daughter of Nettine, a Belgian court-banker, and was Court Banker during the late 1760s, never had the same powers as his predecessors, such as the Huguenot Samuel Bernard or Jean Paris de Montmartel. The Court Banker's functions were further changed in 1778 when the office became solely responsible for the financial services of the Department of Foreign Affairs. Nonetheless, Court Bankers featured amongst the dozen men who both oversaw and were directly involved in credit operations for the Treasury. The most prominent during the 1770s was Nicolas Beaujon, Court Banker until 1778 and thereafter Receiver General, first for La Rochelle and then Rouen. Amongst his associates were Jacques Marquet de Bourgade and Jean-Baptiste Magon de la Balue. Marquet de Bourgade was a confidant of Minister Joly de Fleury, while Magon de la Balue had briefly been Court Banker during 1769. The banker Lecouteulx de Canteleu, was later amongst his close acquaintances. Both Marquet de Bourgade and Magon de la Balue accumulated their considerable fortunes through being bankers and through involvement in war finance.

The great variety of annuities placed on the Parisian market attracted investments from all corners of Europe, making Paris a magnet for foreign private bankers who settled there during the second half of the eighteenth century. According to a contemporary, 'Paris has an incredibly wide-ranging sphere of banking activities; it could be said that there is no city in the universe that is superior to it in this respect.'[83] The Crown, constantly in need of money, enticed investors with long-term securities, such as *rentes perpétuelles* (perpetual bonds) or *rentes viagères* (life annuities). The yields on such securities could vary between 5 and 10 per cent, making them far more profitable than English Consols, which offered only a 3 per cent return. However, these high returns were not risk-free: French funds did not enjoy the same degree of confidence as British Consols (which were backed by Parliament), and could suffer cuts, reductions or, even worse, partial cancellation. This occurred, for example, in 1770 when the Controller-General Terray, alarmed by the large deficit in the French budget, decided to lower interest rates on some *rentes* and suspend reimbursement on part of the debt.[84]

Inevitably, the state's partial default forced the French authorities to offer more attractive conditions to subsequent investors. The loans offered in 1771 and 1772 thus offered higher yields, between 9 and 12 per cent, as did the shares of the *Compagnie des Indes Orientales* (East India Company). With the

[83] Quoted in P. Vilar, *Or et monnaie dans l'histoire* (Paris, 1974), p. 342.

[84] See E. N. White, 'Was There a Solution to the Ancien Régime's Financial Dilemma?' *Journal of Economic History* 49, 3 (1989) pp. 548–9.

accession to the throne of Louis XVI and the appointment of Turgot as Controller-General of Finances, more attention was paid to restoring the credibility of public funds. However, the first steps towards re-establishing public credit had hardly been taken—as witnessed by a sharp decrease in yield of the East India Company—when the outbreak of the American war, and France's subsequent intervention in support of the American colonies, again undermined the state of the public finances. Instead of raising new taxes, the General Controllers of finances, from Turgot to Necker, preferred to issue new loans.

Two groups of foreign bankers were increasingly active on the French capital market: the large community of Swiss bankers, many of whom were resident in Paris, and the Dutch bankers who had a deep knowledge and a long experience of foreign loans—whether in Sweden, Russia, or Great Britain. French bankers and speculators were also actively involved in the annuities mania. However, focusing on foreign private bankers clearly illustrates the attraction of the French financial market, which offered a wide array of financial products making the Paris market a valid alternative to the more solid, but less profitable, London market.[85]

The Geneva bankers were renowned for being masters of large investments in life annuities, which could yield more than 10 per cent a year. Their success stemmed from a scheme known as the *Trente demoiselles de Genève* (thirty maidens of Geneva) that took advantage of the loopholes in an old financial product, the life annuity: the facts that they yielded a flat interest rate, irrespective of the age of the holder; and that the buyer of life annuities could choose his contingent life. Geneva bankers selected as contingent lives young girls who had survived smallpox and other deadly diseases. With the help of statistics and early demographic studies, they were able to choose appropriate lives with a small margin of error. They thus 'scientifically' increased the likelihood of receiving payments of life annuities for a very long time. This mechanism was completely legal and for the 1788 loan, Geneva bankers largely chose nominees of life annuities aged between 5 and 10 years.[86] The only risk was that the young contingent life might die earlier than expected, and the only costs were the notarial documents required to prove that the third party was alive.[87] Geneva bankers pooled these annuities and resold them to investors interested in these highly attractive products.

[85] On the temporary superiority of the French capital market for government debt compared to the English one, see C. P. Kindleberger, 'Financial Institutions and Economic Development. A Comparison of Great Britain and France in the Eighteenth and Nineteenth Centuries', *Explorations in Economic History* 21, 2 (1984), pp. 118–19.

[86] See Velde and Weir, 'The Financial Market and Government Debt Policy in France, pp. 32–3.

[87] Another obstacle to investment in life annuities consisted in the long delays with which the *payeurs de rentes* (the officers in charge of the distribution of returns on life annuities) operated.

The golden age of investments in life annuities was without any doubt the 1780s, when more than 640 millions borrowed by the French Crown were in life annuities, almost as much as during the rest of the century (653 million livres).[88] The loan issued by Controller-General Calonne in December 1783 consisted of 100 million livres of life annuities. Parisian bankers were this time heavily involved, with such houses as Rilliet & Cie, Girardot, Haller & Cie, Etienne Delessert, and many others, as well the Lyons bankers Fulchiron, Jean-Louis Grenus. The Geneva banking community was represented by banks which had had a long experience in the field since Necker's issue of life annuities during the American war: Bontems & Mallet, Passavant, de Candolle, Bertrand & Cie, and François Calandrini. As Geneva bankers largely bought life annuities from Parisian and Lyons bankers, they took up some 25 per cent of the entire 1783 loan.[89]

The market for life annuities had actually been offered to the Dutch bankers. In 1771 Controller-General Terray sold the right to place life annuities on the Amsterdam market, up to the value of 2 millions, to the Amsterdam bank Horneca, Hogguer & Co. However, it was precisely because of the reticence of Dutch investors that Geneva bankers, above all Bontems & fils, decided to venture into this business, considered too risky and unsound by their Dutch peers.[90] Dutch investors, who were particularly cautious about their investments, changed their attitude towards French annuities when their country became engaged in a war against the United Kingdom in 1780, triggering an outflow of capital from that country. The activities of Jan Jacob Brandts, Amsterdam merchant and *rentier*, are revealing in that respect. Between 1783 and 1790, Brandts increasingly invested in life annuities and lottery tickets issued in France. His 1782 balance showed 44,567 florins in annuities, rising to more than 100,000 in 1790.[91] Besides their investment function, life annuities were also used as security to obtain credit on the Amsterdam market. Moreover, Amsterdam brokers, such as Johannes Bouman and Pierre Stadnistki, jointly operated and bought large amounts of annuities that would be sold in small batches to clients eager to broaden and diversify their portfolios.[92]

Generally annuities were paid in alphabetical order, therefore many bankers, to have their annuities paid, employed a market operator with a name beginning with 'A'. Moreover, it must be said that sometimes Geneva bankers were also unlucky with their investment, as was the case of the death of Pernette Elisabeth Martin, who died at 8, carrying with her more than two millions of life annuities. For this episode and on the mechanism of life annuities see H. Lüthy, *La banque protestante en France: de la révocation de l'Édit de Nantes à la Révolution. II, de la banque aux finances (1730–1794)* (Paris, 1961), pp. 469–87.

[88] Velde and Weir, 'The Financial Market and Government Debt Policy in France', p. 28.

[89] Lüthy, *La banque protestante en France, II*, pp. 532–8.

[90] Lüthy, *La banque protestante en France, II*, pp. 487–90.

[91] See J. C. Riley, 'Dutch Investment in France, 1781–1787', *Journal of Economic History* 33, 4 (1973), pp. 745–7.

[92] Riley, 'Dutch Investment in France, 1781–1787', pp. 752–5.

Despite being outnumbered by the Swiss, the presence of Dutch bankers in Paris was far from negligible. Balthazar-Elie Abbema had fled from Amsterdam after that city had been occupied by the Prussian army in 1787 and chose Paris as a safe refuge. There he succeeded in being appointed a member of the Board of Directors of the Compagnie des Indes, and he actively took part to the political life of the Jacobin club where he pleaded for French intervention against the Austrian Empire to free the Dutch provinces. Together with another Dutch banker, Jean-Konrad de Kock, he sat on the Dutch committee that was in charge of the supply operations for the French forces engaged in Holland. His brilliant career was fatally jeopardized by his friendship with General Dumouriez, whose treason resulted in the arrest and death of the two Dutch bankers.[93]

The French Revolution brought an end to the career of another successful Dutch banker in Paris: Jean-Baptiste Vandenyver. Born in Amsterdam, he moved to Paris at the age of 28, rapidly obtained naturalization, in 1757, and he sat on the Board of Directors of the Caisse d'Escompte. His activities ranged from credits offered to Dutch merchants and French colonial planters, to large trade operations with the island of Haiti. In 1791 he decided to retire and leave the firm to his sons who were both engaged in the activities of the Jacobin club. Notwithstanding these powerful political connections, Vandenyver was sent to the guillotine after he was found guilty of treason against the Republic for running operations for the exiled Madame du Barry.[94]

There was a third group in the French financial scene of the eighteenth century that played a role akin to that of private bankers, and these were the notaries. They were pivotal in the development of the credit market in Paris: whereas bankers proposed and made available the government debt to *foreign* investors, Parisian notaries made it possible for *domestic* investors to take part in the many loans issued during the eighteenth century.[95] They offered information to borrowers and lenders who were not familiar with the credit instruments related to government debt. Moreover, they were in a unique position to offer insightful information about the trustworthiness of lenders and borrowers because they dealt with a wide range of people, extending well beyond the personal connections available to a private Parisian.[96] They also opened the credit market to people residing outside Paris and eager to invest their capital or simply to deposit it in the notaries' strongboxes. This included not only male provincial investors, but also women who could invest part of

[93] On these two Dutch bankers, see J. Bouchary, *Les manieurs d'argent à Paris à la fin du XVIIIe siècle* (Paris, 1939), vol.1, pp. 119–41.

[94] Bouchary, *Les manieurs d'argent*, 1, pp. 143–71.

[95] On the relevance of notaries to French credit markets, see P. T. Hoffman, G. Postel-Vinay, and J.-L. Rosenthal, *Priceless Markets. Political Economy of Credit in Paris, 1660–1870* (Chicago, 2000).

[96] Hoffman et al., *Priceless Markets*, pp. 117–34.

their dowries and capital that would otherwise remain completely idle within the household.

During the eighteenth century, notaries dealt not only with government debt subscriptions, but also with cash deposits. In fact, clients entrusted them with large sums of money and expected them to know about the most profitable investment opportunities. Notaries could either invest these sums in government debt or lend them to other clients. In this way they started to act not only as simple brokers of bonds, but also as bankers granting credit. However, this activity was not riskless, since clients usually wanted to be able to withdraw their funds at short notice: in the mid-eighteenth century twelve notaries went bankrupt as a result of the risks incurred by lending on the security of their clients' deposits.[97] Under the threat of stricter regulations, the Parisian notaries began to act more cautiously—there were 'only' three bankruptcies between 1762 and 1787.They largely reverted to their original duty of laying out their clients' investments in government debt, which offered lower profit margins but was incomparably safer than lending on the security of clients' deposits. When this change occurred, the market for government loans was booming, and even if they had to sacrifice their banking activities, notaries remained essential to the functioning of the credit market in Paris up until the coming of the French Revolution.[98]

Frankfurt: Private Bankers and Court Jews

As in Amsterdam, banking in Frankfurt during the eighteenth century was intermeshed with merchanting although, from the mid-century, there was an increasing specialization of function within the commercial communities of this German city. By 1790 some forty-five houses in Frankfurt were regarded as banks, despite most of their businesses still displaying a strong marker of their commercial origins. Their operations comprised significant and continuing trading interests by accepting commissions, undertaking the carriage of goods, and engaging in speculative wholesaling transactions. However, these enduring commitments to merchanting had been increasingly coupled from the mid-century with a clear specialist involvement in the provision of credit. This involved undertaking payment clearances by transfer and remittances through the supply to customers of bills drawn on all the European financial centres.

Frankfurt's sobriquet of 'Little Amsterdam' after 1750 did not solely rest upon its importance as a primary centre of continental European trade credit and payments clearance, since its financial market had risen to be second only

[97] Hoffman et al., *Priceless Markets*, pp. 140–5.
[98] Hoffman et al., *Priceless Markets*, pp. 150–3.

to that of the Dutch city in this respect over the seventeenth century. Rather, during the second half of the eighteenth century, Frankfurt's increasingly specialist bankers became involved in sovereign lending, with the first loan being made in 1754. The leading firm was Gebrüder Bethmann, a Christian house established as wholesaling merchants in 1748. Its transformation was marked by one of its eighteenth century partners—Simon Moritz von Bethmann—being described as the 'epitome of a German court financier'.[99]

German court agents and bankers had their origins in the activities undertaken by the Jewish Hoffaktor or Hofjude. These individual Jewish merchants had collectively risen in importance over the century after the Thirty Years War by occupying the vacuum caused by the retreat of mercantile bankers from German princely finance. From the late seventeenth century, rulers of the German states, especially those in central and southern Germany, turned to Hoffaktoren to liberate their finances from political control, especially with regard to maintaining a standing army. In this respect, the court Jew played a major part during the eighteenth century in these rulers' attempts to establish their absolute power. Consequently, the Hoffaktors' positions had all the dangers of Machiavelli's warning regarding placing trust in princes. This was because their situations—financial and personal—arose solely from their particular relationships with rulers, to the extent that some were legally executed upon the death of the lord they had served. Generally, Hoffaktors fulfilled the consumption needs of the court and financed them, for which they drew upon their own resources and those of their Christian depositors. Furthermore, they usually leased upon an advance payment the local mint which they supplied with bullion. With respect to their war-financing functions, clear examples can be found in the activities of Joseph Süß Oppenheimer, who resourced the standing army as well as the Württemberg court of Duke Karl Alexander during the early eighteenth century, and Feidel David, who relayed English subsidies to the Landgraf of Hessen-Kassel at the mid-century.

Many of Frankfurt's Jewish merchants acted as Hoffaktoren, while Bethmanns had their origins in the earlier trading activities of an uncle—Jakob Adami. This general commerce was maintained by Johan Philipp and Simon Moritz von Bethmann and grew substantially with the French occupation of the city during the Seven Years War. Johan and Simon seized upon the opportunity to victual the French forces as well as undertaking financial operations to enable their payment. This first major step in financing a non-German state paved the way for the Bethmanns undertaking international loans within a matter of years. Critical to their development as an issue house was the Austrian loan of 1778. Initially, they attempted to place it amongst close friends but this proved to be a failure and so they adopted Amsterdam methods and the practices of Saxon

[99] A. E. G. Heyn, *Private Banking and Industrialisation. The Case of Frankfurt am Main, 1825–1875* (New York, 1981), pp. 41–4.

bankers. The loan of 20,000 florins was divided, as in Amsterdam, into *partial-obligationen* or debt certificates of 1,000 florins each, which were publicly advertised for sale. Furthermore, interest coupons were attached to each sub-bond. Going beyond their own intimate circle to tap general private savings for the loan gave the Bethmanns the success they sought, which resulted in their taking away further Austrian issues from the Amsterdam market. Between 1768 and 1793, Bethmanns at Frankfurt raised 17.2 million florins for the Habsburgs. Like Hopes, Bethmanns charged their international clients a commission for their issuing services—5 to 5.5 per cent—and also drew a further commission for servicing the arising securitized debt (interest and amortization payments). On occasion, they operated with other houses, as in the case of a loan to the duke of Saxony in 1791, which they undertook with J. F. Goutard & Söhne.[100]

Among other Frankfurt houses of importance before the French revolutionary wars were B. Metzler seel. Sohn & Co., which issued a loan for Liege in 1791 and Willmer & Co., which undertook a comparable operation for Prussia in 1792. As yet Mayer Amschel Rothschild did not feature amongst Frankfurt's prominent Jewish bankers. He had begun as a small specialist dealer in antiques, coins, and medals, which led him into the provision of exchange in a petty way. The subsequent development of Mayer Amschel's business was increasingly related to commodity dealing, which remained his principal activity until 1810. The first indication of the Rothschilds' financial future was Meyer Amschel replacing Feidel David as Hoffaktor to the Landgraff of Hessen-Kassel. His connections with the Hessen court only really developed from 1796 and Mayer Amschel was not to become the senior court agent until 1806. Nonetheless, by 1797, he was one of the wealthiest Frankfurt Jews. Over the previous seven years, he had increasingly concentrated upon the provision of banking services through a network that came not only to span the German states, but also extended to Amsterdam, London, Paris, and Vienna. The outbreak of the French wars led him into military contracting, initially for the Austrian army, while, from 1797, he and his son, Nathan, developed a trade in importing English cottons. In parallel, from 1796, Mayer Amschel had a growing involvement in the financial operations of William of Hesse-Kassel, which resulted in his first participation in a sovereign loan—to Denmark—in 1800.[101]

[100] M. North, 'The Great German Banking Houses and International Merchants, Sixteenth to Nineteenth Century', in Teichova et al., *Banking, Trade and Industry*, pp. 39–42; and Heyn, *Private Banking and Industrialisation*, pp. 43–7. For Bethmanns, see J. P. Freiherr von Bethmann (ed.), *Bankiers sind auch Menschen. 225 Jahre Bankhaus Gebrüder Bethmann* (Frankfurt, 1973); W. Forstmann, *Simon Moritz von Bethmann 1768–1826. Bankier, Diplomat und politische Beobachter* (Frankfurt, 1973); and F. Zellfelder, *Das Kundennetz des Bankhauses Gebrüder Bethmann (1738–1816). Frankfurt am Main im Spiegel der Hauptbücher* (Stuttgart, 1994).

[101] N. Ferguson, *The World's Banker. The History of the House of Rothschild* (London, 1998), pp. 45–9, 51–2, 66–8.

3

War and Economic Transformation, 1793–1815

Some historians have applied the label, the 'Second Hundred Years' War', to the period 1688–1815,[1] but Europe's foreign trade expanded over these years—though that growth was repeatedly punctuated by the impact of recurrent hostilities. However, it is doubtful whether the continent's trade continued to expand during the culmination of this second prolonged Franco-British confrontation, between 1793 and 1815. As previously, the belligerents employed economic devices and mechanisms to achieve their war aims, beginning in 1793 with the French National Convention's annulment of the Anglo-French 1786 free-trade treaty.[2] The economic conflict thereafter heightened, especially from 1803, with the progressive development of Napoleon's Continental Blockade and Britain's ripostes through Orders in Council. Napoleon's Continental System assumed its final form during 1806–7. A further increase in the French tariff, coupled with prohibiting the import of cotton textiles, were followed by the Berlin decrees, augmented in the 1807 Milan decrees.[3] These measures, their British counters, and those imposed by other states increasingly disrupted trade.

The trade blockades of 1806–7 were to be the apogee, during the Napoleonic wars, of harnessing economics in support of military strategy and tactics. But, almost as soon as the French Revolutionary armies had entered the field some sixteen years earlier, their campaigns had had major economic consequences. One was the progressive disruption of Europe's commercial

[1] J. Meyer and J. Bromley, 'The Second Hundred Years' War (1688–1815)', in D. Johnson, F. Crouzet, and F. Bedarida (eds), *Britain and France. Ten Centuries* (Folkestone, 1980), but see also J. Black, *British Foreign Policy in the Age of Walpole* (Edinburgh, 1985), pp. 1–12.

[2] J. B. Williams, *British Commercial Policy and Trade Expansion, 1750–1850* (Oxford, 1972), pp. 190–1, 346.

[3] See A. S. Milward and S. B. Saul, *The Economic Development of Continental Europe, 1780–1870* (London, 1973), pp. 267–70; F. Crouzet, 'Wars, Blockade and Economic Change in Europe, 1792–1815', *Journal of Economic History*, 24 (1964); F. Crouzet, *L'économie britannique et le blocus continental 1806–1813* (Paris, 1958); and Williams, *British Commercial Policy*, pp. 347–9.

and financial networks established over the preceding two centuries. Beginning with Amsterdam during the mid-1790s and then Hamburg and Frankfurt from 1806, the major mercantile and financial market centres lost dynamism. Paris was shaken by the revolution and, especially, the Terror of 1793–4, but it recovered gradually thereafter and its appeal became ever stronger from the turn of the century, to the detriment of provincial towns, particularly Lyons; while at the international level, it was soon to assert itself as second only to London.

London's importance increased, which was in part due to the migration of German merchants to the City. Many of the houses that they established in London were to become the leading merchant banks of the nineteenth century, such as Brandts, Fruhling & Goschen, Huths, Rothschilds, and Schroders'. They were the second component of the London private banks, alongside the private deposit banks, which had emerged in the late seventeenth century. The period's most significant changes thus took place in Britain, with the advent of London as not only the most important financial centre, but also the fulcrum of a new world economy increasingly shaped by industrialization; and the rapid expansion of country banks, a type of banking institution still without equivalent in continental Europe.

A CHANGING INTERNATIONAL FINANCIAL ORDER

Amsterdam's already waning trade was stifled from 1795, when the British blockade of continental Channel ports was extended beyond the Scheldt in response to the Revolutionary armies occupying the Low Countries.[4] Partners in Hope & Co., safely in London, transferred the servicing of their house's foreign state loans to former associates and competitors: Polish to Raymond and Theodore de Smeth, and Swedish to Hogguer, whereas Russian issues went to Martin Dorner in Hamburg. Although the French Revolutionary terror abated and the new Batavian Republic's leaders attempted to re-establish a stable and calmer business environment in Amsterdam, the city's merchants were subject to compulsory loans and levies.[5]

Dutch investment no longer flowed abroad in substantial quantities. The government controlled security issues and became the major drawer on both new savings and existing wealth. Between 1795 and 1814 Dutch state debt

[4] Until 1813, smuggling was the only way for British goods to gain entry into the northern Netherlands: see Williams, *British Commercial Policy*, pp. 178, 349–50.

[5] M. G. Buist, *At Spes Non Fracta. Hope & Co. 1770–1815. Merchant Bankers and Diplomats at Work* (The Hague, 1974), pp. 50–2.

increased by about 261million guilders.[6] The new government's progressive 'crowding out' of foreign loans on the Amsterdam capital market was coupled with the negative effects upon Dutch investors of repudiations by borrowing states. France suspended servicing of its international debts in 1793, followed by partial repudiation in 1797. Similarly, Austrian debt servicing went into abeyance from 1795, only to be resumed for Dutch holders in 1802. But by 1804, this was undertaken from Vienna in inconvertible banknotes, which proved to be the overture to the Habsburg bankruptcy of 1811. These blows to Dutch rentiers' foreign financial assets were compounded by others, arising from Danish, Russian, Spanish, and Swedish repudiations in part or in full.[7]

After the Treaty of Amiens (March 1802), which ended the European hostilities, albeit for what proved to be a short period, the Hope partners hesitantly re-established themselves in Amsterdam, having to be guarded about their personal ties to Britain. The house's continued standing and resources enabled it to play a significant part in the finance of Napoleonic Europe—for both the Emperor and his ennobled family members.[8] The resulting relationship, substantially based upon Napoleon's respect for Hopes' honesty, shielded the house from Amsterdam police officials, Batavian radicals, and envious competitors. But with the resumption of war and as the Continental Blockade's constrictions became more pervasive and cut deeper, Hope's commercial dealings declined, especially from 1808 when French troops occupied Spain. Their business malaise was also due to Henry Hope's death and subsequent bitter disagreements amongst the partners. Nonetheless, Hopes proved able to survive, although in a reconfigured form which was unlike any of its late eighteenth-century peers, like Hogguers, Muilman, and de Smeth.[9]

The decline of Amsterdam's importance as a financial and mercantile centre was not initially shared by Hamburg, its long-time rival. Indeed, the city's merchants substantially benefited from their Dutch counterparts' growing difficulties. Furthermore, Hamburg's traditional neutrality attracted an inflow of migrants and flight capital, especially from the Batavian Republic and France, which also brought much of the trade previously conducted in Amsterdam, Antwerp, and Le Havre. The basis for sustained prosperity continued to be colonial commerce, with Hamburg's mercantile community dealing in New World commodities imported either from Iberian ports, particularly Corunna, or the neutral United States. This business was matched, as previously, with trading in the Baltic, especially with Russia. While continuing to supply the

[6] J. C. Riley, *International Government Finance and the Amsterdam Capital Market 1740–1815* (Cambridge, 1980), pp. 195–6, 202, 211–14.

[7] Riley, *International Government Finance*, pp. 198, 204–5, 207, 209, 210.

[8] This is discussed below, see pp. 96–8.

[9] Buist, *At Spes Non Fracta*, pp. 55–69.

continent's interior via the Elbe and Weser rivers, Hamburg also became, during the 1790s, *the* entrepôt for Europe and its most important exchange market. One marker of the latter was the way that Johann Heinrich Gossler, a new partner in the long established mercantile house of Joh. Berenberg, Gossler & Co., began in 1798 increasingly to specialize in discounting and the provision of acceptance credits.[10] However, the firm, despite its standing, lacked the resources and international connections of John Parish & Co., founded by the son of an English migrant who had settled in Hamburg in 1756.[11]

Hamburg's neutrality and its merchants' ability thereby to trade with Britain were ultimately untenable in the titanic struggles of the French Revolutionary and Napoleonic wars. Flourishing commercial and financial intercourse with Britain led to the imposition of a French embargo in 1799. It caused a commercial crisis during which 150 of the city's mercantile firms went bankrupt. The embargo was lifted after the payment of a hefty fine but, almost immediately thereafter, Hamburg's trade was gravely affected by the formation, and actions, of the League of Armed Neutrality. The city was occupied by Danish troops and Prussian forces closed the Elbe and Weser to British commerce. This was a countermeasure to the British government requiring neutral vessels crossing the Atlantic and bound for continental Europe to call first at a British port. The Danish occupation continued until 1801. Any subsequent business recovery experienced by Hamburg merchants following the Peace of Amiens was undermined from 1803 when French troops moved into Hanover. They closed the Elbe and Weser estuaries to British shipping, and Britain responded by extending its naval blockade of the continent. The effects of the consequent progressive strangulation of Hamburg's trade from 1803 were compounded by France exacting forced loans.

Over the second half of the 1800s, undertaking business in Hamburg became even more difficult. In late 1806, French forces occupied the city, which became subject to the Continental System, and, with French armies in Portugal from 1807, its Brazilian trade was diverted to London. Attempts by both British and Hamburg merchants to sustain trade by systematic smuggling from the offshore base of Heligoland were stymied in 1810 by France annexing the city.[12] The French occupation of Hamburg between 1810 and 1814 had at least some benefits for its Jewish minority. Moses Marcus and Gerson, the partners in the bill-broking bank of M. M. Warburg & Co. that

[10] S. R. Cope, *Walter Boyd. A Merchant Banker in the Age of Napoleon* (Gloucester, 1983), p. 73; and E. Rosenbaum and A. J. Sherman, *M. M. Warburg & Co., 1798–1938. Merchant Bankers of Hamburg* (London, 1979), p. 1.

[11] P. H. Emden, *Money Powers of Europe in the Nineteenth and Twentieth Centuries* (New York/London, 1938), pp. 20–2.

[12] Williams, *British Commercial Policy*, pp. 351–8; R. Roberts, *Schroders. Merchants & Bankers* (Houndsmills/London, 1992), pp. 14–19; and Rosenbaum and Sherman, *M. M. Warburg & Co.*, pp. 1–13.

had been established in 1798, enjoyed greater personal liberty. However, in 1812, the city's French administration attempted to extort Ff500,000 from its Jewish community through, in certain instances, holding to ransom its wealthiest members, including Gerson Warburg.[13] Greater Jewish toleration throughout Napoleonic Europe came to end with the peace—the decisions of the Congress of Vienna—and was not to be re-established within Germany until 1871.

Private bankers in Frankfurt, especially those involved with state loans, also initially benefited from Amsterdam's increasing difficulties. While Hamburg took the place of Amsterdam from 1795 as the continent's international credit market, Frankfurt became Europe's major capital market for sovereign borrowers. This was despite the city being temporarily occupied by French forces in October 1792. By 1797 there was organized securities trading on the Frankfurt Börse and, within three further years, twenty loans were quoted.[14] Bethmanns, the leading house, floated loans in 1801 and 1802, although its partners found that war conditions increasingly deterred subscribers. Consequently, from the turn of the century, Bethmanns largely abandoned securities business and reverted to mercantile dealings on commission. These were for clients largely involved in the manufacture of brass, silk, wire, and wool throughout western and central Germany. This forced change of strategy increased Bethmanns' annual profits by about 25 per cent despite Frankfurt, like Hamburg, being occupied by French troops from 1806 and the city's trade consequently being affected by the Continental Blockade.[15] Bethmanns' retreat into wholesaling may also have been partly a result of Mayer Amschel Rothschild's rising importance on the Frankfurt financial market. During the mid-1790s, he secured a role in the substantial investment activities of William of Hesse-Kassel. This gave him a basis for participating during 1800 and 1801 in Danish loans along with Bethmanns and Rüppell & Harnier. In 1804, Mayer Amschel gained a monopoly of Danish finance, while his widening financial undertakings were buttressed by his being appointed agent to many German princely courts, above all the Emperor in 1800.[16]

[13] R. Chernow, *The Warburgs. The Twentieth-Century Odyssey of a Remarkable Jewish Family* (New York, 1993), p. 6; but see, Rosenbaum and Sherman, *M. M. Warburg & Co.* for a somewhat different account of Gerson's ransom.

[14] A. E. G. Heyn, *Private Banking and Industrialisation. The Case of Frankfurt am Main, 1825–1875* (New York, 1981), pp. 43, 45.

[15] M. North, 'The Great German Banking Houses and International Merchants, Sixteenth to Nineteenth Century', in A. Teichova, G. Kurgan-van Hentenryk, and D. Ziegler (eds), *Banking, Trade and Industry. Europe, America and Asia from the Thirteenth to the Twentieth Century* (Cambridge, 1997), p. 42; and W. Forstmann, 'Frankfurt am Main: A City of Finance. Banking Systems in Frankfurt in the 18th and 19th Centuries', in H. Diederiks and D. Reader (eds), *Cities of Finance* (Amsterdam, 1996), pp. 184–5.

[16] N. Ferguson, *The World's Banker. The History of the House of Rothschild* (London, 1998), pp. 66–8.

Unlike continental Europe, British overseas trade expanded throughout the French wars although it is difficult to establish its precise dimensions. When only the first decade of the French Revolutionary and Napoleonic Wars (1794/6–1804/6), is considered, Davis's painstaking reconstruction of trade values at current prices indicates a very marked increase. British domestic exports grew by 72 per cent, imports by 47 per cent, and re-exports by 20 per cent,[17] with only the latter being relatively affected by the mounting Anglo-French economic confrontation. Nonetheless, almost continuous warfare distorted British overseas trade, clearly evident when changes in its geographical pattern are reviewed. The most rapid growth was in dealings with not only North America and the Caribbean, a continuation of eighteenth-century trends, *but also* with northern Europe—with Hamburg and the Baltic.

The Baltic area gained much consequence during the first decade of war as a market for British re-exports. This significant change in Anglo-European commerce was almost as much a result of wartime trade diversion as trade generation. This was even more the case with exports of British produced goods to northern Europe. Countries of the Baltic littoral had only ranked fifth as a market for British manufactures during the mid-1780s but, by the mid-1800s, they were second in importance to the United States.[18] One of the major reasons for northern Europe's considerable significance over the decade from the outbreak of war in 1793 is that much of Britain's trade with the whole of the continent came to be conducted through its ports, principally neutral Hamburg. Furthermore, Hamburg was the wartime exchange market for clearing Anglo-European payments until 1806.

The wartime increase in Hamburg's already established role in Anglo-Continental dealings led the city's merchants to deepen their connections with London. For instance, C. M. Schröder & Co. sent their vessels to Britain's principal port from 1797, and Bernard Heinrich Schröder II took up residence in London during that year. He acted as a commission agent on the family's behalf and was probably responsible for their vessels when they were moored in the Pool of London. His coming to London was an aspect of the expansion of the network of the filially-related Schröder houses. They had opened in Amsterdam at the close of the 1780s, and Christian Matthias Schröder's development of an interest in intra-Baltic trade led to further family houses being established in St Petersburg at the turn of the century and in Riga in 1812. A permanent Schröder house was opened in London in 1800 by Johann Friedrich, a son of the leading partner in the family firm who became a member of Lloyds (the insurance market) within a year of his arrival. In

[17] Excluding trade with Ireland. Calculated from R. Davis, *The Industrial Revolution and British Overseas Trade* (Leicester, 1979), Table 37, p. 86.

[18] Again, excluding trade with Ireland. Calculated from Davis, *British Overseas Trade*, Tables 38–40, pp. 88–93.

1802, he was joined by one of his five brothers, Johann Heinrich, a full partner in J. F. Schröder & Co. from 1804. Initially, Friedrich and Heinrich focused on the sugar trade, an established Hamburg–London staple, but also accepted bills and, with Hamburg's increasing commercial difficulties from 1803, may have moved into the Russian trade.

Schröders were somewhat exceptional in having a wide and formalized, family-based European trading network during the first decade of the nineteenth century. However, they were not the sole Hamburg mercantile family to institutionalize their London connections during the Revolutionary and Napoleonic wars. Brandts, established in 1805, is another example, its business having developed through a prior connection with Rougement & Behrens, leading City merchants of Huguenot origin.[19] The Brandt and Schröder London branch houses joined a community of about forty merchants trading with Hamburg, many of whom had German origins.[20]

Other merchants of Hamburg birth came to London by more tortuous routes and some for more pressing reasons. Johann Huth, the founder of Frederick Huth & Co., arrived in 1809, having fled from Spain on Napoleon's invasion possibly carrying the Princess of Asturias' jewels. He had gained his commercial experience in the long established Hamburg-Iberian trades under Juan Urbieta coupled with further training at the Handelsakademie. This was followed by a senior clerkship at Urbieta's Corunna house and acting as supercargo on voyages to South America, including to the continent's Pacific coast. As a result of French blockades and invasion, Corunna was Hamburg's principal Spanish connection and staging post for trade with the Americas for a short period after 1783. When Johann Huth started afresh in London, he began, not unusually, as a commission agent and, applying his experience, specialized in trade with Latin America's Pacific coast. He only re-established his direct Spanish connections during 1814 after Wellesley's victories in the Peninsula war.[21]

The migration of continental European merchants and bankers to London was not solely due to the push forces generated by enveloping French occupation and the consequent trade distortions of Napoleon's Continental Blockade. One major attraction arose from a new, vital dynamic within British overseas trade: the growth of exports of manufactured cottons, the value of which at current prices soared by nearly 2,000 per cent between the mid-1780s and the mid-1800s.

In terms of individual items, cottons had only ranked third amongst British domestic exports on the eve of the French wars. They were then completely

[19] Roberts, *Schroders*, pp. 15, 28–31; and S. D. Chapman, *Merchant Enterprise in Britain. From the Industrial Revolution to World War I* (Cambridge, 1992), pp. 134–5.

[20] Chapman, *Merchant Enterprise in Britain*, p. 133.

[21] A. J. Murray, *Home from the Hill* (London, 1970), pp. 4–22, 24–112.

overshadowed by the traditional woollen trade and exported iron goods. Prior to the outbreak of war, cotton yarn and cloth had been taken principally by three markets in almost equal shares: Africa; north-western Europe; and the United States. By the first years of war, 1794–6, the United States had become the prime outlet for these goods, absorbing 45 per cent, followed by the West Indies (22.2 per cent) and north-western Europe (11.8 per cent). A decade later, when cotton exports totalled £15.9 million at current prices and accounted for 42 per cent of all exported British produced goods, the United States was still their predominant mart (28.6 per cent) but only just. Northern Europe, to where 27.3 per cent was consigned, was very nearly as large a buyer and, though the value of cottons sent to the West Indies more than tripled between 1794–6 and 1804–6, this region's share had declined to 16.2 per cent by the latter years.[22] Overall, during the water-powered phase of cotton manufacturing in Britain, the industry's exports went principally to Europe and the New World. Yet, from the outbreak of war until 1806, those destined for continental European markets increasingly went through northern ports, particularly neutral Hamburg. The only other route for either legitimate trade, or organized smuggling, was via the Mediterranean, and southern Europe's proportional take of expanding British cotton exports increased somewhat from 8 per cent in 1794–6 to 10.3 per cent in 1804–6.[23]

As Chapman has demonstrated, the remarkable growth of manufactured cotton exports from the 1780s brought about the rise of a new echelon of northern, provincial merchants and merchant-industrialists in Britain. It gave the Atlantic ports, above all Glasgow and Liverpool, a further, dynamic to their international dealings. Amongst the many other commercial and financial changes induced by the astounding international success of British machine-spun cotton yarn, one involved Frankfurt and Hamburg merchants settling permanently in Manchester, the industry's emerging marketing centre. By the turn of the century, there were eight German merchants resident in this north-western town while as a counterpart fifteen Frankfurt Jewish firms imported Lancashire's cotton textiles. Direct access to the prime wholesale source of cotton yarn and cloth cut out chains of middlemen and, of course, their commissions. Buying prices could be even keener if deals were made towards the year-end when Manchester merchants and cotton masters were keen to reduce stocks before striking the annual balance in their ledgers. This situation was exploited by Nathan Meyer Rothschild, initially on behalf of his father's Frankfurt house.

After a brief apprenticeship with Levi Barent Cohen, one of only some dozen Askenazi merchants in London, Nathan Meyer worked in Manchester

[22] Again, excluding trade with Ireland. Calculated from Davis, *British Overseas Trade*, Tables 41–3, pp. 94–6.

[23] Williams, *British Commercial Policy*, pp. 362–71.

from about May 1799 to by-pass both English exporters operating through continental correspondents and sales at German fairs.[24] He was joined by his brother Salomon, and handled orders that had been personally obtained in France, Germany, the Low Countries, and Switzerland, not only in Lancashire's cotton capital but also at other textile centres: Leeds, Nottingham, and Glasgow (travelling to Scotland for this specific purpose in November 1800). By 1801, the Rothschild brothers had become textile manufacturers, and the overall business reached such a size within a further four years as to require a further partner, Nehm Beer Rindskopf. He was the son of one of Mayer Amschel's business associates and took charge of sales.[25] Other members of the Rothschild family and its trading network followed, some of whom settled in Glasgow or London. Members of two Frankfurt mercantile families of Huguenot origin—the Du Fays and Souchets—likewise saw the profitable advantages of direct dealings in British-manufactured cottons.

London remained Britain's principal port and had a far more liquid credit market than possibly any other centre, and was more open to foreign merchants because of the City's cosmopolitan character. These factors may have been responsible for Nathan Meyer Rothschild turning more to the metropolis from 1805. In London, Nathan had initial backing from two Dutch Jewish houses—Salomon Solomans and Goldsmid & Eliason—as well as Harman & Co., all within his father's commercial and credit networks.[26] A very particular, personal motivation was Nathan's attachment to Hannah Barent Cohen, who he married in 1806. Her dowry assisted his financial position; likewise, her father's legacy in 1808. By about this stage in his business's development, credit provision had become Nathan's growing interest while his mercantile dealings included colonial goods. In association with his father-in-law, these were smuggled along with Baltic products to feed continental markets. Banking only started to gain total ascendancy from 1810, although it was not to have a clear focus and be totally metropolitan-based for yet a further year.[27]

The wartime augmentation of London's mercantile and financial community was also due to the effects of the West Country woollen industry's stagnation. It led some other sons of Exeter merchants to follow in the footsteps of Francis Baring.[28] One example is Heath & Co., established in

[24] B. Williams, *The Making of Manchester Jewry, 1740–1875* (Manchester, 1976), pp. 17–19; and S. D. Chapman, *N. M. Rothschild 1777–1836* (privately printed, 1977), pp. 5, 19.

[25] Ferguson, *World's Banker*, pp. 51–7.

[26] Chapman, *Merchant Enterprise in Britain*, pp. 133–5, 145–6.

[27] Ferguson, *World's Banker*, pp. 57, 62.

[28] John Baring I had come to Exeter from Bremen in 1717 to be involved in one of the poles of the Anglo-Continental wool trade. He was naturalized in 1723 and six years later married the daughter of a wealthy Exeter import merchant who brought him a sizeable dowry. With the advice of their London agent, his three sons Charles, Francis, and John II reorganized the family business at the close of 1762, establishing two interlocking partnerships: John & Charles Baring & Co. in Exeter and John & Francis Baring in London.

London by John Heath. His commercial training had involved a sound grounding in continental practice—an apprenticeship with Doxat & Aubert, Genoa, followed by a partnership in Robert Aubert & Co., Geneva—both possibly secured by the connections of his mother, Rose Mary Michelet, a Huguenot. A brother, Charles, after receiving a comparable mercantile grooming, went into partnership with John in a new Genoese firm in 1781. However, John returned to England shortly after the outbreak of war. In making this circuitous but educative transfer to the metropolis, the Heaths were joined by some members of another West Country merchant family—the Gibbs—who had complementary interests in the Iberian trade. Lyle Gibbs became a member of John and Charles Heaths' Genoese partnership and only rejoined his own family's house in 1820 which, by then, had moved to London.[29]

The financing of trading from London was assisted by war-induced changes in the Bank of England's policies. The exchanges turned against Britain from spring 1795, partly due to the re-establishment of the French currency after the assignat hyperinflation. French monetary reconstruction during 1795 and 1796 drew bullion legally and illegally from London, both directly and indirectly via Hamburg. From the beginning of 1796, Bank of England directors restricted discounting, mainly with a view to contract the Bank's note issue and prevent an internal gold drain. For newcomers to the metropolis' mercantile community, the rationing of discounts at Threadneedle Street was undertaken 'without regard to the respectability of the party . . . or the solidity of the Bills'.[30]

The problems of British mercantile finance became more acute with the full development of the Napoleonic Continental Blockade, especially from the Peace of Tilsit (7 July 1807) until spring 1809 and, again, from summer 1810 to late 1812.[31] These commercial difficulties of 1809 to 1812 have been seen by Chapman to have resulted in a generational change within Britain's mercantile communities, both metropolitan and provincial, coupled with consequent structural alterations in trade finance and marketing. The bankruptcies of 1810 and 1811 were accompanied by retirements from overseas dealings by older, established merchants. The resulting vacuum was filled by young commission agents, frequently operating abroad. Concurrently, the most wealthy, committed metropolitan merchants shifted further away from

[29] [Sir William R. Drake], *Heathiana* (London, 1880), pp. 5–20; J. A. Gibbs, *The History of Antony and Dorothea Gibbs* (London, 1922), pp. 14–17; and C. A. Jones, *International Business in the Nineteenth Century. The Rise and Fall of a Cosmopolitan Bourgeoisie* (New York, 1987), pp. 34–5.

[30] Sir John H. Clapham, *The Bank of England. A History*, I, *1694–1797* (Cambridge, 1944, rep. 1970), p. 269.

[31] See J. Moyr and E. Savin, 'Stagflation in Historical Perspective: the Napoleonic Wars revisited', *Research in Economic History*, 1 (1976) but also H. V. Bowen, *War and British Society 1688–1815* (Cambridge, 1998), pp. 72–7 for an overall appreciation.

direct involvement in trade. Instead, they concentrated to a greater degree upon providing credits through accepting bills drawn by merchants of lesser means within their clienteles. This further development of London acceptance houses, or merchant banks, was only to become distinct by the early 1830s but a major stage in their evolution took place during the final difficult decade of the French wars.[32]

BRITISH WAR FINANCE

Merchant banking also further emerged in London from 1793 as a result of the government's greatly increased need to borrow. The unredeemed, funded National Debt rapidly expanded from the outbreak of war, rising from £231.5 million, nominal, 1792 (financial year-end), to £478.1 million, nominal, 1802. Thereafter, the introduction of property and income taxes tempered state indebtedness' explosive growth somewhat but, nonetheless, the unredeemed total stood at £733.6 million nominal, in 1816.[33]

Annual state budgets were cast over the winter months and, as projected wartime deficits yawned, the Chancellor of the Exchequer was repeatedly faced with the task of negotiating the long-term borrowing required for coming fiscal years. Established loan contractors played their accustomed role. Peter Thellusson & Sons were responsible for the 1793 loan, while Parisian relations of partners in this house were being employed in a somewhat comparable fashion by Necker to support French military forces. The contract for a £11 million loan in February 1794 was obtained by Godschall Johnson & Co., in association with both John Julius Angerstein and James Morgan.[34] Morgan also operated on the Stock Exchange through Garroways and was a partner in W. & J. Morgan, bill brokers.[35] His particular business network is a pointer to the connections utilized by loan contractors when compiling a loan tender. Stock-market dealings, first 'bear' then 'bull', in long- and short-term state securities were deployed sequentially to establish the necessary contexts for, first, an advantageous bid price and, then, the subsequent, profitable retailing of a loan's script.

By the 1790s, the government was also relying upon significant City banking connections, including those of Robarts, Curtis & Co., a major London agency house, which could utilize its provincial links to bring in country banks

[32] Chapman, *Merchant Enterprise in Britain*, pp. 29, 68–74.

[33] B. R. Mitchell with P. Deane, *Abstract of British Historical Statistics* (Cambridge, 1962, rep. 1971), Public Finance, Table 3, p. 392 and Table 5, p. 402.

[34] Cope, *Walter Boyd*, p. 48.

[35] Morgan and Thomas, *The Stock Exchange*, pp. 48–9.

and their customers to fill a subscription list. The other formal financial intermediaries that featured in loan contracts from 1793 (and until 1810) were Benjamin and Abraham Goldsmid, bill brokers.[36] However, they were far from commercial banking specialists since their firm, established during the mid-eighteenth century, had an interest in bullion dealings and also, like Morgan, stock-market connections. The establishment of a physically housed stock market in 1802, albeit one based upon election and subscription, appears to have occurred when its members were coming to rival bankers and merchants as loan contractors. The parallelism may be purely coincidental, although, by 1802, the British funded debt at £497 million had doubled in size since the end of the American War of Independence and constituted by far the most actively traded group of securities on the secondary market.

The use of the stock market by all government loan contractors, together with the importance of their connections for filling their lists, is evident in the activities of Smith, Payne & Smiths. This City bank headed the successful group for the 1802 loan. On this occasion, it had outbid six other competitors: a Stock Exchange syndicate, a coalition of bankers, three lists submitted by individual banking houses—Everett, Walker & Co., Esdaile & Co., and Robarts, Curtis & Co.—and Barings. The Smith list drew upon the family wealth of the bank's partners as well as that of their customers. It was augmented by the resources mobilized through the associated Smith banks in Hull, Lincoln, and Nottingham and the connections of others such as the Thistle (Glasgow) and Mansfield & Co. (Leicester), for which the London bank acted as a metropolitan agent. Like other loan contractors, the Smith partners had groomed the market during 1801–2 when attempting to secure the new loan on the cheapest terms. They sold their bank's holdings of government securities, looking to depress prices in order to try and obtain the new loan on the cheapest possible terms. When the contract was gained, their market position was reversed from 'bear' to 'bull' since rising prices for the 'funds' would assist in distributing the new loan's script.[37]

The rewards from state loan contracting during the French wars are far from clear but could, at times, be substantial. For instance, they comprised 46 per cent of Barings' total profits, £45,115, for 1799 and accounted for a third of £55,419 made by this merchant banking house over 1801.[38] Barings' gains from new loans in 1813 were much higher, spectacularly higher. Returns from this business were determined by market sentiment. For instance, when it collapsed in 1810, Barings made a short-term loss of £43,000 upon a contract

[36] S. R. Cope, 'The Goldsmids and the Development of the London Money Market during the Napoleonic Wars', *Economica*, n.s., 9 (1942).

[37] Leighton-Boyce, *Smiths*, pp. 93–4, 95–6; and Morgan and Thomas, *The Stock Exchange*, p. 50.

[38] J. Orbell, *Baring Brothers & Co., Limited. A History to 1939* (London, 1985), p. 17.

for £22.3 million and, more gravely, the house's contracting partner on this occasion, Abraham Goldsmid, committed suicide.[39]

Over the first decade of the French wars, a new merchant banking house, Boyd, Benfield & Co., was able to break into the somewhat restricted circles of government long-term finance. Its entry was due to Walter Boyd's business links with the Austrian Netherlands which assisted the Emperor's attempts to raise funds in London so as to maintain a Habsburg army in the field.

Boyd, a Scot, had become a banker in 1782, managing the 'Banque particulière dans les Pays-Bas autrichiens' in partnership with J. W. Kerr which, within three years, involved overseeing four branches in Flanders. They took this accumulated expertise to Paris in mid-1785 while retaining connections with the Austrian Netherlands and also the United Provinces, including with Hope & Co. On the outbreak of the French Revolutionary wars, Boyd formed a new merchant banking house in London, backed by Paul Benfield, a dubious Indian financier and previous customer.

Through his continuing contacts in the Austrian Netherlands, particularly the Brussels bank of Veuve Nettine et Fils, Boyd became involved from early 1794 in the diplomatic negotiations for raising an Austrian loan in London.[40] These particular circumstances were eventually to enable him to contract loans for the British government. The objectives of Boyd and the British state became more intermeshed when, in August 1794, Pitt decided that his war policy required keeping Austrian forces in the field. The Emperor responded by requesting loans of £6m., which created additional difficulties for the British government. It was doubtful whether this amount could be raised within the City since Britain's own projected war costs involved raising a new long-term loan of £18 million, and its issue would rapidly follow upon that of a £13 million loan negotiated during February 1794. Boyd joined forces with established loan contractors—bankers, merchants, and stock brokers—and brought in others. They all agreed on 12 December 1794 to meet both the government's further needs and raise £6 million for Austria, should Parliament agree to guarantee its servicing.

What is known of the various contractors' backing groups for the 1795 £18million loan reveals something of the compositional structure and interconnections of the new issue market for British long-term state finance during the early years of the French wars. Boyd, Benfield's list amounted to £5.7 million, and the house also agreed to take £300,000 via E. P. Saloman's list, although the latter largely comprised fellow stock-market brokers and jobbers. Boyd himself had drummed up subscribers within the metropolitan banking community, led by Smith, Payne & Smiths, his own bankers, which took

[39] P. Ziegler, *The Sixth Great Power. Barings 1762–1929* (London, 1988), p. 58.

[40] K. F. Helleiner, *The Imperial Loans. A Study in Financial and Diplomatic History* (Oxford, 1965), pp. 3–6; and Cope, *Walter Boyd*, pp. 3–6, 12, 26, 37–47.

£650,000 on behalf of its customers. Otherwise, Boyd's list largely featured City merchants, headed by John Julius Angerstein and Godschall Johnson & Co., these established loan contractors each contributing £350,000, while £180,000 came from the Bank of England's directors and staff. Furthermore, the wide net of potential subscribers included country bankers. Some had been recruited by the City bank, Glyn Mills, which had canvassed during the previous year on behalf of one of the major loan contractors.[41] This is a guide to the 'monied interests' during the early war years but it has to be borne in mind that it was shaped by Boyd's successful prior negotiations with established competitors.[42]

Typically for British war finance during the decade after 1793, the December 1794 borrowing arrangements undertaken by Boyd involved not just the issue of £18m three per cent Consols but also a 'douceur' to attract subscribers. The latter consisted of £33.3 four per cent Consols and a 8*s.* 6*d.* Long Annuity for every £100 of three per cent Consols taken up, this package known on the stock market as 'Omnium'. If the loan had been issued through competitive tendering, rather than a forced arrangement, rival contractors would have bid in terms of the price for the annuity component. The mounting pressures of war finance with its foreign entanglements had produced the underlying issuing compact of December 1794 between the Treasury and Boyd's amalgam of contracting groups. Only settled after a heated Commons debate during late May 1795, the compact was that Britain would guarantee interest payments on an Austrian loan of £4.6 million and the Emperor agreed to put 200,000 men in the field against France.[43]

Boyd moved further into state finance by successfully bidding, indeed overbidding, for the English portion—£1.1 million—of the Irish loan and lottery of March 1795. Five months later, his relationship with Pitt became even closer through meeting a Treasury request for accelerated instalment payments upon the £18 million 1795 loan. These possibly amounted to £4.1 million, but Boyd required a further discount of 5 per cent on them. Thereafter, Boyd tried to capitalize upon his rapid ascendancy within British state finance by attempting to secure all the new long-term debt issues during 1796. With Robarts, Curtis & Co., he secured what was to be the first major loan issue of 1796. The circumstances surrounding the contract with Boyd for the 1796 loan led to a Commons inquiry but the subsequent debate had a favourable outcome for Boyd. It confirmed that, when government was making arrangements to issue a further loan, it was necessary to gain the contractors' agreement to its predecessor should there still be outstanding instalments.[44]

[41] Pressnell, *Country Banking*, p. 431.

[42] Cope, *Walter Boyd*, pp. 89–90.

[43] Helleiner, *Imperial Loans*, pp. 28–9, 50; and Cope, *Walter Boyd*, pp. 55, 57–9, 67–8.

[44] Helleiner, *Imperial Loans*, pp. 60–2; and Cope, *Walter Boyd*, pp. 74–6, 81–8. Boyd Benfield's list for the 1796 loan is reproduced in Morgan and Thomas, *The Stock Exchange*, p. 47.

Mounting war costs forced the government in April 1796 rapidly to seek another long-term loan. Reluctantly, Boyd, with Abraham Goldsmid, E. P. Saloman, and Robarts, Curtis & Co., took the contract for the £7.5 million loan on terms less favourable than their December 1795 agreement. Boyd, Benfield's share of the loan was £2.4m., for itself and the house's customers. However, further parliamentary criticism was provoked by the way that the contract had been placed. Dark clouds began to gather around Boyd, Benfield from summer 1796 but the house was supported secretly by Pitt which delayed its demise until the second half of 1798.

Government long-term borrowing in December 1796 consisted of the public issue of £18 million 5 per cent annuities. Terms were agreed with the Bank of England and, to secure success, Pitt appealed directly to the City. It became known as the 'Loyalty' loan and was subscribed within a day at the Bank's Court Room. The East India Company contributed £2 million, the Bank as an institution £1 million, and Bank directors and staff £500,000. City mercantile and banking houses took about £100,000 a piece, including Boyd, Benfield and its bankers, Smith, Payne & Smiths.[45] Nevertheless, the very rapid filling of the loan was also due to the subscriptions channelled through some London banks' provincial agency connections. Robarts' list included four named client country banks and others who preferred to remain anonymous, who, collectively, put up £300,000 through two of this London bank's partners. Similarly, two of the staff of Smith, Payne & Smiths pledged £400,000 on behalf of sixty-one houses, customers, and correspondents.[46]

Yet, the promise that the Loyalty loan's quick subscription appeared to offer for future government borrowing was severely undercut in February 1797 by the French invasion scare's impact upon the market. In these adverse circumstances, a new loan for £14.5 million went uncontested to the Boyd group joined by Thellusson. They also gained the right to undertake a projected second British guaranteed Austrian loan, upon which Parliament had placed a ceiling of £3.5 million. It proved to be little of a prize. The Emperor's withdrawal from the war on 18 April 1797 both further weakened the stock market and reduced the Austrian component of the new loan contract to £1.62 million, which funded previous advances.[47]

Government long-term borrowing during February 1798 took the form of voluntary contributions made through a City committee of bankers and merchants (including Barings), headed by the Lord Mayor.[48] Anxious to maintain his house's status and mask its declining substance, Boyd joined

[45] Cope, *Walter Boyd*, pp. 134–5.

[46] Pressnell, *Country Banking*, pp. 431–2.

[47] Helleiner, *Imperial Loans*, pp. 89–94; and Cope, *Walter Boyd*, pp. 138–41.

[48] The Bank of England, contributed £0.2m., see Clapham, *Bank of England*, II, *1797–1914*, p. 43.

the canvassers and also personally subscribed £3,000, even pledging comparable sums in every subsequent year of war.

Boyd's continuing apparent supremacy in British state finance resulted in his group securing the £17 million loan of April 1798, although this was the result of overbidding.[49] The award of the contract marked the public apogee of his merchant bank's standing. Thereafter, Boyd's growing personal financial embarrassment led to his former associates excluding him from negotiations for a £3 million loan, required by Pitt in December 1798. By June 1799, Boyd was insolvent but, nevertheless, attempted to play a role in gaining a £15.5 million loan through associating himself with one of the six rival contractors' groups.[50] He made a last, faint mark upon long-term state finance when his former business partners, in conjunction with Barings and Robarts, secured the contract for the £28 million loan of 1801. Boyd made a profit of £4–5,000 on the portion passed to him, a gain which met his living expenses.[51]

During the first decade of the nineteenth century, Stock Exchange members, or those with strong connections with the market, were at the head of those who secured new loan contracts—the Goldsmids in 1804 and 1805, and a group led by David Ricardo in 1807 and again in 1811. Thereafter, competition for new government long-term loans was nominal as each group involved made an identical bid.[52] While stock-market traders came more to the fore during these years, bankers remained important as government loan contractors. Furthermore, leading metropolitan merchant bankers had the ability to draw upon a very wide range of support—not just in the provinces but also overseas. Smiths and Barings collectively obtained a portion of the 1804 £15 million loan and, despite the growing problems of Anglo-European commerce, a significant amount of script was placed through the merchant bank's connections with various continental financial and trading centres. Nine years later, Barings in conjunction with Barnes, a Stock Exchange member, undertook a £28 million loan, which was again distributed throughout Europe. The same procedure was adopted by Barings for the 1815 £30 million loan: on this occasion the merchant bank acted with Smith, Payne & Smiths.[53] Widening the catchment area for British long-term war finance had been considered during the first decade of hostilities but rejected. This was possibly due to the rapidity of the French advance while some established loan contractors may have lacked the necessary mercantile contacts. Continental European placements of script from at least 1804 also had benefits with regard to the financing of Britain's allies in the war against France.

[49] R. W. Hidy, *House of Baringin American Trade and Finance, English Mrechant Bankers at Work, 1763–1861* (New York, 1941), p. 26; and Cope, *Walter Boyd*, p. 151.

[50] Cope, *Walter Boyd*, pp. 159–60.

[51] Hidy, *House of Baring*, p. 26; and Cope, *Walter Boyd*, pp. 164–5.

[52] Morgan and Thomas, *The Stock Exchange*, pp. 49–50.

[53] Hidy, *House of Baring*, pp. 28, 52–3.

FINANCING THE WAR IN EUROPE

A significant portion of British war expenditure from 1793 was disbursed within continental Europe to maintain armies in the field, as in Flanders and Hanover and, later, for Wellesley in the Peninsula. Even more important was the long-established policy of subsidizing allies. One estimate of the total amount involved from 1792 to 1816 is of the order of £57 million,[54] equivalent to over a tenth of the increase in the funded National Debt during the war. Merchants and merchant bankers played key roles in making subsidy payments by having the commercial and financial connections for remitting sums across the exchanges, effectively, efficiently, and at the lowest cost.

In the case of the first Austrian Imperial loan, Boyd, Benfield transferred £400,000 from London to Vienna during spring 1795 within less than a month. Initially, the operation, which hinged on Hamburg, was somewhat compromised by the London merchant bank's newness and, thereby, unknown standing. However, as Martin Dorner in Hamburg agreed to participate, John Parish & Co. could not stand back and also took over the portion initially earmarked for Schubach. The balance, a quarter of the amount, went through other houses in Augsburg (de Halder), Frankfurt (Bethmanns), and Leipzig (Frege), together with merchants and merchant bankers in Leghorn (d'Honoré) and Vienna (Fries). Nearly all these undertook the responsibility for transfers from Hamburg. The Genoese house involved was Heaths, not of the standing of Bethmanns or Fries but its engagement is a marker of a growing position within European merchant banking.[55] Boyd faced even greater problems with the subsequent remittance of £2.75 million, the bulk of the loan proceeds. At first, £1.6 million was transferred by bills, but when the Hamburg exchange inevitably fell, the balance went in specie. In order to ensure its safe conveyance, British frigates carried the bullion to Hamburg.[56]

Making the remittances for the Imperial Austrian loans ultimately proved to be long-drawn-out affairs and, at times, fraught with difficulty because of war conditions. Barings was requested by the British government to transfer £150,000 to Vienna in 1800 which, despite the smallness of the sum, the house managed only with great trouble. However, another similar operation during summer 1806, but totalling £500,000, was accomplished without any hesitancy on this merchant bank's part.[57] These particular movements of bills and bullion occurred along with many others financing the armies and mercenaries of allied German princes. The sums involved amounted

[54] Hidy, *House of Baring*, p. 28.
[55] Helleiner, *Imperial Loans*, pp. 47–8; and Cope, *Walter Boyd*, p. 66.
[56] Cope, *Walter Boyd*, pp. 68–70.
[57] Ziegler, *The Sixth Great Power*, p. 56; and Helleiner, *Imperial Loans*, p. 146.

to £800,000 in 1793, £2.35 million in 1794, £970,000 in 1795, and £30,000 in 1796.[58]

War subsidy payments and comparable transfers did not just flow from Britain to her allies. For instance, Mayer Amschel Rothschild was involved in undertaking remittances on behalf of Elector William to Austria during 1809.[59] However, the Rothschilds were far more important in the closing years of the Napoleonic wars in support of Wellington's invasion of France and in relaying British official payments to Austria, Prussia, and Russia. Nathan, with his brother James across the Channel, had smuggled gold from England to France and transferred specie from Hamburg to France since 1810. The scale of the related transactions in London, or the consequent use of bills arising from the finance of Britain's Peninsula army, may have brought Nathan to the attention of John Herries, the British Commissary-in-Chief. Certainly, on 11 January 1814, Nathan gained the contract to supply secretly £600,000 in French coin to Wellington in France. He accomplished this in concert with his brothers and they went on to play a major part, in parallel with Barings, in making the remittances to Britain's allies that helped to secure Napoleon's defeats in 1814 and 1815.

The Rothschilds developed a very effective courier system for conveying coded information about exchange movements. They also applied their particular knowledge of the timing of subsidy payment transfers in order to benefit from exchange transactions. Furthermore, although the Rothschild house made no spectacular financial coup from the news of the victory at Waterloo, the brothers matched their exchange operations with speculations in British government long-term debt. In some respects, this was a continuation of the style of business that the family had conducted since 1809. Mayer Amschel had invested some of Elector William's wealth in Consols through Nathan.[60]

Merchant bankers' international connections and inter-connections, especially those of Barings and Hopes, led them to become involved in the finance of Napoleonic Europe. The houses had been associated since 1770 and the bonds between them further increased thereafter. For instance, Alexander Baring, Sir Francis' son, completed his initial commercial training with Hopes, even remaining in Amsterdam during the opening years of the French wars along with Pierre César Labouchère. Hope partners, in London from October 1794, worked through Barings or Harman & Co., and they joined Alexander Baring in an American real estate purchase. This transaction also coincided with Alexander marrying Anne Louisa, a daughter of the vendor, the millionaire Senator William Bingham. The ill-fated land deal, part of the business generated by Alexander while he was in America from 1795

[58] Helleiner, *Imperial Loans*, p. 61, fn.20. [59] Ferguson, *World's Banker*, pp. 73–4.
[60] Ferguson, *World's Banker*, pp. 71–2, 100–1.

to 1802, and its wider context, were to lead to Barings gaining an entrée to United States government finance. The personal ties between Barings and Hopes further developed through Labouchère marrying Dorothea, daughter of Sir Francis. After the Peace of Amiens, Hope & Co. was re-established in Amsterdam, initially on the basis of capital supplied by Barings, with Labouchère a partner but not his brother-in-law, Alexander Baring, as had been originally planned.[61]

The involvements of Barings and Hopes in the finances of Napoleonic France commenced even before the Anglo-Dutch house had resettled in Amsterdam. The starting point was Portugal's need to pay a war levy to France, imposed on 29 September 1801. The first approach for assistance came through a Baring business connection in Lisbon but the affair was eventually executed by Hopes. The Amsterdam house had been the official channel for the flow of Brazilian diamonds via Portugal since 1791 and had been contacted in 1796 and, again, in March 1800, regarding a comparable long-term advance upon the gemstones. Consequently, Hope partners had greater experience in the diamond trade while having been long involved in the issue of sovereign loans. Furthermore, the promise of a successful affair chimed well with the Hopes' plans for re-establishing their house in Amsterdam. The loan was supported by the British government, anxious to secure for its 'oldest ally' the greatest possible freedom of manoeuvre within Napoleonic Europe.

The negotiations were undertaken by Labouchère together with George Baring, Sir Francis' youngest son. They resulted in Barings and Hopes being appointed Portuguese court bankers but the scheme nearly miscarried because of the Dutch government's opposition to new foreign loans on the Amsterdam market. A threat by Barings to establish an Antwerp house, whether of substance or a negotiating ploy, had no effect and, consequently, the bonds for the 13 million guilder loan were signed in Lisbon as opposed to Amsterdam where they were to be floated. The business proved to be a poor introduction to issuing European state loans for Barings since, at the end of 1802, the house had only disposed of about 1.5 million out of its share of 5 million in the loan. When France demanded a further war levy from Portugal in July 1805, eventually amounting to Ff16 million, Hopes merely acted as remitters, although enticed by an interest in the important brazilwood trade.[62]

During the brief period of peace from March 1802 to summer 1803, Barings and Hopes became immersed in facilitating the United States' purchase of

[61] Henry Baring married Maria Matilda Bingham in 1802: Hidy, *House of Baring*, p. 29; Orbell, *Baring Brothers & Co.*, p. 14; and Buist, *At Spes Non Fracta*, pp. 40, 49–54.

[62] Hidy, *House of Baring*, p. 27; Orbell, *Baring Brothers & Co.*, pp. 17–18; Ziegler, *The Sixth Great Power*, pp. 55–6; and Buist, *At Spes Non Fracta*, pp. 51, 5–56, 384, 387, 389, 392, 397, 399, 402, 405–8.

Louisiana from France. Partly as a result of their connections with Bingham, Barings had become advisers to the United States, undertaking affairs for the American Federal government from 1795. The rising head of the family house, Alexander Baring, was in Paris from Christmas, 1802, until the following spring. He advised President Jefferson's representatives and, very shortly after the agreement of 30 April 1802, agreed to take from the French government, for Ff52 million the $11.25 million six per cent bonds by which the United States had secured Louisiana. The arrangement's ratification was overtaken by the fresh outbreak of war but the scheme went ahead. Yet, in the changed circumstances, Hopes came to lead the operation for financing the purchase, especially as Barings was specifically warned by the British Prime Minister about the remittances of Ff2 million a month to France that it involved.[63]

Hopes in Amsterdam became involved in generating funds for the subsidies that Spain reluctantly and tardily paid to Napoleonic France from May 1803. The house floated two Spanish loans upon the Amsterdam market, although the second encountered the Dutch government's opposition as King Louis required a domestic loan. Like the financing of the Louisiana purchase, the underlying arrangements became increasingly intricate and one of its threads involved Barings. Discussions concerned loan operations involving other ways by which Spain could make payments to France. This brought Hopes into contact once more with the dubious financial operations of Gabriel-Julien Ouvrard, a furnisher of *matériel* to French forces. His English counterpart, the bankrupt Boyd, featured for a while within the tangled negotiations. These increasingly focused upon Spain's major resource, Mexican silver. Ouvrard developed a number of schemes to capitalize upon this asset and one involved London and Barings from mid-1806 until 1807. The basis was Mexican silver shipments predominantly to the United States for acquiring raw cotton, foodstuffs, and tobacco for export in neutral vessels to Europe. The proceeds would give the Spanish government funds at Amsterdam, Antwerp, London, Nantes, and Rotterdam, all for making payments to Paris.

WAR AND THE LONDON MONEY MARKET

Henry Burgess, editor of the *Circular to Bankers,* maintained in retrospect that the rediscounting of bills of exchange became prevalent during the French Revolutionary and Napoleonic wars due to the government then being 'the great cormorant customer for all accumulating money'.[64] Consequently,

[63] Orbell, *Baring Brothers & Co.*, pp. 15–16.

[64] *Circular to Bankers*, 8 (12 Sept. 1828).

London bankers took bills to the Bank of England from 1797, with some thirty-three houses rediscounting at Threadneedle Street by 1811–12. Country bankers turned even more to London, the hub of the economy. Generally, this was undertaken through two already established channels: either the services of an agency bank or the founding of an associated City house. A further, largely new development was country bankers' employment of another London specialist—a bill broker—who attempted to marry the demand for, and supply of, short-term funds within the changing wartime economy. These thickening connections, involving the augmentation of existing links and the growth of new ones, were evidence of the consequences of the government's wartime 'crowding out' of borrowing. They laid the foundations for the unique emergence post-war of a national discount market in London.

The increased volatility of Consols on the stock market, with their prices responding to news, more likely rumours, of defeat, or invasion, or a possible peace or victory, provided the conditions for highly speculative trading. The mechanism, 'contango', for sustaining speculative operations in Consols until the parties involved either made a profit, or had to cut their losses, was not subject to the usury laws' ceiling of 5 per cent on interest rates. Banks, primarily London-based but also some country houses, made highly profitable advances enabling stock-market speculators nominally to close their continuing bargains.[65]

The stock market and the embryonic London money market became more intermeshed and not just through speculative bargains in long-term government stocks but also by dealings in the state's short-term paper. With almost continuous warfare, Britain's unfunded, unredeemed debt mounted, noticeably from 1801 and markedly from 1809.[66] This growth was of securities closely analogous to bills of exchange but which offered opportunities to London banks for greater profitability than could be had from dealings in instruments of private credit. Importantly, trading in both three-month Exchequer bills and Navy bills was not subject to the usury laws since it consisted of buying, or selling, fixed-interest paper. Exchequer bills, together with Navy bills, were traded on the stock market, along with the 'funds'. After 1793, London banks turned to dealing in them, which became the main focus of their wartime short-term business.[67] This development is clear, for example, in the turnover in Exchequer bills of the City bank, Smith, Payne & Smiths: it increased to £0.47m. during 1806 and 1807, and mounted again to more than £0.5m. in 1813–14.[68] The resulting general shift in London banks' assets

[65] Pressnell, *Country Banking*, pp. 95–6, 428, 432–4.

[66] Mitchell with Deane, *Abstract of British Historical Statistics*, Public Finance, Table 3, p. 392 and Table 5, p. 402.

[67] Pressnell, *Country Banking*, pp. 95, 97, 420–6.

[68] Leighton-Boyce, *Smiths*, p. 100.

adversely affected the positions of country banks by severely affecting their ability to turn to the metropolitan market for liquidity.

After the outbreak of war, and especially from the suspension of cash payments in 1797, country banks made firmer connections with the metropolis, the economy's centre of wealth. This was done both to share in the profits from dealings in state securities upon the stock market and to try to sustain their own liquidity levels. The suspension of cash payments had removed any limit on their note issues and, thereby, allowed, potentially, the country banks to undertake discounting on a far greater scale. There was a rising demand for credit facilities not only within agrarian areas but also in the thickening industrial regions, like the west Midlands and the textile districts of south-east Lancashire and the West Riding.

One aspect of the further development of provincial–metropolitan links was the greater growth of country banks' corresponding relationships with London banks, especially those in the City. This was largely taken up by metropolitan houses that had become specialists in it, although after 1793 others also turned to this particular market niche. For instance, Glyn, Mills held only four country bank agencies in 1790 but thirteen in 1800 and twenty-eight in 1810. Initially, these accounts had been obtained through the personal connections of the City bank's partners. As they developed, Glyns took on more clerks to handle the business while the house acquired a growing expertise in this particular aspect of banking. By 1815, Glyns had correspondence relationships with some thirty-five banks located in the Cotswolds, Cumberland, East Anglia, the East Riding, the Home Counties, Lancashire, the Welsh Marches, the east Midlands, the north east, the Potteries, south-central and south west England, and Scotland. A few of these country banks had transferred their London agency to Glyns—a possible indication of competition to provide such services amongst the relatively static number of metropolitan banks with City origins over the war period.[69]

Firmer, enduring connections came through the establishment of interlocking partnerships between country bankers and major City agency banks. These are evident amongst some of the major London specialists in the country agency business—Esdailes had thirty-nine country correspondents in 1802, Robarts twenty-six, Masterman fourteen—and are even more manifest in the case of City banks that held just a few such accounts.[70] Direct, personal relationships between the provinces and the City, according to Pressnell's estimates, constituted the substance of the metropolitan

[69] R. Fulford, *Glyn's 1753–1953. Six Generations in Lombard Street* (London, 1953), pp. 59, 95–101, 246–55.

[70] I. S. Black, 'The London Agency System in English Banking, 1780–1825', *London Journal*, 21 (1996), p. 116.

connections of about a third of the some 660 country banks in business during 1813.[71]

The London agency system was important in a number of respects. It not only provided a means for both investing surplus provincial resources in government debt and profitably supporting stock-market transactions, but it also facilitated, as before 1793, local and inter-regional inter-bank payments.[72] Nevertheless, during the war, transactions in government securities, short-term and long-term, were a greater source of profit for London banks than bill dealings on behalf of country banks, which were subject to the constraint of the usury laws. Indeed, much of the London banks' wartime assets came to comprise Exchequer bills, which could be sold to the Bank of England when there was liquidity pressure.

The growth of personal interlocks between City banks and country houses from the late 1790s failed to resolve one important aspect of the wartime provincial liquidity problem. This arose from the Bank of England not rediscounting 'long' bills—those with more than sixty-five days to run before maturity. These were typical of provincially drawn paper but, because of the Bank's discounting rules, lacked eligibility with London bankers even if they were interested in taking private bills. The resulting void in credit facilities was filled to some degree by the growth of bill broking within the metropolitan market.

Specialist London bill brokers had emerged from the late 1780s and, in the particular case of Benjamin and Abraham Goldsmid, they may have acted as discounters as opposed to being solely agents during the monetary ease of the early 1790s. Bill broking became far more important from the suspension of cash payments in 1797, and there are clear indications that it was an established speciality some sixteen years later. However, most of the nineteen bill-broking firms active in 1813 were small-scale undertakings, often conducted by failed bankers or those who worked in association with banking houses. The major exception was Thomas Richardson, a bill broker from 1802, who was joined in partnership by John Overend in 1805 and by Samuel and John Gurney in 1807. It is also possible that Alexander & Co. and James Bruce undertook bill agency business of some significance during the second decade of the French wars.

Richardson had been a clerk with Smith & Holt, who were, first, London wool factors, then bill brokers or bankers, and had supplied bills to the Gurney Norwich & Norfolk Bank from its formal establishment in 1775. With his accumulated experience, Richardson saw an opportunity at the turn of the century in handling ineligible, 'long' bills for which he would only charge brokerage to the party seeking discounts. His terms were innovative since

[71] Pressnell, *Country Banking*, p. 115.

[72] Black, 'London Agency System', pp. 124–7.

brokers had previously also charged a commission of one-quarter per cent to those purchasing bills through their agency. By 1810, Richardson's tariff for those requiring discounts—bank drafts at one-eighth per cent and private paper with maturities greater than sixty-five days at one-eighth to one-half per cent—had become almost standard in the London market. On this basis, Richardson took Gurney bill business away from Smith & Holt so that, by mid-1809, he was supplying all of their bill investments, totalling £1.45 million, the Norwich & Norfolk Bank having little opportunity locally for mobilizing its resources. Furthermore, he came to specialize in 'long' paper ineligible at the Bank of England, with such bills comprising the great majority—more than 66 per cent in 1810—of those he negotiated.

The bill broker's expertise lay in assessing the quality of the bills that passed through his hands, which required knowledge of the creditworthiness of everyone who had signed them. At the beginning, Richardson's contacts were solely with East Anglia, Lancashire, and Yorkshire but, from 1807, his insight, and business, was assisted by information directly obtainable through the Gurney Quaker network. John Gurney's function as Richardson's partner was largely to obtain Norfolk bills from Kings Lynn (probably arising in part from North Sea coastal trade), and arrange return remittances from Norwich. Richardson himself clearly discharged a monitoring function, returning unsafe bills to those who sought their discount, and there is independent testimony that few losses were incurred by those who bought bills through him. The paper that Richardson handled was taken largely by rural, primarily Norfolk, country banks, above all the Gurney network, their collective resources—£6–8 million—swollen by the deposited proceeds of wartime agricultural prosperity.

Investment in bills, on average £1.5 million, and selected for quality by Richardson, provided higher returns than the interest paid by London agency banks on balances. Richardson paid the sellers of bills with maturing bank drafts or cash from the London correspondent of the country bank that bought them. In all this, Richardson was an agent, not a principal. His dominance of the London bill market after 1800, totalling about £10 million, was not solely due to his links with the Gurneys and other country banks. Much of his business increasingly came through metropolitan mercantile connections. In the case of merchants' paper, Richardson had many competitors, and the supply of merchants' bills involved a problem, but one which assisted him and his peers. Variations in the demand for discounts from individual merchants, or even groups of mercantile houses with a common trading specialism, could have a seasonal pattern. This often caused considerable difficulties, especially when a large volume of their paper needed to be discounted at the Bank of England over just a few weeks. Although the Bank discounted freely from 1797, it did so, except for the finest paper, on the basis of discrimination, with sectional limits for the various trading groups within its clientele. Consequently, merchants turned to bill brokers, Richardson and the like, to iron out their individual 'humps' of illiquidity arising from the yearly pattern of their activities.

WARTIME INFLATION AND ENGLISH COUNTRY BANKS

More than two decades of warfare from 1793 generated inflation. Yet, although marked price rises were a common European experience over these years, there were divergences in inflation's impact, for example, as between country bankers in England and Wales, the Scottish provincial banking companies, and financial intermediaries in Revolutionary France.

English wholesale prices peaked in 1813 at about 72 to 84 per cent above their immediate pre-war level.[73] The underlying trend rate of inflation, at 2.5–2.8 per cent per annum, might appear modest but contemporaries were struck by noticeable price rises at the outbreak of war and, especially, the sharp increases experienced at the turn of the century and, again, during 1812 and 1813. Others also looked to the depreciation of sterling on the exchanges as an indication of the fall in the value of money—a small decrease during the first decade of hostilities but a sharp decline thereafter. Culprits were found in many quarters but there was a focus upon the considerable expansion of country bank note issues after the suspension of cash payments on 26 February 1797, and the mushroom growth in the number of provincial banking houses, especially from 1800.

The course of prices over the war period—a trend rise to 1813, falling away thereafter—is broadly paralleled by the upsurge and then reduction in the numbers of English and Welsh country banks. As with prices, precise data are unavailable while those series that are to hand conflict, largely because it is uncertain whether they enumerate banks alone or embrace all banking offices (i.e., also include branches and agencies). Nonetheless, the general movement is clear: a relatively small increase in the number of country banks before 1800—from about 280 in 1793 to about 312 in 1798—followed by a very rapid augmentation of their ranks thereafter to total about 761 in 1813. Subsequently, moving with the deflation of the final war years, their numbers declined, down to about either 699 or 626 in 1815.[74]

[73] For a discussion of the various available price indices for the period and their complications, see M. W. Flinn, 'Trends in Real Wages, 1750–1850', *Economic History Review*, 27 (1974), pp. 399–404; and T. R. Gourvish, 'Flinn and Real Wage Trends in Britain, 1750–1850: A Comment', *Economic History Review*, 29 (1976), pp. 136–9.

[74] Pressnell, *Country Banking*, pp. 8, 11 (Table I), p. 127 (Table VI).

The outcome suggested by note-issuing licences, not a totally reliable guide, is that by 1808 there was at least one private note-issuing bank in every English and Welsh county with the exception of Radnor.[75] Yet, many of these provincial houses established over the war years were not inflation mayflies. For instance, out of the 146 private houses that subsequently became part of Lloyds Bank, fifty-four (37 per cent) had been formed before 1793 but forty-eight (33 per cent) were set up between 1793 and 1815.[76] The founders of the wartime banks eventually acquired by Lloyds were, therefore, houses of some substance and longevity, and they had a diverse range of backgrounds. Many were coal-factors, drapers, and merchants and, consequently, had business interests broadly comparable with one of the principal occupational groups from which formal bankers had emerged during the half-century before 1793. Besides these individuals, there were also agricultural processors—tanners—and those with a stake in the land, along with a government agent for packet-boats, a wealthy solicitor, and an innkeeper. The publican in question possibly turned to banking on the basis of a chest of French gold coin left in safekeeping with his forebears by the Young Pretender sixty-two years earlier during 1745.[77]

Not surprisingly, many banks established after 1793 within developing industrial districts had partners whose interests lay in, or connected to, manufacturing. For instance, Birmingham, which had four banks in 1793, gained a further four during 1804 and 1805. These were formed, variously, by a gun maker and by metal merchants, whose individual banking interests were subsequently augmented by those of an American merchant and a copper manufacturer. Established and new houses collectively made Birmingham the largest provincial wartime banking centre, only rivalled by Bristol and Exeter, which each had seven banks in 1804.[78] As a result, the west Midlands enjoyed the greatest provision of formal banking facilities during the French wars, with approximately one banking office per 12,000 inhabitants in 1801 compared with one per 21,000 for England and Wales as a whole, including London.[79]

There are many sound reasons for regarding the wartime expansion of country banking within England and Wales as the product of the same formative factors that had been in play since 1750, if not earlier. However,

[75] Pressnell, *Country Banking*, pp. 148, 152 (Table IX). Radnor gained a note-issuing bank from 1808—the Kington & Radnorshire Bank—with offices in Kington and Knighton on the county's Shropshire border. See W. F. Crick and J. E. Wadsworth, *A Hundred Years of Joint Stock Banking* (London, 1936, 3rd edn, 1958), pp. 174–5.

[76] Calculated from R. S. Sayers, *Lloyds Bank in the History of English Banking* (Oxford, 1957), Appendix 1, pp. 276–88.

[77] Sayers, *Lloyds Bank*, pp. 3–4.

[78] D. J. Moss, 'The Private Banks of Birmingham, 1800–1827', *Business History*, 24 (1982), p. 80; Pressnell, *Country Banking*, pp. 129–30; and Crick and Wadsworth, *A Hundred Years*, pp. 51–3.

[79] R. Cameron, 'England, 1750–1844', in R. Cameron et al., *Banking in the Early Stages of Industrialization* (London, 1967), p. 26.

prolonged war conditions from 1793 made a difference, especially in two respects. First, country bankers played greater roles within the collection and disbursement of state revenues (assisting in the payment of troops and administering fiscal changes), which led to a significant number of country bankers experiencing considerable increases in the volumes of the official balances that passed through their hands. As previously, such boosted resources could be profitably employed for periods of time before either their transmission to the Treasury or their disbursement.[80] Second, and more importantly, the suspension of cash payments from 26 February 1797 allowed 'continuous credit expansion' which, as Pressnell has commented, proved to be 'a fertile ground for breeding new banks'.[81]

Suspension went along with small payments, reflected in the growth from 1797 of private note issues. For the fiscal year 1808–9,[82] stamp duty statistics indicate a total private issue of about £14.5 million (from which has to be deducted notes held in bankers' reserves, possibly as much as 10 per cent of the aggregate). There was also an uncertain, further amount, comprising notes either outstanding or issued illegally.[83] The Bank of England's issue in public hands then amounted to about £17.6 million but its notes largely circulated within London and the Home Counties.[84] The indications are that the Bank's note issue was always greater in volume than that of all English and Welsh private bankers during the French wars although, after 1800, the differential narrowed as country banks' circulations markedly expanded.[85]

Country banks issued notes because it was profitable, with some partners claiming that their circulations were the largest single source of their respective houses' net earnings. In lieu of an issue, there were the significant costs of obtaining Bank of England notes, although this did not deter bankers in Lancashire and Norwich. There was also the difficulty from 1799 of obtaining gold guineas, most of which had gone into private wartime hoards. Beyond the cotton textile districts of Cheshire and Lancashire, country bankers frequently equated banking with note issuing. A prominent West Country banker argued that, without a note issue, they would be merely bill brokers. Furthermore, a note circulation came to be seen in contemporary eyes as a symbol of status and prestige for a banking house. And, it was a very effective advertisement, with many bankers testifying that the publicity given by their particular notes had attracted customers. This was all within the context of deposits in a

[80] Pressnell, *Country Banking*, pp. 63–9.

[81] Pressnell, *Country Banking*, p. 8.

[82] Pressnell considered that stamp duty statistics could only be employed with any degree of certainty for just a single fiscal year—1808–9.

[83] Pressnell, *Country Banking*, p. 145.

[84] Bank of England, *Bank of England Liabilities and Assets*, p. 6. On the Bank's note circulation, see Clapham, *Bank of England*, II, *1797–1914*, p. 5.

[85] Pressnell, *Country Banking*, p. 159.

modern sense and, thereby, cheques, not having any great national significance before the 1830s.[86]

North of the Trent, particularly in Lancashire and Cheshire, but also to a degree within the emerging Black Country and the West Riding, private issues played little part in the wartime circulation. Instead, the monetary media consisted of Bank of England notes and, especially, locally drawn bills of exchange. Two months bills for £5, but more likely during the war period for £10 or £20, passed between Lancashire manufacturers and traders as cash. They were accepted because of their long lists of endorsements, the signatures sometimes filling two additional sheets of paper attached to a bill. Consequently, almost the whole north-western business community was liable at times for this paper's ultimate payment. The corollary was that there were no more than six note-issuing banks throughout Lancashire during the war period and, likewise, no more than eight in Cheshire.[87]

The consequent, forced reliance upon uninstitutionalized credit webs within the north-west industrial district during the unfolding of the first phase of the growth of powered cotton-spinning explains why, in general, early Lancastrian textile manufacturers lacked bank accounts. Only the major firms tended to use the services of formal bankers, but they largely did so after 1810 and they turned to London houses, even though this involved the maintenance of a minimum balance. The failure of the banking habit to develop significantly went with the lack of further formalization of regional credit provision that had any solidity during the war period. It acted, ultimately, as a financial constraint upon the growth of south-east Lancashire's developing staple industry, especially over the two decades from 1810 when the industry's profit margins narrowed.[88]

While always trying to meet the needs of a customer, country bankers issued their notes with a cautionary eye upon profits, especially when a discount transaction or an advance was involved. Generally, they would only provide their own notes for local payment needs since this gave some guarantee of them staying profitably in circulation. The local, or even regional, mutual full acceptance of notes led country banks to open accounts with one another for at least the purpose of note clearing. Evidence from Birmingham indicates that some of

[86] Pressnell, *Country Banking*, pp. 156–8, 162.

[87] Pressnell, *Country Banking*, pp. 152 (Table IX), 170–4. The antipathy to private notes in particular and to formal banks more generally within the developing cotton textile districts of south-east Lancashire and north-east Cheshire was a continuing echo of the adverse experience of the 1788 crisis caused by the Livesey, Hargreaves crash, especially for the holders of their dishonoured five-guinea notes.

[88] S. D. Chapman, 'Financial Restraints on the Growth of Firms in the Cotton Industry, 1790–1850', *Economic History Review*, 32 (1979), pp. 51–2, 57; S. D. Chapman, 'The Peels in the Early English Cotton Industry', *Business History*, 11 (1969), pp. 79, 81, 84, 87; and L. H. Grindon, *Manchester Banks and Bankers* (Manchester, 1877).

its wartime banks extended these arrangements to houses within this town's wide rural hinterland.[89] The next developmental step was the emergence within the provinces of more formalized note clearing arrangements, already begun by the Gurneys in Norfolk during the late eighteenth century. Over the opening decades of the nineteenth century, there were certainly weekly clearings operated by some banks in Kent and Somerset and this was probably a regular provincial practice in most other districts. At Birmingham, a daily local clearing was established for balances below £200 in either notes or coin.[90]

Note exchange arrangements acted as a check upon over-issue as had become already apparent in late eighteenth-century Scotland. They also allowed country bankers to economize upon both the volume of their issues in relation to their respective circulations and their individual holdings of Bank of England notes. Furthermore, banknotes, along with cash and a London balance, constituted a country bank's principal reserve, primarily employed for note redemption. Its extent was determined by individual business experience so that there was no general national ratio. Some provincial bankers might include bills, particularly those drawn on London, within what they termed their 'reserves' while others considered that holdings of short-term government securities also fell under this heading, despite volatile wartime prices.

As later during the nineteenth century, houses in agricultural areas probably held proportionately lower 'reserves' than their counterparts within the developing industrial districts. Yet, it was already becoming clear that the economy's structural transformation, as well as wartime liquidity pressures, were leading to areas of manufacturing and commercial development becoming 'credit hungry'. Consequently, although bankers within emerging industrial districts might, from day to day, be subject to more sudden demands than their counterparts in the shires, they were also likely to have businesses involving regular customer pressure for discounts. The available evidence of actual practice is very slight but indicates reserve ratios at 5 to 10 per cent, which was very much lower than contemporaries thought was the case, even allowing for the imprecision of what constituted a provincial banker's 'reserve'.[91] But, it also has to be borne in mind that English and Welsh country banking was not homogeneous. The nature of individual businesses varied greatly, depending upon the particular economic and social complexion of the community served, its preference for monetary media and its other demands for financial services and accommodation.[92] The arising heterogeneity led to considerable variance in banks' reserve levels, safe or otherwise.

[89] Moss, 'Private Banks of Birmingham', p. 85.
[90] Moss, 'Private Banks of Birmingham', p. 85.
[91] Pressnell, *Country Banking*, pp. 195–7, 203–5 (Table XVII).
[92] H. V. Bowen and P. L. Cottrell, 'Banking and the Evolution of the British Economy, 1694–1878', in Teichova et al., *Banking, Trade and Industry*, pp. 92–3.

The suspension of cash payments in February 1797 did not prevent the failure of country banks—three went out of business during 1797, followed by seven bankruptcies between February 1798 and September 1799, all in rural areas and probably due to low grain prices. Equally but conversely, poor harvests at the turn of the century were a contributory factor to the collapse of six further houses over the fourteen months from June 1800. The consequences of a temporary peace and then renewed warfare also led to an intermittent stream of bank failures, seventeen in all from February 1802 to June 1805. However, this occurred within a context of a markedly rising number of country banks, so that the overall failure rate was not increasing but, rather, falling. Country bank fatalities continued at about one every four months until the 1810–11 crisis. The difficult mercantile financial dimensions of these years due to Napoleon's Continental system, growing trading problems with the United States and the failure to develop alternative export markets in South America have already been considered.

The banking crisis within England and Wales began in July 1810 with the collapse of a London house, Brickwood & Co., caused by the problems of a client—a West Indian broker—but provoked by a run sparked by rumour. Crisis banking difficulties continued thereafter until early 1814, involving the failure of forty-one country houses at an average rate of more than one a month. One dimension was failures within predominantly agricultural districts, the south, and west during both 1810–11 and 1812–13. A provincial aspect of crisis closures was the corrosive force of rumour-mongering, met by attempts to check its sapping work often taking the form of public meetings at which declarations of confidence in local houses were passed.

Bank failures continued during the final years of the war period. The average rate of forced bank closures, at 1.7 a month from May 1814 until June 1815, was higher than during the immediate period of the 1810–11 crisis and its prolonged aftermath. Once more, failures were largely within agricultural districts and this spatial pattern appears, in general, to have been cast by the deflationary effects stemming from the decline of the state's wartime role within the economy.

What is somewhat remarkable is the relatively small number of 'industrial' banks forced to close throughout the period from the suspension of cash payments in February 1797 until June 1815. If the broadest definition is taken, while excluding the consequences of the demise of a provincial house's London agent, then only about fifteen 'industrial' country houses collapsed over these seventeen years. This would strongly suggest that wartime failures after 1797 were not generally associated with the problems of banking within 'credit hungry' manufacturing and commercial districts. Instead, but in terms of general context as opposed to the individual country bankers' particular abilities, it was the difficulties arising from conducting banking within localities predominantly based upon the 'old' economy of agriculture and wool that were mostly likely to force banks to close their doors.[93]

PRIVATE BANKS IN REVOLUTIONARY FRANCE

Wartime inflation had its greatest effect, albeit for a few years, upon banking in Revolutionary France. Accelerating price increases, which became a hyperinflation, were powered by the rising issue to state creditors, including rentiers, of assignats backed by nationalized church property. This circulation began in August 1790 and its volume sharply increased during 1795 while there was a general rise in French prices from 1792, which, by 1795, had gained all the characteristics of hyperinflation.[94] The spur to formal banking came from the need to turn assignats into paper of smaller denomination, undertaken by *caisses patriotiques* that sprang up in considerable numbers from spring 1791. Within less than nine months, France had some 1,666 'patriotic banks', found in nearly every large village and town throughout the country.[95] From merely exchanging assignats for their own *billets de confiance*, many became fractional-reserve banks of issue, filling the void in the circulation as accelerating inflation induced both the hoarding and export of specie. Unlike the bankrupt state's chronic misuse of assignats, their note issues played only a very small role in generating inflationary pressures during the first half of the 1790s.

French revolutionary banking proved to be a short-lived development since it was opposed from the outset by the radical elements of the 'First Terror'. Their anti-market, anti-capitalist attitudes led to a campaign against the 'patriotic banks' almost from the moment that they appeared and culminated in them being made illegal on 8 November 1792. The Jacobins and sans-culottes also saw almost any banker but particularly those in Paris as anti-revolutionary, if only on the grounds that, with their international connections, they had assisted the flight of wealth from inflation torn France. Consequently, leading Parisian bankers, for instance Mallet, were imprisoned and some, such as Vandenyver, went to the guillotine, while those who retained their liberty either emigrated or went to ground. Likewise, the Paris Bourse was closed on 27 June 1793 to suppress speculation, the activities of the Caisse d'Escompte

[93] The preceding paragraphs have been drawn from Pressnell, *Country Banking*, pp. 461–71.

[94] C. Aubin, 'Les assignats sous la Révolution française: un exemple d'hyperinflation', *Revue Economique*, 42 (1991); E. N. White, 'Measuring the French Revolution's Inflation: The Tableaux de Dépréciation', *Histoire et Mesure*, 6 (1991); and S. E. Harris, *The Assignats* (Cambridge, MA, 1930).

[95] E. N. White, 'Free Banking During the French Revolution', *Explorations in Economic History*, 27 (1990).

were ended two months later and on 7 September 1793 bankers' assets were frozen and sequestrated.

The consequent absence of active financial intermediaries aggravated monetary reconstruction. The hyperinflation of 1795 had spent itself by the closing months of the year, with only specie now being the generally accepted medium of exchange. This preference during 1796 led to France returning de facto to a metallic currency. Nevertheless, despite domestic dishoarding, the return of flight capital, and other inflows generated by either the fruits of military victory or exchange speculation, France experienced a shortage of specie that appears to have persisted after 1800. The lack of cash was regarded by contemporaries as a contributory factor to the economy's depression during the late 1790s, and particularly a cause of agricultural distress. It was also reflected in high interest rates—1.5 to 2 per cent a month.

The monetary and banking gap was filled to some extent from 1796 by the establishment of a number of public banks in both Paris and the provinces. They largely followed in the tradition of the pre-revolutionary Caisse d'Escompte and, indeed, the first, the Caisse de Comptes Courants, established on 26 June 1796, had former directors of the Caisse d'Escompte amongst its shareholders. These restricted corporate banking experiments paved the way for Napoleon's establishment of the Banque de France during January and February 1800, largely undertaken by bankers, such as the Mallets, Lecouteulx, and Perrégaux, who had featured amongst supporters of his 18 Brumaire coup. Almost immediately, the Banque de France took over the Caisse de Comptes Courants and, on 14 April 1803, gained a monopoly of the note issue within the Parisian region. However, the expansion of its circulation quickly threatened a further bout of monetary depreciation and resulted in the Banque becoming subject to greater control in 1806, through its governor and his two deputies being made responsible to the state. Monetary reform also involved the creation of a new currency—the issue of the bimetallic franc from 1802—supported by an overhauled fiscal system.[96]

Unlike their peers in England, French private bankers had little further opportunity to participate in supplying monetary media as, from 1817, nine departmental banks of issue were progressively established in the main provincial commercial and industrial cities and towns. Furthermore, the French general public, after the inflationary experience of 1792–5, would only take specie and retained its long-standing antipathy towards 'l'état de finances'.

[96] A. Plessis, 'La création de la Banque de France et la genèse des banques nationales d'émission en Europe au XIXe siècle', in O. Feiertag and M. Margairaz (eds), *Politiques et pratiques des banques d'émission en Europe (XVIIe–XXe siècle)* (Paris, 2003), pp. 25–51; F. Crouzet, 'Politics and Banking in Revolutionary and Napoleonic France', in R. Sylla, R. Tilly, and G. Tortella (eds), *The State, the Financial System and Economic Modernization* (Cambridge, 1999), pp. 20–52.

In Paris, the top echelon of bankers quickly re-coalesced, not least with the return to business of the Swiss, notably Genevan, bankers who had settled in Paris at the end of the Ancien Régime. Four banking houses came to dominate the scene: Mallet, Perrégaux, Delessert, and Hottinguer.[97]

The Mallets were already the second, and soon to be the third, generation of their family in Paris. The first bank had been founded in 1713 by Isaac Mallet, back from Geneva, where his ancestors had taken refuge one and a half centuries earlier. In 1794, the bank took the name of Mallet Frères, after a partnership agreement had been renewed between the brothers Guillaume and Isaac-Jean-Jacques, the founder's grandsons, and their cousin Jacques Torras. Mallet Frères was not one of the largest banks in the capital, but the length of time that it had been in existence and its soundness made it a prestigious house, and it was as such that it became co-founder of the Banque de France. Jean-Frédéric Perrégaux, who had arrived in Paris in 1765 from Neuchâtel, opened his own banking house in 1781. In 1788, he hired Jacques Lafitte, a Catholic, who became his partner in 1795. The bank barely interrupted its activities during the Revolution and emerged as the most important of the Parisian banking houses under the Empire. It took the name of Perrégaux, Laffitte & Cie following the death of Jean-Frédéric Perrégaux in 1808.

The Delesserts were originally from the canton of Vaud. Etienne Delessert settled in Paris in 1777, after a detour via Lyons. He survived the Revolution and kept his fortune, despite being imprisoned in the second year, very probably because of transferring funds abroad. In 1795, his son, later joined by his brothers, succeeded him at the head of the bank, of which he remained a limited partner. The House of Delessert's power came chiefly from its subsidiary in Le Havre, more directly involved in trading activities. Jean-Conrad Hottinguer, born into Zurich's circle of big traders, set up in Paris in 1784. He left France for the United States in 1794, but returned to Paris in 1796 and re-established his bank in 1798. He was also the largest importer of cotton in continental Europe.

Others followed during the early years of the nineteenth century. Michel-Frédéric Pillet-Will left his partners in Lausanne and, in 1811, settled in Paris, where he formed a partnership with Charles Vernes. In 1812, Henri Hentsch sent his partner Jean-Antoine Blanc from Geneva to Paris, where he joined him one year later; in 1821, Jean Ador and Auguste Dassier founded the banking house Ador, Vernes & Dassier; Barthélemy Paccard followed in 1825, joined two years later by his colleague, Louis Dufour. The other great wave of

[97] See L. Bergeron, *Banquiers, négociants et manufacturiers parisiens du Directoire à l'Empire* (Paris, 1978) and L. Bergeron, *Les Rothschild et les autres . . . La gloire des banquiers* (Paris, 1991); A. Plessis, 'Le développement des activités financières à Paris au XIXe siècle', in Diederiks and Reader, *Cities of Finance*, pp. 168–70. For Mallet, see *Deux siècles de banque. Mallet Frères et Cie, 1723–1923* (Paris, 1923).

foreign immigration, from Germany, only really started under the Restoration, though James de Rothschild arrived fairly unnoticed in Paris in 1812, within the framework of fund-transfer transactions organized by his brother Nathan. He founded his own bank, de Rothschild Frères, in 1817 and quickly emerged as the dominant force within the Parisian *haute banque*.

The changing constituent houses of *haute banque* were surrounded within Paris by lesser undertakings, possibly numbering more than fifty at the beginning of the nineteenth century and rising to seventy within fifteen years. However, within the provinces, particularly at seaports and internal market centres, banking from 1792 became again largely a mercantile adjunct, although with some exceptions at Lyons, the centre of the silk trade and a half-way stepping stone for Huguenots between Geneva and Paris.[98]

[98] Crouzet, 'Politics and Banking'; see also, Crouzet, *La grande inflation: la monnaie en France de Louis XVI à Napoléon* (Paris, 1993).

4

Golden Age, 1815–1870

The early to mid-nineteenth century was undoubtedly the golden age of private bankers—for two main reasons. One was the expansion of banking activities, at both national and international levels. The growth of world trade, the resumption of international capital flows, railway construction, and the advance of industrialization all required increasing amounts of capital, which banks either provided directly or, more commonly, endeavoured to raise. The second reason was that private bankers faced little or no competition from joint-stock banks. This was a unique period in their history, an era dominated by Rothschilds and Barings and a group of powerful houses befitting the French appellation of *haute banque*. Competition from public banks was very limited in previous centuries, but so was the level of banking activities. Conversely, the business of banking grew exponentially from the late nineteenth century, but it was increasingly undertaken by joint-stock banks. Private bankers were in command between 1815 and 1870, shaping the world of banking and finance, including through the establishment of the joint-stock banks that were to dominate the field. International private bankers were still at the helm in London and Paris, issuing foreign loans and financing world trade. However, commercial banking, which had taken root in Britain in the eighteenth century, gradually expanded in Europe as a distinct activity, not least to meet the demands of domestic industry.

LONDON AND THE FINANCING OF THE EUROPEAN POLITICAL SETTLEMENT

Restoration Bourbon France inherited no significant debt problem. State loans raised before 1789 had been substantially wiped out by, first, the assignat hyperinflation and, second, the Directory's decision in 1797 to cancel two-thirds of the principal sum. Thereafter, Napoleon had added little by attempting to restrict state indebtedness to Ff.50 million. He accomplished this by financing his regime principally through increased taxation, imposing levies upon conquered territories and pursing rapine military policies abroad.[1] Consequently, the French public debt in 1815 amounted to merely Ff1.5 billion, of which Ff63 million consisted of *rentes* with the greater part, Ff.40 million, dating from before 1789.

However, the restoration of the Bourbons in 1814 and 1815 required resources. The French government soon discovered that the Parisian *haute banque* was reluctant, after the experience of the previous twenty-six years, and, most recently, the uncertainties of the Hundred Days followed by the Bourbons' not entirely firm grasp of the throne. Consequently, the requirement in the 1816 budget to issue Ff6 million (£240,000) of long-term debt, in conjunction with short-term borrowing, appears to have been only eventually met by the sale of 5 per cent *rentes* on the Amsterdam market at prices as low as 57 per 100 nominal. Otherwise, the government had to turn to the Banque de France, while its provisional governor, Jacques Laffitte, also lent Ff10 million personally and privately to the state at 5 per cent.

The 1817 budget required the flotation of further *rentes*, some Ff.30 million. Leading Parisian bankers advised the government to approach their London peers, in particular Barings and Hopes, which had emerged as the foremost international financial houses over the course of the war.[2] This London–Amsterdam financial axis was more tightly knit after 1813. Alexander Baring had acquired the London and Amsterdam Hope houses for £250,000. After the unification of the Austrian Netherlands and the Northern Provinces, he re-opened Hopes in Amsterdam on 1 January 1815 under the management of Hieronymous Sillem and Adriaan van der Hoop.[3] Barings' partners were familiar with *rentes*, having placed Ff.25 million during 1816 on behalf of Allied army contractors through the irrepressible Gabriel-Julien Ouvrard.[4] This was to raise funds for covering a part of the annual maintenance costs, some Ff.150 million, of the Allied armies occupying France.

French state finances' need for foreign assistance was even greater in order to pay the Ff.700 million (£28 million) war indemnity to the Allied coalition in five annual instalments. Their armies of occupation would only leave France once this had been accomplished. After employing a substantial part of Napoleon's gold hoard for the first instalment, the French government announced that no further sums could be handed over to the Allies. A solution

[1] F. Crouzet, 'Politics and Banking in Revolutionary and Napoleonic France', in R. Sylla, R. Tilly, and G. Tortella (eds), *The State, the Financial System and Economic Modernization* (Cambridge, 1999), p. 46.

[2] D. C. M. Platt, *Foreign Finance in Continental Europe and the United States, 1815–1870. Quantities, Origins, Function and Distribution* (London, 1984), p. 8.

[3] M. G. Buist, *At Spes Non Fracta. Hope & Co. 1775–1815. Merchant Bankers and Diplomats at Work* (The Hague, 1974), pp. 68–9.

[4] R. W. Hidy, *The House of Baring in American Trade and Finance. English Merchant Bankers at Work, 1763–1861* (New York, 1941), p. 58.

was ultimately found in foreign borrowing. This was approved by an initially reluctant British government, and Wellington persuaded the other Allies to give their agreement. Barings and Hopes issued the loans during 1817 and 1818, after securing the contracts in competition with six others, including Ouvrard and Rothschild.[5] Employing bankers from states that had defeated France caused Gallic repugnance,[6] but they argued that some advantages would accrue from raising foreign funds. The mobilization of international capital to finance the indemnity payments could reduce any adverse impact that might otherwise be inflicted upon the franc and French credit. Indeed, in many respects Barings and Hopes proposed using the techniques for minimizing the adverse exchange effects on the franc that they had previously employed to maintain sterling's standing. These had coupled British wartime subsidy payments to Allies with placing abroad tranches of long-term British loans.

Issues of French *rentes* on the London market were only one aspect of financing the French war indemnity payments. After securing Barings' co-operation, members of the Parisian *haute banque*,[7] led by Jacques Laffitte, governor of the Banque de France, collectively took a quarter of each of the two loans floated during 1817. Their sizeable participations were retailed within France, and the loan contracts indicate the French bourgeoisie's increasing confidence in *rentes*. In the February and April 1817 agreements, bankers in Amsterdam, London, and Paris took *rentes* at 55 per 100 nominal, two points below their probable price on the Dutch market during 1816. The contractors' price for the third indemnity loan in July 1817 was 61.5, and the Parisian houses took half as opposed to a quarter of the issue. French investors' growing confidence in *rentes* and, thereby, in their government, was clear by May 1818: a Ff.14.6 million domestic flotation, priced at 66.5, was oversubscribed ten or fifteen times. Within fifteen months French investors were more than ready to place their savings in French state debt, while speculative international dealings in *rentes* had spread from Amsterdam and London to Antwerp, Berlin, Frankfurt, and Vienna.[8]

Barings were not perturbed by the changes in the membership of the syndicates that issued *rentes* during 1817 and 1818. They had expressed the hope to the British government in July 1817 that they would 'be able to

[5] Hidy, *House of Baring*, pp. 59–60; and P. Ziegler, *The Sixth Great Power. Barings, 1762–1929* (London, 1988), pp. 78–80.

[6] See R. J. Baker, 'The Périer Bank during the Restoration (1815–1830)', *Journal of European Economic History*, 2 (1973), p. 649.

[7] Baguenault et Cie, Delessert et Cie, Greffulhe et Cie (headed by a personal friend of the Bourbons), and Hottinguer et Cie.

[8] Platt, *Foreign Finance*, pp. 8–11. See also F. Redlich, 'Jacques Laffitte and the Beginnings of Investment Banking in France', *Bulletin of the Business Historical Society*, 22 (1948); and Ziegler, *The Sixth Great Power*, pp. 80–5.

withdraw altogether, and to leave these operations in future, where they should be, entirely in the hands of the French Houses'.[9] Nonetheless, financial and monetary conditions during 1818 resulted in Barings and Hopes being responsible for the loan financing the fifth and final indemnity payment. After making a domestic loan issue in May, their French partners no longer had sufficient free resources, whereas Allied governments wished to have the assurance of the British houses' involvement. Yet, facilitating the Ff.265 million payment proved to be a complicated and an almost disastrous affair. *Rentes* fell on the Paris Bourse, down to 60 by mid-December 1818, which was considerably below the price—76—at which the contractors had taken the loan. The price slide led Barings and Hopes to join Parisian bankers in a market support operation, which necessitated the renegotiation of the issuing contract on three occasions. Nevertheless, Barings' initial balance sheet for the French indemnity loan operations showed an 'enormous and unheard of' profit of £720,000.[10]

SOVEREIGN LOANS

Barings failed to capitalize on the leading position in European state finances that it had won by undertaking the French indemnity loans. The house was involved with other issues that were part of the financial concomitant of the Congress of Vienna but did not play a dominant role. Cooperation between bankers for floating major loans spread the risks involved, and had been developed by Hopes on the Amsterdam market during the late eighteenth century. Yet, Barings' flotations of state loans from 1818 in association with other houses besides Hopes may be due to other factors. Its capital base had become volatile, and was markedly declining—from £620,000 in 1821 to merely £280,000 in 1823. Furthermore, Alexander Baring not only withdrew capital but was increasingly absent. In 1825, he personally acknowledged his partial retirement, this despite his personal commitment to making state loan issues. As a result, the house's affairs were being largely directed by the ultra-cautious Swinton C. Holland, who focused upon mercantile business rather than high finance.[11] He took the view that 'The Stocks for Public securities of all countries . . . are a dangerous commodity to deal in, by those who do not understand them, and the wisest . . . are often deceived by them.'[12]

[9] Alexander Baring to Lord Liverpool, 27 July 1817, quoted in Hidy, *House of Baring*, p. 60. See also, J. Orbell, *Baring Brothers & Co., Limited. A History to 1939* (London, 1985), p. 23.

[10] Hidy, *House of Baring*, pp. 61–3; and Ziegler, *The Sixth Great Power*, pp. 84–5.

[11] Orbell, *Baring Brothers & Co.*, pp. 23, 26, 27; and Ziegler, *The Sixth Great Power*, pp. 86, 93–4.

[12] Quoted in Ziegler, *The Sixth Great Power*, p. 95.

Barings were increasingly replaced by Rothschilds as bankers to the needy governments of restoration Europe. Initially, this would have appeared to have been an unlikely outcome. Despite their accumulated expertise, acquired from wartime financial transfers on behalf of states, the Rothschilds had had little opportunity to profit from it immediately after Waterloo. A political cloud hung over James's head in Paris, while many houses, not just Barings, competed over transferring French maintenance payments to the Allied armies of occupation. Consequently, the Rothschilds in Frankfurt and Paris acquired only a small share of this business—for Austria and Prussia—and had to cooperate with other bankers, which rankled.[13]

The first major post-war state securities operation was undertaken on the London Stock Exchange by Nathan, the first amongst equals within the family. Despite remonstrations from his brothers and father, Nathan, employing closely-guarded 'insider' information, speculated that the price of Consols would rise on the market during 1817. And, he was very successful, making a profit of more than £0.25 million. Two years later, he issued a £12 million loan for a British government whose post-war reconstruction of state finances was being hamstrung by Parliament.[14]

The Rothschilds moved into post-war continental European state finance from early 1817, through arranging a small loan for Prussia. As at the turn of the century, this was largely placed with the Elector of Hesse-Kassel. The Frankfurt house, located close to the new German Confederation's political forum, also undertook relatively petty loans for small German states. Between 1817 and 1829 these amounted to £2.2 million.[15] However, they were not the affairs that caused the British parliamentary committee in 1819 to seek Nathan's expert evidence on foreign loan issues and their impact upon the initial exchanges. He was called because of his innovative arrangements for a major Prussian loan of £5 million floated in London the previous year. Like Hopes and Bethmanns during the late eighteenth century, Nathan had taken the business of successfully issuing state bonds to a higher plane.

After Waterloo, it was clear that the largest source of liquid funds in Europe was the London capital market. In order to appeal to British investors, Nathan made his 1818 Prussian loan as closely analogous to familiar Consols as possible in negotiations with the Hohenzollerns' representatives. It was secured on royal assets which, were subject to parliamentary oversight as far as an absolutist state would allow. Investors' confidence was further assured by the loan having a sinking fund. Besides giving the loan the greatest backing that could be obtained, Nathan assisted its marketability in other ways. First,

[13] N. Ferguson, *The World's Banker. The History of the House of Rothschild* (London, 1998), pp. 121–4.

[14] Ferguson, *The World's* Banker, pp. 126–7, 130.

[15] Ferguson, *The World's* Banker, pp. 131, 135.

the loan was denominated in sterling so that British investors need not be concerned by the complexity of exchange rates, as was the case with their post-war holdings of *rentes*. Second, like Amsterdam issues of the late eighteenth century, its servicing was to be primarily undertaken from the market where it had been issued rather than the seat of the borrower. Last but not least, Nathan arranged servicing in local currencies at the other financial centres where tranches had also been floated: Amsterdam, Frankfurt, Hamburg, and Vienna. He used the same techniques for his second major Prussian loan—of £3.5 million—issued during 1822. His innovative approach to issuing the 1818 and 1822 Prussian loans was adopted by all other houses, becoming the model for sovereign loan flotations during the nineteenth century.[16]

The 1818 Prussian sterling loan marked the beginnings of the Rothschilds' connections with the finances of major European absolutist states. Furthermore, these developing relationships shaped in turn the geographical structure of the Rothschild family bank during the second quarter of the nineteenth century. Branch houses in Vienna and then Naples were founded. Two profitable Austrian lottery loans undertaken in 1820 with David Parish led Salomon to settle in Vienna, where he became an intimate of Metternich. The Austrian occupation of Naples to quell a revolt was followed not only by Rothschilds undertaking a stream of loans for this Italian state, including a £2.5 million issue in 1824, but also to Carl taking up permanent residence in the major Italian city-port.[17] Furthermore, the Rothschilds displaced Hopes in long-term Russian state finance, floating a £6.6 million loan in 1822 (on which they lost heavily).[18] Their portfolio of client major European states was completed in 1823 by James gaining the contract for the issue of Ff.462 million *rentes* against the competition of the Parisian *haute banque*. The Rothschilds' compass was further extended through Nathan making a £1.5 million loan on behalf of Portugal with the assistance of the Bank of England.[19]

The European sovereign loan boom was capped by issues for the new South American republics, beginning with £2 million for Columbia in March 1822, undertaken by a London firm of Caribbean merchants. In some respects, these flotations were a repeat of the attempt made between 1806 and 1809 to open up the continent to British trade. The stream of high yielding stocks floated for Brazil, Buenos Aires, Chile, Guatemala, and Mexico between 1823 and 1825, which collectively raised *c.* £20 million, was to fare generally no better. They were undertaken by a diverse range of contractors, some of whom like

[16] Ferguson, *World's Banker*, pp. 132–4.

[17] M. C. Schisani, 'How to Make a Potentially Defaulting Country Credible: Karl Rothschild, the Neapolitan Debt and Financial Diplomacy (1821–26)', *Rivista di Storia Economica*, 2 (2010), pp. 233–78.

[18] This was despite the loan being backed by an underwriting syndicate. See P. L. Cottrell, 'The Business Man and Financier', in S. and V. D. Lipman (eds), *The Century of Moses Montefiore* (Oxford, 1985), p. 30.

[19] Ferguson, *World's Banker*, pp. 135–6, 139, 140, 142.

B. A. Goldschmidt and J. & S. Ricardo had been involved in British war finance. Others, such as Reid, Irving & Co. and T. Wilson & Co., were attempting to extend their business affairs.

Barings had been involved in Ouvrard's wartime 'Mexican piastre affair' and from 1814 developed a mercantile interest in South America by building upon late eighteenth-century foundation. The house was amongst the first to express an interest in republican issues, offering a commitment of £10,000 to a likely Chilean loan in 1820 and bidding for a Colombian flotation the following year. Acceptance credits for trade with the Plate estuary may have led Barings in 1824 to take over on commission a £1 million six per cent loan for Buenos Aires that had been negotiated locally. Despite Buenos Aires being the Latin American trading node most familiar to London merchants, the loan proved to be a disaster, especially when speculators were unable to make good their commitments. Barings mounted a market support operation but this proved unsuccessful. The house was left with much of the stock and a badly damaged reputation.[20]

Rothschilds were more circumspect than Barings about South American sovereign borrowing. It was only after T. Wilson & Co. had successfully floated the first Brazilian loan in 1824 that Nathan agreed to act for the Brazilian Empire, building upon his 1823 Portuguese loan which was secured on Brazilian revenues. He issued a £2 million loan during 1825.[21] His timing was faultless, just as the price of Consols began to fall together with those of all the foreign stocks that had been floated in London over the previous eight years.

Reversal turned to rout during the closing months of 1825 as the actual value of many South-American mining companies became apparent. The lack of safety nets for most Latin-American loan issues was revealed in January 1826 when coupon payments on Colombian debt ceased with the failure of B. A. Goldschmidt.[22] Barings' Buenos Aires loan was further affected by its borrower declaring war on Brazil, resulting in holders receiving no interest payments from mid-1827. As Mexican financial agents from September 1826, Barings attempted to ensure that interest was paid on this state's loans, advancing funds in mid-summer 1827 but, ultimately, was unable to provide continuing support.[23] The aftermath of the South American loan boom proved to be bitter and protracted. For instance, Barings reinstituted the servicing of Buenos Aires debt in 1844, but partially and merely for a year. Regular coupon payments, albeit under a debt composition, were only finally resumed in January 1859.[24] Amongst the South American sovereign borrowers of the

[20] Hidy, *House of Baring*, p. 66; Orbell, *Baring Brothers & Co.*, pp. 25–6; and Ziegler, *The Sixth Great Power*, pp. 100–3.

[21] Ferguson, *World's Banker*, pp. 141–2.

[22] L. H. Jenks, *The Migration of British Capital to 1875* (New York, 1927), p. 57.

[23] Hidy, *House of Baring*, p. 66.

[24] Orbell, *Baring Brothers & Co.*, p. 26; and Ziegler, *The Sixth Great Power*, pp. 110–11.

mid-1820s, only Brazil's international creditworthiness was maintained—by a resumption of debt servicing in 1829.[25]

FINANCING THE RECOVERY OF INTERNATIONAL TRADE

The volume of European overseas trade in 1815 was probably no greater than it had been in 1790. Furthermore, British and continental European international commerce between 1815 and the late 1820s was adversely affected by continuing war-induced distortions and deflation. In the case of Britain, war's disruptive effects were clearly evident in every component of its visible trade. Re-exports at current prices rose to £16 million in 1814–15 as a result of the speculative boost given by the coming of peace. Yet, as more normal patterns of trade resumed, they declined to £8.1 million at the peak of the mid-1820s boom.[26] Exports of British produced goods also fell, from £44.5 million in 1814–16 to £35.3 million in 1824–6, with only flows to the Middle East and the Orient having any dynamism.[27] Textiles, particularly cottons, continued to dominate the composition of British exported manufactures.[28] However, competition from emerging rivals in both continental Europe and the United States added to that within home industries. It aggravated the fall in prices and narrowed already slim profit margins. Furthermore, the growth of European manufacturing led to Britain becoming increasingly a supplier of machine-spun cotton yarn to the continent's weavers.

Continental European trade was also disrupted by the collapse in 1814–15 of the wide 'internal' market developed under the Napoleonic system. For example, the French economy's recovery was to take a decade and a half. Consequently, total French exports in 1820 were only half the value of British, although they then began to grow at a faster rate. Like Britain, manufactured textiles characterized French post-war exports, of which silk was the most important. Wool and cotton products shared to varying degrees the competitive edge of French silks given by the quality that arose from the employment of cheap labour, especially for hand finishing.

International trade growth, despite its hesitant *and* volatile character, required finance. It was increasingly supplied by a small number of largely London-based merchant bankers. After the searing experience of the 1809–10

[25] J. F. Rippy, *British Investments in Latin America 1822–1949* (Minneapolis, 1959).

[26] Excluding trade with Ireland. R. Davis, *The Industrial Revolution and British Overseas Trade* (Leicester, 1979), Table 39, p. 91.

[27] Excluding trade with Ireland. Davis, *British Overseas Trade*, Table 38, p. 89.

[28] Davis, *British Overseas Trade*, Table 9, p. 21.

crisis, these houses increasingly turned to specializing in extending trade credits. This significant change in their affairs was also a response to the demand for new forms of finance arising from how British overseas trade was being increasingly conducted, especially across the North Atlantic. Exports to the United States were handled more and more by petty merchants, brokers, and agents. They were largely British born and worked from home or overseas locations on commission rather than mobilizing their own small capitals. The various firms of this heterogeneous group could only conduct trading on a substantial basis by marrying their expertise to externally provided credit.[29] This was supplied by the small group of London merchant banks as acceptances, the metropolitan houses involved guaranteeing by their undoubted standing the payment of the bills involved.

The merchant banks' backing was made clear by their acceptance on presentation of the international trade bills with which they were individually connected. It led to this clutch of significant providers of commercial finance within the City becoming known as 'acceptance houses', and the paper involved as 'acceptances'. The bills were readily traded on the London market and so were liquid over the period, normally sixty to ninety days, between their acceptance and maturity. The bills' international standing was further assisted by sterling going onto gold by legislation passed in 1816 and 1819, which became operative between 1821 and 1823. Sterling also became *the* currency because of the considerable weight of British overseas dealings within world trade coupled with the insistence of British trading agents on only working in their own currency. All was mutually supported and reinforced by the growing width and depth of the City as a post-war international financial centre.

The London market's growing finance of world trade, particularly its North Atlantic component, was further developed over the 1820s as the acceptance houses increasingly granted bill finance drawn under letters of credit. Merchant banks used their respective networks of foreign correspondents and agents to support the payment of the acceptances as they arose.[30] Furthermore, some acceptance houses institutionalized their extra-British links by opening branch houses throughout the world beyond Europe. This development began in the still nascent Latin-American trades, in which communications were difficult due to the physical distances involved and, as a consequence, the greatest trust and confidence was required in overseas agents. For instance, A. Gibbs & Sons, a London firm that increasingly specialized in South American dealings, opened branch houses in Lima (1822) and Santiago (1826). Overseas correspondents and the growth of branch-house networks extended the payment functions performed by London acceptances by enabling foreign debtors to settle their positions through them. One result was a payment flow of specie, or

[29] S. D. Chapman, *Merchant Enterprise in Britain* (Cambridge, 1992), pp. 69–74.
[30] R. Roberts, *Schroders. Merchants and Bankers* (Basingstoke and London, 1992), p. 27.

securities, or bills drawn on other British houses. London acceptors' businesses increasingly came thereby to comprise an amalgam of trade finance and exchange operations.[31] Critical for the soundness of all these developments was more effective and speedier communications. These were initiated during the late 1810s by American packets sailing from Liverpool on timetabled services to New York, with the vessels' access to blue water aided by steam paddle tugs. This regularity and rapidity contrasted markedly with the concurrent early mercantile voyages from the Mersey to China and India, following the abrogation of the East India Company's monopoly trading privileges. These took between ten and fifteen months.[32]

The importance of acceptance credits—'bills on London'—grew from the mid-1820s and, especially, in British trade to Europe and the United States. Increasingly, importers of British goods bought directly from their manufacturers, using bills drawn under letters of credit from London merchant houses.[33] Thereby, the deals were based on the creditworthiness of the acceptor rather than the buyer.[34] The result was that the buyer obtained a keener price, particularly appreciated by American shippers in Manchester during the 1820s.

The importance of London extenders of bill finance, whether by letters of credit or otherwise, varied depending upon a house's particular stature. Equally, the importance of acceptances within the total business of merchant banks varied widely as, for instance, between Barings, Rothschilds, and Schroders.

Schroders' acceptance business developed out of financing the wartime trade of either other Schröder family firms or houses whose members were linked to the Schroders by marriage. The London house's acceptances rose from 1813, aided by the French evacuation of Hamburg in 1814. By 1817 it was extending credits to New York firms for their trade between Savannah, Georgia, and Amsterdam. Although still rooted in Schröder filial connections, this development signalled the provision of credits for 'third' party dealings.

[31] C. Jones, *International Business in the Nineteenth Century. The Rise and Fall of a Cosmopolitan Bourgeoisie* (Brighton, 1987), pp. 63–4.

[32] T. Baines, *History of the Commerce and Town of Liverpool* (London, 1852), pp. 569, 572, 587, 637, 654; R. G. Albion, 'Planning the Black Ball Line', *Business History Review*, 41 (1967); and R. G. Albion, *The Rise of New York Port 1815–60* (New York, 1939), pp. 38–43. One consequence of lengthy communications with the Orient was a different mercantile and financial structure once the trade was freed, for which, see M. Greenberg, *British Trade and the Opening of China 1800–1842* (Cambridge, 1951); B. B. King, 'The Origin of the Managing Agency System in India', *Journal of Asian Studies*, 26 (1966–7); and Chapman, *Merchant Enterprise in Britain*, pp. 107–18.

[33] See S. D. Chapman, 'The Fielden Fortune: The Finances of Lancashire's most Successful Manufacturing Family', *Financial History Review*, 3 (1996), pp. 13–15.

[34] E. J. Perkins, *Financing Anglo-American Trade. The House of Brown, 1800–1850* (Cambridge, MA and London, 1975), pp. 9–11.

The London house was reorganized at the beginning of 1818: Johann Heinrich took charge, initially in partnership with Francis Gill, in a firm styled J. Henry Schroder & Co. The anglicization of the name marked its commitment to the City, although its affairs continued to be primarily family based. They involved shipments of indigo and sugar to a brother in St Petersburg, taking tallow in return. Johann Heinrich paired his London 1818 partnership with his own newly established firm in Hamburg, which he ran alone until 1826. The London–Hamburg Schroder axis, linking two of the world's predominant ports, was initially concerned with the sugar trade, a long-standing family interest. There are indications that its affairs also included granting acceptance credits to merchants beyond the family circle. Furthermore, with over half of Hamburg's imports coming from Britain, largely textiles, and it supplying in return wool to West Riding manufacturers, Schroders traded alongside other London houses of Hamburg origin, such as Rückers and Brandts, the latter also having significant family connections with Russia.

During the trade upswing of the mid-1820s, J. Henry Schroder & Co. expanded on the basis of the capital of a new partner, Herman Otto von Post, who replaced Gill. The larger equity probably assisted widening interests, including American cotton, French wine, and Latin-American dealings. An indication of the business's growth and spread is that, by 1829, it required nine clerks, all German. They found a City training the best possible foundation for a subsequent career in international commerce and finance.[35]

Until the late 1820s, Schroders was an acceptance house with standing in the finance of only a small number of particular trades. Towering above it were Barings and Rothschilds, whose outstanding acceptances at the end of 1825 have been estimated by Chapman at £520,000 and £300,000 respectively.[36] These two houses were the leading London acceptors, although the provision of trade credit played different roles in their respective affairs. Barings remained committed to commercial dealings, from which the house's growing supply of acceptance credits stemmed. This was despite its post-war merchanting being sapped by managerial problems. In the case of Rothschilds, trading in goods was clearly declining as Nathan increasingly specialized in, and further developed, the business of floating state loans.

During the 1820s, N. M. Rothschild & Co.'s commercial affairs largely concentrated on importing from the Caribbean and the United States, together with Russia (copper) and Spain (mercury). Its relatively small interest in the related provision of acceptance credits is indicated by bills payable only comprising 5 per cent of liabilities in 1828. On the other hand, bills received made up 25 per cent of assets. Four years later, Nathan described his bill transactions at the Royal Exchange to a parliamentary committee. He spoke of

35 Roberts, *Schroders*, pp. 26–7, 31–2, 35–6, 38–40.
36 S. D. Chapman, *The Rise of Merchant Banking* (London, 1984, 1988 edn), Table 2.2, p. 17.

buying weekly about £6,000–10,000 of provincial bills which were sent to the continent in return for paper drawn on London. In this, as Ferguson has stressed, Nathan's prime concern was not to profit from trade finance per se but to conduct exchange operations and ship specie internationally. This built upon the bullion smuggling operations at the height of the Napoleonic wars that he had undertaken with James. However, by the early 1830s, profiting from exchange movements could be based on not only the Rothschild family group of five houses, but also Nathan's own salaried agents in Europe—as in Madrid and St Petersburg—and in New York, together with his parallel network of corresponding American and European banks.[37]

Nathan's forte in handling bullion movements came to the fore during the British domestic banking crisis of winter 1825–6.[38] The situation became so dire that Bank of England directors advised the government that a suspension of cash payments might be required. Putting aside personal and political animosities, Nathan supplied the Bank with gold from 17 December 1825, largely drawn from James in Paris, and continued to do so for almost a year, involving imports from practically every world source. This aid built upon N. M. Rothschild & Co. having acquired bullion in significant quantities from Paris since the beginning of the year. The Bank of England paid for the gold out of its significant holdings of silver, demonetized in Britain but not in bimetallic France. The crisis operation was the culmination of Nathan's cultivation of the Bank of England since summer 1823, as a result of which he became its bullion broker, displacing Mocatta & Goldsmid, which had dealt for the Bank almost since its foundation.[39]

Barings, although lacking a family-based group of houses spanning Europe apart from Hopes in Amsterdam, had, in 1815, a continental network of correspondents who provided business links to every major political capital and commercial port. Dating from Sir Francis Baring's role within the East India Company, the house also had considerable trading interests in the Orient. While Schroders became best known in the City as Russia merchants, Barings were most closely identified with the North Atlantic trade and were considered London's leading 'American' house. Its post-war New World connections were largely with the wealthiest merchants in Baltimore, Boston, New York, and Philadelphia.

[37] Ferguson, *World's Banker*, pp. 291–3, 297, 300, 302.

[38] See below, pp. 145–6.

[39] Ferguson, *World's Banker*, pp. 145–6. For the general context, see E. Victor Morgan, *The Theory and Practice of Central Banking 1797–1913* (Cambridge, 1943; rep., London, 1965), pp. 80–2, 91–2; J. H. Clapham, *The Bank of England. A History*, II, *1797–1914* (Cambridge, 1944, rep. 1970), pp. 95, 82–6, 94–5; F. W. Fetter, *Development of British Monetary Orthodoxy 1797–1875* (Cambridge, MA, 1965), pp. 111–15, 116–18; and B. Hilton, *Corn, Cash, Commerce. The Economic Policies of the Tory Governments 1815–1830* (Oxford, 1977), pp. 202–4, 207, 208–9, 210, 215–17.

Before the late 1820s, Barings, unlike other American houses, had no resident agents in the United States through whom to develop further the provision of trade finance. Rather, there was a continued reliance upon traditional correspondent relationships, which during the immediate post-war period had provided some new business developments. These largely consisted of financing, by letters of credit, the United States' trade with China and India. Barings' considerable mercantile links with America were augmented by those with the Federal government, governments of individual states, and, from March 1817, the second Bank of the United States. These were strengthened when the house placed £200,000 Bank of New York stock in 1823, acquiring an interest in Virginian state stock, and taking on, albeit reluctantly, a participation in other American banking shares.[40]

Although not publicly evident, Barings lost direction after 1815. Total commission income, including from acceptances, halved over the post-war decade. As noted above, despite having a background in the American trades, Swinton C. Holland took an exceedingly cautious approach. His day-to-day inflexible control between 1815 and 1827 resulted in the loss of a considerable number of first-class connections, including John Jacob Astor, a client since 1811. Management was one problem, arising from absent Baring family partners, especially Alexander. Another, and more serious, was a marked erosion of trading capital, the backing for the house's contingent liabilities, i.e., acceptances. Barings' trading equity contracted sharply from 1821, falling to an amount probably considerably less than its outstanding acceptances by the close of 1825.[41] This negative development was congruent with Holland's very careful approach to business. A fatal reckoning never came but the house was vulnerable.

The sudden death in 1827 of Holland forced the issue of the much-needed managerial restructuring of the City's best-known American acceptor. Overseen by Alexander Baring, leadership within the family went to Thomas Baring II, a son of Sir Thomas, who had been educated at Winchester and then trained in business with Hopes as, first, a clerk and, then, a partner. He was put in harness with two others as the house's managing partners: Humphrey St. John Mildmay, Alexander's son-in-law, who had been an army officer before acquiring from 1824 commercial and financial expertise within Barings; and Joshua Bates, a New Englander, who had been a general agent in Europe, establishing his own London firm by which, possibly, he came into contact with Barings through Pierre César Labouchère. It was a combination clearly indicating that Barings were to re-focus upon North American dealings.[42]

[40] Hidy, *House of Baring*, pp. 53, 65, 70, 72, 74, 75; Orbell, *Baring Brothers & Co.*, p. 24; and Ziegler, *The Sixth Great Power*, pp. 75, 76.

[41] Orbell, *Baring Brothers & Co.*, pp. 22–3, 26–7.

[42] Hidy, *House of Baring*, pp. 79–85; Orbell, *Baring Brothers & Co.*, pp. 27, 28–9; and Ziegler, *The Sixth Great Power*, pp. 112, 119–21, 122–4, 125.

THE RISE OF THE LONDON MERCHANT BANKS

Trade finance and foreign issues were the two financial activities which, in the footsteps of Barings, Rothschilds, and Schroders, gave rise to a group of private banks, the merchant banks, which were to play a crucial role in the City of London, and more generally in international finance over the next century and half. However, the balance between the accepting and the issuing businesses was far from being equal. In 1910, Baron Schroeder divided the business of his merchant bank into two parts with respect to the rate of return that each generated. There was what he called the regular but low yielding 'bread and butter' work of granting acceptance credits—sterling bills on London—for financing international trade and payments, and, but considerably less often, the highly profitable 'jam' of undertaking securities flotations, nearly always on behalf of a foreign borrower.[43] Granting acceptance credits had developed from the house's origins as international merchants, which had provided the initial knowledge about a considerable range of goods, their markets, and those who dealt in them, especially their personal standings. However, the opportunities for what Baron Schroeder considered the 'jam' only began to be considerable from the mid-1850s when Britain became a major exporter of capital.

The United Kingdom clearly occupied a dominant position in international trade, providing more than 20 per cent of world trade in 1850 and about 25 per cent in the 1860s—approximately twice France's share (11 per cent in 1850 and 13 per cent in 1860). The bulk of this trade was handled directly by the City—throughout the nineteenth century, the City of London remained much more of a trading centre than a financial centre—and was also financed through bills of exchange drawn on London. The volume of acceptances remains difficult to assess with any precision before the last quarter of the century. Acceptances connected with the United States, probably half the total until the late 1860s, might have increased from £15–£20 million in 1836 to about £30 million in 1856 and £40 million in 1876. Their share then diminished as a result of the tariff of 1864 and merchant bankers' diversification into other areas, especially Europe.[44] Barings remained the market leader and its acceptances started to rise sharply from the mid-nineteenth century. Rothschilds, for their part, were primarily concerned with the issuing business.

Behind the two leaders, a host of other firms entered the London accepting business. The ranks of the London merchant banks were swelled by waves of immigration. After the arrival during the French wars of men who founded houses which subsequently rose to prominence (Horstman, Wm Brandt, Fdk

[43] National Monetary Commission, United States, *Interviews on the Banking and Currency Systems of England, Scotland, France, Germany and Italy* (Washington DC: Government Printing Office, 1910), evidence of Baron Schroeder.
[44] Chapman, *Rise of Merchant Banking*, p. 105.

Huth, Frühling & Goschen)[45], the following decades saw, amongst others, the foundation of George Peabody & Co. and C. J. Hambro, Sons & Co. The former was founded in 1838 by George Peabody, from Massachusetts. It became J. S. Morgan & Co. in 1864, after Peabody's retirement and following the admission ten years earlier of another American, Junius Spencer Morgan (John Pierpont Morgan's father) as a partner. Hambro was founded in 1839 by Carl Joachim Hambro, son of a merchant and banker from Copenhagen and former American consul in Denmark. Kleinwort, Sons & Co. was established two decades later by Alexander Kleinwort. He set up on his own in London in 1858, having previously left Hamburg to work in an English merchant bank in Havana, Cuba. Kleinworts was to become the City's leading accepting house in the early twentieth century.

British overseas investment grew substantially during these years without, however, experiencing the expansion that was to characterize the period 1870–1914—especially the boom of the early 1870s, the 1880s, and the decade preceding the First World War. Britain exported about £2 million to £6 million per year on average in the 1840s, £15 to £16 million in the 1850s and £30 million in the 1860s. Unlike the accepting business, the issuing business, especially government loans, remained in the hands of an elite group of merchant banks dominated by N. M. Rothschild, followed by Baring Brothers. Hambro issued a £4 million Anglo-Sardinian Loan in 1851—despite competition from the Rothschilds. Frühling & Goschen was involved in the Egyptian loans, and Morgan in Chilean loans in the 1860s. A few newcomers were more involved in the issuing than in the accepting business. This was especially the case with the international Jewish banking dynasties, mainly of German origin, which spread throughout Europe and the United States from their richest reservoir, Frankfurt. The Rothschilds were of course the most illustrious amongst them, but there were others, such as the Bischoffsheims, the Erlangers, the Seligmans, the Speyers, and the Sterns, who installed members of their families in London, Paris, New York, San Francisco, Brussels, and Amsterdam.[46] Stern Brothers had its hour of glory in the 1860s through their involvement in Portuguese bonds. Erlangers managed to issue a £3 million loan on behalf of the Confederate States in 1863 during the American Civil War.[47] Speyers and Seligmans did not make their mark in London before the 1870s, when a new wave of merchant bankers, including Lazard and Ernest Cassel, were to settle in the City.

[45] See, Ch. 3, pp. 84–7.

[46] See P. Emden, *Jews of Britain. A Series of Biographies* (London, 1944) and *Money Powers of Europe in the Nineteenth and Twentieth Century* (London, 1937).

[47] Chapman, *Rise of Merchant Banking*, pp. 45, 85–6.

THE FORMATION OF THE PARISIAN *HAUTE BANQUE*

The founding of the Parisian *haute banque* dates back to the closing years of the eighteenth century, with the increasing attraction exerted by Paris on provincial bankers, such as Claude Périer, and the return to business of Swiss bankers, such as Mallet, Perrégaux, Delessert, and Hottinguer.[48]

A second wave of foreign immigration, from Germany, started under the Restoration. James de Rothschild, arrived in Paris in 1812, founded his own bank, de Rothschild Frères, in 1817, and quickly emerged as the dominant force within the Parisian *haute banque*. Other bankers from Frankfurt came to settle in Paris too. The Protestant Bethmanns, who had played a leading role in placing foreign securities, especially Austrian, in Frankfurt's financial centre during the second half of the eighteenth century, sent a representative, whilst the Gontards made longer-term commitments there from 1827, while maintaining the hub of their activities in Frankfurt. Others, often of Jewish origin, followed in their wake: the Oppenheims from Cologne, through their alliance with the Foulds,[49] the de Habers from Karlsruhe, and the Seligman-d'Eichthals from Munich.[50]

Like their London counterparts, the members of the Parisian *haute banque* were primarily engaged in trade finance and, a little later, in foreign issues. Paris played a crucial role in the financing of France's domestic and international trade. Not only was almost all international trade handled in the capital, but numerous foreign merchants, especially Swiss, regularly drew bills of exchange on Paris. Paris's international role was further enhanced by France's key position in the multilateral system of payments: in spite of its relatively modest foreign trade, it was the only country in continental Europe that had balanced trade with Latin America and a positive trade balance with the Anglo-Saxon countries. The franc was an international currency because, on the one hand, the British and Americans were trying to obtain bills of exchange on Paris to pay for some of their purchases and, on the other hand,

48 See Ch. 3, pp. 111–12.

49 L. Bergeron, *Les Rothschild et les autres . . . La gloire des banquiers* (Paris, 1991), pp. 38–82. M. Stürmer, G. Teichmann, and W. Treue, *Wägen und Wagen. Sal. Oppenheim jr. & Cie. Geschichte einer Bank und einer Familie* (Munich and Zurich, 1989), p. 41.

50 Even though they stayed in Cologne, where they had been the first Jews to settle in 1798, the Oppenheims founded, in partnership with Berr-Léon Fould, the bank B.L. Fould & Fould-Oppenheim in Paris in 1813, forging a solid and lasting alliance between the two families, consolidated by the marriage in the same year of Hélène Oppenheim to Benedict Fould, son of Berr-Léon. The settlement of the Habers, from Karlsruhe, was more direct. Maurice Haber (1798–1874), son of Salomon (banker to the Baden and Prussian courts since 1794, which earned him the title of Baron of Baden in 1829), arrived in Paris in 1822, equipped with a share from his father, and formed a partnership with Felix Worms from Romilly. Another distinguished personality of German origin in the Parisian *haute banque* was Adolphe d'Eichthal, son of Aron-Elias Seligman, banker to the king of Bavaria and made Baron d'Eichthal in 1814 for services rendered as a supplier during the Napoleonic Wars.

the merchants of continental Europe used Paris's centre to clear their debts with the Anglo-Saxon countries.[51]

This new role offered the opportunity of creating a very active capital market. Capital accumulated in Paris. Deposits, which represented up to 80 per cent of the liabilities of certain banks, included, besides the accounts of members of the aristocracy and the bourgeoisie, as well as the funds of numerous French industrial and commercial firms, the proceeds from sales made in France by foreign merchants, who used them on the spot to make payments and to obtain new credits. This capital replenished itself. In particular, it lay at the root of the role that Paris would henceforth play in placing and then issuing foreign loans.[52] Even though France, along with Britain, was the main capital-exporting country, the number of loans floated on the Paris market only progressed slowly during the first half of the nineteenth century. The three loans to the Kingdom of Naples between 1821 and 1824, managed by the Rothschilds, were mostly issued in Paris and the Spanish loan of 1823 was concluded under difficult conditions by the Parisian banker, Guebhart. In addition, four Belgian loans and two others on behalf of the city of Brussels were issued between 1831 and 1844, while papal loans were very easy to place in France between 1831 and 1839.

The Parisian *haute banque* was also involved in early industrial financing. From the outbreak of war until the crisis of 1810, factory-based cotton manufacturing in Alsace, Normandy, Paris, and Picardy increased, especially finer muslins for revolutionary fashions. Expansion occurred despite a considerably higher price for raw material inputs than in Leipzig or Liverpool. Parisian bankers took direct stakes in this developing industry. Delessert opening a spinning mill in 1801 while other members of the *haute banque* became connected with cotton manufacturing by marriage. Their links were largely with the more technologically advanced concerns. These were mostly located in Alsace, established by co-religionists, and built up before 1789 on the basis of finishing, dyeing, and printing. The Mallet and Vernes families became connected with C. Oberkampf, the Périers with the Berckheims and Dietrichs, and the Neuflizes with the Dollfuses. Interests in the new forms of production, or filial connections with them, expanded these bankers' business horizons, opening up new opportunities for financial exploitation.

The Davillier family built up extensive textile interests. The Périers went further through their direct involvement with the Anzin coal mines and the Chaillot engineering works. Claude Périer, the progenitor of Périer Frères,

[51] M. Lévy-Leboyer, *Les banques européennes et l'industrialisation internationale dans le première moitié du XIXe siècle* (Paris, 1964), pp. 437–40.

[52] Lévy-Leboyer, *Les banques européennes*, pp. 441–2.

had, under the Ancien Régime, been a merchant-manufacturer in Grenoble but, shortly before his death, was one of the founders of the Banque de France. Two of his sons, Casimir and Scipion, together with some of his former business partners, established the family's Parisian banking house during 1801, the year of their father's death. They continued with their industrial interests, principally the Anzin collieries acquired by Claude during the revolutionary period. From 1815 they became the principal plank of the banking house's activities. Furthermore, the family's pre-1815 manufacturing interests had gone beyond cottons and coal to include woollens and the processing of beet sugar. These were augmented in 1818 by Scipion buying the Chaillot foundry, not only a supplier of equipment to the Anzin mines but also one of the first producers of steam engines in France.[53] The only major Parisian banking house after 1815 with business interests analogous with those of the Périers was that of William Ternaux. He financed a major woollen enterprise, building upon the success of his 'cashmere' shawls.

The Périers had not been alone amongst Parisian bankers in developing the wartime import substitute industry of beet-sugar processing. Delessert too established a sugar refinery. Equally, there were some other provincial French bankers and quasi-bankers, comparable to Claude Périer, who had significant industrial connections even if they did not migrate around the turn of the century to the capital. Waterloo completely altered the institutional environment for continental European economic development. Yet, Parisian bankers maintained their industrial interests after 1815 and, as in the case of the Périers, extended them.

A new departure in their constellation of business interests during the late 1810s was the development of corporate insurance companies to fill the void opened by the tumult of the past quarter of a century. Laffitte, with Delessert and the Périers, established the Compagnie Royale d'Assurances Maritimes in 1816 with a capital of Ff. 10 million, whereas a group of other bankers, possibly including James de Rothschild, founded in 1818 the Compagnie d'Assurances Générales.[54] Insurance was a profitable business and, furthermore, was complementary to and compatible with the activities of a private bank. Led by Delessert, the *haute banque* also established in 1818 the Caisse d'Épargne et de Prévoyance de Paris, the first French working-class savings bank. Initially, it worked from within the premises of the Compagnie Royale until, in 1820, the Banque de France provided permanent premises. The Banque's *régents* acted as either administrators or directors of this pioneering savings bank, and the

[53] Barker, 'The Périer Bank', pp. 641–6, 655 (Table 1); Barker, 'French Entrepreneurship during the Restoration; The Record of a Single Firm, the Anzin Mining Company', *Journal of Economic History*, 21 (1961); and B. Gille, *La banque et le crédit en France de 1815 à 1840* (Paris, 1959), pp. 55, 252.

[54] On James's association, see the implied connection in Ferguson, *World's Banker*, p. 294.

politicians amongst them during the mid-1820s opposed plans for the conversion of *rentes* that would compromise the bank's investment earnings.

By the mid-nineteenth century, the Parisian *haute banque* consisted of some twenty to twenty-five very wealthy houses, most of which were on or near the Chaussée d'Antin. They were distinct from other private bankers in Paris because of their greater resources, considerable social standing, cosmopolitan character, and involvement with international business. Members of the *haute banque* formed a particular echelon of elite society, yet, in the case of those who were either Protestant or Jewish, they were somewhat aloof. This is because they continued to attach great importance to sustaining their connections with their foreign origins despite the passage of time.[55] This character trait led to marriages either with family relations beyond France or the sons and daughters of 'friends' amongst their widespread business connections.

Although clearly constituting a very separate cluster of bankers, members of the *haute banque* were heterogeneous apart from having in common considerable capital regularly employed in major affairs, including those with international dimensions. During the 1850s and 1860s, the wealthiest by far was James de Rothschild, who had a capital of *c.* Ff. 50 million. This was more than ten times the average capital of an *haute banque* house (about Ff.4.5 million) mobilized, for example, by either Mallet Frères & Cie or Périers. Considerably smaller was Mirabaud, Paccard & Cie, the capital of which had declined to Ff2.8 million by 1861.[56] These were the sums engaged in daily business transactions but the personal assets of a house's partners could be considerably larger and were available during times of strain and crisis. Greater family resources, accumulated over the past century in the case of some, or over the past half century for others, marked out the *haute banque* from the very few Parisian private bankers whose business capitals were considerably larger, such as the Ff.12 million of the partners in the Caisse Lécuyer. This is clear when the fortunes amassed by members of the *haute banque* over their lifetimes are considered. For example, the estates at death of Jean-Pierre Pescatore (1855), Frédéric Pillet-Will (1860), August Dassier (1862), and Jean-Henri Hottinguer (1866) amounted to Ff.16 million, Ff.15 million, Ff.25 million and Ff.14 million, respectively.[57]

The composition of the *haute banque* changed over time. Three houses were forced to cease payments in 1848: Delessert; d'Eichthal; and Laffitte,

[55] Amongst the French Catholic members of the *haute banque* were: Davillier, Durand, Lafitte, Périer, Pillet-Will, and Seillière.

[56] A. Plessis, 'The Parisian "haute banque" and the International Economy in the Nineteenth and Early Twentieth Centuries', in Y. Cassis and P. L. Cottrell (eds), *The World of Private Banking* (Farnham, 2009), p. 131.

[57] N. Stoskopf, *Les patrons du Second Empire, 7, Banquiers et financiers parisiens* (Paris: 2002).

Blount & Cie. Furthermore, some only lasted for a generation (Ador, Vernes & Dassier; Odier; and Girard & de Waru), or two (Ardoin, Hubbard & Cie; and Lefebvre). Equally, the increasing demand for financial services during the 1850s and 1860s led to the foundation of some new houses that Mollier has termed collectively the 'nouvelle *haute banque*'. Their affairs were focused in particular upon the expanding Paris Bourse of the Second Empire.[58]

Members of the 'nouvelle *haute banque*' concentrated on one of the three major components of the business undertaken by the *haute banque*—finance—and this was coupled with trading in goods and extending trade credits. This trio of activities, often interrelated, had been fully established amongst the *haute banque* by the 1830s.[59] As such, their affairs were closely comparable to those of the developing merchant banks in London. Like their British peers, the particular importance of any one of the three major aspects of their activities—commerce, banking, and finance—varied considerably between each *haute banque* house.

International engagements were one of the characteristics of their business that distinguished this grouping from other Parisian private bankers, especially as during the Second Empire, Paris increasingly competed with London in loans to governments and the financing of companies abroad. From 1840 to 1870, Britain and France exported very similar amounts each year.[60] Britain was certainly in the lead in the 1830s and 1840s—especially until 1848—with an annual average of £6 million, compared with a very slightly negative balance of payments in France. Yet France definitely had the upper hand in the early 1850s, as well as during the 1860s, exporting in some years more than twice the amount that Britain did, even though more loans, to which foreign banks and investors subscribed, were issued in London than in Paris. However, this capital did not have the same destination: French capital flowed mainly towards Europe, whereas British capital flowed towards the high seas. Europe absorbed more than two-thirds (67.4 per cent) of French investment between 1852 and 1881, but less than a third (29 per cent) of British investment between 1865 and 1881.[61]

[58] Donon, Aubry, Gautier & Cie; Bischoffsheim Goldschmidt & Cie; Heine; Kohn Reinach & Cie; and Lévy-Crémieu & Cie. See J.-Y. Mollier, *Le scandale de Panama* (Paris, 1991); and A. Plessis, 'Le développement des activités financières à Paris au XIXe siècle', in H. A. Diederiks and D. Reeder (eds), *Cities of Finance* (Amsterdam, 1996), p. 173.

[59] Lévy-Leboyer, *Les banques européennes*, p. 434.

[60] See supra, p. 127. For France, see the estimates of M. Lévy-Leboyer, 'La balance des paiements et l'exportation des capitaux français', in M. Lévy-Leboyer (ed.), *La position internationale de la France. Aspects économiques et sociaux* (Paris, 1977), pp. 119–20.

[61] R. Cameron, *France and the Economic Development of Europe 1800–1914* (Princeton, 1961), p. 88; M. Simon, 'The Pattern of New British Portfolio Foreign Investment, 1865–1914', in A. R. Hall (ed.), *The Export of Capital from Britain, 1870–1914* (London, 1968), pp. 39–40.

Yet, the extent to which all the member houses were involved in European and intercontinental transactions has been questioned. Plessis has argued, albeit tentatively, that it is probable that the Catholic houses, of which there were many, lacked extensive foreign connections and, therefore, were not, collectively, a substantial component of cosmopolitan high finance.[62] The Catholic *haute banque* through being substantially of domestic origins lacked the extra-national linkages—particularly to the German states and Switzerland—of the Jewish and Protestant (Huguenot) houses. While only James de Rothschild was a member of a trans-European family-based partnership of five houses, all of the *haute banque*, though to varying extents, had business networks across Europe and beyond.

Family connections and a shared faith constituted the basis of some of the major linkages in *haute banque* networks. Others arose from day-to-day business, especially the provision of credits to finance French exports and imports. Trade finance involved agents, clients, and correspondents and, frequently, the constituents of a house's network fell under all three heads. One particular example of an *haute banque* network has been revealed by Plessis' analysis of Mallets' 'inventories' at the close of 1860. These itemize the agents and clients who had current accounts with the Parisian house. Most of those beyond France—400—were located elsewhere within Europe and the forty in Switzerland possibly reflect Mallets' early eighteenth-century Swiss Huguenot origins. The house's most important European linkages, by number of agents and clients, were with Britain (75) and Scandinavia (75). Beyond Europe, the network extended to India, the Levant, Mauritius, South America, and the United States. Its various components primarily reflected Mallets' particular foreign interests but they also had some basis in the geographical structure of French overseas trade, with Britain being France's most important trading partner. However, with just over half of all Mallets' agents and clients resident in France, Plessis has concluded that the house had a somewhat restricted engagement with international business. Yet, it may also equally indicate Mallets' support, through the provision of credits, of French exporters and importers (as at Le Havre) rather than solely the house's financing of domestic trade and business.[63] Indeed, it is frequently overlooked that London merchant banks during the mid-nineteenth century regularly extended credits for financing British exports, a business largely obtained through agents and clients in the thickening industrial districts of the Midlands and the North.

[62] Plessis, 'The Parisian "haute banque"', p. 131.
[63] Plessis, 'The Parisian "haute banque"', pp. 130–4.

PRIVATE BANKERS AND INDUSTRIALIZATION IN THE RHINELAND

One of Europe's many centres of industrialization was the Rhineland, a Prussian province after 1815. A long-established view of the onset of economic growth in the German states stresses its rapidity, with the drivers considered to be Prussia's launch in 1834 of what proved to be a widening custom union amongst the German states—the Zollverein—and the impact of railway building, particularly upon the coal and iron industries. This interpretation needs to be tempered. First, half of Prussian exports by value consisted of manufactures on the eve of the commencement of the Zollverein. Second, an emphasis on domestic developments during the second quarter of the nineteenth century masks the importance of an international triangular trading relationship. Growing British imports of grain from the Baltic generated within eastern Prussia a rising income for purchasing manufactures from the central Rhineland, the producers of which worked up British pig iron, and cotton and woollen yarns. Rhenish manufactures could be sold profitably on the markets of the German states beyond the Elbe but not generally elsewhere before the 1840s because of the force of British competition.[64]

As manufacturing expanded in the Rhineland, developing out of proto-industry, local providers of financial services grew in number—from about 50 in the mid-1820s to 110 by the early 1850s, and to 141 a decade later. These totals include moneychangers and bill dealers. There were far fewer specialist private bankers, possibly sixteen in the mid-1830s, and between forty and fifty by 1850, predominantly clustered in and around Cologne and Düsseldorf.[65] Most had begun as commission merchants and shippers, dealing in textiles and colonial goods. Their commercial dealings resulted in many having regular contact with the financial markets of Amsterdam and Frankfurt. Some institutionalized their extra-regional links while merchanting was still their dominant business activity. The Oppenheims in Cologne, for example, gained a relatively early formalized connection with the Paris market in 1813. It was gained through the marriage of Helene Oppenheim to Benoît Fould, the contract for which was paralleled by an agreement to establish Fould & Fould-Oppenheim with a capital of Ff.80,000. Almost a quarter of a century later, in 1836, Gebrüder Oppenheim & Co. opened in Amsterdam.[66]

[64] See R. Dumke, 'Anglo-deutscher Handel und Frühindustrialisierung in Deutschland, 1822–1865', *Geschichte und Gesellschaft*, 5 (1979).

[65] R. Tilly, *Financial Institutions and Industrialization in the Rhineland 1815–1870* (Madison, 1966), pp. 46–7.

[66] For a history of Sal. Oppenheim jr. & Cie., see M. Stürmer, G. Teichmann, and W. Treue, *Striking the balance. Sal. Oppenheim jr. & Cie. A Family and a Bank* (London, 1994). See also G. Teichmann, 'Private Banks and Industry in the Light of the Archives of Bank Sal. Oppenheim jr. & Cie, Cologne', in Cassis and Cottrell (eds), *The World of Private Banking*.

The increasing focus of the Oppenheims and their peers on banking developed as transport improvements reduced both the profitability of trading on commission and the size of business inventories. However, the shift of emphasis in their affairs from commerce to banking often occurred over many decades. For instance, Seydlitz & Merkens, considered one of Cologne's major banking houses in 1819, was not to specialize wholly in providing financial services until the 1840s.[67]

Retained profits from trading frequently provided the capital for a commercial enterprise to concentrate more on providing banking services. It has been estimated that the average capital of Rhenish private bankers by the mid-1840s was about 400,000 thalers (£57,142).[68] Their wealth was displayed to their clients and the wider community by their real estate interests. In some cases, these investments were more than demonstrations of how accumulated profits had been placed. Some proto-banking houses, such as Herstatts and Oppenheims, were substantially involved in financing the secularization of church lands that had begun during the French occupation of the Rhineland and was continued by the Prussian administration.[69] Equally, the estate of Salomon Oppenheim jr. on his death in 1829 amounted to 220,751 thalers (£31,535), of which his personal residences alone accounted for 31,686 thalers (£4,526).

Whilst a Rhineland banker's wealth probably constituted about a third of his house's liabilities, the balance comprised a range of elements. Like local merchants, private bankers took deposits on which they paid 4 per cent interest—a rate higher than that given by the region's public savings banks. Deposits were accepted from close family members, more distant relations, and the house's clients. A further major source of funds was, collectively, small savings deposits. However, the 1847 commercial crisis and the revolutions of the following year caused bank failures, which, in turn, led to what proved to be the permanent withdrawal of petty savings deposits. Contemporary estimates indicate that deposits with Cologne's private bankers declined from about nine and ten million thalers (£1.3 million–1.4 million) immediately prior to the 1847 crisis to four to five million thalers (£570,000–700,000) during 1848. Two years later, they had only recovered to six to seven million thalers (£860,000–£1 million).[70]

Other sources of a banking house's funds were clients' working balances and, in the case of major private bankers, temporary balances arising from servicing the securities of joint-stock companies, particularly those of railway companies, that they had played a part in issuing. Furthermore, liquidity could be maintained in most years by re-discounting bills with a larger bank. This

[67] Tilly, *Financial Institutions and Industrialization*, p. 52.
[68] Tilly, *Financial Institutions and Industrialization*, p. 60.
[69] Tilly, *Financial Institutions and Industrialization*, pp. 55–6.
[70] Tilly, *Financial Institutions and Industrialization*, pp. 64, 66.

might involve sending bills to the Frankfurt market—to, for instance, the Rothschild house. Some leading private banks could replenish their funds by re-discounting bills even further afield, with the Oppenheims turning to their connected family banks in Amsterdam and Paris, or through their particular business links to Brussels or Vienna.

Rhenish private bankers met most of their clients' requirements for finance through current account advances, usually in the form of overdrafts. The agreements for these facilities varied considerably. Long-established clients are likely to have had overdrafts on which there were no stipulated time limits, but relatively new customers might be required to clear debit balances within two to six months.[71] In developing this particular form of financing for commercial and industrial clients, the Rhineland's private bankers came to establish the way that credit was to be typically extended by subsequent generations of German bankers. Yet, it was hazardous and required bankers to ascertain, as far as possible, potential clients' creditworthiness since overdrafts were illiquid assets. This imperative led to an emphasis upon a likely client's wealth, demonstrated most visibly, as with his banker, by his landholdings. That selection criterion went with one another—establishing a potential borrower's reputation, particularly his track record for repaying debts. Such an approach to assessing risk, employed by many other European bankers, both private and corporate, emphasized potential clients' characters and personal habits—their 'honour' and particularly their aversion to gambling. This approach to gauging risk placed considerable weight on adherence to bourgeois mores, for both the banker and his client alike. And, it had a corollary. It was extremely difficult for a banker to require a new client to provide security for credit since this would call into question his reputation. Indeed, should it become more generally known that a banker was requiring security, this could undermine more widely his potential client's creditworthiness and, so, further endanger his business's finances.[72]

FINANCING RAILWAYS CONSTRUCTION

As elsewhere in Europe, joint-stock companies could only be established in Prussia through gaining a charter of incorporation from the government. But,

[71] Tilly, *Financial Institutions and Industrialization*, pp. 81, 83–4.

[72] See especially, M. Pohle, 'Risk, Information and Noise: Risk Perception and Risk Management of French and German banks during the Nineteenth Century', *Financial History Review*, 2 (1995), especially pp. 33–5. See also M. Pohle, 'Personal and Impersonal Exchange. The role of Reputation in Banking: Some Evidence from Nineteenth and Early Twentieth Century Banks' Archives', in P. L. Cottrell, E. Lange, and U. Olsson (eds), *Centres and Peripheries in Banking. The Historical Development of Financial Markets* (Aldershot, 2007).

before 1848, the state's Junker-dominated government and bureaucracy was antipathetic to stock and bond capitalism in general, and to corporate railway concerns in particular. A market in joint-stock securities was considered to be a direct threat to the maintenance of government credit. More generally, state officials thought that it would lead to a detrimental outflow of mortgage funds (and workers) from the land and trade. Consequently, when some Rhenish business leaders advocated during the mid-1830s the state's construction of a regional railway network, the Prussian government rejected their proposals because of the size of the investment required and the attendant risks,. The state's opposition was not solely a question of the conservatism of the political elite and their officials. It was thought by ministers and their staffs that railway development might challenge both the state-owned postal service, and the state-owned turnpike roads that had been laid after 1815 to improve communications between Prussia's dispersed provinces.[73] However, the impact of the abortive revolutions of 1848 resulted in a greater meeting of minds. This was due to the bourgeoisie and the Junkers finding common grounds in opposing the street mob, and to the Junker landlords of eastern Prussia coming to appreciate the railway's advantages for carrying grain from their estates to markets in the west.

Despite all the difficulties that had had to be resolved, 700 kilometres of railway track were laid in Rhineland-Westphalia before 1848. This had required an investment of *c.*42 million thalers (£6 million), largely raised by Rhenish bankers, especially those of Cologne. Furthermore, they had played major roles in gaining the charters of incorporation for embryonic railway companies, and attempted to ensure a harmony of financial interests between themselves and these companies once their lines were open for traffic.

The spur to establishing a regional railway network came not only from pressures to improve the area's transport system but also the Belgian initiative to construct an 'Iron Rhine' to retain thereby as great a share as possible of the transit trade between the North Sea and the German states. The first German railway, the Rhenish Railway, mooted in 1835 but only eventually chartered in 1837, linked Cologne with Brussels, and Antwerp via Aachen. Its junction with the developing Belgian system aided the raising of capital. The Oppenheim bank through J. R. Bischoffsheim placed the company's shares on the Antwerp and Brussels Bourses, and induced both the Banque de Belgique and the Belgian government to become shareholders. The Belgian interest in the Rhenish Railway was not a special case. Rhineland bankers frequently found it necessary to make agreements with their counterparts in major financial centres—in Berlin and Frankfurt, and Brussels and Paris—for placing the

[73] D. Ziegler, 'German Private Banks and German Industry, 1830–1938', in Cassis and Cottrell, *World of Private Banking*, pp. 160–1; and Tilly, *Financial Institutions and Industrialization*, pp. 96–102.

securities of railways and other local joint-stock companies. The need to tap savings beyond the Rhineland resulted in just a few of the region's bankers being responsible for obtaining these funds since only they had the required connections. It gave prominence to four or five houses in Cologne, led by Oppenheims, and one or two in Aachen, Düsseldorf, and Elberfeld, as, for example, von der Heydt-Kersten u. Söhne.

Rhenish bankers continued to be closely connected with the railway companies whose financing they had played leading roles in chartering and establishing. They became members of their directorates and administrative councils through being major shareholders. These positions gave them a continuing close knowledge of the companies' affairs, which aided how they managed the deposits that these corporations placed with them. A further gain came during the 1850s, when sixty-six industrial joint-stock companies were established in Rhineland-Westphalia. With seats on their boards and on those of the railway companies, bankers were able to guide buying orders from one client enterprise to another.

The 'railway private bankers' of Cologne were somewhat exceptional in the entrepreneurial roles that they played from the mid-1830s. They had counterparts in only a few of the German states' other financial centres—Breslau and Leipzig, and, somewhat later, Berlin—but not in Frankfurt. This city's leading bankers had appreciated the promise of railway construction at the same time as their peers in Cologne, in the mid-1830s. However, few were to develop thereafter a sustained engagement with local railway building and railway companies, and, thereby, with these affairs' significant links to the development of the coal and iron industries. As a consequence, the Frankfurt market came principally to trade in the securities of railway and manufacturing companies located elsewhere in the German states—in the Rhineland, or in Baden, Bavaria, and Wurttemberg, the governments of which issued loans to finance state-owned railway systems.[74]

In common with the major private bankers of continental Europe, members of the Parisian *haute banque* played significant roles in promoting and financing the construction of railway networks. This particular involvement was to shape to some significant degree the emergence of corporate banking within France from the early 1850s, while giving rise to both competition and cooperation amongst the *haute banque*. The new departure in their affairs began in 1835, when Emile Pereire gained James de Rothschild's support for constructing the first public line—Paris-St Germain—subsequently extended to Versailles. Following established procedures on the Paris bond market, the funds were raised by a syndicate of bankers that included Adolphe d'Eichthal and Auguste Thurneyssen. The pioneering railway's success immediately

[74] Ziegler, 'German Private Banks', pp. 161–3.

sparked competition, Benoît Fould promoting a rival line on the Seine's left bank.[75]

During the mid-1840s, the outlines of the French railway system began to be established in the form of radial spokes from Paris. Those projected to connect the capital with the Channel coast were also supported by British finance, interested in securing routes by land and sea that would link to London. The aim of English railway companies in Kent and Sussex to secure the London–Paris traffic played a part in the transfer of British savings to finance railway building in northern France. These flows were paralleled by those arising from the connections between London's merchant banks and the *haute banque*, such as the close relationship between Barings and Hottinguers.

The Parisian banks played an active role in the process of launching companies as soon as they had reached a certain size, in other words from the end of the 1830s, and then during the first real boom of the French railways between 1844 and 1846. They were instrumental in making the financial arrangements for investments—either as bidders or as guarantors that the capital required for building the line could be raised—an indispensable condition for accepting a bid. Their financial commitments were far from insignificant.[76] At the height of the boom, in 1845 and 1846, the capital issued by the railway companies[77] totalled 919 million francs, approximately three-quarters of the entire railway capital issued since the first concession of 1833. At that time, the amount subscribed by nine of the main banking houses[78] reached 225 million francs; in other words, nearly 25 per cent of the grand total. Some subscriptions constituted long-term investments, starting with the Rothschilds' 51 million francs—out of 200—in the Nord. For the most part, however, the bankers played the role of middlemen, whether simply by acting as brokers, or by reallocating, usually with a premium, all or part of these issues to their clientele. Yet these subscriptions also represented opportunities to influence companies and to be on their first board of directors.[79]

The main *haute banque* houses were all involved and both competed and cooperated with each other. Before the Crédit Mobilier was founded in 1852, they were central to three of the four large groups that took shape during this period.[80] James de Rothschild's group[81] controlled the Nord railway company.

[75] Ferguson, *World's Banker*, pp. 441–2; and R. E. Cameron, *France and the Economic Development of Europe 1800–1914* (Princeton, 1961), pp. 206–7.

[76] See G. Ribeill, *Révolution ferroviaire. La formation des compagnies de chemin de fer en France 1823–1870* (Paris, 1993), pp. 112–15.

[77] The Nord, the Paris-Strasbourg, the Paris-Lyon, the Lyon-Avigon, and the Midi.

[78] Rothschilds, d'Eichthal, Thurneyssen, Laffitte-Blount, Bartholony, Hottinguer, Mallet, Fould-Oppenheim, and Gouin.

[79] Ribeill, *Révolution ferroviaire*, p. 113.

[80] Ribeill, *Révolution ferroviaire*, pp. 97–102.

[81] Supported, among others, by Sanson Davillier, Adolphe d'Eichthal, and Francis Lefebvre.

Charles Laffitte's and Edward Blount's group,[82] backed by British capital, obtained several concessions, including Paris-Rouen and Rouen-Le Havre, but were also party to several agreements with the other groups. Finally, the group led by François Bartholony[83] controlled the Paris-Orléans and the Centre. The fourth group, run by the engineer Paulin Talabot, did not, as noted, include any member of the Parisian *haute banque* and remained relatively weak financially speaking, a weakness that was compensated for by support from the Rothschilds. Its positions were strong in the Sud-Est and it endeavoured to control the route linking Paris to the Mediterranean. From the mid-1850s, the *haute banque* continued to be widely represented on their boards of directors but it quickly ceased to play a significant role within these companies, since the bulk of power was entrusted to salaried managers.

The staple business of the English commercial banks, whether private or joint-stock, metropolitan or provincial, was the provision of credit. Nonetheless, some bankers became involved in affairs that led them to undertake investment financing. In the case of Britain's pioneering public railway—the Stockton & Darlington—it was the outcome of difficult circumstances. The line's promoters, the Peases, were unable to raise the required capital by a local share flotation. Consequently, they turned to fellow Quakers for finance: the Gurneys, private bankers in Norfolk, and the Gurney's bill brokers in London, Richardson, Overend. It is an example of private bankers' involvement at the dawn of a new transport technology but, equally, an instance of a private capital market drawn together by a shared faith.[84] The interest of Quaker bankers in railway development continued to have some considerable importance. For instance, in 1840, the Quaker partners of Wilson, Marriot & Co., Kendal, took up debentures in the Great North of England Railway on behalf of their house, themselves personally, and their local co-religionists. These investments were related to a Quaker financial network, the Kendal bank's partners having close relations with the Pease private bank east across the Pennines in Darlington. Following the opening of the Stockton & Darlington in 1825, Joseph Pease had become a railway banker, a development that included being treasurer to the Great North of England Railway.[85]

[82] Charles Laffitte was the nephew of Jacques Laffitte, and Edward Blount was a Scottish banker settled in France and very actively involved in promoting the railways. They were partners from 1834 to 1848 in the bank, Laffitte, Blount & Cie.

[83] Formed mainly of houses of Genevan and generally Swiss origin, including Pillet-Will (ousted in 1839), André & Cottier, Paccard, Dufour & Cie, and Adolphe de Waru.

[84] M. C. Reed, *Investment in Railways in Britain, 1820–1844. A Study in the Development of the Capital Market* (Oxford, 1975), pp. 115, 207, 237–8; and P. L. Cottrell and G. Ottley, 'The Beginnings of the Stockton & Darlington Railway: People and Documents, 1813–25. A Celebratory Note', *Journal of Transport History*, n.s., 3 (1975).

[85] Reed, *Investment in Railways*, pp. 254–5; Dawes and Ward-Perkins, *Country Banks*, pp. 186–7; and M. W. Kirby, *Men of Business and Politics. The Rise and Fall of the Quaker Pease Dynasty of North East England 1700–1943* (London, 1984).

Other private bankers, besides those who were Quakers, also played leading roles during the first phase of railway building in England. John Moss, a Liverpudlian private banker, was a promoter of the Liverpool & Manchester, drawn into the enterprise through his relationship with Joseph Sandars, a corn merchant who had put forward the venture. Moss went on to be the chairman of the Grand Junction Railway.[86] Samuel Brooks, who had founded the Manchester banking house of Cunliffe, Brooks & Co., was amongst the promoters in 1835 of the Manchester & Leeds, a progenitor of the Lancashire & Yorkshire Railway. He chaired its first board meeting, and his house became bankers to the railway, together with another Mancunian private bank, Loyd, Entwistle, and a joint-stock concern, the Manchester & Liverpool District Bank. Members of the Cunliffe family, Brooks' partners, were also both shareholders in the railway and providers to it of personal loans. Equally, the Loyd family had sizeable equity interests in the Lancashire & Yorkshire while supplying, personally, loan finance. Furthermore, Cunliffe, Brooks lent to the railway company on overdraft, in particular to ease its cash flow, especially when a share dividend was to be distributed. These particular banking facilities could amount to as much as £100,000. Despite the significant personal financial interests in the railway company of the partners in Cunliffe, Brooks and their respective families, the relationship between this private bank and the railway could be strained. On occasions, the house refused to lend, and, at other times, increased its charges for handling the railway company's account without any prior warning.[87]

Examination of the first railway companies' finances has found that some became reliant upon overdrafts or loans from their bankers. Banks, including private houses, offered loans, but in many instances were acting as agents for members of their clienteles. This would appear to have been the case with respect to loans made by two Liverpool private banks, Heywoods, and Leyland & Bullins, to constituent lines of the Lancashire & Yorkshire during the 1840s.[88] Many railway companies were forced to turn to loan finance because their ability to raise equity capital was constrained by legislation. Statutory restrictions led to the growing practice from the late 1830s amongst railway companies of issuing loan notes to bearer through country bankers as well as provincial share brokers.[89]

Some of the private banks that advanced short-term funds to the Lancashire & Yorkshire eventually lost its custom because of competition from joint-stock institutions. The Yorkshire Banking Co. displaced the Pontefract private

[86] Reed, *Investment in Railways,* p. 206; and Dawes and Ward-Perkins, *Country Banks,* pp. 140–1.

[87] S. Broadbridge, *Studies in Railway Expansion and the Capital Market in England 1825–1873* (London, 1990), pp. 92, 94, 99.

[88] Reed, *Investment in Railways,* p. 206; and Broadbridge, *Studies in Railway Expansion,* p. 95.

[89] Reed, *Investment in Railways,* pp. 237–8.

banking house of Leatham Tew & Co. in 1852, and the Bradford Quaker bank of Harris & Co. five years later. Although the Yorkshire Banking Co.'s management was not prepared to make advances comparable in size to those provided by either Cunliffe, Brooks or Loyd, Entwistle, they charged a lower commission and were always responsive to the railway company's financial requirements. Indeed, within a further decade, the Lancashire & Yorkshire no longer banked with Cunliffe, Brooks, the railway company's directors having turned to further joint-stock banks, both established and newly promoted.[90]

By the late 1860s, the only major continuing presence of Quaker private bankers' pioneering investments in railway development was that of the Peases. Five members of this family sat on the boards of railway companies, led by Henry, a director of five, including chairman of the Stockton & Darlington.[91] The only other comparable representation of country bankers within the railway industry was that of Charles Mangles, recently a partner in the family's Guildford banking house. He was the chairman of the London & South Western and a director of three of its subsidiary companies. However, he had ceased to be a practising banker in 1864, when his family's banking house had been converted into a limited joint-stock institution—the South East Banking Co.[92]

Unlike their country peers, London private bankers played hardly any role in financing the development of the railway system. The one great exception was George Carr Glyn, a partner in the family's City house from 1819. His considerable involvement with railway construction and operations stemmed from having been, along with other family members, a leading investor in the St Katherine Dock Company in 1825.[93] This had brought him into contact with some of those who five years later would promote the London & Birmingham Railway. He became a director of the company and in 1837 its chairman. Although relinquishing the chair in 1852 because of ill health, George Carr Glyn remained a director of the company, now styled the London & North Western, until 1870. His involvement went further and wider, being one of the supporters for establishing in 1842 the Railway Clearing House, modelled on the bankers' Clearing House in London. The manifold connections that George Carr Glyn developed with the growing railway system led to his family's London house becoming *the* railway bank. In 1845, Glyns held the accounts of 110 railway companies, which collectively

[90] Broadbridge, *Studies in Railway Expansion*, pp. 93–4.

[91] See *Bradshaw's Railway Manual...for 1869* (London, 1869), appendix, p. 87.

[92] *Bradshaw's Railway Manual...for 1869*, appendix, p. 84; and Dawes and Ward-Perkins, *Country Banks*, pp. 249–50.

[93] See R. A. Ashbee, 'George Carr Glyn and St. Katherine Dock', *The Three Banks Review*, 129 (1981); and R. Fulford, *Glyn's 1753–1953, Six Generations in Lombard Street* (London, 1953), pp. 118–19.

provided the house with deposits of £1.5 million, nearly a third of the total. This particular business remained very substantial: in 1872 railway companies' credit balances amounted to more than £4 million, accounting now for more than a third of Glyn's deposits (£11.6 million).[94]

THE EMERGENCE OF JOINT-STOCK BANKS

Some European private bankers were challenged, albeit only to some degree, by the initial growth from the mid-1820s of various joint-stock institutions. Changes in the ways that banks could be legally established were the result of either liberalizing legislation or personal initiatives, especially those of bankers. Both were reactions to the experience of the previous quarter of a century, but, in the case of continental Europe, an additional factor was the need for reconstruction after an era of sustained warfare.

There were two contrasting developmental streams within the inception of corporate banking from the 1820s. One was British and led within a decade to the considerable expansion of joint-stock deposit banking. It followed from legislation whose drafters had attempted to address the problem posed by the run of failures of English and Welsh private banks that culminated in the 1825–6 crisis.

The other stream was continental European. Its mainspring was the recognition of the need to establish corporate financial institutions for supporting directly and more effectively economic structural transformation—industrialization. Its origins can be traced back to at least the foundation of the Wiener oktroyirte Commerzial-, Leih- und Wechselbank (Chartered Bank of Vienna) in 1788 by Prince Joseph Schwarzenburg.[95] During the early 1820s, the necessity for mobilizing resources more widely and channelling them into entrepreneurs' hands was advocated by, particularly, Jacques Laffitte, a member of the Parisian *haute banque*. However, his conception of corporate banking was put into practice not in France but in The Netherlands by King William to give his new country a more robust economic foundation. It was an approach to corporate banking that was to be subsequently nurtured by the Pereires, who ultimately realized it in their foundation of the Crédit Mobilier in 1852. This banque d'affaires, despite its speculative nature, came to be a model for emulation by many others across Europe during the mid-century.

[94] See Anon, 'George Carr Glyn and the Railways', *The Three Banks Review*, 46 (1960); and Fulford, *Glyn's*, pp. 122–33.

[95] See H. Freudenberger, 'The Schwarzenberg Bank: A Forgotten Contributor to Austrian Economic Development, 1788–1830', *Austrian History Yearbook*, 27 (1996).

The British government's preparedness from the early 1820s to act, beginning with banking in Ireland, led to rapid advances. However, the developments that were to lead to the creation of the Crédit Mobilier were continually checked. Before the 1850s, apart from The Netherlands and, then, Belgium, continental European governments displayed considerable antipathy to corporate banking. The only major exceptions to this pervasive attitude were the creations of either national banks to assist state finance or transitory, specific institutions to quell financial crisis. One nominal exception was the Bavarian National Bank of 1819, which was allowed by its charter to extend loans on mortgages to industrial enterprise.[96] Consequently, within this general context, the first major challenge to private banking to be considered is British legislators' interest in securing banking stability.

The progressive changes affecting the constitution of English, Irish, and Welsh banks from 1821 took place as a result of liberalizing legislation introduced by government. Elsewhere in Europe, those who sought to found corporate financial undertakings could only do so by obtaining a particular concession from the state. This situation brought them up against the conservative attitudes of those in power, frequently to their frustration.

The apparent need to mobilize capital more widely through the fund-raising powers of a joint-stock bank for investment in developing productive purposes largely arose from contemporaries' perceptions of the British economy's advance from the mid-eighteenth century. This was especially the case in fields such as the manufacture of cotton textiles, the smelting of iron, generating steam power, and transport improvements. To this growing technological gap across the Channel was added after 1793 the negative consequences of nearly a quarter of a century of a Europe-wide military and economic struggle. This, by and large, affected detrimentally the economies of continental Europe considerably more than those of Britain.

BANKING REFORMS IN ENGLAND AND WALES

Post-war banking reform in England and Wales—the liberalizing legislation of 1826—had some of its origins not in the further difficulties of rural country bankers from 1819 but in those of their Irish counterparts. Small and weak private banks in south-western Ireland were gravely affected by financial crisis during 1820. The government reacted the following year by passing legislation that permitted, beyond a 50-mile radius of Dublin, the establishment of banks with more than six partners, in effect the foundation of provincial joint-stock

[96] D. S. Landes, *The Unbound Prometheus. Technological Change and Industrial Development in Western Europe from 1750 to the Present* (Cambridge, 1969), p. 207.

banks although without their shareholders having the privilege of limited liability. The 1821 Irish Act's provisions, especially those restricting the Bank of Ireland's corporate monopoly powers to a specified 'metropolitan area', foreshadowed the 1826 Act for England and Wales. Indeed, there was soon an attempt to put the Bank of England on the same footing, but changes in banking regulation in England and Wales were put on the back burner for some years as Parliament again considered Irish problems.[97]

The growing debate during the mid-1820s concerned with the constitution of banks was brought to a head by the severe 1825–6 crisis. Its fuse was lit by the adverse cyclical turn of the exchanges over the closing months of 1824, followed by the development of liquidity pressures within the London market, clearly evident by spring 1825. Although country banks had been considered to comprise 'a flexible capital market for turning facilities into facts', this view was increasingly challenged from summer 1825. The Castle Bank, Bristol, made redemptions in Bank of England notes as opposed to the gold that customers had requested. The matter was raised in Parliament, where it was decided that, following resumption, country bankers, like the Bank of England, were required to redeem their notes in specie when stipulated by customers. The outcome of debate at Westminster, which clearly implied that provincial houses' gold reserves should be increased, was followed within a month by some country bankers refusing to provide accommodation. Domestic unease, then stringency, was rapidly followed by the North Atlantic trade collapse and the pricking of the speculative South-American lending bubble.

In August, there were bank failures in the agricultural districts. They were largely of minor importance and so of no significance beyond their immediate business hinterlands. However, the closure of Sir William Elford's bank at Plymouth during early November, following a run, had some national importance because he was a leading spokesman for country bankers.[98] A crisis of panic proportions—it was later to be regarded as the British financial catastrophe of the first half of the nineteenth century—erupted following the bankruptcy of Pole, Thornton & Co. on 12 December. It was a London bank that was the agent for a large number of country houses. It had previously survived a run with the aid of a £400,000 loan from the Bank of England. But a bank's junior partner decided to cease employing the facility for assisting its forty-three weakened country correspondents. With Pole's closure, pressure immediately came upon its connected provincial banks and, very quickly, engulfed not only other houses in the same towns but also in their immediate districts.

[97] J. H. Clapham, *The Bank of England. A History*, I, *1694–1797* (Cambridge, 1944, rep. 1970), pp. 87–8; and L. S. Pressnell, *Country Banking in the Industrial Revolution* (Oxford, 1956), p. 507.

[98] Pressnell, *Country Banking*, pp. 505–6.

Contagion rapidly spread, fed by rumour, some of which was retailed in the press, and country bankers turned to their respective London agents for greater assistance.[99] But five of these metropolitan houses almost immediately failed, which affected directly and grievously, in turn, at least thirty-seven further provincial banks. Within three days of Pole's doors closing, there were few places in England and Wales where a country bank had not stopped payment. Other endangered provincial houses were supported by local public declarations of confidence, sometimes based upon audit or led by a mayor. Over the six months following Pole, Thornton's bankruptcy, sixty country banks failed, the numbers swollen by an almost separate northern banking crisis that had broken out in February 1826.[100]

Contemporaries blamed the Bank of England, country bankers, and London bankers alike for the crisis. They also argued that banking needed to be overhauled in order to meet the greater, growing financial needs of commerce and industry.[101] Yet, the circumstances of many of the failures put the spotlight on the adequacy of private banks' ultimate reserves—their respective partners' equity stakes—rather than the totality and diversity of banking conduct and practice, let alone particular abuses of it. The stricture that provincial banking required greater capital, first stridently aired by Thomas Joplin, a doughty campaigner for joint-stock banking, had some basis because, generally, during the mid-1820s country banks had a capital of at most £10,000, with merely twenty-six out of some 550 having the legal maximum of six partners. Lord Liverpool and Robert Peel saw a solution to the provincial banks' apparent lack of equity and, in their analysis, these houses' instability, by passing legislation to permit the introduction of joint-stock banking in England and Wales on what they regarded as the Scottish model.[102]

While the domestic banking crisis continued to rage, Bank of England directors reacted on 12 January 1826 to the signals of government intentions by constituting a committee to investigate the opening of branches. This anticipated by a day the receipt at Threadneedle Street of a memorandum from Lord Liverpool and the Chancellor, Robinson.[103] It was pithy and to the point. Unless it opened branches, the Bank would lose all its monopoly privileges. Furthermore, 'small' notes were to be abolished and the introduction of joint-stock banks, but without limited liability, was contemplated.

[99] For some examples, see R. S. Sayers, *Lloyds Bank in the History of English Banking* (Oxford, 1957), pp. 207, 208–9.

[100] Pressnell, *Country Banking*, pp. 482–8; Anon, 'Letters from a Young Lady', *Three Banks Review*, 6 (1950); and Hilton, *Corn, Cash, Commerce*, pp. 204–10, 215.

[101] For example, see R. Mushet, *An Attempt to Explain from Facts the Effects of the Issues of the Bank of England upon its Own Interests, Public Credit, and Country Banks* (London, 1826).

[102] On the alleged superiority of the Scottish model, see Ch. 2, pp. 61–3.

[103] On Robinson's minor role, see W. D. Jones, *Prosperity Robinson. The Life of Viscount Goderich 1782–1859* (London, 1967), pp. 113–17.

Directors vacillated for nearly a month, and then compromised by agreeing that their institution's corporate privileges should be restricted in like manner to those of the Bank of Ireland in 1821.

The bills for both the liberalization of the constitution of banks and the regulation of notes were rapidly introduced during February 1826. The Banking Act of 26 May 1826[104] followed the 1821 and 1825 Irish statutes in permitting the establishment of banking co-partnerships of more than six individuals beyond a sixty-five-mile radius of London but restricting the nature of the bills and notes that they could draw on the metropolis.[105]

With the prolonged business depression that followed in the wake of the 1825–6 crisis, it is understandable why only fourteen English joint-stock banks had been established by 1830. Nevertheless, while relatively few in number, this group contained various clear indications of future developments that were to lead to the eventual demise of private country banking. One of the first joint-stock banks was the conversion of Vincent Stuckey's important private interests—five West Country houses. However, it was an intimate affair, with no prospectus published to attract the stakes of its first thirty-nine shareholders in an initial nominal capital of £65,000.[106] Nearly all early joint-stock banks were small, local undertakings and so, apart from having shareholders, very comparable in nature to existing private country banks. Besides Stuckey's converted house, the other major institutions were the converted Norfolk & Norwich Banking Co. and the establishment of two large joint-stock banks in the North West: the Bank of Manchester and the Manchester and Liverpool District Bank. This was the region whose residents had displayed antipathy towards private banknotes and formal banks from the late 1780s.

The establishment of sizeable joint-stock banks in the cotton-manufacturing districts of Cheshire and Lancashire ran in parallel with the wider and greater competitive threat to country bankers arising from Joplin's activities. Immediately following the 1826 legislation, he busied himself with the establishment of new banks in northern England in places either where there was no formal banking outlet or, as in Yorkshire, where the 1825–6 crisis had created banking voids. During this initial round of activity after legislative liberalization, Joplin formed the first 'true' joint-stock bank in Lancaster, attempted to establish a comparable concern in the Lake District, and, then, participated in the foundation of the Bradford Banking Co. and the Huddersfield Banking Co.[107]

After undertaking these local promotions, his scheme for a national joint-stock bank got underway and was given further force over the opening months

[104] 7 Geo IV *c.*46. [105] Clapham, *Bank of England*, II, *1797–1914*, pp. 76, 91, 103–7.

[106] On the development of Stuckey's Bank, see P. T. Saunders, *Stuckey's Bank* (Taunton, 1928); and, for a biographical sketch of Vincent Stuckey, see T. E. Gregory, *The Westminster Bank through a Century* (London, 1936), II, pp. 144–57.

[107] W. F. Crick and J. E. Wadsworth, *A Hundred Years of Joint Stock Banking* (London, 1936), pp. 115, 145, 203.

of 1829.[108] By spring 1830, as Joplin's project came closer to fruition, with powerful financial and political backing, some country bankers conjured with the idea of establishing their own 'National Bank' upon a 'federal principle' from which joint-stock rivals would be disbarred as shareholders.[109] Joplin's endeavour, re-entitled the National Provincial Bank of England, was finally launched during May 1833 as the economy began to expand once more. Its directors purchased country banks, such as Turner & Co. at Gloucester, and negotiated for others, like Rotton, Scholefield & Co., Birmingham, and C. Forster & Sons, Walsall.[110] Somewhat comparable to the country bankers' attempted counter in 1830, Joplin had envisioned the National Provincial as a confederation with each component bank having its own local shareholders and a board of directors but, ultimately, this found no favour. His idea, a melding of local and national banking, was finally abandoned by the National Provincial's board in spring 1835, which led Joplin to give up his 150 shares in the institution. Instead, the bank's development was shaped by Daniel Robertson, its general manager from 1835, who had previously gained experience with the Commercial Bank of Scotland and the Glasgow Union Bank. By 1836, the National Provincial had forty branches and twenty-three sub-agencies throughout England and Wales, so forming a unique nationwide network beyond the Bank of England's protected metropolitan area. Many of its outlets comprised former private houses.[111]

Using the diverse data for the number of private English and Welsh country banks in business poses considerable problems. They indicate decline from the 1825–6 crisis but with most of the fall—the disappearance of between eighty-four and seventy-nine houses—taking place over the period of the national banking panic and its immediate aftermath (1825–7). Thereafter, they are in conflict with, on the one hand, official statistics indicating continuing erosion and, on the other, the *Post Office Directory* series indicating some recovery in numbers during 1828 and 1829 to postpone the onset of country banking's decline until 1830.[112]

Private banks continued to decline over the course of the mid-nineteenth century. Their numbers in both the City and West End of London fell, while the discount houses in and near Lombard Street had to contend with corporate competitors from the late 1850s. The number of country banks fell

[108] *Circular to Bankers*, 17 (14 Nov. 1828); 30 (13 Feb. 1829); 31 (20 Feb. 1829).

[109] *Circular to Bankers*, 86 (12 Mar. 1830).

[110] *Circular to Bankers*, 250 (3 May 1833); 265 (16 Aug. 1833); and 283 (20 Dec. 1833).

[111] See the evidence of D. Robertson to the Select Committee on Joint Stock Banks (1836). H. Withers, *National Provincial Bank 1833 to 1933* (London, 1933), pp. 17, 35, 44, 49–50, 56; and Reed, *National Westminster*, pp. 10–11.

[112] Pressnell, *Country Banking*, p. 11. The previous section has also drawn from P. L. Cottrell and L. Newton, 'Banking Liberalization in England and Wales, 1826–1844', in Sylla et al., *The State, the Financial System and Economic Modernization*, pp. 79–83, 89–90, 91, 92–6.

from 430 in 1830 to 311 in 1842[113] and from 252 in 1855 to 206 in 1870.[114] All in all, the number of country banks appears to have halved between 1830 and 1870.

A range of factors were responsible for the diminishing importance of private provincial banking in England and Wales over the mid-nineteenth century. As in 1825–6, country banks failed during commercial and financial crises—in 1836, 1840, and 1866. For instance, seven closed their doors during 1866. However, they were susceptible not only to violent shocks, as before 1830, but also to new, long-term forces of competitive attrition that developed from the 1830s.

By 1830, fourteen provincial joint-stock banks had been established under the 1826 Act, and in 1843, 117 were in business. Some private country bankers recognized almost immediately that they would be unable to compete profitably with their joint-stock counterparts. A few retired there and then. Others decided to convert their houses into joint-stock concerns, beginning with Vincent Stuckey's cluster of private banks in Bristol and nearby towns. His initiative was followed by many of his peers so that at least a fifth of the 117 joint-stock banks in business in 1843 had private country bank origins.[115]

Private country banking's vitality was also sapped to a degree during these years by the beginning of the fall in the use of private banknotes, and by some, but not all, of the terms of the Bank of England's 1844 charter. The private note issue, put into circulation by both country banks and provincial joint-stock banks, peaked in 1839 at £11.7 million[116] and the 1844 Bank Charter Act capped the private note issue at this level during early spring 1844. This provision arose from the legislators' intention to make the Bank of England the sole issuer of notes. The Act's purpose in this respect was also to be accomplished by no new bank being allowed to circulate notes. However, the statute's framers were more lenient to existing private country banks than joint-stock institutions. Unlike joint-stock banks, private houses retained their full note-issuing powers when they amalgamated and the arising new partnership had no more than six members. This was an important concession since there were 208 note-issuing private country banks in 1844 as opposed to 65 houses without circulations.[117]

[113] Pressnell, *Country Banking*, p. 11. This is the figure given by the official statistics. According to the *London Post Office Directory*, they fell from 628 to 480. However, the *Directory* gives the number of country bank offices rather than solely banks. Both series point to a reduction in numbers of about one quarter between 1830 and 1842 (28 per cent in the case of the official series, 23 per cent in the case of the *Directory* series).

[114] S. Nishimura, *The Decline of Inland Bills of Exchange in the London Money Market 1855–1913* (Cambridge, 1971), p. 80. The figures are drawn from *Banking Almanac*.

[115] See Cottrell and Newton, 'Banking Liberalization in England and Wales'.

[116] B. R. Mitchell with P. Deane, *Abstract of British Historical Statistics* (Cambridge, 1971), p. 450.

[117] Crick and Wadsworth, *Hundred Years*, p. 20.

The growth of joint-stock banking resumed from the 1860s, with the number of corporate institutions rising from 98 in 1857 to 117 in 1870. Renewed expansion followed in the wake of the government's liberalization of company law. The 1844 code regulating joint-stock banks was largely repealed in 1857, and in the following year further legislation allowed joint-stock banks with limited liability to be established by an almost nominal process of registration. The 1844 code's few remaining restrictive clauses were repealed in the 1862 Act that consolidated the reformed company law.[118] Despite the radical changes to the company code between 1855 and 1862, which also permitted an increase in the number of partners in a private bank from six to ten, country banks continued to decline—from 237 houses in 1857 to 206 in 1870.

By the 1870s, private country banking was 'down but not yet out'. It remained something of a force in the rural counties of England and Wales.[119] That private banks might be able to survive in the shires had begun to be clear at the mid-century. In 1850, the counties with the greatest number of private country banks included Devon, Hampshire, and Norfolk, together with those in central and northern Wales. Yet, the counties having the largest number of banking houses in both 1850 and a quarter of a century later were Lancashire and Yorkshire.[120] Their continuing substantial presence there was not solely due to these two northern counties being either the greatest in geographical extent or having sizeable populations.[121] Rather, private country banking proved able to continue in three major cities—Hull, Liverpool, and Manchester—while retaining a significant presence in one other—Leeds. Private bankers' ability to find viable niches in the financial markets of these major ports and commercial centres of the northern industrial regions is further pointed up by the opening of some new houses—four in Liverpool between 1839 and 1855, and three in Manchester between 1833 and 1843.

[118] P. L. Cottrell, 'London's First "Big Bang"? Institutional Change in the City, 1855–83', in Cassis and Cottrell, *World of Private Banking*, pp. 70, 77–9. In response to the numerous failures of joint-stock banks—twenty-three between 1836 and 1843—legislation was passed in 1844 requiring new, but not existing, joint-stock banks to obtain a charter. This would only be granted if their promoters had met a range of stipulations including specified minimum equity capitals and specified minimum share denominations. Indeed, the 1844 regulatory code was regarded as so draconian that merely four provincial joint-stock banks were established while it was in force up to 1857.

[119] See W. Newmarch, 'The Increase in Banks and Branches in the United Kingdom', *Banker's Magazine* (Oct. 1879), and reprinted in *Journal of the Statistical Society of London*, 42 (1879).

[120] Dawes and Ward-Perkins, *Country Banks*, pp. 11–12.

[121] Populations in 1851: Lancs.: 2,031,000; Yorks.: 1,798,000; Devon: 567,000; Norfolk: 443,000; Hants.: 405,000; and the Principality of Wales: 1,007,000.

As well as some new entrants into private country banking in Lancashire and Yorkshire there was a remarkably low failure rate amongst existing houses in the counties where they were most numerous—only one in Devon in 1865, two in Lancashire (1857 and 1880), and one in Norfolk in 1870. Their closures were followed by two others in Liverpool much later, in 1916; but these were the consequence of their respective partners deciding to cease business. Indeed, nearly all the private banks in Devon, Hampshire, Lancashire, Norfolk, Yorkshire, and Wales in 1850 continued in business until either the late nineteenth century or the early twentieth century, when they were acquired by joint-stock institutions during the amalgamation movement.

Private banking was still a force in London throughout the mid-century, though with a decreasing influence. The number of metropolitan houses declined from seventy in 1830 to thirty-seven four decades later. Over this period, those in the West End that had members of the nobility, gentry, and the clergy as clients fell in number from twenty-one to fifteen. The number of counterparts in the City—in and near Lombard Street—contracted to a far greater extent, from forty-nine houses to twenty-two by 1870.[122]

Compared with private country banks, London houses proved to be, in general, resilient to the shock of commercial and financial crisis after 1825–6. None failed during the 1857 crisis, and only two 'City' private banks ceased business as a direct result of the 1866 crisis, despite it being thought by contemporaries to have been the worst since 1825–6. Rather, metropolitan private bankers, especially those in the City, proved unable to stop the expansion of joint-stock banks.

A declaratory clause in the Bank of England's 1833 charter had allowed the establishment of non-note-issuing joint-stock banks within the London area. Beginning with the London & Westminster Bank, four were founded during the 1830s, followed by a fifth in 1841 and a further five over the 1850s. Their managements pioneered and further developed a new banking based upon mobilizing the deposits of the expanding metropolitan middle classes, even deliberately attracting small placements. These were gained by paying interest—a radical departure in London practice—while the opening of branches within the inner metropolitan area enlarged the banks' respective catchment areas for deposits.[123] By mid-1851, the five London joint-stock banks held deposits totalling £14.06 million and had, collectively, nineteen offices. The building of grand and substantial head offices physically marked their arrival in the capital's banking market. These were totally

[122] See F. G. Hilton Price, *A Handbook of London Bankers*... (London, 1st edn: 1876; enlarged edn, 1890–1); I. S. Black, 'Private Banking in London's West End, 1750–1830', *London Journal*, 28 (2003); and P. L. Cottrell, 'London Private Banks at the Mid-Nineteenth Century' in O. Feiertag and I. Lespinet-Moret (eds), *L'économie faite homme. Hommage à Alain Plessis* (Geneva, 2011).

[123] W. T. C. King, *History of the London Discount Market* (London, new imp., 1972), p. 173.

different in size and style to the private banks' Georgian houses. Face to face contact with a private banker in his parlour was now beginning to be superseded by the joint-stock banks' spacious but impersonal banking halls, gained by entrances deliberately designed to give easy access to the public.[124] All in all, it was a new approach to banking that was to be followed in many respects by the Crédit Lyonnais and the Société Générale in Paris during the 1860s and 1870s.

Joint-stock deposit banking expanded in the metropolis despite the attempts that had been made to check it by both the Bank of England and London's private bankers. The Bank of England refused the London & Westminster a drawing account, would not discount bills payable at the bank, and opposed its bill in parliament for it to be able to sue, and be sued, in the name of one of its senior staff. These particular measures went with the Bank of England's directors insisting that all London joint-stock banks should not be able to accept bills of exchange of less than six months—this despite provincial joint-stock banks having been freed from such an onerous restriction in 1833. The opposition of metropolitan private bankers was longer lasting—for two decades—and took the form of refusing London joint-stock banks entry to the Clearing House.

However, joint-stock deposit banking was further facilitated by the reform of taxation in 1853. The ad valorem duty on cheques was replaced by a one-penny flat rate. And, in the following year, joint-stock banks began to be admitted to the London Clearing House. Furthermore, their penetration of the metropolis included acquiring the staff—'the brains'—and, sometimes the premises, of failed private banks. This aspect took on a new form from 1859 when a joint-stock bank—the Union—for the first time took over a private bank—the West End house of Brooks & Dixon.[125]

The confrontation between joint-stock institutions and private banks in the capital became more intense during the first half of the 1860s. The liberalization of company law led to the promotion of a number of limited joint-stock banks in London. Furthermore, the wave of metropolitan corporate foundations occurred as provincial joint-stock banks acquired London private banks. This particular aspect of the competitive struggle began with the Bank of Manchester's purchase of its London agents, Heywood, Kennards & Co. It was maintained that this takeover caused 'the private banking interests in Lombard Street . . . to be . . . thoroughly irate . . . [T]he example may be followed, and several of the private banks will be absorbed'.[126] Their anger proved to be well based as, soon after, the London & Westminster bought the business of Jones Loyd & Co, one of the major houses on Lombard Street.

[124] See I. S. Black, 'Spaces of Capital: Bank Office Building in the City of London, 1830–1870', *Journal of Historical Geography*, 26 (2000).

[125] Gregory, *Westminster Bank*, I, p. 278, n. 3.

[126] *Bankers Magazine* (1863), p. 206.

The takeover was considered to be 'the greatest blow that has ever yet fallen on the system of private banking'.[127]

Joint-stock institutions' acquisition of City private banks was one factor that led to their number falling by ten between 1861 and 1865. The other was the reaction of the partners in some houses to the increasing number of joint-stock banks within the metropolis and their growing power—amalgamation. Mergers were not a new development; some had occurred during the 1850s both amongst West End and City private banks. However, during the first half of the 1860s they took place between some of the most important houses on Lombard Street—those that were major agents for provincial banks, both joint-stock and private. In 1860, Lubbocks combined with Robarts, followed in 1864 by two further, equally significant, mergers: Hanburys with Barnetts; and Glyns with Curries.[128] Amalgamation was a response to the rapidly changing business environment. Yet, doubts about its effectiveness are indicated by the Mills family's willingness in early 1866 to sell their equity interest in Glyns to a consortium of Scottish joint-stock banks.[129] The sale, planned to be finalized at midsummer, was negated by the banking market's collapse following the failure of Overend, Gurney in early May.

The development of a metropolitan money market in which the discount houses—bankers' banks—were the principals was unique. In other European financial centres, major and minor, there was to be no such 'buffer' between the banks and the quasi-central bank. The full emergence of London's very particular money market took nearly a quarter of a century, enabled initially by a number of unrelated institutional developments. The grounds were laid during the late 1820s by partners in metropolitan banking houses as a result of the searing experience of the 1825–6 crisis. They decided both to cease re-discounting bills and to lend 'at call' temporary cash balances to bill brokers. Bill brokers' ability to employ call money profitably was aided in 1829 by the Bank of England's decision to allow them discount accounts. Their regular access to the Bank of England was followed in 1833 by three months bills of exchange being exempted from the usury laws that capped the private rate of interest at 5 per cent, a liberalization which within a few further years was extended to bills of longer dates. Initially, only four broking firms dealt in bills and money: Alexander & Co.; Bruce Buxton & Co.; Overend, Gurney & Co.; and Sanderson & Co.. The most important of them by far was the 'house at the corner'—Overends.[130]

[127] *Daily Telegraph* (2 Apr. 1864), quoted in Gregory, *Westminster Bank*, I, p. 283.

[128] Cottrell, 'London Private Banks', pp. 202–3.

[129] Fulford, *Glyn's*, pp. 188–9.

[130] King, *London Discount Market*, pp. 68, 82, 89, 90, 119; and Clapham, *The Bank of England*, II, *1797–1914*, pp. 135–7.

The amount of call money placed with the discount houses grew substantially from the late 1830s, with the practice of lending 'at call' becoming increasing common amongst London banks, joint-stock and private, due in part to the decline of the market in Exchequer bills. By the mid-1850s private country banks were also placing call money with the discount houses. This contributed to bringing about the complete shift from bill broking to bill dealing. The leading discount houses, the foremost being Overends, also accepted private deposits and, moreover, had provincial agents through whom they obtained bills from throughout Britain.[131] In these various ways, the London money market married the economy's credit–deficit regions, primarily the industrial districts of the Midlands and the North, with the cash surpluses of the agricultural shires of the South and East. Bills related to manufacturing were re-discounted on the London money market with the call money and other deposits placed with the discount houses. Furthermore, banks in agricultural areas could increase the size of their investments in bills by purchases made either through their London agents or directly from the discount houses.

Joint-stock discount companies with limited liability were formed from 1856. The need for the market's principals to have greater equity capital was increased by the Bank of England's somewhat faulty diagnosis of the 1857 crisis's cause—the discount houses' inadequate reserves—and its remedy—the '1858 shuttings rule', which closed their running accounts with the Bank. Further corporate discount houses were established in 1860–1 and from 1863, but only two, the City Discount and the Joint Stock Discount, had substantial resources and so were somewhat comparable to the very profitable National Discount that had been founded in 1856. As was the case with some of the new London joint-stock banks, a number of the new corporate discount houses were conversions of private houses. Equally, some houses responded to the formation of corporate competitors by amalgamating, the most important merger being that of Alexander's with Cunliffe & Co. on 1 January 1864.

The triumph of limited liability in the London money market appeared to occur in mid-1865, with the conversion of the 'house on the corner'—Overend, Gurney—into a corporate concern. However, within less than year it became very apparent that this particular adoption of limited liability had been a desperate attempt by Overends' relatively new partners to sustain a business that over the past decade had very substantially diverged from bill dealing into highly speculative financing. As a consequence, the house's assets were immobilized—'locked up'—to a significant degree. Overends were not alone amongst the discount houses in having moved away from the business of dealing in money and credit, and the consequences were increasingly made

[131] King, *London Discount Market*, pp. 115, 122, 174–6, 182.

plain from late 1865. Two of the new corporate concerns collapsed—the London Mercantile and the Joint Stock Discount—and their closures proved to be the overture to the failure of Overend, Gurney on what quickly became known as 'Black Friday'—10 May 1866. The shutting of the doors of the venerable 'house on the corner' sparked a banking crisis that came to be considered the worst in Britain since 1825–6.[132]

Overend's demise led to the National Discount being the major player in the London money market from the mid-1860s until almost the close of the century. Its only significant corporate competitor was General Credit & Finance, a reconstituted finance company with some links to the French Société Générale. The sole private house of any stature after 1866 was Alexanders. Nonetheless, Overends' failure had created such a void in the money market that eleven new private houses were started during the late 1860s, of which three had partners who had been involved with the 'house on the corner'. Several of the new private discount houses were to develop, albeit slowly, into major businesses, like Gillett Brothers, which was founded by some of the partners in a private, Quaker Oxfordshire country bank.[133]

THE BIRTH OF 'MIXED BANKING'

The problem of post-war national reconstruction was particularly pressing within the United Kingdom of the Netherlands, which was created in 1814–15. The sovereign, William I, was anxious to translate his first-hand experience of British economic change, particularly in the southern half of his new kingdom where transformation was already occurring. In the post-1815 world, although initially unfettered by substantial fiscal burdens, this region required both capital to further its economic structural development and greater access to international markets. However, the realization of William's vision was initially hamstrung both by Parliament, which was more concerned with reducing the taxes and state indebtedness that had risen substantially over the war period, and the Amsterdam financial market's conservatism. To these impediments were added the attitudes of the management of the recently established Nederlandsche Bank, which refused to assist the king in executing his designs. William turned to the plans of a group of private bankers in Brussels, led

[132] King, *London Discount Market*, pp. 229–61; P. L. Cottrell, 'Railway Finance and the Crisis of 1866: Contractors; Bills of Exchange and the Finance Companies', *Journal of Transport History*, n.s., 3 (1975); R. A. Batchelor, 'The Avoidance of Catastrophe: Two Nineteenth-century Banking Crises', in F. Capie and G. E. Wood (eds), *Financial Crises and the World Banking System* (London, 1986); and G. E. Wood, 'The Lender of Last Resort Reconsidered', *Journal of Financial Services Research*, 18 (2000).

[133] R. S. Sayers, *Gilletts in the London Money Market 1867–1967* (Oxford, 1968).

by François Opdenbergh. They sought to set up a local joint-stock bank. With royal assent, the Algemeene Nederlandsche Maatschappij ter Begunstiging van de volksvlijt/Société Générale pour favoriser l'Industrie Nationale des Pays-Bas was established in December 1822. It changed its name to Société Générale de Belgique after the country's independence in 1830, soon becoming a 'mixed bank', in other words both a deposit bank and an investment bank.[134]

The Société Générale's decision to opt for mixed banking at the beginning of the 1830s had not really been planned but had been forced on it by the freezing of its short-term claims on companies in the Hainaut region. As Ginette Kurgan has written: 'By deciding, under the weight of circumstance, not to insist that debts be repaid, but to acquire holdings in companies by requiring that they transform themselves into limited companies, the bank embarked on a new course, largely anticipating the creation of the French and German universal banks in the second half of the 19th century.'[135] All the same, the first imitation occurred within Belgium itself, with the founding in 1835 of the Banque de Belgique on the model of the Société Générale, with which it immediately tried to compete.

THE 'NEW BANK' IN FRANCE

In France, the father of the new joint-stock bank was Jacques Laffitte, who possibly had the greatest range of commercial and industrial investments amongst the *haute banque*. In 1821, he proposed the formation of a company with a capital of Ff.240 million to finance a programme of canal construction, but the scheme was rendered abortive by the government, which would not approve the société anonyme's charter, a decision also possibly influenced by Laffitte's membership of the liberal opposition. Instead, building was financed through the Compagnie des Quatre Canaux, officially authorized in 1823. The confrontation between the interests and attitudes of the leading Parisian bankers and those of the French Bourbon state again became evident in 1825 with Laffitte's attempt to establish the Société Commanditaire de l'Industrie. This venture had even broader aims, not only the finance of new canal

[134] H. van der Wee and M. van der Wee-Verbreyt, 'Belgian Banking in the Nineteenth and Twentieth Centuries: The Société Générale and the Générale de Banque (1822–1997), in Sylla, et al., *The State, the Financial System and Economic Modernization*; H. Houtman-De Smedt, 'Société Générale from 1822 to 1848. From "Bank of the Crown Lands" to "Mixed-Type Bank"', in H. van der Wee (ed.), *The Generale Bank 1822–1897* (Tielt, 1997); G. Kurgan-van Hentenryk, *Gouverner la Générale de Belgique. Essai de biographie collective* (Brussels, 1996).

[135] Kurgan-van Hentenryk, *Gouverner la Générale de Belgique*, p. 15.

building but also the support of industry, especially mining and metals, and of land-improvement schemes. It had the *haute banque*'s backing, with the Périers alone subscribing Ff.1 million to its capital of Ff.100 million and, furthermore, drew in some of the major banking houses of Frankfurt, Geneva, and London. Despite being constituted as a *commandite* (limited partnership), Laffitte's scheme for mobilizing capital to aid economic development required state authorization. This was only forthcoming under impossible conditions, and the proposed company was also rendered still-born by the effects of the November 1825 financial crisis in France.[136] Joint-stock banks did not make their appearance in France before the 1840s.

As the economy recovered during the early 1850s, railway finance gained a new dimension through Emile Pereire's creation of the Crédit Mobilier, initially conceived as a 'railway bank'. The Mobilier's foundation followed very rapidly Emile's establishment during early 1852 of the Crédit Foncier, involving the amalgamation of embryonic mortgage banks in Marseilles, Nevers, and Paris. The Mobilier's launch was supported by members of the *haute banque*, in particular Benoît Fould but also Ernest André, Charles Mallet, and Baron Seillière.[137]

The Crédit Mobilier has come to be seen by some as the motor of the mid-nineteenth century's financial revolution. This view emphasizes the Mobilier as *the* initiator of corporate investment banking and, thereby, introducing a 'new' banking that challenged the *haute banque* and their peers in Europe's other major financial centres. Such an interpretation gives too great an importance to the Mobilier. Although it had a significant impact on continental European finance during its initial relatively brief 'life'—it had to be reconstituted in 1867—the Mobilier was not the first corporate investment bank and its foundation had not marked a revolutionary change in high finance. The Société Générale had pioneered corporate investment banking from the mid-1820s, first in the Kingdom of the Low Countries and, from 1830, in newly established Belgium. Although the Mobilier gave further prominence to the Pereire brothers, Emile and Isaac, its foundation was accomplished with the backing of members of the *haute banque*, Catholic, Jewish, and Protestant. As with the establishment of corporate banks in the German states during the 1850s, the Mobilier's creation was largely an evolutionary step, substantially taken by private bankers looking to amass the greater resources required for the ventures of the mid-century, above all railway building.

[136] B. Gille, *La banque en France au XIXe siècle* (Geneva, 1970), pp. 114–16; and B. Gille, *La banque et le crédit en France de 1815 à 1848* (Paris, 1959), pp. 109–13.

[137] J. Autin, *Les frères Pereire. Le bonheur d'entreprendre* (Paris, 1984); E. Chadeau, *L'économie du risque. Les entrepreneurs 1850–1980* (Paris, 1988).

Nonetheless, the chartering of the Crédit Mobilier was disruptive, particularly in one respect. It led very quickly to competition between the Pereires, especially Emile, and James de Rothschild for both the control of existing railway companies and for gaining concessions, above all the proposed Grand Central. Within a few years, there was an intense struggle over how the French trunk lines were to be completed and supported by branches. The Pereires held sway over the Midi (Bordeaux-Cette) and, through the Mobilier, two other companies.[138] James de Rothschild in association with François Bartholony and Paulin Talabot controlled the Nord along with three other lines.[139] James was able to oppose the Pereires on a number of fronts. Faced with the Pereires' plan to control the entire Austro-Hungarian railway network, James obtained concessions in Lombardy, Venetia, Hungary, and Serbia. In early 1855, Alphonse de Rothschild was elected a *régent* of the Banque de France. Gaining this prestigious position, the first occupied by a Jew and which outwardly placed the Paris Rothschild house amongst the *haute banque*, was followed a year later by James forming the Réunion Financière. This loose alliance of bankers and those with a railway interest enlarged James's grouping of associates as it included Edward Blount, Auguste Dassier, Mathieu Hentsch, Adolphe Marcuard, Count Pillet-Will, and the house of Paccard, Dufour et Cie.[140]

The Réunion's aim of chartering a bank that would confront the Crédit Mobilier was stymied by the government temporarily banning the foundation of further financial corporations in order both to reduce speculation and facilitate state borrowing. However, the bank—the Société Générale pour favoriser le développement du Commerce et l'Industrie en France—was successfully established during the business upswing of the mid-1860s. Its support amongst private bankers now included both Louis Bischoffsheim and Périer, while leading industrialists, merchants, and politicians also backed the bank's launch. Although the fruition of the Réunion's eight-year old plans, James de Rothschild was not amongst its public sponsors. Nonetheless, the Société Générale subsequently operated in tandem with the Paris house of Rothschild.[141]

The Société Générale joined a growing number of joint-stock banks in Paris. Corporate banking in France had begun as a response to the very considerable financial problems caused by the 1848 revolution. The Comptoir d'escompte de Paris, initially a temporary emergency institution, continued in business

[138] The Est (Paris-Mulhouse; Paris-Strasbourg; and Strasbourg-Basel), and the Ouest (Paris-Cherbourg; Paris-Rouen; Paris-St Germain; and Rouen-Le Havre).

[139] Lyon-Genève; Lyon-Mediterranée; and Paris-Orleans.

[140] Cameron, *France and the Economic Development of Europe*, p. 166; Ferguson, *World's Banker*, pp. 594–5.

[141] Cameron, *France and the Economic Development of Europe*, p. 173; and Ferguson, *World's Banker*, p. 609.

and gained a charter in 1854. Five years later, the Société générale de Crédit industrial et commercial was founded by an Anglo-French alliance of Arlès Dufour and Armand Donon on the one side and William Gladstone of Thompson, Bonar on the other, while also having the support of David Hansemann. It had the objective of fostering the use of the cheque in France, which was also the initial aim of the Société de dépôts et de comptes courants, established in 1863 by the same promoters. The setting up of the Société de dépôts et de comptes courants was aided by the partial liberalization of the French company code, as was the foundation during the same year of the Crédit Lyonnais by Henri Germain in the major industrial city on the Rhône.

The Crédit Lyonnais opened a branch in Paris within a year of its creation, followed by another in Marseilles in 1865. The initial aim for its Parisian outlet was to participate in what its directors termed 'les grosses affairs'. This objective was joined by a second after the Société Générale had successfully gained the custom of some sections of the capital's bourgeoisie by opening offices from 1865 in the outer 'quarters' of Paris. The management of Crédit Lyonnais followed suit, as well as completing a very grand building on the Boulevard des Italiens in 1878 that has been described as a 'véritable temple de la finance'.[142] The Crédit Lyonnais' full entry into Paris, together with the business strategy that its management came to share with its counterparts at the Société Générale, marked an important change in how French banking was to be conducted in the future. This very significant turning point was re-inforced by the managements of both banks opening overseas outlets from the 1870s. The consequences were even wider and greater due to the thickening affairs of the corporate specialist and overseas banks that had been established in Paris during the Second Empire.

The rapid gains made by corporate banks, particularly the Crédit Lyonnais and the Société Générale, were one important factor in initiating the beginning of the end of the Parisian *haute banque*, particularly its Catholic houses. Yet their decline from the late 1860s, considered by Plessis to have been 'relatively rapid and apparently inexorable', contrasts markedly with provincial private banking's continuing vitality.[143] Although national and regional joint-stock banks progressively opened offices on the high streets of cities and towns throughout France, those of the private bankers continued to be found in the side streets and back roads, even on the eve of the First World War.[144] Local private banking was buoyant in France. During the 1830s and 1840s, many French bankers were primarily merchants, of whom a great many were small-scale economic actors. Their principal activities were either dealing in

[142] Plessis, 'Le développement des activités financières à Paris', pp. 175–6.
[143] Plessis, 'The Parisian "haute banque"', pp. 135–6.
[144] See S. Nishimura, 'The French Provincial Banks, the Banque de France, and Bill Finance, 1890–1913', *Economic History Review*, 48, 3 (1995).

commodities or trading on commission, but they also discounted bills. As such they were regarded as bankers, and they were very numerous. Their ranks had been swelled significantly from the 1820s; for example, in central France in the Nivernais, there were six private bankers in 1827 and twelve four years later. It has been estimated that by 1870 there were over 3,000 nationally, so that somewhat more than 1,000 of France's 35,000 communes had at least one discount banker (*escompteur*).[145]

Provincial private banking came to be sustained to a significant degree by the expansion of the Banque de France's branch network, especially after 1848. The Banque's first Napoleonic branches had been rapidly closed. Instead, the three departmental joint-stock banks of issue established soon after the Restoration were joined during the mid-1830s by another six, including in Lyons, Marseilles, and Toulouse. These initiatives, together with government pressure, caused the Banque's *régents* to change their attitude towards branches that they had previously considered difficult to manage and likely to be unprofitable. Over the decade from 1836, the Banque de France opened thirteen.

The *régents*' branching policy developed further as a result of the 1848 revolution's impact. The related financial crisis, when all banks suspended specie payments, was met by the government establishing comptoirs d'escompte in the larger cities. These intermediated between those seeking to discount bills—merchants and industrialists—and the Banque de France. Another outcome of the 1848 revolution was that the Banque de France absorbed the departmental banks of issue, giving it a monopoly of note issue. By 1857, the Banque de France had thirty-seven branches, and its new charter required its *régents* to open in every département when called upon by the government. This led the Banque de France to have sixty branches in 1870, a significant expansion of its network although one that was not yet nationwide. During the last year of the Second Empire more than twenty-five départements lacked a Banque de France branch.[146]

Yet, there is a question over the extent to which the managements of the Banque de France's branches were prepared to discount, or re-discount, the bills of private bankers and 'near-bankers' that populated the provinces. Before 1848, it is clear that they would only consider bills payable in either Paris or those provincial cities and towns where the Banque had branches. This restriction was accompanied by other regulations so demanding that it has been concluded that 'they prevented many legitimate bills from being

[145] See A. Plessis, 'Banques locales, succursales de la Banque de France et financement de l'économie sous le Second Empire', in P. Fridenson and A. Straus (ed.), *Le capitalisme français. XIXe-XXe siècle. Blocages et dynamisme d'une croissance* (Paris, 1967).

[146] R. Cameron, 'France, 1800–1870', in R. Cameron (ed.), *Banking in the Early Stages of Industrialisation* (London, 1967), pp. 104–5, 109.

presented'.[147] It would appear that there were three reasons why many Parisian private bankers had been declined an account with the Banque: they were newly established and therefore lacked a 'track record'; or they had small establishments; or they were persons in whom the *régents* had little confidence. However, the Banque de France's policy changed substantially after 1848, with a considerably greater preparedness on the part of its *régents* to extend facilities to private bankers.[148]

GERMAN UNIVERSAL BANKS

Financing railways and steam-based industry was risky and difficult. These fundamental issues were fully appreciated from the outset by Rhineland private bankers and businessmen. For instance, the problems of placing 6,000 shares of the Rhenish Railway Company in 1839 had caused Camphausen to draft plans for an industrial investment bank.[149] And, the perceived need for corporate financial institutions with considerably greater resources than those of private bankers played a part in the founding of chartered joint-stock banks in some German states from the mid-1830s, beginning with the Bayerische Hypotheken- und Wechselbank (1835), followed by the Leipziger Bank (1839), the Oldenburgische Spar- und Leih-Bank (1845), and the Dessauer Bank (1847). However, Camphausen's idea of a corporate Rhineland investment institution was not to be realized before 1870. Instead, the region's private bankers benefited only to a degree from the reconstituted Bank of Prussia, the incorporation of Schaaffhausen & Cie as a crisis measure, and the founding of the Kölnische Privat-Bank. Rather, Rhenish bankers played significant roles in establishing banks beyond their immediate region—both chartered institutions and companies in which only the shareholders enjoyed limited liability (Kommanditgesellschaften auf Aktien).

Although the Prussian state was more prepared after 1848 to charter industrial and railway joint-stock companies, it remained substantially opposed to the founding of corporate banks in order to protect both the state's finances and the Bank of Prussia's position. Some of the consequences of this negative stance can be traced in the reactions of Hansemann and the Oppenheims.

Hansemann's path to founding a bank in Berlin with share capital began with his response to the impact of the 1848 revolutions upon the finances of

147 Cameron, 'France, 1800–1870', p. 105.

148 A. Plessis, 'Le développement des activités financières à Paris au XIXe', in Diederiks and Reader (eds), *Cities of Finance*, p. 170.

149 Tilly, *Financial Institutions and Industrialization*, p. 110.

the petty bourgeoisie. Seeing a solution in the Belgian Union du Crédit, he sought in 1849 to establish a comparable institution for supporting Berlin artisans and shopkeepers especially during business downswings. After being refused a charter, he realized that a credit bank could be founded in the guise of a commercial or trading enterprise. A bank in this form would not require a charter because, following French commercial law, it could be constituted as a *commandite* partnership. Its 'sleeping' members would have limited liability while the 'active' managers bore full personal responsibility for discharging its debts. He developed this scheme during 1851 with Mevissen's aid. Over its first five years of business, Hansemann's Disconto Gesellschaft generally followed a conservative business strategy, a policy that led the Prussian state to take the stance of what has been termed 'benign disdain' towards its affairs. The Prussian Bank, for example, would not recognize the Disconto Gesellschaft as a financial institution and therefore would not discount its bills.

The situation changed dramatically in 1856 with Hansemann's reconstitution of the Disconto Gesellschaft as a *commandite* partnership that had publicly issued shares, the holders of which had limited liability (Kommanditgesellschaft auf Aktien). His scheme involved two series of share issues amounting in total to ten million thalers (£1,428,571). As a *commandite*, the bank's managers—its directors—were those who were fully liable for the institution's debts, an accountability that Hansemann considered would result in their adherence to responsible business policies.

The Disconto Gesellschaft's shares were very rapidly subscribed. And within a month, there were two promotional groups, one including Mevissen and the Oppenheims, vying to found a chartered bank in Berlin. Their applications to the Prussian government provoked a seven-month long debate amongst the king, his ministers, and officials on the policy for new bank foundations, whether corporate (Aktiengesellschaften), or *commandite* (Kommanditgesellschaften auf Aktien). One outcome was a refusal at the end of March 1856 to charter either of the proposed Berlin institutions. But, this caused the proponents of banking in Berlin with greater capital to fall back on utilizing the Kommanditgesellschaften auf Aktien for their schemes following Hansemann's success. It led to the foundation of the Berliner Handelsgesellschaft, promoted by Mevissen with Conrad Carl, Paul Conrad, Johann Gelpcke, and A. Mendelssohn amongst others. Although the Prussian cabinet then considered outlawing banks constituted as Kommanditgesellschaften auf Aktien, no restrictive action was ultimately taken due to leading ministers' various political manoeuvres. Furthermore, during the month and a half of cabinet discussions over the early summer not only had two such banks been formed in Berlin, but also others in Breslau, Königsberg, and Magdeburg.[150]

[150] These paragraphs are drawn from J. M. Brophy, 'The Political Calculus of Capital: Banking and the Business Class in Prussia, 1848–1856', *Central European History*, 25 (1992).

The Oppenheim interest in founding a chartered joint-stock bank in Berlin in 1856 was but one aspect of their various involvements after 1848 with establishing corporate banks. The Cologne banking house was a founder of the Crédit Mobilier in Paris in 1852, due in part to the partners being related by marriage to one of the venture's leading promoters, Benoît Fould. The Mobilier became, during the mid-nineteenth century, the prototype of corporate investment banking. Its directors formed comparable institutions elsewhere in Europe, while the Mobilier became, during the mid-nineteenth century, the prototype of corporate investment banking—a model for others to emulate—and its directors formed comparable institutions elsewhere in Europe.

The Oppenheim's schemes in the Rhineland were stymied by the Prussian government's refusal to charter a bank, whilst they were opposed in Frankfurt due to its private bankers seeking to insulate themselves from competition. However, they obtained a banking charter in 1852 from the government of the Grand Duchy of Hesse-Darmstadt. This was on the condition that their new institution—the Bank für Handel und Industrie in Darmstadt (the Därmstadter Bank)—raised funds to complete the railway between Mainz and Aschaffenburg.[151] The Oppenheims were joined in its promotion by Mevissen of the Schaaffhausen'sches Bankverein, other Cologne bankers—Ludwig Deichmann and Viktor Wendelstadt—and a representative of their south German correspondents, Moritz von Haber. Four years later, the Oppenheims were the leaders in founding the Banque Internationale, Luxembourg. It had the objective of further developing financial channels between Paris, the south German states and the Habsburg Empire. Their main partners in the affair were Mevissen and a Frankfurt private bank, von Erlanger u. Söhne.

The development of private banking in the Rhineland had an importance not only for the region but also for how German banking came to be practised. Rhenish bankers established the practice of extending credits through current account advances, and came to link this with issuing securities—shares and bonds. They thereby laid the basis for 'mixed' banking: the combining of the provision of credit with investment finance. In turn, it led to the growth of personal interlocks between banks and their corporate clients: bankers became members of the directorates and administrative councils of the joint-stock companies that they had played leading roles in promoting. The mould for German 'universal' banking was made when some Rhineland bankers founded what was to prove to be three of Germany's major corporate credit banks: the Berliner Handelsgesellschaft, the Därmstadter Bank, and the Disconto Gesellschaft. Furthermore, Rhenish bankers were not to be their own gravediggers through establishing corporate competitors. They and their peers elsewhere in

[151] See R. E. Cameron, 'Founding the Bank of Darmstadt', *Explorations in Entrepreneurial History*, 8 (1955–6).

the German states continued to flourish during the mid-nineteenth century, and thereafter occupied a particular market niche in a symbiotic relationship with the corporate credit banks.[152] The resilience of private banking and local banking was still very evident a century after the foundation of the first German corporate credit banks.[153]

[152] See H. Wixforth and D. Ziegler, 'The Niche in the Universal Banking System: The Role and Significance of Private Bankers within German Industry', *Financial History Review*, 1 (1994).
[153] R. G. Opie, 'Western Germany' in R. S. Sayers (ed.), *Banking in Western Europe* (Oxford, 1962), p. 55.

5

The Onset of the Corporate Economy, 1870–1914

Since the mid-nineteenth century, banking history has no longer been the history of private banking. Private banks had first to share an increasing proportion of the business of banking with joint-stock banks, whose growth potential appeared limitless. And as the nineteenth century wore on, they looked increasingly marginalized, at best retaining a lucrative niche, at worst becoming a picturesque anachronism. Private bankers themselves were aware of the fate awaiting them. As early as 1864 the *Daily Telegraph* commented that the sale of the famous English private bank, Loyd, Jones & Co., to the Westminster Bank was a 'big confession that the era of private banks has passed and that the day of joint stock banking is fully and finally acknowledged. It is an avowal that one kind of banking must give way to the other, which is the better.'[1] The prediction did of course in the end materialize, though the process would greatly vary, whether in speed, extent, or significance, depending on country, region, and type of bank. The conventional wisdom about the accelerated decline of private banks in the last third of the nineteenth century only reflects part of the truth.

The history of private banking after 1870 does not fit easily into a simple 'decline and fall' framework of analysis. It is more complex and thus more interesting. The continuing relevance of private banking between 1870 and 1914 is potentially a far richer starting point. Private banking remained a key component of the banking world on three levels. The first is the world of the *haute banque*, the old established private banks mostly involved in the financing of world trade and the issue of foreign loans—what is known in Britain as merchant banking. The *haute banque* was able not only to survive, but to hold its own against the rise of the joint-stock banks. Admittedly, it was far more successful in London than in continental Europe. However, given the crucial part played by the merchant banks in the working of the

[1] Quoted in T. E. Gregory, *The Westminster Bank through a Century*, 2 vols (London, 1936), vol. 1, p. 283.

City of London, by then the undisputed financial centre of the world, there is a solid case in favour of the continued significance of private banks up to the First World War. The second level is the less glamorous world of the local and regional private banks. They provided essential banking and financial services to the many areas of continental Europe which remained untouched by the spread of the new joint-stock banks and often played a decisive role in the financing of small and medium-sized enterprises. And the third is the survival of private bankers, as opposed to private banks. The most prominent amongst them displayed a high capacity for adapting to a business world dominated by giant companies and were often able to retain commanding positions; while in the highest echelons of the profession, especially in the realm of international finance, the game continued to be played according to the unwritten rules and code of conduct of the banking aristocracy.

PRIVATE BANKS IN THE CITY OF LONDON

The decline of private banks in the last quarter of the nineteenth century was nowhere as steep as in Britain: in 1909, in the City, there were only two banks left which could be called 'private banks' in the old sense of the term.[2] And yet nowhere did private banks flourish more than in the City of London! This paradox reflects the peculiarities of the English banking system: its extreme specialization and the divorce between domestic and international banking, still prevailing in the late nineteenth century.[3] In Britain, the decline of private banks was the decline of private *deposit banks*, which had continuously lost ground ever since the appearance of the first joint-stock banks in the late 1820s. These were the banks commonly called *private banks* as opposed to the private firms engaged in international banking, which were known as *merchant banks*.[4] The largest, richest, and best connected London private banks, which formed an integral part of the banking aristocracy, were able to resist until the last decade of the nineteenth century. The leading private banks in the City were members of the London Clearing House: their number fell only slightly between 1870 and 1890, from thirteen to ten;

[2] H. Withers, R. H. Palgrave et al., *The English Banking System*, Washington, National Monetary Commission, 61st Congress, 2nd Session, Senate Document No. 492 (1910), p. 51. Glyn, Mills Currie & Co. and Robarts, Lubbock & Co. are the banks in question. These figures do not include private banks in the West End.

[3] P. L. Cottrell, 'The Domestic Commercial Banks and the City of London, 1870–1939', in Y. Cassis (ed.), *Finance and Financiers in European History 1880–1960* (Cambridge, 1992).

[4] For the sake of convenience, we will distinguish between private banks and merchant banks in the course of this chapter even though both groups were, of course, private banks.

it then fell sharply to five in 1891, and to a single one in 1914. The private banks in the West End, which were mainly linked to the aristocracy whose fortunes they managed survived a little longer, until just after the First World War for the most prestigious of them.

The London private banks remained major players in the 1870s and 1880s. They were all old-established family concerns whose partners had become extremely wealthy individuals and from the mid-nineteenth century had started to integrate into the English aristocracy. In terms of size, the London private banks were still comparable to the purely London joint-stock banks, such as the City Bank or the London and Westminster Bank: in 1884, the deposits of thirty-five London private banks have been estimated at £68 million, as against £77 million for twenty-one London joint-stock banks.[5] Even taken individually, the London private banks were by no means small, with capital and reserves usually around £500,000, and as much as £1.5 million for the outstanding London private bank of the period, Glyn, Mills, Currie & Co.[6] Significantly, Glyn's did not surrender its independence until 1939, when it was sold to the Royal Bank of Scotland.

Apart from a few exceptions, such as Coutts & Co., bankers to the royal family, the other powerful houses were part of family networks including London and provincial banks. The most impressive was undoubtedly the Barclay group, led by Barclay, Bevan, Tritton & Co. in the City, with banks in London, Norwich and East Anglia (Gurney & Co.), Cornwall, Tyneside, Yorkshire etc., and with capital and deposits in excess of £28 million in 1896.[7] The Smith group was smaller, though no less distinguished. The first Smith bank was founded as early as 1688 in Nottingham by Thomas Smith; other banks were later established in Hull, Derby, Lincoln, and Newark, as well as in the City of London under the name of Smith, Payne and Smiths.[8] Taken together, the Smith banks commanded over £9 million deposits in 1898.[9]

For the London private bankers, competition was stiffening and size was increasingly becoming a matter of concern as a result of the movement to concentrate English banking that gathered pace in the 1880s, and especially the 1890s. While an average of seven amalgamations a year took place between

[5] W. F. Crick and J. E. Wadsworth, *A Hundred Years of Joint Stock Banking* (London, 1936), p. 34.

[6] Deposits of the leading London private and joint-stock banks in 1891 (figures from the *Bankers' Magazine* and *The Economist*). *Private banks*: Glyns: £14.02m.; Barclays: £7.98m.; Coutts: £6.37m.; Smiths: £4.42m.; Robarts, Lubbock: £2.91m.; Hoare: £2.71m.; Child: £2.65m. *Joint-stock banks*: Westminster: £26.12m.; Union Bank of London: £14.34m.; London Joint Stock: £11.36m.; London and Provincial: £6.62m.; City: £6.17m.; London and South Western: £5.57m.

[7] M. Ackrill and L. Hannah, *Barclays. The Business of Banking 1690–1996* (Cambridge, 2001), p. 57.

[8] See supra, Chap. 2, pp. 47–8.

[9] J. Leighton-Boyce, *Smiths, the Bankers, 1658–1958* (London, 1958).

1862 and 1889, the figure reached eleven between 1890 and 1902.[10] Before 1890, amalgamations were mainly a result of the 1862 company law, which extended the principle of limited liability to banks. The collapse of Overend Gurney & Co. in 1866 undoubtedly dealt private banks a severe blow; while the failure of the City of Glasgow Bank in 1878, with heavy losses falling on shareholders carrying unlimited liability, led several private banks to convert into limited companies.

The Baring crisis[11] was certainly one of the major causes of the acceleration of the movement after 1890, especially as far as the absorption of private banks was concerned, with the highest ever number of amalgamations, eighteen, being recorded in 1891. But other causes should not be overlooked. The ruling interest rates from 1892 and 1895 were extremely low and may have led bankers to look for more remunerative ways of using their funds in the provinces. In 1890, the Chancellor of the Exchequer, George Joachim Goschen, complained that the banks' reserves were too small, especially those of the private banks, which did not publish balance sheets. Lastly, several banks, following Lloyds, undeniably engaged in a race for size, encouraged by the atmosphere of the time.[12] The upshot was the emergence of a dozen giant joint-stock banks with head offices in London and a wide network of branches around the country, dominated by Lloyds Bank, the London City and Midland Bank, and the London County and Westminster Bank, all with deposits approaching £100 million in 1913.

As the small provincial banks were absorbed by the big joint-stock banks, London private bankers were progressively deprived of one of their basic activities, which was to act as London agents for the country banks and carry out various financial operations on their behalf in London. To what extent these growing difficulties affected their profits is impossible to say. Fear of future difficulties and the attractiveness of takeover offers no doubt played a part. In 1884, for example, Lloyds Bank, then of Birmingham, paid Barnetts, Hoare & Co., of Lombard Street, the equivalent of seven years' profit to take them over and thus secure membership of the London Clearing House, whereas five years was considered a perfectly fair maximum as a general rule.[13] Nor should the pervasive effect of the mood of the moment be underestimated: in the 1890s, not a year went by without the announcement that one or more old-established bank had disappeared. As the *Bankers'*

[10] J. Sykes, *The Amalgamation Movement in English Banking* (London, 1926), p. 97. See also F. Capie and G. Rodrik-Bali, 'Concentration in British Banking, 1870–1920', *Business History*, 29, 3 (1982), who revised downwards these figures by distinguishing between amalgamations between banks and disappearances of banks, though remaining in agreement with Sykes chronology.

[11] See infra pp. 175–6.

[12] Sykes, *Amalgamation Movement*, pp. 48–9.

[13] R. S. Sayers, *Lloyds Bank in the History of English Banking* (Oxford, 1957), p. 148.

Magazine wrote of the takeover of the West End bank, Herries, Farquhar & Co by Lloyds Bank in 1893: 'It was only last month that we had to record an important bank amalgamation, and now another has been arranged . . . Year by year, the private firms are growing fewer in number and the large joint stock companies are becoming more powerful . . . Who would have ever thought of Herries Bank ever amalgamating with Lloyds, or indeed with any bank from the City? . . . Herries! The name is familiar to most business men because there is about it an air of antiquity, and a history that commands respect.'[14]

Survival could have been envisaged, at least in the medium term, through a few significant mergers between some of the leading houses anxious to preserve their 'private bank' character. Yet such a strategy proved problematic. In the late 1870s, a possible amalgamation between Glyn's and Coutts had already been mooted. However, the project fell by the wayside, as did a similar attempt in 1901.[15] There was later talk of the possible formation of a strong coalition of West End banks with Coutts, Herries, and Drummond.[16] In 1900, Smith, Payne and Smiths was approached by Glyn's with a view to an amalgamation which would also include Coutts, Drummond, and Childs and it was thought that Beckett, of York and Leeds, and Lambtons of Newcastle, might also join the new group.[17] All these projects, and others, failed for reasons which seem to have been mainly connected with the private bankers' state of mind, which was made up of a great deal of pride and a definite feeling of superiority. Even merging banks belonging to the same family network could prove an insurmountable obstacle. Thus all the projects for regrouping the various Smiths banks were systematically blocked by the senior partner in Lombard Street, Samuel George Smith, until his death in 1900. The Smith banks were taken over by the Union Bank of London in 1902.

One attempt, however, proved hugely successful: the simultaneous amalgamation, in June 1896, of twenty private banks, all connected by family ties, under the leadership of Barclay, Bevan Tritton & Co. in London and the Gurney & Co. group in Norwich and East Anglia, under the name of Barclay & Co. Limited. Described by the *Bankers' Magazine* as a *coup d'état*, the amalgamation established the new bank from the start as one of the country's major financial institutions. The Barclay people wanted to carry out their 'survival operation' without renouncing the private nature of their business: the bank had only 110 shareholders at its foundation and its board of directors was entirely made up of partners of the constituent banks. As Ackrill and

[14] *Bankers' Magazine*, 60 (1893), pp. 745–6.

[15] R. Fulford, *Glyn's 1753–1953. Six Generations in Lombard Stree*t (London, 1953), pp. 225–6.

[16] *Bankers' Magazine*, 60 (1893), p. 746.

[17] Leighton-Boyce, *Smiths*, p. 297.

Hannah put it, the new bank offered a 'corporate home for private bankers'.[18] Nevertheless, the new bank immediately threw itself into the race for amalgamations, absorbing fourteen banks between 1897 and 1906. And as the bank grew in size, its private type of structure was proving increasingly inadequate. At the start of the century, the private deposit bank finally ceased to be viable, even strictly in the hands of private bankers, as soon as it exceeded local or regional dimensions.

Glyn, Mills, Currie & Co was the only private bank in a position to go it alone and chose to preserve, in Algernon Mills words, 'a characteristic which we alone of all the large and serious banks possess, namely of having only one door'.[19] From 1864—when Glyn, Mills & Co. merged with Currie & Co—to 1896, the bank was de facto run by Bertram Currie (1827–96), one of the leading bankers of his day. Generally considered to be the City's most eminent financial authority, Bertram Currie was regularly consulted by Chancellors of the Exchequer, especially Gladstone with whom he was on close friendly terms. A pillar of monometallism, he was a delegate to the 1892 Brussels international monetary conference. In 1895, he took the initiative in founding the Gold Standard Defence Association and was its first chairman. With Lord Rothschild, he played a decisive role in the rescue of Baring Brothers in 1890, thus avoiding a major financial crisis. Under Bertram Currie, Glyn's was the first private bank to publish a half-yearly balance sheet. For that purpose, the firm was registered as a joint-stock bank in 1885, though the capital remained in the partners' hands. The decision proved advantageous to the bank as the magnitude of its business had been generally underestimated in the City. In 1889, the fifth year of publication, the accounts showed an increase of total assets of more than 50 per cent since 1885.

Even after Currie's death, the bank still had sufficient prestige to remain independent. And though increasingly outdistanced in terms of size by the leading joint-stock banks, it was able to retain a substantial business. In domestic banking, Glyn's had a large number of major industrial customers, including the shipbuilding and armament concerns John Brown and Vickers, two of the country's largest companies, as well as British Westinghouse, conceived on a gigantic scale in 1899 by George Westinghouse, the founder of the American parent company, Westinghouse Electric and Manufacturing Company. Characteristically, its involvement in industrial finance extended to acting as an issuing house on behalf of customers.[20] For the key to Glyn's survival probably lies in its unique position in English banking, a combination of deposit banking, investment banking, and merchant banking. More than any other English clearing bank, Glyn's remained engaged in international

[18] Ackrill and Hannah, *Barclays*, p. 59.

[19] Fulford, *Glyn's*, pp. 226–7.

[20] See P. L. Cottrell, *Industrial Finance 1830–1914. The Finance and Organization of English Manufacturing Industry* (London, 1980), pp. 228–36.

finance—if only through the overseas banks it had promoted in the 1860s—and was thus part of a far more promising field, as far as private firms were concerned, of British finance in the late nineteenth century.

For private bankers engaged in international finance, the 1870s were the dawn of a golden age which was to last until the First World War. Far from declining or simply resisting the trend towards consolidation, merchant bankers expanded enormously the scale of their activities, taking advantage of the pivotal role played by the City of London in the growth and globalization of the world economy.[21] In many respects, this was a continuation of the transport revolution of the mid-nineteenth century and the ensuing boom in world trade which, admittedly, grew more slowly after 1873. Nevertheless, it was not before 1870 that the City established itself as the undisputed financial centre of the world, following in particular France's defeat in the Franco-Prussian War of 1870 which temporarily put to an end the convertibility of the Banque de France's banknotes.

London's position as the financial centre of the world meant, firstly, that the bulk of world trade was financed through the medium of bills of exchange drawn on London; and secondly that, with over 40 per cent of the world's total exported capital in 1913 raised on its markets, London was the leading centre for the issue of foreign loans and equities. The acceptance and issuing businesses, it should be remembered, were the two pillars of merchant banking. Their development offered tremendous business opportunities, both to existing firms and to newcomers, as did the many other financial services offered by the City. London was home to the world's largest stock market (the nominal value of the securities quoted on the London Stock Exchange was larger than the New York and Paris Stock Exchanges combined), insurance market (with Lloyds of London), shipping market (with the Baltic Exchange), and others, not least merchanting (in addition to being a financial centre, the City remained a major commercial centre).[22]

Consider, first, acceptances, the 'bread and butter' of merchant bankers' income. Estimates of their total volume show an increase from between £50 to £60 million in 1875–6 to about £140 million by 1913 (though they recorded a sharp fall in the early 1890s (from £90 to £50 million) following the Baring Crisis). The merchant banks were probably responsible for some 70 per cent of this total, i.e., around £100 million.[23] This was a large sum, though hardly

[21] On the City of London, see in particular Y. Cassis, *La City de Londres, 1870–1914* (Paris, 1987); R. Michie, *The City of London. Continuity and Change, 1850–1990* (Basingstoke and London, 1992); D. Kynaston, *The City of London, I: A World of its Own 1815–1890* (London, 1995), *II: Golden Age, 1890–1914* (London, 1995). For an international comparative perspective, see Y. Cassis, *Capitals of Capital. The Rise and Fall of International Financial Centres 1780–2009* (Cambridge, 2009).

[22] On this latest point, see especially Michie, *City of London*.

[23] S. Chapman, *The Rise of Merchant Banking* (London, 1984), pp. 105–7, 209.

higher than the deposits of the largest clearing bank of the day, the London City and Midland Bank, which reached £93.8 million in 1913 and £125.7 million in 1914. This puts the merchant banks' position into perspective. Even in their golden age, they were able to thrive as private banks by occupying what would be called today a 'niche' market—though acceptances were far from an insignificant 'niche' and formed one of the essential 'mechanisms' of the City.

Foreign issues also increased dramatically in the second half of the nineteenth century. British overseas investment has been estimated at about £195 to £230 million in 1854.[24] By 1913, it had jumped to some £3.5 to £4 billion, with major booms of capital exports taking place in the early 1870s, the 1880s, and the decade preceding the war. The two biggest borrowers were governments and railway companies. Loans to governments—including dominion and colonial governments and municipalities—made up as much as 63 per cent of British capital invested overseas in 1875, but only 29.9 per cent by 1913.[25] Railway securities, on the other hand, rose from 25.4 to 40.6 per cent (representing some £1.5 billion), as the world's railways mileage more than quadrupled—from 205,000 to 925,000 kilometres—between 1870 and 1906. American railways took the lion's share in the 1870s and 1880s, leading to close collaboration between private bankers on both sides of the Atlantic. Investment in all types of companies operating abroad rose considerably in the two decades preceding the First World War, with the most spectacular mania taking place in South African gold and diamond mining.

Private banking houses, in the first place merchant banks, were able to maintain their hold on the huge London issuing business, being responsible for 37.2 per cent of all new issues between 1870 and 1914. Admittedly, they lost market share—from 53 per cent between 1870 and 1874 to 35 per cent in years 1910–14—mostly to the joint-stock banks and the overseas banks. Nevertheless, they remained, by a significant margin, the largest single intermediary in the London market, where a vastly increased amount of new overseas issues were floated in the pre-war years.[26]

As a result, the number of merchant banks and other private banks involved in international financial operations increased substantially during this period. Estimates vary, as such banks were involved in a variety of activities. Merchant bankers, for example, continued to call themselves very discreetly, and very imprecisely, 'merchants'. Furthermore, a great many firms describing themselves as 'private banks' consisted of brokers (bill brokers, bullion brokers, and so on), money-changers, arbitrageurs, and other 'financiers'. The total number of such private banks increased from forty-five in 1885 to 105 in 1914–15,

[24] P. L. Cottrell, *British Overseas Investment in the Nineteenth Century* (London, 1975), p. 13.
[25] A. R. Hall, *The London Capital Market and Australia, 1870–1914* (Canberra, 1963), p. 13.
[26] Hall, *The London Capital Market and Australia*, p. 72.

according to some estimates, but from thirty-nine in 1890 to sixty-three in 1910 according to more conservative ones.

Part of this increase was due to new arrivals from abroad. Waves of immigration had contributed to the development of British commercial and financial enterprises since the beginning of the nineteenth century. As far as the leading houses are concerned—Lazard Brothers, A. Rüffer & Sons, Arthur H. Brandt & Co., König Brothers, Neumann, Luebeck & Co., Robert Fleming & Co.—they all settled in London between 1870 and 1914. Independent financiers such as Ernest Cassel also arrived during this period. However, in all financial centres, the number of small private banks, most of them actually brokers, increased with the globalization of the world's capital markets. What characterized the City of London was the unique position enjoyed by the top merchant banks. Despite a relatively modest size, a small group of private firms continued to have the upper hand on the most important international financial operations conducted in the world's leading financial centre, keeping at bay the competition from joint-stock banks, overseas banks, and foreign banks.[27]

There was a high degree of continuity at the top of the merchant banking hierarchy throughout most of the nineteenth and twentieth centuries. Several of the 'prime movers', to use Alfred Chandler's terminology, established during the late eighteenth or early nineteenth century, were able to maintain their competitive advantage. This was certainly true of Rothschilds and Barings, but also of Morgans, Schroders, and Hambros. Latecomers have been relatively few—Kleinworts and Samuel Montagu in the 1850s, Lazards in the 1870s, Warburgs in the 1930s—while steep decline and extinction proved equally rare, Stern Brothers being the most notable case. This does not mean that no change took place during a century and a half. Some firms proved more dynamic than others at a certain stage of their history and, as we shall see, the ranking occasionally changed. But these were the houses which sustained long-term market dominance and at times moved ahead of the pack.

In the early 1870s, N. M. Rothschild & Sons was the undisputed number one merchant bank in the City of London. It had retained this position in 1914, though the contest was then a little closer. Capital is the clearest measure of the Rothschilds' superiority, though other indicators point in the same direction. In 1873, it stood at £6.5 million, higher than any British bank, including the joint-stock banks, and nearly three times higher than that of their nearest rival, Baring Brothers, which then reached £2.2 million.[28] Forty years later, in 1913,

[27] See Y. Cassis, 'London Banks and International Finance, 1890–1914', in Y. Cassis and E. Bussière (eds), *London and Paris as International Financial Centres in the Twentieth Century* (Oxford, 2005), pp. 107–18.

[28] N. Ferguson, *The World's Banker. The History of the House of Rothschild* (London, 1998), p. 1043; P. Ziegler, *The Sixth Great Power. Barings, 1762–1929* (London, 1988), p. 376.

N. M. Rothschild's capital had only slightly increased, to £7.8 million, but it was still substantially larger than Kleinwort's £4.4 million, the new number two.[29] It should also be remembered that until the early years of the twentieth century, the various Rothschild houses were part of a single family partnership, whose capital reached the staggering sums of £34 million in 1874 and £37 million in 1904, when the partnership was finally dissolved.[30]

There has been some discussion about the decline of the English Rothschilds and the re-ordering of the City hierarchy. Early assertions of their continued dominance up to the First World War have subsequently been questioned, in particular in view of their low level of acceptances—an activity which the Rothschilds had never really cared for—and the extreme caution attributed to Natty, later Lord Rothschild, the senior partner between 1879 and 1915.[31] Niall Ferguson's archive-based study of the House of Rothschild has done much to clarify the issue, if only by providing hitherto unavailable figures, revealing the true magnitude of their operations. The decline of N. M. Rothschild & Sons in the thirty to forty years preceding the war must be put into perspective: it was a relative decline—in the sense that the firm grew more slowly than some of its competitors—rather than an absolute decline. Ferguson observes that apart from the 1870s, which were exceptional years, the firm's performance after 1879 was not markedly worse than during the period 1830–69.[32] The lasting strength of established powers should never be underestimated, especially in the case of such an overwhelming financial power as the Rothschilds.

Whatever their conservatism, the Rothschilds were still prepared to make large investments in selected areas. It was in the 1880s and 1890s that they built their mining empire—in gold, diamonds, non-ferrous metals, and oil. In many respects, this was a joint venture between the London and Paris houses, though each was more particularly involved in certain fields. N. M. Rothschild & Sons were mainly active in the South African gold and diamond industry—through the Exploration Company, a highly profitable mining syndicate they established in 1886, through their own investments in a number of gold mining companies (Consolidated Goldfields of South Africa, Rand Mines), and, most spectacularly, through their financial backing of Cecil Rhodes who, in 1888, succeeded in concentrating the bulk of the South African diamond extraction in the hands of De Beers Consolidated Mines, of which N. M. Rothschild were the second biggest shareholder. In the late 1880s, with the Paris house, they

[29] Ferguson, *World's Banker*, p. 1045; J. Wake, *Kleinwort Benson. The History of Two Families in Banking* (Oxford, 1997), p. 472.

[30] Ferguson, *World's Banker*, p. 1039.

[31] See, for example, S. D. Chapman 'Aristocracy and Meritocracy in Merchant Banking', *British Journal of Sociology*, 37, 2 (1986); Y. Cassis, 'Merchant Bankers and City Aristocracy' and S. D. Chapman, 'Reply to Youssef Cassis', in *British Journal of Sociology*, 39, 1 (1988).

[32] Ferguson, *World's Banker*, p. 809.

took a controlling interest in the Rio Tinto Company, which at the time accounted for more than 10 per cent of the world copper production, with the London house acting as the company's bankers. In 1911–13, Rio Tinto and De Beers were Britain's two most profitable companies, with respectively 38 and 34 per cent return on shareholders' equity.[33]

The Rothschilds were also able to maintain their traditional dominance of government bond issues. Between 1865 and 1914, they handled, solely or in partnership, nearly three quarters of the foreign public sector issues floated on the London capital market.[34] Competition increased in the twentieth century, especially from the revitalized Barings, the ambitious Morgans, and the formidable Ernest Cassel, who took over some of the projects they deemed to be too risky, especially in Egypt, but the Rothschilds maintained their supremacy until the First World War. To this must be added the immense prestige of the house and of its senior partner, Nathaniel Mayer (Natty), the first lord Rothschild. He might not have possessed his grandfather Nathan's financial genius, but for nearly forty years, until his death in 1915, he was the City's most influential banker, at the crossroads between finance, politics, and society.

For most of the nineteenth century, Baring Brothers had been N. M. Rothschild's great rivals—though not quite their equals. Firmly ensconced in second place in 1870, they had slipped back a little by 1914. Between these two dates, the bank grew very rapidly at first, was almost bankrupt in November 1890, and then made a quite remarkable recovery. Until 1890, Baring Brothers was the largest acceptance house in the City—its acceptances had grown from £6.7 million in 1870 to £15 million in 1890.[35] While it was no match for Rothschilds on the government loan market, it dominated that of the American railways that was booming in the 1870s and 1880s, with 28.7 per cent of all issues floated by merchant banks in London between 1865 and 1890; only J. S. Morgan came close with 21.6 per cent.[36] Baring Brothers was also one of the first merchant banks to float a British industrial company: in 1886, they handled the conversion of Guinness, the famous brewing company, into a public company by issuing £6 million of preference and ordinary shares. The firm and the individual partners made a total benefit probably in excess of £500,000.[37]

It was in Argentina, however, that the bank was most active, handling about a quarter of the inflow of British capital into the country, which surged from £25 million in 1885 to £150 million in 1890. Dealing in Argentinian securities

[33] Y. Cassis, *Big Business. The European Experience in the Twentieth Century* (Oxford, 1997), pp. 87–8.

[34] Ferguson, *World's Banker*, p. 814. Government loans represented over 90 per cent of the issues handled by N. M. Rothschild & Sons between 1852 and 1914.

[35] Ziegler, *Sixth Great Power*, pp. 180, 202.

[36] See D. Adler, *British Investment in American Railways, 1834–1898* (Charlottesville, 1970).

[37] Ziegler, *Sixth Great Power*, pp. 199–200.

was risky but potentially highly profitable. Baring Brothers and above all its senior partner, Edward Charles Baring, from 1885 the first Lord Revelstoke, lost all sense of prudence. Barings earned a lot of money in Argentina, but their over-commitment brought about its collapse in 1890.[38] The bank was locked up in too many illiquid assets, in this case Argentinian issues no longer taken up by the public, especially the doubtful Buenos Aires Supply and Drainage Company, which Revelstoke imprudently decided to back in November 1887. The bank was no longer able to pay the £16 million of acceptances that fell due on 15 November 1890.

The bankruptcy of such an important and prestigious bank would have had devastating consequences not only in London but all over the world. A rescue operation was immediately organized by the governor of the Bank of England, William Lidderdale, through concerted action by the banking community. Lidderdale strengthened the Bank of England's position by borrowing £1 million worth of gold from the Russian government and £3 million from the Banque de France, through the Rothschilds. He obtained the support of the British Cabinet, which refused to intervene directly but promised to support the Bank by leaving sufficient funds in its own account. Finally, he set up a guarantee fund to cover any losses that might result from the liquidation of Baring Brothers, to which all the main banks contributed. The Bank of England put in £1 million; Glyn, Mills, Currie & Co., and N. M. Rothschild & Sons £500,000 each; Raphael & Sons £250,000; A. Gibbs & Sons and Brown, Shipley & Co. £200,000; Barclay, Bevan, Tritton & Co., Smith, Payne & Smiths, Robarts, Lubbock & Co., J. S. Morgan & Co., and C. J. Hambro & Sons £100,000. The joint-stock banks were also called on to contribute: the London and County Banking Company, the London and Westminster Bank, and the National Provincial Bank each put in £750,000. The London Joint Stock Bank and the Union Bank of London put in £500,000 each.

The London private bankers thus played a key role in the rescue of Barings, though the contributions to the guarantee fund can be interpreted in a number of ways. It is true that the weight of the joint-stock banks could now clearly be felt. Yet apart from the governor of the Bank of England, the two key people on whom the success of the entire operation ultimately depended were two private bankers, Bertram Currie and Natty Rothschild; and their financial contributions, as well as that of their fellow private bankers, were far from insignificant. In many respects, this reflected the position of private bankers in

[38] On the Baring Crisis, see in particular Sir J. Clapham, *The Bank of England. A History*, 2 vols. (Cambridge, 1944); Fulford, *Glyn's*; G. Chandler, *Four Centuries of Banking* (London, 1964); L. S. Pressnell, 'Gold Reserves, Banking Reserves and the Baring Crisis of 1890', in C. R. Whittlessey and J. S. G. Wilson (eds), *Essays in Money and Banking in Honour of R. S. Sayers* (London, 1968); Ziegler, *Sixth Great Power*; Kynaston, *The City of London, I: A World of Its Own*, 1993; Ferguson, *World's Banker*; J. H. Flores, 'Information Asymmetries and Conflict of Interest During the Baring Crisis, 1880–1890', *Financial History Review*, 18 ((2011), pp. 191–215.

the City: they were already outdistanced in terms of size, but still had the upper hand in terms of influence, and of leadership of the profession.

Baring Brothers was reorganized as a limited liability company—Baring Brothers & Co. Ltd. Its capital was fixed at £1 million, taken up by members of the family, friends, and friendly firms, including Hopes, of Amsterdam, and Hottinguers, of Paris, which took respectively £50,000 and £40,000. There is no doubt that Barings remained a private bank. As Rodolphe Hottinguer wrote to Francis Baring: 'I hope that it will quite soon be possible to do away with the word limited imposed by circumstances . . .'[39] The new bank was helped back onto its feet. The fact that it was not fundamentally insolvent at the time of this crisis—its assets could be liquidated easily—certainly played a role in this rebirth, as did the determination of the younger generation which took control—first and foremost John Baring, the second Lord Revelstoke. From the beginning of the twentieth century, it was once more a force to be reckoned with in the world of international finance, especially in Argentine matters and in Russia, where it regained the government's confidence—another example of the resilience of established financial powers.

J. S. Morgan & Co. experienced steady growth as an issuing rather than as an accepting house, though the firm of course continued to finance trade. This strategy was decided upon by Junius Morgan and his partners as early as 1873. Their first issue for a foreign country had been for Chile in 1867 and their first incursion into Europe was an £8 million Spanish government loan, which was brought out in 1869. More important, however, in terms of both prestige and profits, was the £10 million loan they issued for France in October 1870 in the midst of the siege of Paris by the Prussian armies. The risk was high (the loan had been refused by Rothschilds and Barings), but so was the reward, the total profit on the transaction netting £1.5 million.[40]

At first, J. S. Morgan's greatest strength was in corporate issues in London, especially American railways, in this, they were second only to Barings. In the United States, Pierpont Morgan, Junius's son, soon established a leading position in railway finance. As far as government loans were concerned, J. S. Morgan usually had to content itself with playing second fiddle during the 1870s and 1880s, being a mere participant in syndicates led by others. However, it had the opportunity to take a leading part in connection with the US Treasury's refunding of the long-term Civil War debt: almost $1.4 billion of federal bonds were issued between 1871 and 1879 and a substantial part sold in London, with Morgans solely or jointly sponsoring some of the offerings.[41]

[39] Baring Brothers Archives, HC 7.1.1615.

[40] K. Burk, *Morgan Grenfell 1838–1988. The Biography of a Merchant Bank* (Oxford, 1989), pp. 33–5.

[41] See V. Carosso, *The Morgans. Private International Bankers, 1854–1913* (Cambridge, Mass., 1987), pp. 176–200.

By the 1880s, J. S. Morgan was successfully penetrating other parts of the world: in the first place, Argentina, where it sponsored its first government loan in 1884, leading to fierce competition with Barings in the following decades, though the two firms remained allied. Morgans benefited from its strong American connection as Argentina sought access to both the London and New York capital markets. J. P. Morgan's prominent position in America proved decisive in British government finance. In 1900, the Chancellor of the Exchequer, Sir Michael Hicks Beach, placed half the £10 million loan—one of several destined to finance the war in South Africa—in New York through Morgans. It was the prelude to a much greater involvement in British war finance. J. S. Morgan was by then one of the leading issuing houses in the City, probably in third position behind N. M. Rothschild and Baring Brothers. However, the bank's ultimate control was moving to America. In 1910, J. P. Morgan & Co. became a partner in the London firm, renamed Morgan Grenfell & Co., with a 50 per cent stake and a claim to half its profits.

C. J. Hambro & Sons established its credentials as an issuing house a little earlier. In the 1870s, it issued four loans on behalf of Sweden and Norway and remained throughout the period closely connected to Scandinavia. But it had its hour of glory in 1881 when Everard Hambro, with the help of Barings, took the lead of a syndicate formed to issue a £29 million Italian loan, making it a point of honour to float it only in London and without the intervention of the Rothschilds.[42] Thirty years later, it had probably been overtaken by Morgans, though it had built a stronger accepting business.

The rise of J. Henry Schröder & Co. and Kleinwort, Sons & Co. was more spectacular. Schroders reached some prominence as an issuing house in the decade preceding the war, especially through South American corporate and municipal issues; it established its reputation with the £15 million Sao Paulo Coffee Valorisation Loan (declined by Rothschilds), destined to stabilize coffee prices.[43] Kleinworts only dipped a toe in the water, underwriting and selling in London the issues of commercial enterprises (notably Sears Roebuck & Co. and F. W. Woolworth & Co.) brought out by Goldman Sachs and Lehman Brothers in New York.[44]

However, it is through their accepting business that both firms moved up among the leaders. By 1913, Kleinworts and Schroders were the City's two largest accepting houses, with respectively £14.2 million and £11.7 million, far ahead of their nearest followers, Barings (£6.6 million), Brown Shipley (£5.1 million), and Hambros (£4.6 million). Barings' collapse in 1890 undoubtedly opened the way for Kleinworts' and Schroders' pre-eminence. However, their success must primarily be attributed to their strong entrepreneurial drive.

[42] B. Bramsen and K. Wain, *The Hambros, 1779–1979* (London, 1979), pp. 309–18.
[43] R. Roberts, *Schroders. Merchants and Bankers* (Basingstoke and London, 1992), pp. 139–43.
[44] Wake, *Kleinwort Benson*, pp. 122–4.

Both firms, especially Kleinworts, were prepared to take greater risks and work with a lower ratio of capital to acceptances than other firms (1:4 for Schroders and 1:5 for Kleinworts as against a commonly agreed practice of 1:3–4).[45] They were also mainly working with the world's two fastest growing economies, the United States and, especially, Germany. The latter connection was to cost them dear with the outbreak of the war in August 1914.

The use of the Chandlerian concepts in the context of merchant banking can, however, be misleading. In no way can merchant banking be described as an oligopolistic industry and prime mover advantages were of little value in a field requiring little investment. In fact, behind this small elite group, a host of highly successful firms were competing for a share of the market. Some dated back to the early nineteenth century. Frühling & Goschen, Antony Gibbs & Sons, Fredk. Huth & Co., Wm Brandt & Co., Brown Shipley & Co. were all founded during the Napoleonic wars, though none of them was ever to reach the very top. The same can be said of latecomers such as Samuel Montagu & Co., M. Samuel & Co., Emile Erlanger & Co., Seligman Brothers, or Speyer Brothers.

Then there were the many firms finding themselves on the borderline of merchant banking, especially the merchant houses engaged in a certain amount of accepting business and slow to abandon trade. Collectively, merchants remained the strongest group in the City until the beginning of the century, with firms such as Blyth, Greene, Jourdain & Co., Curtis Campbell & Co., J. K. Gilliat & Co., Edward Johnston & Co., Ogilvie, Gillanders & Co., Rathbone Brothers, and others, which were massively represented on the boards of directors of the major financial institutions, including the Bank of England.[46] With the decline of merchanting, some of these firms went into an irreversible decline and eventually disappeared. Others turned themselves into 'investment groups', controlling a variety of overseas subsidiaries in trading, manufacturing, mining, or financial enterprises, which involved a degree of banking and financial activity.[47] However, the distinction was firmly established with the foundation of the Accepting Houses Committee in 1914. With the old-established private deposit banks nearly all gone, the Accepting Houses Committee's twenty-one members now formed the very heart of the City *haute banque*.[48]

[45] Roberts, *Schroders*, pp. 130–2; Wake, *Kleinwort Benson*, pp. 125–6.

[46] On their position in the banking world, see Cassis, *City Bankers*, pp. 58–60, 85–9.

[47] S. D. Chapman, 'British Based Investment Groups before 1914', *Economic History Review*, 38, 2 (1985). See also his *Merchant Enterprise in Britain from the Industrial Revolution to World War I* (Cambridge, 1992); and G. Jones, *Merchants to Multinationals. British Trading Companies in the Nineteenth and Twentieth Century* (Oxford, 2005).

[48] For a list of the first members of the Accepting Houses Committee, see infra, Ch. 6, p. 219.

THE PARISIAN *HAUTE BANQUE*

Private international bankers were in a different position in continental Europe. For one thing, the scope for international financial operations was more restricted than in Britain, and for another joint-stock banks were able to secure a larger share of this business. However, conditions were far from identical across Europe. The *haute banque* remained stronger in France than in Germany, and was also able to prosper in smaller countries with old banking traditions such as Switzerland.

The turning point in the history of the Parisian *haute banque* can be fairly accurately dated. Its dominance over French international finance reached its peak in 1871–2, with the issue of the war indemnity loans, amounting to Ff.5.2 billion (£208 million), which was the levy required by Bismarck to pay for France's defeat by Prussia in the 1870 war. This was a huge sum, by past and future standards: the Allies had only required 700 million francs in 1815, and not until the First World War would issues of such magnitude be floated on the European capital markets. The French *haute banque*, led by de Rothschild Frères, was able to keep control of these issues, with the new joint-stock banks very much in the position of junior partners, though the latter's influence was to increase in the process. Alphonse de Rothschild, then aged forty-four, was the man in command. Head of the French house since his father James's death in 1868 and a *régent* of the Banque de France, he was constantly consulted by members of the government and senior civil servants, and had a meeting with Bismarck in his capacity as special adviser to Thiers, the head of the French government.

The preamble was the payment of 200 million francs levied on Paris for its resistance to the Prussian army—the siege of Paris lasted from September 1870 to January 1871. The Germans would only accept Ff.100 million in banknotes with the rest being paid in bullion and drafts on major bankers. The Banque de France provided a Ff.210 million advance to the city of Paris for six months, while a banking syndicate guaranteed the immediate delivery of the required bullion and drafts. The syndicate was entirely made up of members of the *haute banque*, with a 40 per cent share for Rothschild and 10 per cent each for six old established houses (Fould, Sellière, Hottinguer, Mallet, André & Marcuard, and Pillet-Will).[49] The big deal, however, was the payment of the Ff.5 billion. Thiers and his finance minister, Pouyer-Quertier, decided to raise the money through two government loans: the first, for a sum of Ff.2 billion was issued in June 1871, the second, for Ff.3 billion, in July 1872. Rothschild and the *haute banque* kept their hold over the first indemnity loan, securing the bulk of the lucrative commissions paid for underwriting it, placing it with

[49] J. Bouvier, *Les Rothschild* (Brussels, 1983), p. 211.

the public, and supplying the bullion and drafts; and of the gains deriving from the difference between buying and selling prices. According to Jean Bouvier, the Rothschilds' commissions must have reached, at the very least, Ff.5.3 million, as against a mere Ff.200,000 for Crédit Lyonnais.[50]

The newly-formed joint-stock banks bitterly resented having been left out. 'It was Rothschild and his friends, in cooperation with the Banque de France, who made the Ff.200 million advance to the city of Paris . . . It was that same group which reserved the two billion loan for itself, and it was by favour that the credit institutions were able, at the last minute, to get all together an insignificant part of the 20 million commission gained by the Rothschild syndicate', complained the Crédit Lyonnais.[51] In order to play a more active role in, and get a larger share of the second indemnity loan, they decided to join forces. On 8 August 1871, they formed a coalition against Alphonse de Rothschild and his London cousin Lionel. The coalition, named the syndicat des établissements de crédit, was led by the Banque de Paris and included all the major joint-stock banks (whether investment banks, such as the Banque des Pays-Bas, which merged with the Banque de Paris in 1872, or deposit banks, in particular the Crédit Industriel et Commercial, the Comptoir d'escompte, and the Crédit Lyonnais) with the exception of the Société Générale which enjoyed closer links with the Rothschilds. The Société Générale, however, joined the group in 1874.

The new syndicate embarked on a press campaign and government lobbying in order to get their share of the issuing business. The move proved successful, though for the time being the Rothschild group remained in control, with nearly two thirds (64.2 per cent) of the various operations connected with the Ff.3 billion loan of July 1872, in particular the underwriting of Ff.1 billion and the delivery of bills to the value of Ff.700 million. Nevertheless, with its 35.7 per cent share, the syndicate, led by the newly formed Banque de Paris et des Pays-Bas, had gained a foothold. From then on, an ever increasing share of the foreign loans issued in France was handled by the *établissements de crédit.*

Of course, the opposition between private and joint-stock banks should not be overemphasized. Private banks continued to be included in the various groupings which presided over French international finance before the First World War and many a private banker remained highly influential. However, as distinct, independent firms, the members of the *haute banque* had to surrender their control over international financial operations. In that respect, they differed markedly from their English counterparts: the Parisian *haute banque* was a smaller group than the London merchant banks, in terms of both number and—with the exception of de Rothschild Frères—size. The

[50] Bouvier, *Les Rothschild*, p. 214. [51] Quoted in Bouvier, *Rothschild*, p. 216.

frontiers of the group had necessarily been shifting since its formation during the Restoration, though by the late nineteenth century departures were no longer compensated for by new entries as longevity was becoming one of its hallmarks. By the late nineteenth century, the *haute banque* had become more narrowly defined and did not include more than a handful of old-established and highly prestigious houses. No official list existed, as membership was based on status rather than function. However, by the turn of the century, the group was usually considered to be made up of the eight following banks: de Rothschild Frères; Hottinguer et Cie; Mallet Frères et Cie; Vernes et Cie; Mirabaud et Cie; de Neuflize et Cie; Heine et Cie; and Demachy et F. Seillière.[52]

De Rothschild Frères remained, by a wide margin, ahead of the field. So much so that in his depiction of the French banking scene before 1914, the contemporary observer, E. Kaufmann, distinguished three groups among Parisian private bankers: Rothschild, the *haute banque*, and the other large Parisian private banking houses, considering de Rothschild Frères as a 'unique house'.[53] Between 1874 and 1904, around 60 per cent of the Rothschilds' combined capital was concentrated in the Paris house. This gave de Rothschild Frères, with minor variations from one year to the next, a capital of more than Ff.500 million (£20 million).[54] This was absolutely huge by French and indeed European standards. Mallet Frères & Cie for example, a full member of the *haute banque* though admittedly not the largest, had a capital of Ff.7.1 million in 1913, including reserves and partners' deposits.[55]

The 'decline' of the Rothschilds in the last quarter of the nineteenth century has already been discussed in connection with the English branch. Their French cousins were broadly in the same position of legendary wealth and immense prestige inevitably leading to a more cautious attitude at a time of increased competition. The difference was that competition came from different quarters in the two countries: from more audacious private houses in England (Morgans, Schroders, Kleinworts, or the financier Ernest Cassel); and from the ever more powerful joint-stock banks in France (Banque de Paris et des Pays-Bas, Crédit Lyonnais, Société Générale, Comptoir d'escompte). This was particularly true for the issue of government loans, where the Rothschilds had reigned supreme until the 1870s, but eventually had to consent to cooperate.

The *haute banque*'s, and especially the Rothschilds', reputation and connections enabled them to secure a loan contract, while the joint-stock banks'

[52] E. Kaufmann, *La Banque en France* (Paris, 1914), pp. 166–74.

[53] Kaufmann, *La Banque en France.*

[54] Ferguson, *World's Banker*, pp. 1039–41.

[55] A. Plessis, 'The Parisian "Haute Banque" and the International Economy in the Nineteenth and Early Twentieth Century', in Y. Cassis and P. L. Cottrell (eds), *The World of Private Banking* (Farnham, 2009), pp. 127–40.

huge resources and network of branches ensured that the loan would be placed with the public. This was particularly the case with the Russian government loans between 1888 and 1914, when France became Russia's main creditor. French investment in Russia increased from Ff.1.5 to Ff.12.6 billion during this period. The Rothschilds had handled all the Russian loans issued in London between 1870 and 1875 (totalling £69 million), though they withdrew from Russian affairs in the 1880s in protest at the Russian government's anti-Semitic policy. They returned, however, and issued several Russian loans between 1888 and 1901, though they entrusted the placing to the big deposit banks. They also had to share about half the Russian affairs of the period with the Banque de Paris et des Pays-Bas which entered the fray in 1888 by securing the French share (60 per cent) of a Ff.450 million government loan, leading a syndicate including all the major French banks.

Besides government loans, where they remained a major force until 1914, the strength of the Rothschilds increasingly lay in their investments. They were still involved in railway companies, in the first place with the Compagnie du chemin de fer du Nord, where they held five directorships in 1869, and six in 1933. In the 1880s and 1890s, in connection with the London house, they acquired extensive interests in minerals, especially in non-ferrous metals and petroleum.[56] In 1880 and 1881, the French house took part in the formation of the Société minière et métallurgique de Peñarroya, taking 40 per cent of its capital, which was fixed at Ff.5 million at its official foundation in Paris in October 1881. In 1913, Peñarroya produced 80 per cent of Spain's silver and 60 per cent of its lead, and by 1917, its capital had grown to Ff.73 million. A second area of interest in non-ferrous metals was in the company Le Nickel, which had been established in Paris in May 1880 with a capital of Ff.6.25 million, in order to develop rich nickel deposits in the French-owned island of New Caledonia, in the Pacific Ocean. The Rothschilds were not among the founders, but had advanced funds to its initiator, the Australian John Higginson, taking a 25 per cent stake in the 1880s. The third area was copper: in 1885, they took a 37.5 per cent interest in the Compagnie du Boléo, formed with an initial capital of Ff.6 million in order to exploit deposits in Mexico.

In oil, the Rothschilds' interests were mainly centred in Russia: in 1886, they purchased the Batum Oil Refining and Trading Company, known as Bnito by its Russian initials, and proceeded to market Russian kerosene, linking Russian suppliers with western European distributors. In 1912, they sold their entire oil interests in Russia to Royal Dutch, becoming the company's largest shareholders. By 1900, the Rothschilds had invested some Ff.58 million in their

[56] This paragraph is mainly based on J. P. McKay, 'The House of Rothschild (Paris) as a Multinational Industrial Enterprise: 1875–1914', in A. Teichova, M. Lévy-Leboyer, and H. Nussbaum (eds), *Multinational Enterprise in Historical Perspective* (Cambridge, 1986), pp. 74–86. See also Ferguson, *World's Banker*, pp. 878–1, and Bouvier, *Les Rothschild*, pp. 255–9.

Russian oil operations and a combined minimum of Ff.11.5 million in Peñarroya, Le Nickel, and Boléo. All in all, the Rothschild capital invested in oil and non-ferrous metals might have been as high as Ff.100 million, nearly a sixth of the capital of the Paris house.[57]

The role of the Rothschilds before 1914 should thus in no way be underestimated. In the end, it derived from the sheer magnitude of their financial means. This consisted in the first place of the fortune of the partners and their families, which was far in excess of the bank's capital, fixed at Ff.50 million in 1905, mainly for fiscal reasons: Alphonse and Gustave, who died respectively in 1905 and 1911, each left estates in the region of Ff.250 million (£10 million). But it also included the vast sums of money entrusted to the bank by crowned heads, aristocrats, and wealthy capitalists, as well as the funds at its disposal for payments on behalf of large companies and foreign governments. The bank could thus rely on huge resources and was by far the largest buyer of bills on the Paris financial market, with a portfolio reaching Ff.500 million. Even in the early twentieth century, a withdrawal of funds by de Rothschild Frères was felt on the Paris capital market. Moreover, like their London cousins, they remained the leaders of their country's financial community.

The other members of the *haute banque* had been overshadowed from the start by the Rothschilds. They were further pushed into the background by the rise of the *établissements de crédit*, especially in the issuing business. However, this did not mean, as is too often assumed, that they were in 'decline'. There is no general study of the Parisian *haute banque*, but the evidence at hand, especially the case studies undertaken by Alain Plessis, suggests a healthy growth. Mallet Frères, for example, saw its total balance sheet increase almost threefold (from Ff.17 to Ff.45 million) between 1860 and 1913, mostly as a result of its international activities. Acceptances, in particular, grew more than tenfold (from Ff.1.5 to Ff.18 million), making up 33 to 40 per cent of total liabilities, as against 9 per cent in 1860, while current accounts increased from Ff.5.5 to Ff.22.5 million, with the proportion of foreign accounts rising from one to two thirds.[58]

This state of affairs was akin to that of many a London merchant bank. Mirabaud was extremely successful during the Belle Époque. With a capital of Ff.6 million, its aggregate profits reached Ff.25 million between 1903 and 1913, on top of the 4 per cent interest paid on this capital. Apart from the traditional activities of the *haute banque*, Mirabaud was actively engaged in company promotion, especially mining, where they had gained expertise through their early association with the Rothschilds (Peñarroya, Boléo) and through the Société Française d'Etudes et d'Entreprises, a fully owned consulting engineering company. They struck gold in 1904, when they bought the concession

[57] McKay, 'House of Rothschild', pp. 81–2. [58] Plessis, 'Haute banque parisienne'.

for a copper mine in Serbia and formed the Compagnie Française des Mines de Bor, with a capital of Ff.5.5 million. The company was to prove extremely profitable, posting a net profit of Ff.2.5 million in 1910 and Ff.5 million in 1912. Moreover, although Mirabaud only held a (controlling) minority stake, they were entitled to a 1 per cent commission on the gross proceeds of the sales of copper and other products, including gold, extracted from the mines.[59]

The members of the *haute banque* held a number of assets that enabled them to play a role out of proportion to the actual size of their firms. The first was their prestige and network of relationships. They were thus in a position to place amongst their wealthy clients the securities issued by the big banks. They partly remained bankers to foreign governments, paying the coupons of the loans they had issued in the past: Hottinguer & Cie, for example, had large deposits from the Russian and Turkish governments. Though on a smaller scale than the Rothschilds, they were entrusted with the funds of very wealthy customers, whether private or corporate, and by the early twentieth century, private portfolio management was becoming their main activity. Their second asset was their massive presence on the boards of the major railway companies, public utilities, insurance companies, investment banks and, last but not least, the Banque de France. In that respect, the Parisian *haute banque* closely resembled its London counterpart. Such directorships were sources of both income and influence. Their third asset was their joint ownership and control of a major financial institution, through which they could remain involved in large financial operations—the Banque de l'Union Parisienne, founded in 1904 by six leading houses (Mallet, Mirabaud, Heine, Hottinguer, Neuflize, and Vernes) in association with the Société Générale de Belgique, which became France's second largest *banque d'affaires* behind the Banque de Paris et des Pays-Bas.

The *haute banque* was only the upper stratum of Paris's private banks. According to E. Kaufmann, there existed around 150 other private banking houses in the French capital in 1913, some of which were sufficiently rich and well established to be often considered as belonging to the *haute banque*, others no more than mere brokers and canvassers.[60] Their functions were varied, reflecting the vitality of Paris as a financial centre in the pre-war years. Those closest to the *haute banque* were primarily concerned with private wealth management. Others were more akin to financiers, being engaged in company promotion, investment (on behalf of rich customers or on their own account), arbitrage, and other financial dealings, often in connection with a

[59] A. Plessis, 'Une maison de la haute banque parisienne, les Mirabaud, et le financement des entreprises de la fin du XIXe siècle à la Seconde Guerre mondiale', in P. Marguerat, L. Tissot, and Y. Froixdevaux (eds), *Banques et entreprises industrielles en Europe de L'Ouest, XIXe et XXe siècles: aspects internationaux, nationaux et régionaux* (Neuchâtel, 2000).

[60] The following passage is based on Kaufmann, *La Banque en France*, pp. 175–9.

specific geographical area. Traditional banking—taking deposits (at attractive rates) and extending short-term loans—had not been entirely given up. A few houses specialized in discounting commercial bills whilst others mainly granted acceptance credits.

As a financial centre, Paris acted as a magnet for foreign bankers. Several private banks were part of international family networks, with branches in other centres, especially London and New York. This was the case with such houses as Lazard Frères, E. N. Raphael, Seligmann Frères, or A. J. Stern. Others worked in close connection with French or foreign big banks: Bardac, for example, was closely linked to the Imperial Ottoman Bank, I. Camondo & Cie (who came from Constantinople) with the Banque de Paris et des Pays-Bas, and Gans & Cie were partly owned by the Deutsche Bank. As in London, the largest merchant houses had diversified into banking. Most prominent among them was Louis Dreyfus & Cie, world-famous grain merchants with strong interests in Russia.

Some of these houses had been established during the first half of the nineteenth century and even though they had lost some ground, their partners and their families had remained part of Paris high society, with occasional incursions into the worlds of politics, the arts, or sciences. There were, however, a few dynamic newcomers who managed to reach the top ranks of the subtle hierarchy of French finance. One of them was Lazard Frères & Cie, founded in 1858 by the brothers Alexandre, Elie, and Simon Lazard, with a capital of just over Ff.1 million.[61] The Lazards were a Jewish family from Lorraine, which traced its origins back to Bohemia. Their business began in the early 1840s in the United States, first as dry goods merchants in New Orleans and then, from 1848, as general merchants in San Francisco. By 1858, they were established in both Paris and San Francisco and had started the classical move from trade to banking and finance. Their banking activities were acknowledged in the partnership agreement of 1864 (which included their cousins Alexandre Weil and David Cahn), and, in 1876, the decision was taken to liquidate their commercial activities, the San Francisco house becoming officially a deposit-taking bank on 11 September 1876. The same year, the London agency, created in 1870 during the Franco-Prussian War, became known as Lazard Brothers.

The next step was taken in 1880 when Alexandre Weill established Lazard Frères in New York (following the same route as other German-Jewish investment banks, such as Kuhn Loeb, J. & W. Seligman, Lehman Brothers, Goldman Sachs, and others),[62] while the San Francisco house was gradually disposed of. There are unfortunately no available figures to take measure of the

[61] See A. Sabouret, *MM Lazard Frères et Cie. Une saga de la fortune* (Paris, 1987), pp. 13–59.

[62] See B. Supple, 'A Business Elite: German-Jewish Financiers in Nineteenth-Century New York', *Business History Review*, 31, 2 (1957).

growth of the business. However, given the lifestyle adopted by the partners in Paris and the estates left by some members of the family (Helène Lazard, Simon's wife, left around Ff.24 million on her death in 1915[63]), there can be little doubt about the prosperity of a business mainly involved in discounting and arbitraging. Private banking could still lead to financial prominence in late nineteenth- and early twentieth-century France.

BERLIN, FRANKFURT, HAMBURG, AND COLOGNE

The notion of *haute banque* does not easily fit the world of German banking—even though several members of the London and Parisian *haute banque* were of German origins. The reasons have to be sought in the socio-political context as much as in the economics of German banking. The concept of *haute banque* might refer to a banking function, but it more accurately describes a social status, which, by the late nineteenth century, had become characterized by great wealth, an aristocratic lifestyle, and connections with the world of high politics. German private bankers were unquestionably very wealthy, but the lack of a capital city of the calibre of London and Paris was a hindrance to their reaching a truly global influence. Of course, as the new Reich's political and financial capital, Berlin experienced a tremendous expansion after 1871. And yet it never really lost its provincial character. In any case, the rise of Berlin to *Weltstadt* coincided with the growth of the newly-formed joint-stock banks, the four 'D' banks—Deutsche Bank, Dresdner Bank, Darmstädter Bank, and Disconto-Gesellschaft. Moreover, even after 1871, Berlin as a financial centre never entirely superseded the role of cities such as Frankfurt, Hamburg or Cologne, which all counted old and powerful private banking dynasties.

As in France, no more than a handful of banking houses could be considered as belonging to the German equivalent of the *haute banque*. There were probably some twenty-five private banks of some significance in Germany during this period, but they were scattered around a number of cities—not only financial centres such as Berlin, Frankfurt, Hamburg, and Cologne, but also lesser places such as Munich, Essen, Nuremberg, Breslau, Chemnitz, or Karlsruhe.[64] Among them, only a few could be considered as forming a banking aristocracy: S. Bleichröder, Mendelssohn & Co. and R. Warschauer & Co. in Berlin; M. A. von Rothschild & Söhne, Jacob S. H. Stern, Lazard Speyer-Ellissen, and Gebrüder Bethmann in Frankfurt; L. Behrens & Co. and

[63] Sabouret, *Lazard Frères*, p. 58.

[64] M. Pohl, 'Festigung und Ausdehnung des deutschen Bankwesens zwischen 1870 und 1914', in *Deutsche Bankengeschichte* (Frankfurt, 1982), vol. 2, p. 263.

M. M. Warburg & Co. in Hamburg; and Sal. Oppenheim Jr & Cie in Cologne. This was the core group whose frontiers inevitably shifted between 1870 and 1914, with the decline—and occasional disappearance—of some, the merger and takeover of others, and the rise of a few newcomers. A second tier of influential private banks included Delbrück, Leo & Co, Gebrüder Schickler (the two were to merge in 1910 to form Delbrück Schickler & Co.), Hardy & Co., and Gebrüder Arnhold in Berlin; A. Levy, and J. H. Stein in Cologne; S. Hirschland in Essen; B. Metzler seel. Sohn & Co. in Frankfurt; and Merck, Finck & Cie in Munich.

The problem faced by the German private banks was that the new universal banks were competing in all fields of banking activity, from the provision of credit to industrial customers and the financing of foreign trade to the issue of securities on behalf of foreign companies and governments. Private bankers had thus lost the relative pre-eminence they enjoyed in the 1870s and early 1880s, although they retained a highly significant role within the German banking system.

In Berlin, Gerson von Bleichröder (he was ennobled in 1872) became the most renowned banker in the aftermath of German unification.[65] As Bismarck's personal banker and adviser, he enjoyed enormous advantages, especially in terms of connections and information. He became more involved in industrial finance: in 1871, he floated the iron and steel concern Vereinigte Königs- und Laurahütte, formed out of the coalmines and ironworks of Count Henckel von Donnersmark; and in 1873, he was involved in the creation of Hibernia, one of Germany's largest coal mining companies. But above all, he played a central role in government finance, both at national and international levels. Bleichröder was instrumental in the nationalization of the German railways network in the 1880s, advising the government and dealing in securities on its behalf. He also took a leading part in the issue of a number of foreign loans, often in connection with Bismarck's foreign policy, especially in Russia—though he opposed Bismarck's Lombardverbot of November 1887, forbidding the Reichsbank from accepting Russian securities as collateral for loans, which lasted until 1894 and led to France replacing Germany as Russia's main creditor.

Bleichröder's political and diplomatic roles are far better documented than his banking and financial activities and it remains impossible to assess his bank's position. Some indication is provided by his fortune, estimated in 1892 at 30 to 40 million marks (£1.5 to 2 million), making him the richest banker in Berlin;[66] and, in his heyday, private banks still held the upper hand in German banking and finance. The bank entered a long decline after Gerson von

[65] On Bleichröder see F. Stern, *Gold and Iron. Bismarck, Bleichröder and the Building of the German Empire* (New York, 1977).

[66] Stern, *Gold and Iron*, p. 477.

Bleichröder's death in 1893, though its reputation enabled it to remain in the forefront until 1914 and take part in a number of international syndicates.

We know little about Mendelssohn & Co., which both preceded and outlived Bleichröder as Berlin's and probably Germany's leading private bank, apart from the fact that they derived their strength from their unique position as bankers for Russia.[67] The vast deposits that Russia maintained with them for the service of its coupons and the manipulation of its loans were a constant and notable source of profits. Mendelssohn also chose not to be involved in industrial finance, a unique policy for a German bank, and it hardly ever had one of its partners sitting on the supervisory board of a limited company. Its affairs were nonetheless very prosperous, with the main partners, Robert and Franz von Mendelssohn, both being millionaires in pounds sterling.[68] The third major Berlin private bank, R. Warschauer & Co., reached great eminence in the three decades following German unification, especially through their Russian and Italian business. However, in need of capital following the retirement of a partner, they were taken over by the Darmstädter Bank in 1904.[69]

As a financial centre, Frankfurt suffered a continued decline after its annexation by Prussia in 1867 and its integration into the German Reich in 1871. In terms of people employed in the financial sector, Frankfurt had fallen behind Berlin by 1882, behind Hamburg by 1895, and behind Munich by 1907.[70] Frankfurt remained a rich city, but the big financial operations were increasingly passing it by: in 1884, when a new Russian bond issue was floated in Germany, subscriptions could only be made in Berlin, and no longer simultaneously in Frankfurt. The number of private banks declined faster than in other German cities (from 148 in 1895 to about 100 by 1914) with, amongst others, J. Dreyfus & Co. and Erlanger & Co. being both taken over in 1908, the former by the Commerz- und Disconto Bank, the latter by the Dresdner Bank.

However, it was the closure of M. A. Rothschild & Söhne and the transfer of its business to the Disconto-Gesellschaft in 1901 which most vividly signalled the city's fallen status. The Frankfurt Rothschilds, though overshadowed by their London and Paris cousins, remained part of Europe's most formidable financial power. The absence of male descendants from this branch of the family was clearly a problem: Amschel Mayer, the oldest of the five brothers

[67] See W. Treue, 'Das Bankhaus Mendelssohn als Beispiel einer Privatbank im 19. und 20. Jahrhundert', in C. Lowenthal-Hensel, *Mendelssohn Studien. Beiträge zur neueren deutschen Kultur und Wirtschaftsgeschichte*, Band 1 (Berlin, 1972); P. Emden, *Money Powers of Europe in the Nineteenth and Twentieth Centuries* (London, 1938).

[68] R. Martin, *Das Jahrbuch der Millionäre Deutschlands*, 19 vols. (Berlin, 1911–14).

[69] Emden, *Money Powers*, p. 251.

[70] C.-L. Holtfrerich, *Frankfurt as a Financial Centre. From Medieval Trade Fair to European Banking Centre* (Munich, 1999), pp. 172–6.

and head of the Frankfurt house, died childless in 1855 and was succeeded by his nephews Mayer Carl (1820–86) and Wilhelm Carl (1828–1901). But the decline of the business and the unwillingness of their cousins in London, Paris or Vienna to return to their homeland must at least partly be attributed to Frankfurt's dwindling fortunes.

Hamburg, by contrast, prospered as a port city to become Germany's second financial centre behind Berlin. Here, the rising force was M. M. Warburg & Co., who officially became bankers—as opposed to moneychangers—in 1863.[71] The business prospered in the following decades, consisting mainly of commission transactions in foreign exchange and commercial bills with large trading houses and banks, together with a still limited amount of new issues. By 1889, it had reached a respectable, though still fairly modest size, with a balance sheet total just exceeding 35 million marks (£1.75 million) and twenty-three employees.[72] The bank really took off, especially as an issuing house, in the 1890s under the guidance of the four brothers, Max (1867–1946), Paul (1868–1932), Felix (1871–1937), and Fritz (1879–1964) Warburg. Their first major operation, which greatly enhanced the prestige of the house, occurred in 1905, with the issue of the Imperial Japanese government sterling loans—they received an underwriting participation of £1 million from the London group for the first loan of £30 million and, with the Deutsche-Asiatische Bank, shared the leadership of the German syndicate for a second issue of £30 million, divided in equal tranches between Britain, the United States, and Germany.[73]

From then on, Warburgs were involved in a series of first-class issues both domestic (they were invited to join the Reich Loan Consortium in 1905) and international, as well as in colonial affairs.[74] By 1913, the bank's total balance-sheet had risen to nearly 120 million marks (£6 million).[75] This breakthrough was to a large extent due to the bank's American connection. M. M. Warburg's close relationships with Kuhn, Loeb & Co., one of New York's leading investment banks, derived from two marriages: in March 1895 Felix Warburg married Frieda Schiff, the only daughter of Jacob H. Schiff, Kuhn Loeb's senior partner; and six months later his brother Paul married Nina Loeb, a daughter of Solomon Loeb, the firm's co-founder and Jacob Schiff's father-in-law. Felix Warburg became a partner in Kuhn Loeb in 1897. Paul Warburg at first stayed in Hamburg, but eventually moved to New York in 1902 and joined Kuhn

[71] R. Chernow, *The Warburgs. A Family Saga* (London, 1993), p. 13.

[72] R. Rosenbaum and A. J. Sherman, *M. M. Warburg & Co. 1798–1938. Merchant Bankers of Hamburg* (London, 1979), p. 91.

[73] Rosenbaum and Sherman, *Warburg*, pp. 101–2.

[74] See Rosenbaum and Sherman, *Warburg*, pp. 103–12; Chernow, *Warburgs*, pp. 141–7; B. Barth, *Die deutsche Hochfinanz und die Imperialismen. Banken und Aussenpolitik vor 1914* (Stuttgart, 1995).

[75] Rosenbaum and Sherman, *Warburg*, p. 107.

Loeb while still retaining his partnership in M. M. Warburg.[76] The transatlantic business generated by this close alliance was immensely valuable, especially for the German house which ranked among Germany's leading private banks by the eve of the war.

Finally, in Cologne, a smaller financial centre, Sal. Oppenheim Jr. & Cie retained a prominent position both in the Rhineland economy and as a bank of national significance. Growth, however, was slow, with a balance sheet total hardly increasing over the entire period, from under 70 million marks in 1875 to over 80 million in 1913, with troughs of fewer than 40 million in 1895 and 1902.[77] From this perspective, one could talk of a relative decline, though the bank's standing remained high, especially as it did not publish its balance sheet. Caution and risk avoidance were clearly the order of the day. Nevertheless, Oppenheim remained strong in industrial finance, especially in the old heavy industries, through its historical links with the iron and steel company Phoenix AG, with which it had been involved since the 1840s and which it supported during the slump of 1873; and through its contribution to the foundation of several other leading concerns in the Ruhr (Union AG, Dortmunder Union, GBAG, Eschweiler Bergwerks, Fortuna AG, Harpener Bergbau). It was less fortunate in the new industries, losing several millions in its electrical industry ventures. The bank's other strength was in insurance, another of its historical fields of interest, with the Colonia insurance company, founded in 1839; the Kölnische Rückversicherung, founded in 1852 and one of the world's largest reinsurance companies by the turn of the century; and the Concordia Lebensversicherung, established in 1853 and the second largest insurance company in Germany in 1914. Unlike Mendelssohn, Bleichröder, and later Warburg, Oppenheim did not play any leading role in government loans after 1871, though it regularly took part in the national and international syndicates.[78]

From the 1880s, the credit banks increasingly played the leading role in international finance. The foundation of the Deutsche Bank in 1870 was specifically designed for that purpose: a group of private bankers led by Adelbert Delbrück decided to join forces for their international business activities, with the specific aim of freeing German international trade from its dependence on British finance. The Deutsche Bank, however, grew increasingly independent and competed directly against its original founders in both domestic and international finance. The issuing syndicates came to be dominated by the Deutsche Bank and the Disconto-Gesellschaft rather than by Mendelssohn and Bleichröder, especially in the new areas of capital exports,

[76] See Chernow, *Warburgs*, pp. 45–56.

[77] M. Stürmer, G. Teichmann, and W. Treue, *Striking the Balance. Sal. Oppenheim jr. & Cie. A Family and a Bank* (London, 1994), p. 486.

[78] Stürmer et al., *Striking the Balance*, pp. 255–90.

such as Latin America, China, or the Ottoman Empire—though personal links still played a part in the financial relationships with the United States and Russia.[79] Private bankers were usually offered a share of the business, and could occasionally take the lead, like Mendelssohn in Russia but for a typical Argentinian loan issued in London, Paris, and Berlin at the turn of the twentieth century, Baring Brothers would have as partners the Disconto-Gesellschaft and the Banque de Paris et des Pays-Bas rather than a private bank.[80] In the same way, overseas banks were specially set up to finance German trade and foster German investment abroad. However, unlike their English counterparts, which were formed by private bankers, these overseas banks were established by the large credit banks, though sometimes with the participation of the leading private banks. For example the Deutsche Überseeische Bank was founded in 1886 by the Deutsche Bank, and the Brasilianische Bank für Deutschland in 1887 by the Disconto-Gesellschaft and its close ally the Norddeutsche Bank; while the three most important shareholders (with 550 shares each out of 5,000) of the Deutsche-Asiatische Bank on its foundation in 1889 were the Deutsche Bank, the Disconto-Gesellschaft, and Bleichröder.[81]

The situation was similar in industrial finance. Private bankers played a decisive role in financing early German industrialization, in many ways paving the way for the credit banks and prefiguring their practices. By the 1880s, they could no longer contemplate an intervention on a scale comparable to that of the credit banks: their resources were simply insufficient to meet the financial requirements of large industrial customers. They managed, however, to retain a high degree of influence, visible through their presence on the supervisory boards of the country's major industrial companies. In 1900, half of the directorships of German leading companies were held by private bankers (as against 42.5 per cent for the 'great' banks and 7.5 per cent for the provincial banks). They were still ahead—by one per cent—in 1913 (respectively 42 and 41 per cent), before losing ground, though not in a significant way, up to the mid-1930s.[82]

The importance of a seat on a company's supervisory board should not be over-estimated: since the introduction of the two-tier structure in the 1870s, power had rested firmly with the *Vorstand*, the executive board. This, however, applies to representatives of both private and 'great' banks. In the event,

[79] R. Tilly, 'International Aspects of the Development of German Banking', in R. Cameron and V. I. Bovykin (eds), *International Banking 1870–1914* (Oxford, 1991), pp. 96–8.

[80] See Cassis, *City de Londres*, pp. 116–23.

[81] See P. Hertner, 'German Banks Abroad before 1914', in G. Jones (ed.), *Banks as Multinationals* (London, 1990).

[82] See D. Ziegler and H. Wixforth, 'The Niche in the Universal Banking System: the Role and Significance of Private Bankers within German Industry, 1900–1933', in *Financial History Review*, 1, 2 (1994), pp. 99–119.

private bankers were able to offer a more personalized service, highly valued by industrial companies. Here, as Harald Wixforth and Dieter Ziegler have convincingly argued, private bankers could exploit a niche and turn their limited resources into an advantage. Having to concentrate on a limited number of clients, they could devote their full attention to them. Private bankers' advice was highly valued because of their independence: they were less likely to intervene in the company's affairs, and they often played the role of arbiters between conflicting interests.

LESSER FINANCIAL CENTRES

An aristocracy of private bankers survived in all European countries until the First World War, though they did not necessarily belong to the international *haute banque*. Such a membership depended either on family links or on the global significance of the financial centres from which they operated. Before 1914, the influence of a financial centre was more closely related to the economic and political weight of the country in which it was located than it has been since the 1980s. Tax-heavens and offshore financial centres, which have contributed to the recent revival of private banking, are a fairly recent phenomenon. In the late nineteenth century, 'multinational' private banks such as the Rothschild, Speyer, Seligmann, Lazard, and others were based in the world's leading financial centres: London, Paris, New York, Berlin. Centres like Amsterdam or Brussels could not really compete while Zurich had not yet emerged on the international scene. As for the financial capitals of larger countries, such as Vienna, St Petersburg, or Milan, they were integrated into financial networks dominated by the capital of one of the great powers. Private bankers from the lesser European financial centres had to fit into this hierarchical order. However, they still formed a banking aristocracy within their own country, while some of them were part of the international elite through family ties, as best exemplified by the Austrian Rothschilds.

A brief tour of Europe's lesser financial centres should start in Brussels, probably ranking fourth in the European hierarchy before the First World War, after London, Paris, and Berlin.[83] Brussels was the most international of the second tier financial centres, mainly as a result of the strong presence of a cosmopolitan *haute banque* and, later in the nineteenth century, the penetration of foreign banks. The Belgian *haute banque* reached its apogee in the third quarter of the nineteenth century, with families such as Lambert, Bischoffsheim, Goldschmidt, Oppenheim, and their networks of relationships both in Belgium

[83] Cassis, *Capitals of Capital*, pp. 125–6.

and across Europe. Like many successful European Jewish private bankers, the Lamberts started as Rothschilds' representatives. The bank was founded in 1843 in Antwerp by Samuel Caïn, known as Samuel Lambert, who joined forces with his father-in-law, Lazare Richtenberger, the Rothschilds' agent in Brussels since 1830. The links between the two families were reinforced in the second generation through the marriage in 1882 of Samuel Lambert's son, Leon, to Gustave de Rothschild's daughter, Lucie.[84]

The second major group revolved around the Bischoffsheims, a German Jewish family from Mainz. Unlike the Rothschilds, the brothers Ludwig-Raphael and Jonathan Raphael established their own banking house, Bischoffsheim, Goldschmidt & Cie, in Antwerp in 1825, then in Brussels in 1837, with branches in London and Paris. The Bischoffsheims were at the centre of an impressive European network of Jewish banking families including Bamberger, Cassel, Goldschmidt, de Hirsch, Montefiore, Speyer, and Stern. One of the main achievements of these private bankers was their contribution to the foundation of some of Europe's most important joint-stock banks, in particular the Banque de Paris et des Pays-Bas, but also, through Ludwig Bamberger, the Deutsche Bank.[85]

Like most of their counterparts in continental Europe, Belgian private bankers lost ground to the universal banks in the late nineteenth century, though a few of them remained highly influential until the First World War and beyond. The most successful was the Banque Lambert. Interestingly, and somewhat paradoxically, it became increasingly autonomous, though still closely linked to the Rothschilds under Léon Lambert (1851–1919) who gave it a fresh impetus, especially by supporting King Leopold's colonial ventures in Congo. Other important private banks included the banque Cassel, established in 1839 by Germain Cassel, a relative of the Bischoffsheims, and the banque Philippson, founded in 1877 by Franz Philippson. By the early twentieth century, both were engaged in industrial finance and colonial enterprises, with Léon Cassel sitting on the board of more than thirty companies and Franz Philippson closely connected with railways companies. Curiously, the Protestant—and Catholic—*haute banque* was a latecomer in Belgium, following the Jewish *haute banque* a generation or so later.[86] The leading houses, Josse Allard, and Nagelmackers Fils & Cie, were also actively engaged in company promotion.[87]

[84] G. Kurgan-van Hentenrijk, S. Jaumain, and V. Montens (eds), *Dictionnaire des patrons en Belgique. Les hommes, les entreprises, les réseaux* (Bruxelles, 1996), pp. 408–12.

[85] E. Bussière, *Paribas. Europe and the World, 1872–1992* (Antwerp, 1992), pp. 19–25; L. Gall et al., *The Deutsche Bank, 1870–1995* (London, 1995), pp. 1–14.

[86] G. Kurgan-van Hentenrijk, 'Entre tradition et modernité: le patronat bancaire en Belgique de 1850 à 1950', in *Les entreprises et leurs réseaux: hommes, capitaux, techniques et pouvoirs, XIXe-XXe siècles. Mélanges en l'honneur de François Caron* (Paris, 1998).

[87] Kurgan-van Hentenrijk, et al., *Dictionnaire des patrons*, pp. 16, 92–3, 409, 480–2, 506–8.

In terms of overall influence within their banking system, the leading Dutch private bankers enjoyed an extremely favourable position until at least the very end of the nineteenth century. This was due to the comparatively weak development of the large commercial banks, and to the country's strong financial culture. But it was also due to the inordinate role played by the *prolongatie* (the call-money advanced to the Amsterdam Stock Exchange) in the money market. Private firms, including brokers, still played a significant part in this market whose amount had reached 400 million guilders (£40 million) by the eve of the First World War—that is, more than twice the country's aggregate fixed deposits.[88] Leading private bankers in Amsterdam, including Hope & Co., Lippmann, Rosenthal & Co., Van Eeghen & Co., Becker & Fuld, Wertheim & Gomperz, stood at the top of a subtle hierarchy of private firms trading in securities. As late as 1890, private banks could still compete in terms of size, with the joint-stock banks: the total assets of firms such as Hope & Co. and R. Mees & Zoonen reached about 20 million guilders (£2 million) as against just over 30 million for the Twentsche Bank, then the country's largest. It was not before around 1910 that the gap really widened.[89]

In 1870, Hope & Co. remained probably the largest and certainly the most prestigious private bank in the Netherlands.[90] By the turn of the century, this was no longer the case, as least as far as size was concerned: its balance sheet total was still a respectable 14 million guilders, though the figure was not substantially higher than in the early nineteenth century and could now be matched by several less famous houses. In addition, Hope's exclusive relationship with Russia, which had been at the heart of its financial predominance, was successfully challenged in the 1890s by Lippmann, Rosenthal & Co. Nevertheless, Hopes remained a highly respected house and as such continued to take part in international issuing syndicates while building up a strong position in the placement of domestic issues. More importantly, in a typical *haute banque* manner, Hope & Co. could afford what Joost Jonker calls a 'profitable isolation' thanks to their vast off-balance sheet operations. The firm derived a substantial commission income from the huge assets under its management and played a key role in the market for short-term loans to the Amsterdam Stock Exchange. By contrast, the most dynamic private bank of the period, R. Mees & Zoonen, was based in Rotterdam, a fast expanding city in the last third of the nineteenth century, with the firm closely linked to this development. Its banking activities were wide-ranging (from deposit taking to corporate finance through foreign exchange and arbitrage) and, in the

[88] J. Jonker, 'Spoilt for Choice? Banking Concentration and the Structure of the Dutch Capital Market, 1900–40', in Y. Cassis, G. D. Feldman, and U. Olsson (eds), *The Evolution of Financial Institutions and Markets in Twentieth Century Europe* (Aldershot, 1995).

[89] J. Jonker, *Mees Pierson. The Link between Past and Future: 275 years of Tradition and Innovation in Dutch Banking* (Amsterdam, 1997), pp. 17–19.

[90] The following paragraph is based on Jonker, *Mees Pierson*, pp. 23–60.

tradition of Rotterdam's merchant banks, they were combined with an equally active insurance business. With a balance sheet total of 30.6 million guilders in 1913 (up from 8.5 million in 1870), R. Mees & Zoonen was probably the country's largest private bank.

In Switzerland, private bankers confined themselves to the more traditional activity of the *haute banque*: private wealth management. Swiss capital markets had not reached global status before the First World War and the country's three main financial centres—Geneva, Zurich, and Basle—played second fiddle in international finance.[91] Nevertheless, Switzerland was steeped in banking, and especially private banking, traditions. This probably explains the long-standing success of the Swiss *haute banque*: private international bankers undoubtedly remained a significant force within the Swiss banking system. The survival of private banking in Switzerland was also a result of a regional specialization: the new credit banks in Zurich, the old private banks in Geneva, with Basle somewhat in between. Zurich only had a handful of private banks and still lagged behind the two other cities in the mid-nineteenth century. From an early stage, merchants and industrialists established joint-stock banks in order to support their expanding activities. The Zürich Bank, established in 1837, was Switzerland's first joint-stock bank. But the Crédit Suisse, founded in 1856 on the model of the French Crédit Mobilier proved far more successful, soon becoming the country's largest bank and laying the foundations for Zurich's financial supremacy.

Geneva, by contrast, abounded in private banking dynasties, some dating back to the Huguenot diasporas of the sixteenth and seventeenth centuries.[92] There were still some fifteen houses belonging to the Geneva Protestant *haute banque* by the late nineteenth century, led by Hentsch & Cie (established in 1796), Lombard, Odier & Cie (1798), and Pictet & Cie (1805), all linked by a dense network of family relationships based on a succession of intermarriages. They managed vast amounts of capital on behalf of a wealthy cosmopolitan clientele, though there are still few details available about the scale of their operations. Although significantly smaller than their counterparts in Paris or London, the Geneva private bankers were able to hold their own within a still very fragmented Swiss banking system, where the big banks did not control more than 27 per cent of the country's total assets (up from 12 per cent in 1880) and had not yet entered the field of private wealth management.[93]

Private bankers were thus able to preserve a niche market where they enjoyed a unique competitive advantage based on their old established reputation for

[91] See Y. Cassis and J. Tanner, 'Finance and Financiers in Switzerland, 1880–1960', in Cassis (ed.), *Finance and Financiers*.

[92] Some indications can be found in J. Seitz, *Histoire de la banque à Genève* (Geneva, 1931); L. H. Mottet, *Regards sur l'histoire des banques et banquiers genevois* (Geneva, 1982).

[93] See F. Ritzmann, *Die Schweizer Banken. Geschichte-Theorie-Statistik* (Bern, 1973).

financial expertise; their international network of relationships, especially, though by no means exclusively, with the Parisian *haute banque*; and the emerging role of Switzerland as a refuge for foreign capital, starting with the Franco-Prussian War in 1870. In addition, Geneva private bankers joined forces to undertake issuing and investing operations which went beyond each bank's individual capacity. Successive ad hoc or permanent syndicates had been formed in the course of the nineteenth century. A step further was taken in 1890 with the foundation, by the ten leading banks, of an investment bank, the Union Financière, which in turn promoted a number of investment companies. New investment opportunities were explored, in particular in American power companies, pioneered by Guillaume Pictet (1860–1926). However, unlike the Swiss Bank Corporation founded in 1872 by a group of Basle private bankers, the Union Financière never developed into a truly large bank and could thus remain under its founders' full control.

At the heart of the Habsburg monarchy, Vienna had grown into an international financial centre of some substance. Banks could rely on a rich private clientele and served a dynamic regional industrial *Mittelstand*. But above all, Vienna was the heart—Budapest never took off—of Austria–Hungary's international financial transactions, from foreign exchange and bill discounting to the all-important reception and distribution of foreign capital.[94] Such financial activity did not benefit private bankers. From the 1880s onwards, their decline was even faster than in Germany, including the *haute banque*, with the disappearance of such names as Sina, Springer, and Wodianer. Schoeller, Austria's second largest private bank, was able to survive, though its real independence was questioned following the sale in 1910 of its industrial empire to the Credit-Anstalt.[95]

The exception was of course S. M. von Rothschild, led by Albert de Rothschild (1844–1911) and after his death, by his son Louis. Not only were the Rothschilds the last surviving major private bank in Austria, they were also a force to be reckoned with alongside the seven large Vienna joint-stock banks (Credit-Anstalt, Boden Creditanstalt, Wiener Bankverein, Länderbank, Anglobank, Eskomptegesellschaft, and Unionbank). The Rothschilds remained the largest shareholders of the Credit-Anstalt, Austria's largest bank, which they had founded in 1855, though they were no longer in control by the late nineteenth century. Their strength also derived, as in London and Paris, from their role in government finance. Until 1886, they enjoyed a monopoly over the issue of Austrian state loans, a monopoly which was then granted to the so-called Rothschild group including, besides S. M. von Rothschild, the

[94] See B. Michel, *Banques et banquiers en Autriche au début du 20e siècle* (Paris, 1976), pp. 49–56.
[95] Michel, *Banques et banquiers en Autriche*, pp. 106–7.

Credit-Anstalt, and the Boden Creditanstalt, together with three Berlin banks—the Disconto-Gesellschaft, Bleichröder, and Mendelssohn.

The Rothschilds suffered a major setback in 1910, when the issue of government stock was entrusted to the Postsparkassen (the Post Office savings banks), signalling the failure of the Rothschild group. Cracks had been apparent from some time, especially following the death of Theodor von Taussig, governor of the Boden Creditanstalt, who had effectively run the group and, together with Albert de Rothschild, ensured its cohesion. Von Taussig was replaced by Rudolf Sieghart, against Albert de Rothschild's will. The group's methods of placing government loans among its circle of 'friends' rather than by public issue looked somewhat obsolete and the government was keen to break the monopoly. The Postsparkassen, established in 1883, with its dense network of branches throughout the country, appeared a good contender and, though formally independent, it was in fact an offshoot of the Ministry of Finance.

The Rothschild group's collapse became apparent when Sieghart broke away from the group and joined the Postsparkassen for the second issue, soon followed by the Credit-Anstalt. Rothschild alone refused to take part. Behind the political intrigues and the business and personal rivalries, the failure of the Rothschild group was further evidence of the decline of private banking, in line with the course of events throughout Europe. However, the Rothschilds being the Rothschilds, they remained highly influential, even in decline. The Rothschild group re-formed in 1911 under Louis de Rothschild, without the Boden-Creditanstalt, but with the Credit-Anstalt, the Wiener Bankverein, and the Länderbank. It no longer enjoyed a monopoly of the issue of government loans (and increasingly turned its attention to industrial finance), but was still able to play a significant role, especially as the handling of government issues by the Postsparkassen did not prove entirely satisfactory. In 1914, the Rothschild group floated a loan on the London market.

Throughout continental Europe the *haute banque* was fighting to retain its place among the small circle of top ranking banking institutions. Sweden was no exception to the rule. Private merchant and banking houses gave way to the emerging joint-stock banks (Skandinaviska Banken, Stockholms Handelsbank) which they had often contributed to establishing. There was, however, an exception to confirm the rule. Sweden's third largest bank, the Stockholms Enskilda Bank, not only remained in private hands but was the powerbase of one of Europe's most formidable banking and business dynasties: the Wallenbergs.[96] The bank was founded in 1856 by Oskar Wallenberg (1816–86), a former naval officer and self-taught economic thinker. Wallenberg was not a private banker in the usual sense of the word. His bank was organized as

[96] The following paragraph is based on U. Olsson, *At the Centre of Development. Skandinaviska Enskilda Banken and its Predecessors 1856–1996* (Stockholm, 1997).

a private joint-stock company, with seventy-two owners carrying unlimited liability. Wallenberg became managing director and enjoyed great freedom of action. But he did not own his bank, having only subscribed to 50 of the 1,000 shares making up the bank's capital. Interestingly, and most unusually in the world of commercial banking, the family acquired a majority ownership in the bank in the following generation, through the efforts of Oscar Wallenberg's two eldest sons, Knut Agathon (1853–1938) and Marcus (1854–1943).

Rather than the survival of a private bank, this was a case of a leading bank returning to family ownership in the age of the corporate economy. The bank considerably expanded in the quarter of a century preceding the First World War, playing a leading role in the bond market and in investment banking. The rise of the bond market derived from the massive import of capital, which was a key feature of Sweden's industrialization in the late nineteenth and early twentieth century. The Stockholms Enskilda Bank was one of the few banks handling these capital inflows thanks to its network of relationships with foreign banks, in particular the Crédit Lyonnais. The bank also became involved in a number of development projects in the fields of industry and natural resources, the modern engineering industry, iron ore mining, and hydroelectric power plants being among its main areas of interest.

PRIVATE BANKERS IN THE REGIONS

Moving from the capital to the regions is moving either to a nearly complete void or to the realm of statistics. European diversity is striking in that respect. In the Mediterranean and Scandinavian countries, provincial private banking never really took off, the gap being filled by savings banks and other types of cooperative and mutual banks. In Britain, private country banks had all but disappeared by the last decade of the nineteenth century, their number falling to 172 in 1884 and to only 35 in 1904, as a result of the amalgamation movement.[97] By then, they had lost their significance as one of the components of the English banking system.

Private country banks undoubtedly made a positive contribution to economic growth at both national and regional levels. Even in the late nineteenth century, they were able to offer what we would call today a more personalized service. Their relationships with long-standing customers were governed by more flexible rules than those applied by anonymous branch managers of fast expanding London-based joint-stock banks. However, their often assumed superiority in assessing risks and more generally in financing local industrialists

[97] Crick and Wadsworth, *Hundred Years*, pp. 34–7.

has not so far been supported by strong empirical evidence. In any case, by the late nineteenth century their practices were increasingly criticized by the new keepers of the banking orthodoxy. Felix Schuster, for example, governor of the Union Bank of London and one of the leading bankers of his day, considered that the Smith banks, which he took over in 1902, were over-committed. The only private country bank of some distinction to survive in the twentieth century was Beckett & Co, of Leeds and York, eventually taken over by the Westminster Bank in 1921.

Local and regional private banks flourished and survived at the very heart of continental Europe, above all in France and Germany, where hundreds, even thousands of small, mostly unknown banks remained part of the local economy until the First World War.

The realm of statistics, however, is fraught with great uncertainties. Estimates of the number of private banks vary within very broad bands and recent research has led to drastic revisions. Take France, a country long seen as under-banked during most of the nineteenth century and lagging behind Britain by a good hundred years. Rondo Cameron's early estimates supported such a view: with 369 banks in 1870 (200 of them private provincial banks) totaling 469 outlets, France had one banking outlet for 82,000 inhabitants—roughly the level reached by Scotland in the late eighteenth century.[98] By contrast, there were some 365 banks in England and Wales in 1870, but with a total of 1,628 outlets.[99] However, new estimates have completely altered this view. Banking was a free profession in nineteenth-century France, open to anybody willing to exercise it, and many a merchant, trader, notary, or wealthy *rentier* did exercise it on a more or less regular basis. With no legal definition of the profession existing before the Banking Act of 1941, a firm regularly engaged in credit transactions, especially discounting, was considered, in economic terms, a bank during the second half of the nineteenth century. Taking deposits, however, had not yet become a decisive criterion, and contemporaries did not make any distinction between bankers and *escompteurs* (discounters)—business people and men of independent means investing part of their fortune in bills of exchange, which were rediscounted at the Banque de France. Taking bankers and discounters together, Alain Plessis reckons that there were no less than 2,000 bankers in France in 1870, possibly as many as 3,000![100]

[98] R. Cameron, *Banking in the Early Stages of Industrialization* (Oxford, 1967).

[99] S. Nishimura, *The Decline of Inland Bills of Exchange in the London Money Market 1855–1913* (Cambridge, 1971), p. 80.

[100] A. Plessis, 'Le "retard français": la faute à la banque? Banques locales, succursales de la banque de France et financement de l'économie sous le second Empire', in P. Fridenson and A. Straus, *Le capitalisme français, 19e-20e siècle. Blocages et dynamismes d'une croissance* (Paris, 1987).

These are of course estimates, the former based on the reports of the branch inspectors of the Banque de France, the latter on *l'Annuaire spécial de la finance*, a well-informed and authoritative banking directory. In any case, there can be little doubt that banking was plentiful in provincial France in the last third of the nineteenth century, with some 2,500 country banks in the early 1870s. Most of them were private banks: about a third were in fact individual firms (though often supported by a relative) and nearly half were partnerships, while some 200 banks were joint-stock companies.[101] The question is whether local private bankers played a positive role in French economic development. The assumption that France was under-banked fitted neatly with the thesis of the country's 'economic backwardness' put forward, mostly by American scholars, in the 1950s and 1960s: the slow pace of French industrialization could at least partly be explained by a lack of banks. This thesis, however, has been rejected by the French 'revisionist' school: economic growth has been judged satisfactory in the long term and firms are considered to have responded adequately to such constraints as technological development, available resources, or internal demand.[102] The revaluation of banking density in France, which was about the same as in Britain, is an integral part of this revision. Quantity, however, does not necessarily mean quality and the role of local private bankers has often been considered at best negligible, at worst detrimental to economic growth.

Local banks no doubt had their weaknesses. On the liability side, their resources tended to be meagre. Nearly half of them—the bulk of the escompteurs and small bankers—worked with very little capital (between Ff.40,000 and Ff.150,000, i.e. £1,600 to £6,000) and reserves. Another quarter were somewhat stronger, with a capital of Ff.350,000 to Ff.800,000 francs, leaving only a few hundred banks with one million or more.[103] Moreover, unlike their British counterparts, they did not seek to systematically collect deposits from the local middle classes, thus leaving the field open for the newly formed big banks. They relied instead on a small number of fairly large deposit accounts, mostly from the notables of their region, whose fortunes they often managed. The Banque de France, for its part, considered that deposits should not far exceed the partners' capital and reserves. On the assets side, they were almost exclusively tied to the local economy and their risks rarely sufficiently diversified. The result was that in time of recession, all their customers were likely to be short of funds or to become insolvent at the same time.

[101] A. Plessis, 'Les banques locales, de l'essor du Second Empire à la « crise » de la Belle Epoque', in M. Lescure and A. Plessis (eds), *Banques locales et banques régionales en France au XIXe siècle* (Paris, 1999), p. 218.

[102] See in particular M. Levy-Leboyer, 'Le patronat français a-t-il été malthusien', *Le Mouvement social*, 3 (1974) and Fridenson and Straus (eds), *Capitalisme français*.

[103] Plessis, 'Les banques locales', p. 220.

Nevertheless, local private banks did contribute positively to France's economic growth. Individual weaknesses should not obscure the overall strength of the regional financial structures which emerged at the end of the Second Empire. Two main factors contributed to the working of the system. One was the relationships linking together local banks of the same region, underpinned by constant credit flows: the major country banks usually had official representatives in the smaller neighbouring towns, while the largest among them also had relationships with Parisian banks, to which they could turn if necessary. The second factor was the spread of the branches of the Banque de France, whose number increased from thirty to seventy-two between 1852 and 1870, mostly in response to calls from local authorities. For the presence of the Banque de France in provincial cities provided a steady source of credit and a reduction in the cost of borrowing. Local banks, though constrained by low capital and reserves, could extend the volume of their transactions by rediscounting accommodation bills with the Banque de France; and they benefited from the same conditions as Parisian banks as one and the same rate was applicable throughout the country. The local branches of the Banque de France were thus, as Alain Plessis puts it, the 'linchpin, the keystone of increasingly developed regional credit systems'.[104]

Taken together, country banks represented a far from inconsiderable force in the 1870s and even in the 1880s. With an aggregate capital of Ff.500 to Ff.600 million and deposits of at least Ff.300 million, their liabilities exceeded those of any of the large banks.[105] They were able to offer a variety of banking services, depending on their own size as well as the type of local demand and credit practices. Basically, however, they discounted bills of exchange and granted loans to local enterprises, usually against strong security, though the Banque de France was highly suspicious of the latter practice in its rediscounting policy.[106]

Competition stiffened from the 1880s, especially as the big deposit banks (Crédit Lyonnais, Société Générale, Comptoir d'escompte) started to build their network of branches across the country. By the turn of the century, there was much talk about a 'crisis' of local banks, culminating in the discussions of the select committee on the financing of small and medium-sized firms set up by Finance Minister Joseph Caillaux in 1911. There is no doubt that local banks lost ground: while bills discounted doubled in value between 1868 and 1912, the share of the *établissements de crédit* increased tenfold, leaving a much reduced part of the business, in relative if not in absolute terms, to local banks.[107] And yet local private banks were far from being wiped out. There were still thousands of them in France on the eve of the First World War.

[104] Plessis, 'Le "retard français"', p. 209.
[105] Plessis, 'Les banques locales', pp. 220–2.
[106] Plessis, 'Les banques locales', pp. 222–4.
[107] Plessis, 'Les banques locales', p. 227.

Some estimates put their number at around 1,000 to 1,200 plus a good 1,200 escompteurs; others go as high as 3,162, two thirds of them with less than six employees.[108] With estimates ranging between 2,500 and 3,000 banks, the number of banks was thus roughly the same as forty years earlier.

One of the main explanations for such resilience lies in the attitude of the big banks. Rather than absorbing existing country banks, they expanded by opening their own branches. The Crédit Lyonnais took over one single bank before 1914, the Comptoir d'escompte only eight. This was not the outcome of a deliberate strategy. The Crédit Lyonnais, for example, was highly pragmatic in this matter and carefully weighed up every possibility of absorbing, or even collaborating with local competitors.[109] Instead, a division of labour was established between the big deposit banks and the local and regional banks: the former did not canvass the entire national territory and had but scant interest in local business. The gap was filled by private bankers who concentrated on specific tasks, in particular agricultural credit and industrial finance.[110]

A typical example was Tarneaud, a family bank established in Limoges in 1809, whose capital reached Ff.1.2 million in 1906. Its clients were mainly engaged in farming and in small-scale related industrial activities, such as food and leather; they also included small firms involved in the paper and wood industries as well as in building and retailing. Tarneaud collected drafts in the smallest villages through a network of correspondents (thus dispensing altogether with branches) and often rediscounted bills presented by these very small escompteurs. The growth of the porcelain industry presented the bank with new business opportunities—advances as well as foreign exchange facilities, which it jointly operated with Lazard Frères in Paris. By the early twentieth century, Tarneaud had retained its leadership in Limoges and succeeded in containing the growing competition from the *établissements de crédit*.

Courtois, in Toulouse, played a similar role in the regional economy, with an even weaker customer base, mostly made up of small traders (grain, hardware, iron, wine) and industrialists (vegetable oil, glass, shoes, cotton spinning). Other banks went further in their involvement in industrial finance, acting as quasi-investment bankers, especially in connection with the 'new industries' of the second industrial revolution. A small bank such as Laydernier in Annecy (its capital was only Ff.400,000 until 1911, when it was raised to Ff.800,000) was involved in the foundation of tramway, hydro-electricity, and

[108] A. Liesse, *Evolution of Credit and Banking in France* (Washington, DC, 1909), quoted by S. Nishimura, 'The French Provincial Banks, the Banque de France, and Bill Finance, 1890–1913', *Economic History Review*, 48, 3 (1995), p. 538.

[109] See Jean Bouvier, *Naissance d'une banque: le Crédit Lyonnais* (Paris, 1968), pp. 148–9.

[110] L. Bergeron, *Les capitalistes en France (1780–1914)* (Paris, 1978), pp. 109–10.

car servicing companies in Haute-Savoie.[111] In Grenoble, the centre of the nascent hydro-electricity industry, Charpenay & Cie (with a capital of Ff.1.5 million in 1911 and Ff.2.5 million in 1913) took an active part in the foundation of more than sixty companies between 1889 and 1921, in particular by placing their securities among its customers.

While the bulk of country private banks remained very small firms, some of them grew into regional banks and adopted modern banking techniques. In his survey of banking in France, the German observer Eugen Kaufmann gave a—non exhaustive—list of twenty-two 'important' private banks in 1910, all with a least two branches. The largest by this measure, Varin-Bernier, had twelve branches. One of the most successful private provincial banks in France, Varin-Bernier was established as early as 1812 in Bar-le-Duc (north-east) and prospered until the 1870s as a typical local bank, providing credit to small firms in the textile and metalworking industries. From then on, under Paul Varin-Bernier, the bank moved away from its declining base, opening branches in the neighbouring departments, granting advances to the iron and steel industry in Meuse and Haute-Marne, taking bills on Paris and the industrial north, embarking on stock-market operations, and eventually opening a branch in Paris in 1921.[112]

For most banks, however, the capital required for such an expansion had to be found outside the narrow circle of the partners and their family. The legal form was usually that of a *société en commandite par actions* or partnership limited by shares. Such an arrangement allowed the partners (whose liability was unlimited) to remain in control while holding but a small fraction of the bank's capital, the bulk being provided by the *commanditaires*, the sleeping partners, whose liability was limited to the amount of capital subscribed. At the Banque Thomas, for example, established in 1863 by Emile Thomas in Longwy with a capital of Ff.400,000, there were 650 shareholders in 1898. The bank rapidly became a key player in the financing of the Lorraine iron and steel industry, its capital rising to Ff.8 million (Ff.4.4 million paid-up) in 1898. Yet the partners, Emile Thomas and his son Henri, held less than 9 per cent, alongside the region's leading steel masters and an array of small holders.[113] There were more than 400 shareholders at Henri Delvider & Cie, in Lille (Nord), a larger bank whose paid-up capital reached Ff.12.5 million and deposits more than Ff.70 million in 1911. Verley, Decroix & Cie, also in

[111] H. Bonin. 'Grosse histoire du Crédit du Nord', unpublished typescript, 1998. A shorter version has been published under the title *Histoire de banques. Crédit du Nord 1848–1998* (Paris, 1998). We are grateful to Hubert Bonin for lending us this typescript.

[112] Bergeron, *Les capitalistes*, pp. 113–14.

[113] See J.-M. Moine, 'Banque locale et financement de l'industrialisation. La Banque Thomas et la sidérurgie du bassin de Longwy (1863–1907)', in Lescure and Plessis (eds), *Banques locales*, pp. 127–72; and L. Bergeron, *Les Rothschild et les autres . . . La gloire des banquiers* (Paris, 1991), pp. 180–7.

Lille, had grown into a truly regional bank by the early twentieth century, and vied for leadership in the Nord with the Crédit du Nord, a public limited company. Its paid-up capital and reserves amounted to Ff.17.5 million in 1913, divided between some 700 shareholders, and its deposits approached Ff.100 million. In this highly personalized institution, the partners' share was around 10 per cent, rising to 25 per cent if their families are included.[114]

The question is whether Thomas, Delvider, Verley Decroix, and several others should still be considered as private banks. The answer is yes: these *sociétés en commandite* were private companies and their partners, usually called *gérants*, had full control, if only part ownership, of the business. However, such a position became untenable beyond a certain level of development, when turning into a public limited company became unavoidable. This was done either through merger or, mostly after the First World War, conversion: the Banque Thomas was taken over by the Société Nancéenne de Crédit, another leading regional bank in 1907; Delvider amalgamated with the Crédit du Nord in 1913; while Verley Decroix turned itself into a public company in 1919.

Statistics concerning the number of private banks are a little more reliable for Germany, though estimates are only available from the 1890s. According to the Banking Directory, there might have been as many as 2,180 private bankers in 1892 and 2,564 in 1902, an order of magnitude not far removed from the estimates relating to French private banks. These figures, however, should be considered as the upper limit as they include a fair proportion of very short-lived private banks as well as firms engaged in other, not strictly banking, activities, especially stockbrokers, agents of foreign banks, merchants, and others.[115] The figure given by the Central Association of German Bankers, 1,800 for 1913, is probably closer to the actual number of private banks proper; while the number of private banks keeping a giro account with the Reichsbank was somewhat smaller: 1,386 in 1902 and 1,221 in 1913.[116]

Whichever set of figures is considered, it is obvious that the number of private banks hardly declined before the First World War. One of the reasons for their survival, besides their contribution to the local and regional economy, which has been emphasized in recent works,[117] has to do with the mode of

[114] Bonin, 'Grosse histoire'.

[115] W. Treue, 'Der Privatbankier an der Wende der 19. zum 20. Jahrhundert', *Tradition*, 5 (1970), p. 228. The figures are based on the *Deutsche Bankierbuch*.

[116] See M. Pohl, 'Festigung und Ausdehnung der deutschen Bankwesens zwischen 1870 und 1914', *Deutsche Bankengeschichte*, vol. 2 (Frankfurt, 1982), p. 262. K. A. Donaubauer, *Privatbankiers und Bankenkonzentration in Deutschand von der Mitte des 19. Jahrhundert bis 1932* (Frankfurt, 1988), p. 13.

[117] See in particular the work of H. Wixforth and D. Ziegler, 'The Niche in the Universal Banking System: The Role and Significance of Private Bankers within German Industry', *Financial History Review*, 1, 2 (1994),' and 'Deutsche Privatbanken und Privatbankiers im 20. Jahrhundert', *Geschichte und Gesellschaft*, 23, 2 (1997). See also Donaubauer, *Privatbankiers und Bankenkonzentration*.

expansion of the big banks. As in France, the latter expanded without engaging into a large-scale, British style amalgamation policy. While the French big banks opened new branches, their German counterparts established 'communities of interest' (*Interessengemeinschaften*), based on cross-shareholding and pooled-profits, with a number of provincial banks. The Deutsche Bank, for example, had such links with fourteen banks, including large provincial banks such as the Bergisch-Märkische Bank, the capital of which stood at 60 million Marks. Mergers and takeovers did take place during the period. But they were the means of expansion used by the larger provincial banks, not the big banks. The Bergisch-Märkische Bank, mentioned above, took over twenty-four small private banks between 1895 and 1913, the Deutsche Bank only six.[118] Private bankers thus undoubtedly suffered from the growth of the provincial joint-stock banks. However, this was not enough to eradicate them: the amalgamation movement remained limited, mainly because private banks were still fulfilling a specific economic function.

While the number of private banks remained stable and their combined total assets increased—from 2.5 to 4 billion Marks—between 1880 and 1913, their overall influence, measured by their percentage of German banks' total assets, considerably weakened—from 21 per cent in 1880 to 10 per cent in 1900 and just over 5 per cent in 1913.[119] Their contribution to economic development, however, has not been in doubt: they primarily catered for local small business. Local private banks fitted into the 'division of labour' within the German universal banking system.[120] The great banks provided 'development assistance to the strong', but they badly neglected small and medium-sized industry.[121] The latter, however, could turn to the regional joint-stock banks or to the local private banks, depending on their size and needs. In Augsburg, for example, local private banks were responsible for 58 per cent (192.6 out of 333.4 million Marks) of the new railways and industrial issues floated on the local Stock Exchange between 1901 and 1908.[122] Local industry was mainly linked to the city's two leading banking houses, Friedr. Schmid & Co., primarily concerned with the textile industry, and P. C. Bonnet. The latter, established in 1823, had total assets amounting to no more than 8.9 million

[118] See M. Pohl, *Entstehung und Entwicklung der Universalbankensystem: Konzentration und Krize als wichtige Faktoren* (Frankfurt, 1982), pp. 62–7, J. Riesser, *Zur Entwicklungsgeschichte der deutsche Grossbanken mit besonder Rücksicht auf die Konzentrationbestrebungen* (Jena, 1906).

[119] Calculated from Wixforth and Ziegler, 'The Niche', p. 103.

[120] D. Ziegler, 'Banking and the Rise and Expansion of Industrial Capitalism in Germany', in A. Teichova, G. Kurgan van Hentenryk, and D. Ziegler (eds), *Banking, Trade and Industry. Europe, Asia and America from the Thirteenth to the Twentieth Century* (Cambridge, 1997), pp. 142–4.

[121] R. Tilly, 'German Banking 1850–1914: Development Assistance to the Strong', *Journal of European Economic History*, 15 (1986).

[122] Donaubauer, *Privatbankiers*, pp. 46–50.

Marks (£445,000) in 1905. Yet its senior partner, Max Schwarz, a local notable of considerable weight, sat on the supervisory boards of twenty-three companies, including the Vereinigte Maschinenfabrik Augsburg und Maschinengesellschaft Nürnberg, later to be known as M.A.N., one of the largest companies in Germany.[123]

THE LASTING INFLUENCE OF PRIVATE BANKERS

One of the main contributions of private bankers in the second half of the nineteenth century was the establishment of the new joint-stock banks, which have dominated the financial world ever since. By taking such initiatives, however, private bankers were more pragmatic than visionary. Few imagined the huge development that the new institutions would rapidly achieve, and the threat to their own position that they would soon represent. They seized the opportunity of raising vast amounts of capital in order to finance large-scale investment, especially in transport equipment. That *private banks* would ultimately be marginalized does not mean that *private bankers* lost on the deal or that they could have chosen otherwise. What is clear is that from the mid-nineteenth century, the fate of private banks has been entirely determined by the development of the joint-stock banks.

Though pragmatism and adaptation were the most common reactions, attitudes varied amongst private bankers. Some took a dim view of the new joint-stock banks, others actively promoted them, while most joined in the general movement. Besides personal inclinations and varying degrees of business acumen, different attitudes reflected different levels of banking development, whether at national or regional levels, and different positions within national banking systems.

Private bankers continued to be active in the foundation of joint-stock banks in the late nineteenth century. They were involved in the second wave of foundations of German credit banks, between 1870 and 1873. These were the *Gründerjahre*, the years of economic boom which followed the foundation of the Reich. The leading German banks at the turn of the twenty-first century—Deutsche, Dresdner Bank, and Commerzbank—were founded in these years, and all three by private bankers.

The Deutsche Bank was founded in Berlin in March 1870 to finance foreign trade and, more especially, to liberate German trade from its dependence on British finance.[124] The initiative came from Adelbert Delbrück, founder and partner of Delbrück, Leo & Co., a solid and respected though not a front-ranking

[123] Donaubauer, *Privatbankiers*, pp. 51, 130–7.
[124] See Gall et al., *Deutsche Bank*, pp. 3–10.

Berlin private bank. The founding committee included two other Berlin private bankers, Victor von Magnus, head of F. Martin Magnus & Co., and Hermann Zwicker, of Gebrüder Schickler. Other founders were Adolph vom Rath, partner in the Cologne bank, Deichmann & Co., as well as two lesser names, Gustav Kutter, representing the Frankfurt bank Gebrüder Sulzbach, and Gustav Müller, representing the Würtembergische Vereinsbank and the Königlich-Würtembergische Bank. Though not on the founding committee, the second driving force behind the project, next to Adelbert Delbrück, was Ludwig Bamberger, a leading politician and currency specialist, and a former banker—he was related by his mother to the Bischoffsheims, and had been involved in the foundation in 1863 of the Banque de Crédit et de Dépôt des Pays-Bas. Most of the Deutsche Bank's share capital (15 million Marks) was subscribed by private banks. Significantly, the leading German private bankers—Rothschild, Mendelssohn, Bleichröder, Oppenheim—did not join in the project.

The Commerz- und Disconto Bank was founded the same year in Hamburg by leading private bankers, merchants, and shipowners, including Warburg, with the aim of supporting the city's trade.[125] The Dresdner Bank was founded two years later by Eugen Gutmann, the son of a small private banker in Dresden. In 1872, he persuaded the barons Karl and Felix von Kaskel to transform their old-established banking house into a joint-stock bank. Of the original capital, three eighths was subscribed by the Kaskels, Gutmann, and a few private individuals, the rest by a consortium of joint-stock banks mainly of the second order.[126]

In France, the Banque de Paris et des Pays-Bas, the country's leading *banque d'affaires* until its takeover by the BNP in the summer of 1999, was created in 1872 through the merger of two banks: the Banque de Crédit et de Dépôt des Pays-Bas and the Banque de Paris. The former had been established in 1863 by the Bischoffsheim group and soon established itself as a leading force in international issues (especially in the Ottoman Empire, Italy, Spain, and Austria) with branches in Amsterdam, Antwerp, Brussels, and Geneva. The latter was formed in 1869 by a group of banking houses in opposition to the Rothschilds' domination of the government loans market.[127]

In Belgium, where the presence of the international *haute banque* was particularly strong, the Banque de Bruxelles was founded in 1871 by Jacques Errera, a partner in the private bank Errera-Oppenheim, with a group of Belgian financiers.[128] In Switzerland, the Basler Bankverein was founded in 1872 in Basle by a syndicate of five private banks—von Speyr & Co., Ehinger & Co., Passavant & Cie, J. Riggenbach, and Bischoff zu St. Alban—in association

[125] Rosenbaum and Sherman, *Warburg*, p. 69.

[126] *Neue deutsche Biographie*; W. E. Mosse, *Jews in the German Economy. The German-Jewish Economic Elite 1820–1935* (Oxford, 1987), p. 225.

[127] See Bussière, *Paribas*, pp. 19–25.

[128] See Kurgan-van Hentenrijk, et al., *Dictionnaire des patrons*, pp. 275–7.

with the Frankfurter Bankverein, with the participation of the Wiener Bankverein, the Berliner Bankverein, and a few other private bankers in the city. After the series of amalgamations, the bank changed its name to Schweizerische Bankverein (Swiss Bank Corporation) in 1895 and was to be the country's largest bank for most of the twentieth century.[129]

The last major move by private bankers was the establishment in January 1904 of the Banque de l'Union Parisienne, by six members of the Parisian *haute banque*—Heine & Cie, Hottinguer & Cie, Mallet Frères & Cie, Mirabaud & Cie, de Neuflize & Cie, and Vernes & Cie—in association with the Société Générale de Belgique. The original capital of Ff.40 million was divided in half between each of the two groups. The association with the Société Générale de Belgique, one of Europe's leading banks, gave the private bankers access to its vast resources while they themselves still enjoyed considerable prestige and influence within the world of international finance.[130]

English private bankers were less involved in the formation of joint-stock banks, and have often been judged more hostile to them, than their continental counterparts. However, the contrast should not be exaggerated. English private bankers' opposition to joint-stock banks took place at a time when hardly any joint-stock bank had appeared in continental Europe. By the last quarter of the nineteenth century, there was hardly any noticeable difference, with the conversion of several English private banks into public companies. Lloyds Bank took this step in 1884 and had become Britain's largest bank by the turn of the century. Parr's Bank followed in 1890 and had risen to sixth place in 1913. In both cases, growth was a result of an aggressive amalgamation policy.[131] Moreover, a number of overseas banks were created under the aegis of private bankers, in the first place Glyn, Mills & Co., amongst them the Bank of Egypt in 1856, the London and Brazilian bank, and the Anglo-Austrian Bank, both in 1863.[132] And the major event of the *fin de siècle* was of course the foundation of Barclays Bank in 1896, the product of the amalgamation of twenty private banks, which became from the outset the country's fifth largest bank with more than £60 million deposits in 1914.

All this raises the question of the type of control that private bankers were able to keep over the banks they had created. It is usually assumed that in the 1860s and 1870s private bankers more or less consciously gave birth to what were going to become their most formidable competitors and would eventually drive them out of business. The general assumption is of course correct

[129] See H. Bauer, *Société de Banque Suisse 1872–1972* (Basle, 1972), pp. 44–51.

[130] See E. Bussière, 'La politique financière de la Banque de l'Union Parisienne de 1919 à 1931', Mémoire de maîtrise, University of Paris IV, 1977, p. 19.

[131] See R. S. Sayers, *Lloyds Bank in the History of English Banking* (Oxford, 1957); Gregory, *Westminster Bank*; Cassis, *City Bankers*.

[132] See P. L. Cottrell, 'A Cluster of Corporate International Banks, 1855–75', *Business History*, 33, 3 (1991), pp. 31–52.

over the long term. Up to 1914, and to a certain extent even up to 1939, things were more complex. Private bankers were variously involved in the creation of joint-stock banks and the degree of control they expected to maintain varied accordingly. At the lowest level, there were the passive investors in a new bank: private bankers were regularly offered opportunities to subscribe to new issues, as part of an issuing syndicate or as a friendly or allied firm. In such instances, their commitment was not greater than with any other portfolio investment. At a higher level, there were the promoters of a new bank, private bankers who jointly launched a new venture as if it were an extension of their own firm, in order to undertake financial operations which were beyond their individual means. They obviously expected, if not complete control, at least close collaboration and a degree of strategic guidance. As for the private bankers who converted their firm into a joint-stock bank, their expectations could vary from a desire to cash in and retire to a determination to remain fully in command and find the means to expand their business and face up to competition.

The chances of retaining control in the short to medium term depended on several factors. The first was the size of the stake held in the company: in the last analysis, major shareholders are in the best position to influence policy. However, being a major shareholder depended in turn on certain conditions. One was of course the retention of the shares originally purchased. Another was the ability, or the desirability, of maintaining a large stake in an expanding company, whose capital was being regularly increased. An amalgamation with another large bank, for example, would inevitably dilute the proportion of capital held by the original subscribers.

A second factor was the provisions of company law, in particular those concerning the competence of the board of directors—what has become known as corporate governance. The difference between the two-tier board existing in Germany and the unitary board existing in Britain and France is a case in point. Since the company law of 1870, responsibility for running German companies has been assigned to two boards: a management or executive board (*Vorstand*) and a supervisory board (*Aufsichtsrat*). However, the original idea of separating by law the day-to-day running of the firm from strategic decision-making did not materialize. Far from limiting itself to daily managerial tasks, the *Vorstand* soon seized upon the responsibility of designing the firm's long-term strategy, while the supervisory board's control became increasingly remote. Real influence over the conduct of business thus usually required membership of the executive board. In Britain and France, by contrast, membership of the board of directors (in French *conseil d'administration*) was sufficient in theory, though this was not necessarily the case in practice. British and French board members, especially bank directors, tended to delegate the daily routine of managing the firm to salaried managers and often confined themselves to supervisory tasks. As a rule, however, British boards were more involved in the running of the firm than their French counterparts.

And a third factor, particularly important in the medium term, was what could be called the dynastic factor, in other words the availability of heirs capable, and willing, to take the torch from their father, possibly from their uncle or father-in-law.

Remaining fully in charge of large joint-stock banks proved difficult for private bankers. In any case, this was not necessarily the most desirable option. Managing a large bank was a demanding full-time occupation: few wealthy private bankers were prepared to trade the easy life of a distinguished semi-amateur for the pressures of a professional job. As Walter Bagehot perceptively put it: 'He would sacrifice a suitable and a pleasant life for an unpleasant and unsuitable life.'[133] And indeed there were few attempts at holding on to full managerial control. Barclays Bank was probably the only case: all its directors were 'practitioners' who somewhat retained their status of private bankers as directors of the local banks from which they had come. These local boards also made it possible to preserve the younger generations' right of entry into the profession. Significantly, Barclays did not appoint a general manager, as was common practice in the other joint-stock banks, simply a secretary, as was usual in private banks. By 1903, a post of general manager had been created and awarded to an outsider, Frederick Goodenough.[134] However, the founding families retained considerable power within the bank until well after the Second World War; and, although this power had considerably declined by the late twentieth century, one of their scions still held the chairmanship in 1998. This is a unique instance in the history of European banking: a very large bank remaining if not in family hands at least under strong family control. How to account for such an outcome? The strength of the founding dynasties undoubtedly played a role, as well as the number of families involved, and the density of their internal network of relationships, based on a succession of intermarriages repeated over three or four generations. But there was also the commitment of the founders, whose firms were merged into the new bank and who had no intention of retiring from active business life.

Attempts at retaining overall strategic control were more common and met with mixed success, ranging from the frustration and disappointment of being excluded from the inner circle to the satisfaction of having a well-oiled machine at one's disposal as can be seen in the contrasting examples of the Deutsche Bank, the Swiss Bank Corporation, and the Banque de l'Union Parisienne.

133 W. Bagehot, *Lombard Street. A Description of the Money Market* (London, 1873), p. 280.
134 See Cassis, *City Bankers*, pp. 23–4.

The founders of the Deutsche Bank, in the first place Adelbert Delbrück, intended to run the bank. As members of the administrative board, they were to take the major policy decisions and delegate their implementation to the managing directors. The latter, however, were not prepared to be treated as mere subordinates.[135] A power struggle ensued and turned to the advantage of the executive board, led by the strong personality of Georg von Siemens but which also included such eminent bankers as Hermann Wallich and Max Steinthal. Not only did the *Vorstand* assume full managerial control, but the Deutsche Bank asserted its independence. The relationships with Delbrück Leo & Co., for example, became increasingly cool, with the issuing business no longer jointly undertaken, and the director general, Georg von Siemens, having the edge over the chairman of the supervisory board, Adelbert Delbrück.[136] Delbrück and his colleagues could not stay for long in command of a rapidly expanding bank, led by ambitious and highly capable professional managers, in a country where managing boards were rapidly gaining in autonomy and socio-professional status. We do not know whether this incurred any loss of income for the private bankers, but it did not affect their long-term existence: two of the main protagonists, Delbrück Leo & Co. and Gebrüder Schickler merged in 1910, and Delbrück & Co. remained, until its acquisition by ABN Amro in 2004, one of Germany's most distinguished private banking houses.

The Swiss Bank Corporation was founded in 1872, two years after the Deutsche Bank, by five Basle private banks, in association with a group of German and Austrian joint-stock banks. However, the founding private bankers had a greater say in the running of the new bank than their counterparts at Deutsche Bank. To begin with, they were in a majority on the board of directors, even though representatives from the German and Austrian banks had of course to be admitted. Significantly, seven out of a maximum of seventeen board members, including the chairman, had to reside in Basle; more importantly, the same rule applied to five of the seven members of the committee of the board. Moreover, no managing director was appointed until 1899, after the Bank had considerably expanded—and changed its name from Basler Bankverein to Schweizerische Bankverein. Responsibilities were henceforth increasingly delegated to professional managers, under the strong leadership of Léopold Dubois.[137] Nevertheless, a proper managing board was not formally set up before 1929. Representatives of the founding banking houses could thus retain some influence. One of them, Johann Jakob

[135] See Gall et al. *Deutsche Bank*, p. 118.

[136] C. Fürstenberg, *Die Lebensgeschichte eines deutschen Bankiers* (Düsseldorf/Vienna, 1968; 1st edn 1938), p. 209.

[137] See M. Mazbouri, *L'émergence de la place financière suisse (1890–1913)* (Lausanne, 2005), pp. 274–83.

Schuster-Burckhardt, a partner in von Speyr & Co., was the bank's longest serving chairman (from 1881 to 1901) and combined an active chairmanship with his own worldwide business interests. The five founding private banks remained strongly interested in the bank's affairs. For example, they originally took 50 per cent of the new issue business, but their share was reduced to 35 to 40 per cent in 1890, when the bank's capital was increased to 15 million francs. As the bank continued to grow, new terms had to be agreed, guaranteeing a minimum of 20 per cent for issues of less than one million francs, and 30 per cent for those that were higher.[138]

The Parisian *haute banque* remained even more in control of its *banque d'affaires*, the Banque de l'Union Parisienne (BUP), even though it had been founded with the Société Générale de Belgique in 1904—a full generation later than the Swiss Bank Corporation. The board of directors included representatives of the six founding private houses, the Société Générale de Belgique, and the old Banque Parisienne, which was taken over by the new bank, as well as a few independent people. More importantly, each of the founding private houses was represented on the board's management committee, a body which met twice a week and was responsible for making the decisions concerning all aspects of the bank's activities. Significantly, the general manager was not in regular attendance of these meetings. Participations in underwriting syndicates and other businesses were usually on a fifty-fifty basis, while the BUP would as a rule support a new issue floated by one of the founding houses.[139]

Most former private bankers were perfectly happy to assume a relatively passive role in their new bank. This was particularly the case in Britain, where the amalgamation movement brought a multitude of private banks within the fold of the expanding joint-stock banks. At Lloyds Bank, for example, 64 per cent of the directors in office between 1890 and 1914 were former private bankers; the proportion was 50 per cent at the Union of London and Smiths Bank.[140] This does not mean that all, or even a majority, of the former partners joined the board: out of twenty-four private banks absorbed by Lloyds during these years, representatives of only nine were admitted to the board, and never more than one per bank. Some rose to prominence. Three of the bank's four chairmen between 1870 and 1914 were former private bankers: Sampson Samuel Lloyd (1820–99), who took the step of turning the family firm into a joint-stock company in 1865, Thomas Salt (1830–1904), and John Spencer Phillips (1848–1909). However, the first two were also engaged in a parliamentary career, and only the latter remotely approached the definition of a modern professional banker. At the Union of London and Smiths Bank,

138 Bauer, *Société de Banque Suisse*, p. 101.
139 Bussière, 'Banque de l'Union Parisienne', pp. 253–69.
140 Cassis, *City Bankers*, p. 55.

by contrast, the chairmanship remained in the hands of a professional banker, Felix Schuster, despite the presence of several members of the Smith family on the board, following the takeover of the family banks in 1902. Some of them were large shareholders, including the deputy chairman, Francis Abel Smith (1861–1908). Fulfilling the duties of a bank director was not a particularly demanding task and consisted at most in supervising a particular aspect of the bank through membership of a committee of the board of directors. As befitted the banking aristocracy, this was perfectly compatible with the pursuit of other interests, whether in the City, in politics, or elsewhere.

Beyond the differences between individual banks, there is the question of the position of private bankers within their country's corporate structure. Put another way: to what extent were private bankers represented on the boards of large companies? And what sort of economic influence, control or even power did they derive from these connections? The situation varied between countries, as does the information available.

The best known case is Britain, where the most prominent merchant banks—and merchant houses—were represented, through their partners, on the boards of the major joint-stock banks, overseas banks, insurance companies, and investment trusts, as well as on the Court of Directors of the Bank of England. The same was true of the most distinguished private banking families whose firm had been taken over by a joint-stock bank.[141] This gave private bankers an impressive collective control over the huge assets of the City's financial institutions. Such a control was probably greater than in any other European country. It was due to several factors. One was the strength of these private firms, already discussed in the earlier part of this chapter. A second factor was the specialization of the English banking system and the division of labour between private firms and large financial institutions. The financial services available in the City of London, which made it the world's leading financial centre before 1914, were mainly offered by private firms, in the first place, the financing of world trade through the medium of bills on London and the issue of foreign loans and equities. Such activities, however, were made possible by the funds available in large financial institutions, especially the cash credit provided by the clearing banks. A third factor was the socio-professional hierarchy prevailing within the British financial world, which clearly separated directors and managers. The salaried managers of the large financial institutions, in charge of the day-to-day running of their company, were ultimately the subordinates of the directors who were, for the most part, partners in a merchant house or a merchant banking private firm. The combination of these economic and socio-professional factors ensured that

[141] Numerous examples of these overlapping directorships can be found in Cassis, *City Bankers*.

private banks, and more generally private firms, remained the cornerstone of the City's financial structure until well after the First World War.[142]

Universal banking, a lesser development of the capital markets, and the higher status enjoyed by salaried managers put German private bankers in an altogether different position. As noted earlier, private bankers retained a certain degree of influence in both international and industrial finance, in the latter case through their memberships of supervisory boards. Some of them—Louis Hagen, Ludwig Delbrück, Eduard von Oppenheim—were among the top ten pre-war 'big linkers', those businessmen, especially bankers, whose multiple directorships put them at the centre of a wide network of bank–industry, and more generally inter-firm relationships.[143] Even so, this was in no way comparable to the situation of private bankers in England: not only did a seat on the supervisory board of a German company offer far fewer opportunities for business control than one on the board of directors of a British company; but the overall balance of power within the German corporate structure was clearly favourable to the credit banks and their executive directors.

France, as is often the case, was somewhat in between. As noted above, one of the strengths of the *haute banque* was its presence on the boards of banks, insurance, railway, utility companies, and others, as well as among the *régents* of the Banque de France. In that respect, private bankers in London and Paris were quite close to each other. Their differences were mainly a question of degree: the position of the *haute banque* and more generally of the Parisian private banking and financial firms was not as strong as that of their London counterparts, whether in terms of number of firms, size of these firms, range of business activities or, especially, collective dominance over the country's financial system. The large French banks, whether the *banques d'affaires* or the *banques de dépôts*, were far more active players in the capital markets than the English clearing banks, taking a leading part in the issuing business and heading vast banking groups through interlocking directorships and controlling stakes in various companies.[144] This, in turn, gave far greater weight to their top executives. From this perspective, private bankers in France and Germany had much in common, in that both ultimately had to defer to the big banks.

[142] This argument has been developed in Y. Cassis, 'Management and Strategy in the English Joint Stock Banks, 1890–1914', *Business History*, 27, 3 (1985).

[143] Wixforth and Ziegler, 'Deutsche Privatbanken', p. 221.

[144] See J. Bouvier, *Un siècle de banque française. Les contraintes de l'Etat et les incertitudes des marchés* (Paris, 1973), pp. 102–29.

6

Indian Summer, 1914–1931

The long nineteenth century ended in August 1914 with the outbreak of the First World War. Hostilities were supposed to last a few months, soldiers were expected back home by Christmas. But the fighting dragged on until 1918, putting enormous economic strains on the belligerents. The war was won on the home front as much as on the battlefields: in the end, the Central Powers were overwhelmed by the Allies' economic and financial superiority. For all, however, the cost had been huge—in economic, financial, social, political, and human terms. The legacy of the war was daunting and the world which emerged after four years of total war had profoundly changed, even though this was not immediately perceptible to contemporary elites, including financial elites, who were keen to restore the old order of the Belle Époque. And yet, the First World War and its immediate aftermath did not mark a turning point in the history of European banks. Banks were of course affected by wartime conditions and had to adapt to a radically altered business environment. Severe banking crises broke out in former neutral countries (Sweden, Norway, Denmark, the Netherlands) in the early 1920s and German banks were seriously weakened by inflation and hyperinflation. But the general trend towards the domination of the big banks, which had started in the 1880s, continued more or less unabated. Moreover, despite the upheavals in the world economy, the old monetary order apparently remained in force with the restoration of the international gold standard in the second half of the 1920s.

As to private banks, they enjoyed a respite. The war did not accelerate a decline which had either already occurred or was yet to happen. If anything, the war years and the 1920s witnessed a revival of international private banking. A handful of select houses were entrusted with financial transactions on behalf of their government, while a coterie of international financiers, mostly private bankers in outlook if not in essence, took charge of the financial and monetary reorganization of post-war Europe. Europe, however, had lost its financial pre-eminence, and a leading position among European private banks henceforth required a powerful American connection. At the lower end of the private banking world, adaptation was the order of the day, though economic disorder could occasionally mean a new lifeline: in Germany, for example, the number of private banks increased during the inflation years.

WAR FINANCE

Banks thrive in peacetime, not in wartime, and nowhere in Europe did bankers welcome the outbreak of the war. Charles Addis, senior manager of the Hong Kong and Shanghai Banking Corporation branch in London, considered it a 'hateful necessity', while for Max Steinthal, chairman of the supervisory board of the Deutsche Bank, 'madness had triumphed'.[1] Private bankers were no exception to the rule. The most prominent amongst them, with their wide network of international relations, were best placed to use informal diplomacy to avoid the catastrophe. They did make a few attempts, but in the end they were powerless. Decisions were taken by others. During the July 1914 crisis, Lord Rothschild, still Europe's greatest banker, was kept out of things and was not consulted by the Foreign Secretary. His desire to preserve peace, reiterated in all his letters to his cousins in Paris, went no further than an account of the official steps taken by the British government.[2]

For most bankers, the outbreak of war led to a reduction in their activities. Disruptions caused to international commerce were an obvious handicap. More generally, the requirements of the war economy, in particular state intervention in economic affairs, cut out many traditional banking services, as government orders tended to be paid in cash. The first and hardest hit, however, were those private bankers directly involved in international trade and finance: the merchant bankers of the City of London. They stood to lose most from the collapse of the financial edifice based on the pound sterling and the universal use of the bill on London. Their two main activities were the acceptance of international bills of exchange and the issuing of foreign loans and securities: both almost came to a halt with the outbreak of hostilities. After the initial crisis, part of the accepting business could resume, in particular with countries not directly involved in the conflict. Foreign issues, on the other hand, were barred by the British government's determination to keep all money available for the war effort.

The problem faced by merchant bankers was simple but huge. An estimated £350 million bills of exchange were in circulation in the London discount market and had to be paid on maturity. However, with the outbreak of war, acceptors were no longer sure of being themselves paid by their clients,

[1] Quoted in B. Barth, *Die deutsche Hochfinanz und die Imperialismen. Banken und Außenpolitik vor 1914* (Stuttgart, 1995), p. 455.

[2] See Y. Cassis, *City Bankers 1890–1914* (Cambridge, 1994), pp. 308–9.

especially those now in the enemy camp. No payment could be expected on a good third of these £350 million: an estimated £60 to 70 million were outstanding acceptance liabilities by German and Austrian firms to London merchant banks (whose total capital was thought to be only £20 million), and there was probably an equal amount outstanding from Russia, with which normal commercial communications had been cut.[3] Given the complex and delicate mechanism of the City, the London financial markets were thrown into a severe crisis in the last days of July and the first days of August 1914.[4] The huge assets of the clearing banks, which provided the cash credit on which the entire system was running, were in danger of becoming illiquid. Their loans to the Stock Exchange—amounting to some £80 million—were threatened by the fall in stock prices and the closure of the London Stock Exchange on 31st July. Their loans to the discount market, as well as their own portfolio of bills of exchange, were put at serious risk by the absence of remittances from abroad. The crisis was somewhat aggravated by the banks calling back in their loans and refusing to pay out sovereigns to their customers, thus creating panic among the general public. Many a City banker must have shared the feelings of Gaspard Farrer, a partner in Baring Brothers, for whom it was 'mortifying in the extreme to find how instantaneously the credit edifice which we have been building for generations could tumble to pieces in a night'.[5] Collapse was avoided by the concerted action of the Bank of England, the banks and the government. A moratorium on the settlements of outstanding bills was announced on 2 August. The Bank Holiday, which fell on Monday 3 August, was extended and the banks did not re-open until the following Friday, while an emergency issue of notes provided liquidity to the system.

For the merchant banks, the crisis required delicate negotiations with the Bank of England and the government, and a measure of financial assistance. In order to take concerted action, a meeting of all the leading firms was convened on 5 August 1914 on the premises of Messrs. Fredk. Huth & Co. The following houses were invited: N. M. Rothschild & Sons; Arbuthnot Latham & Co.; Baring Brothers & Co. Ltd; Arthur H. Brandt & Co.; Wm Brandt, Sons & Co.; Brown, Shipley & Co.; Cunliffe Brothers; Frühling & Goschen; Antony Gibbs & Sons; C. J. Hambro & Son; Horstman & Co.; Kleinwort, Sons & Co.; König Brothers; Lazard Brothers & Co.; Morgan, Grenfell & Co.; Neuman, Luebeck & Co.; A. Rüffer & Sons; J. Henry Schröder & Co.; Seligman Brothers; Wallace Brothers & Co.; as well as Fredk. Huth & Co., the inviting house. This was the first step towards the formation of a merchant

[3] R. Roberts, *Schroders. Merchants & Bankers* (London, 1992), p. 153.

[4] See E. V. Morgan, *British Financial Policy, 1914–1925* (London, 1953); M. De Cecco, *Money and Empire. The International Gold Standard, 1890–1914* (Oxford, 1974), pp. 127–70; R. Roberts, *Saving the City. The Great Financial Crisis of 1914* (Oxford, 2013).

[5] Quoted in P. Ziegler, *The Sixth Great Power. Barings, 1762–1929* (London, 1988), p. 320.

bankers' pressure group, which was formally constituted on a second meeting on 10 August and took the name of the Accepting Houses Committee. They elected as chairman, Frederick Huth Jackson, one of the most prominent members of the profession: senior partner of Fredk. Huth & Co., he had been a director of the Bank of England since 1892, and served as chairman of the Institute of Bankers between 1909 and 1912. Members of the executive committee included representatives of the other houses most exposed to German clients—Brandts, Frühling & Goschen, Hambros, Kleinworts, and Schroders.[6] Negotiations led to an agreement between the Bank of England and the government, announced on 13 August. With the support of the Treasury, the Bank would discount any approved bill of exchange that had been accepted before 4 August. The result was a huge amount of bills—a total of £120 million—pouring into the Bank of England. As for acceptors who were not in a position to pay when bills matured, the Bank would lend to them at 2 per cent above Bank Rate and would not claim balances that they had not recovered within a year after the war. These measures revived the commercial bill market, though at the expense of an unprecedented increase of the cash stock.[7]

Merchant banks benefited unevenly from this relative revival. The extent of their involvement in Central European trade and finance was of course a determining factor. For a house like Baring Brothers, whose acceptances mainly related to North and South America as well as the Far East, remittances were only briefly interrupted by the outbreak of war. Business could resume shortly afterwards though at a lower level than in 1913: from £6.6 million in December of that year, acceptances fell to £3.7 million a year later, recovered to £6.3 million in 1915 and averaged £4.5 million for the rest of the war.[8] Schroders, by contrast, had a much rougher time, with acceptances falling from £11.7 million in 1913 to £5.8 million in 1914 and £1.3 million in 1918, having bottomed out at £634,000 the previous year. In addition, Schroders had to borrow £5.1 million from the Bank of England, at a high interest rate, to cover unpaid acceptances. Servicing the debt was a heavy drain on already dwindling resources and although the loan was mostly repaid within two years, interest payments ate up some 80 per cent of the firm's wartime revenues, leaving an average net income of just £9,000—as against £315,000 for the years 1905–13![9] With Schroders, Kleinworts were the hardest hit of the City merchant banks: over half their £14.2 million acceptances were due from Germany, Austria, and Russia, and they also had to borrow heavily from the Bank of England to meet their commitments. The volume of their acceptances had nearly halved by 1916, though £7.8 million was by no means an

[6] Roberts, *Schroders*, p. 154.
[7] R. S. Sayers, *The Bank of England 1891–1944* (Cambridge, 1976), pp. 77–8.
[8] Ziegler, *Sixth Great Power*, p. 324.
[9] Roberts, *Schroders*, pp. 160–2.

insignificant amount. Profits figures are not available, but the partners' capital rose by a mere 6 per cent between 1913 and 1918—to £4.7 million—whereas it had more than doubled in the previous nine years.[10]

For the few houses involved in government finance, the war offered highly profitable business opportunities. The war was financed through taxation, borrowing, and inflation. While the Treasury and the Bank of England took charge of borrowing at home, through the issue of war loans, War Bonds and Treasury Bills, the leading merchant banks could still offer unique expertise and contacts for borrowing abroad and lending to allied governments. Not so, however, the Rothschilds. The First World War definitely marked the end of their supremacy in state loans, which had started to be dented at the beginning of the century. The Rothschilds desperately lacked a strong presence in the United States, where the sinews of war now lay. To make matters worse, the three partners, all in their seventies, died in the space of three years—Natty, Lord Rothschild, the undisputed head of the house, in 1915, his brother, Leo, in 1917, and the third brother, Alfred, in 1918—leaving no obvious successor in command. The bank suffered heavy losses during the first war years—nearly £1.5 million in 1914 and more than £100,000 in 1915—and its capital decreased from £7.6 million in 1913 to £3.6 million in 1918, partly because of these losses and partly as a result of capital withdrawals following the partners' deaths.[11] By then N. M. Rothschild & Sons was no longer the largest merchant bank in the City, having been overtaken by Kleinworts in terms of capital, and by Baring Brothers in terms of total assets.

The lion's share went to the house of Morgan, which led practically all the public loan operations of the British and French governments in the United States until 1917, when the United States entered the war. In January 1915, J. P. Morgan & Co. was formally appointed purchasing agent for Britain. This broke with normal practice, which was for the War Office and the Admiralty to negotiate themselves the purchase of war material, whether with British or with foreign suppliers. However, the new scale of demand required an agent who already had expertise and contacts in the United States. Morgan's task was to secure the best terms for the British government and to stimulate, when necessary, productive capacity. The agreed commissions, which were reviewed in the course of the war, were 2 per cent on the net price of all goods up to £10 million and 1 per cent in excess of that.[12] As the British government's intermediary with the New York firm, Morgan Grenfell benefited greatly from

[10] J. Wake, *Kleinwort Benson. The History of Two Families in Banking* (Oxford, 1997), pp. 138–41, 472–6.

[11] N. Ferguson, *The World's Banker. The History of the House of Rothschild* (London, 1998), pp. 982–3.

[12] K. Burk, *Morgan Grenfell 1838–1988. The Biography of a Merchant Bank* (Oxford, 1989), pp. 127–8.

these arrangements. Their net profits reached £439,000 in 1915 and averaged £185,000 for the rest of the War.[13]

Another firm to greatly benefit from the war was Baring Brothers. Barings' net profits topped £1 million in 1915 and reached an average of £589,000 for the next three years,[14] more than any other merchant bank. The bulk of this income derived from their 'Russian accounts'. As the Russian government's official bankers in London, Barings were involved in the negotiations between the Russian and British governments to secure the increasingly large loans required to sustain the Russian war effort. Barings made themselves several advances to the Russian government (always guaranteed by the British government) and orchestrated several interventions in order to rehabilitate the Russian exchange on London. Their commissions were usually a quarter of a per cent, for transactions virtually risk-free. Given the huge amounts involved, they added up to handsome profits. They received, in particular, a 1/16 per cent commission on the £300 million loan granted by the British government to Russia in September 1915, followed by a further £150 million twelve months later; their task consisted in collecting the Treasury Bills, discounting them at the Bank of England and crediting the proceeds to a newly opened account, the *Compte Spécial*.[15] Barings continued to offer their services to the Kerensky provisional government after the February Revolution of 1917, though most credit was refused, given the regime's highly unstable situation. Business of course came to a halt after the October Revolution.[16] The weakest link in the Allies' chain proved to be the richest source of profits!

In the other two major belligerent countries, Germany and France, private bankers could not fulfil such functions, having surrendered the leading role in international finance to the big banks well before the outbreak of war. As in Britain, borrowing played a major part in the financing of the war by the French and German governments. The big banks were deeply involved in the placing and holding of War Bonds and Treasury Bills, though a small share of business was left to the leading private banks. The Cologne private banking house Sal. Oppenheim, for example, was responsible for 0.24 per cent (about 233 million Marks) of the subscriptions to the nine war loans issued by Germany between September 1914 and October 1918, which must have earned it around 3.5 million Marks.[17]

[13] Burk, *Morgan Grenfell*, pp. 128–9, 268–9.

[14] Ziegler, *Sixth Great Power*, p. 377.

[15] See Baring Archive, 'History of the Russian Business of Barings, 1914–1985'; see also Y. Cassis, 'Banquiers, guerre et révolution: *Baring Brothers* et le rétablissement du change à Londres sur Petrograd, 1915–1918', in M. Porret et al. (eds), *Guerres et Paix. Mélanges publiés en l'honneur du Professeur Jean-Claude Favez* (Geneva, 2000), pp. 191–203.

[16] Ziegler, *Sixth Great Power*, pp. 328–31.

[17] M. Stürmer, G. Teichmann, and W. Treue, *Striking the Balance. Sal. Oppenheim jr. & Cie. A Family and a Bank* (London, 1994), pp. 308–9.

A major difference between the three countries, however, was the almost total absence of foreign borrowing by Germany. Unlike Britain and France, Germany was unable to make use of the American capital market. Despite the presence of a powerful contingent of German-born investment bankers, American business favoured the Allies, the more so as they became rapidly engaged in their supply of war material while trade with the Central Powers almost entirely vanished as a result of the sea blockade. Moreover, American opinion grew decidedly anti-German with the beginning of the U-boat warfare in February 1915. From the summer of 1914 to April 1917, the foreign loans marketed in the United States amounted to $1,250 million for Britain, $640 million for France, and a trifling $35 million for Germany.[18] In France, de Rothschild Frères still played a significant role. In June 1915, in order to avoid the embarrassment that the signature of a French government was not sufficient without a material guarantee, the Rothschilds, rather than the French government, borrowed $40 million through J. P. Morgan.[19]

Likewise in neutral countries, private bankers only played a marginal role in war finance. The exception, up to a point, might have been Holland, where private bankers remained serious players in international finance, but little is known about their activities during this period. In Switzerland, the most powerful among them, the Geneva private bankers, took part in the nine federal loans (totaling 830 million francs) issued by the Syndicate of Swiss Banks between 1914 and 1918, mostly through their joint subsidiary, the Union Financière. The Union Financière also granted a number of loans to the Entente powers. Switzerland, however, also had to borrow abroad. For that purpose, it relied on one of Geneva's leading private banks, G. Pictet & Cie. Pictet were able to use their American connections and, together with Lee Higginson, they negotiated the three loans (amounting to $70 million) that the Swiss Confederation took out in the United States to ensure its provision of fresh supplies.[20]

The situation was different in Sweden, where the family controlled Stockholm Enskilda Bank remained one of the country's leading banking institutions—despite being increasingly outdistanced, in terms of size, by its two major competitors, the Handelsbanken and the Skandinaviska Banken. However, the Stockholm Enskilda was far more engaged in international activities than the other major banks, with its foreign assets increasing by more than 100 million kronor between 1913 and 1918. Moreover, the bank's connections with government were reinforced by the appointment in 1914 of its chairman, K. A. Wallenberg, as Swedish Minister of Foreign Affairs.

[18] V. Carosso, *Investment Banking in America. A History* (Cambridge, Mass., 1970), p. 212.

[19] Y.-H. Nouailhat, *France et Etats-Unis (août 1914-avril 1917)* (Paris, 1979), pp. 268–9.

[20] *Pictet & Cie 1805–1955* (Geneva, 1955), pp. 57–8. See also H. Bauer, *Société de Banque Suisse 1872–1972* (Basle, 1972), pp. 198–9; and L. Ruggia, 'Les relations financières de la Suisse pendant la première Guerre Mondiale', in Y. Cassis and J. Tanner (eds), *Banques et crédit en Suisse (1850–1930)* (Zurich, 1993), pp. 77–95.

Although K. A. Wallenberg relinquished his chairmanship during his three years in office, his brother Marcus remained the bank's managing director throughout the period, between 1911 and 1920.[21]

Knut Wallenberg's appointment as foreign minister was the highest office reached by a private banker during the war. In all countries, however, private bankers were called on to hold official or semi-official functions falling within their fields of expertise. This was not a privilege, or duty, reserved for private bankers. The importance of the economic front in waging a total war hugely increased the level of state intervention and led to far greater collaboration between business and government. Among the more prominent figures were Walther Rathenau, chairman of the giant electrical concern, AEG, who established in August 1914 the Raw Materials Section of the German War Ministry; or Louis Loucheur, a building contractor and former *polytechnicien*, who became French minister of armaments in 1917. But a myriad of others were appointed to—usually unpaid—senior positions in ministries, participated in various committees, and were entrusted with ad hoc missions.

Leading private bankers, with their financial expertise, wide international connections and closeness to political circles, were thus able to play a more influential role than their actual bank. In some cases, this could take the form of old style financial diplomacy. Max Warburg, for example, was entrusted with semi-official missions. In 1915, he was requested by the Foreign Ministry to go to Sweden in order to try and influence the Swedish government, through its foreign minister—and fellow private banker—Knut Wallenberg; and in March 1918, the new Reich Chancellor, Count von Hertling, asked him to go to Holland in order to make contact with the new resident American Minister with a view to sounding out peace possibilities.[22] Likewise Lord Revelstoke, Baring Brothers' senior partner, was given the honorary title of Minister Plenipotentiary and was a member, as British financial expert, of Lord Milner's mission at the Allied Conference in Petrograd in January 1917.[23]

INDIAN SUMMER: THE 1920s

Financial diplomacy took a new dimension in the aftermath of the First World War. The problems inherited from the war and the early post-war years ultimately required political decisions. Yet many of these problems were of

[21] U. Olsson, *At the Centre of Development. Skandinaviska Enskilda Banken and its Predecessors 1856–1996* (Stockholm, 1997), pp. 124–9.

[22] E. Rosenbaum and A. J. Sherman, *M.M. Warburg & Co., 1798–1938* (London, 1979), pp. 115–19.

[23] J. Orbell, 'Baring, John, 2nd Lord Revelstoke (1863–1929): Merchant Banker', in D. Jeremy (ed.), *Dictionary of Business Biography*, 5 vols (London, 1984–6), vol. 1, pp. 164–7.

an economic and financial nature, often of a high degree of technical complexity. The financial effects of the war were at the heart of the matter: the monetary disorders of the early 1920s, culminating in the German hyperinflation of 1923; the problems posed by monetary stabilization and the restoration of the Gold Standard; and the questions of German reparations and Allied war debts, which poisoned international relations until 1931. This is not the place to discuss these well-known episodes of European history.[24] What is interesting from our perspective is that a group of international private bankers were, in these particular circumstances, able to play a role incommensurate with the size of their firm.

Status and Power

Despite the overwhelming position of the big banks in the German economy, the most important figures during the Peace Conference and the discussion of the reparations question were two private bankers, Max Warburg and Carl Melchior, both partners in M. M. Warburg & Co., who were prominent than the directors of the Deutsche Bank.[25] The reason was not only the experience of international affairs that leading private bankers traditionally had, but also Warburg's powerful American connections. Carl Melchior was appointed a member of the principal delegation, while Max Warburg joined the financial delegation which accompanied the German negotiators to Versailles.[26] John Maynard Keynes was Melchior's opposite number during the conference and has immortalized in a memoir his 'defeated enemy'.[27]

A few private banking houses were still in a position to offer their government financial assistance in times of crisis. The role played by Lazard Frères during the speculation against the franc in 1924 was their first claim to fame—and to a possible succession to the Rothschilds' leadership. France, like other belligerents, had financed war through public borrowing and inflation, with the national debt increasing nearly fivefold and the wholesale price index three-and-a-half-fold between 1913 and 1919. France continued to borrow heavily in the immediate post-war years, confident that Germany would pay for war damage and reconstruction: the national debt nearly doubled between 1919 and 1921. The payment of German reparations, however, was to prove a rather vexed question while the United States was adamant that there should

[24] See C. H. Feinstein, P. Temin, and G. Toniolo, *The European Economy Between the Wars* (Oxford, 1997).

[25] G. Feldman, 'The Deutsche Bank from World War to World Economic Crisis, 1914–1933' in L. Gall et al., *The Deutsche Bank, 1870–1995* (London, 1995), p. 185.

[26] Rosenbaum and Sherman, *Warburg*, p. 121.

[27] J. M. Keynes, *Two Memoirs. Dr. Melchior: a Defeated Enemy; and my Early Beliefs* (London, 1949).

be no link between reparations and Allied debts. The French government's problems were compounded by the size of its floating debt and the insufficiency of its tax income. The franc began to slide, reaching 11 to the dollar in 1919 (down from 5.18 in 1913) and, after much fluctuation, 19 in 1923.[28] By late 1923, speculation mounted against the French franc. The German, Austrian, and Hungarian currencies had been stabilized and speculators, having pocketed hefty profits, were ready to move on to a new target. The franc looked the most likely casualty. Real possibilities of a financial recovery appeared increasingly doubtful amidst a persistent budget deficit, government indecision in tackling the situation, and uncertainties over reparations payments following the passive resistance to the Ruhr occupation by France and Belgium in 1923. The franc fell to 23 to the dollar by mid-January 1924 and to 29 by 8 March: France faced the risk of a total collapse of its currency.

Government legislation on capital flows had little effect. The counterattack against speculators had to be fought on the capital markets and was led by Lazard Frères, in particular two of its partners, Raymond Philippe and Michel Lazard, together with a circle of trusted friends including the financier Octave Homberg, the private banker Robert Wolff, a partner in Alfred Salomon Cahen & Cie, and Maurice Bokanowski, a deputy in the French National Assembly and Wolff's brother in law. Speculation was mainly, though by no means exclusively, German and Austrian, in particular through the Amsterdam branch of Mendelssohn & Co. and the Unionbank of Vienna—the so-called Mannheimer–Bosel syndicate, from the names of the respective heads of the two banks. But 'Anglo-Saxon' as well as French speculators were also involved in what is unlikely to have been a politically motivated and coordinated action in order to exert diplomatic pressure on France. Effective action required ample financial means. On 5 March, the team from Lazard Frères met with the Prime Minister, Raymond Poincaré, and the Finance Minister, de Lasteyrie. A $100 million credit, backed by the Banque de France, was granted by J. P. Morgan on 12 March, to serve as a war chest. The dollar had reached 27 francs on 8 March, and slightly fallen by 10 March. On the 12th, on the official announcement of the Morgan loan, it fell below the highly psychological 20 franc mark, then to 19 on the 15th, and 18 on the 24th. By late April, the exchange rate was about 12 francs to the dollar. Another crisis, however, was soon to resurface before the eventual stabilization of the franc in 1926 at 25.5 to the dollar and the return to gold at this rate in 1928.[29] But Lazard would no longer be part of those events.

[28] See S. A. Schuker, *The End of French Supremacy in Europe. The Financial Crisis of 1924 and the Adoption of the Dawes Plan* (Chapel Hill, 1976). Good overview in C. Kindleberger, *A Financial History of Western Europe* (London, 1984), pp. 346–55.

[29] J.-N. Jeanneney, *L'argent caché. Milieux d'affaires et pouvoir politique dans la France du XXe siècle* (Paris, 1981).

The end of the First World War marked the advent of New York as 'a hub of international finance',[30] competing with London for world supremacy. In particular, the United States had become a creditor nation, and given the abundance of capital in New York, American private banks provided greater financial assistance to European governments than European private banks. No single firm monopolized the issues of any one country, though the house of Morgan was in the forefront. In particular, they led the syndicate which floated the American share of the Dawes Loan ($110 million) granted to Germany in October 1924. The loan—the largest granted to Germany—was an essential part of the Dawes Plan which opened the way to economic recovery by offering a temporary solution to the reparations question (annual increments were introduced and additional payments were linked to a prosperity index). The role of American investment banks in the promotion and underwriting of foreign government issues, which reached unprecedented levels in the 1920s, is beyond the scope of this book. One aspect of their history, however, is highly relevant to European private bankers—the persistence and long-lasting success of family-owned and controlled private investment banks, despite the strong competition from newly-founded security affiliates of commercial banks and investment trusts.[31]

The 1920s were undoubtedly J. P. Morgan & Co.'s apogee. The bank was still the largest private banking house in the United States, and probably the world, with its total assets amounting to $680 million in 1929, in other words more than four times that of the City's largest merchant banks. It undeniably lagged far behind the large national banks in terms of size. But it was the country's top investment bank, capable between 1919 and 1933 of putting on the market, usually in cooperation with other banking houses, more than $6 billion worth of stock, including two billion in both public and private foreign securities. Furthermore, its close association with Morgan Grenfell in London and Morgan Harjes in Paris guaranteed it a strong international presence. J. P. Morgan & Co.'s prestige was derived, in addition to the volume of its operations, from its position at the hub of the world of business and politics, particularly in the field of financial diplomacy during the 1920s. The other large private banking houses—Kuhn Loeb & Co., Kidder Peabody & Co., Dillon Read, Lee Higginson & Co. and others—remained highly influential at both national and international levels. Kuhn Loeb, with assets of over $120 million in 1929—approximately the size of Baring Brothers or Schroders in London—remained firmly in second place. Dillon Read & Co., formed in 1921, was particularly active in issues on behalf of large German companies,

[30] See M. Wilkins, 'Cosmopolitan Finance in the 1920s: New York's Emergence as an International Financial Centre', in R. Sylla, R. Tilly, and G. Tortella (eds), *The State, the Financial System, and Economic Modernization* (Cambridge, 1999).

[31] Carosso, *Investment Banking in America*, pp. 271–99.

including $100 million on behalf of the steel giant, Vereinigte Stahlwerke, between 1926 and 1928.[32]

Despite the rise of the big banks, a powerful group of private banks thus retained a dominant position in two of the worlds' leading financial centres after the First World War—the investment banks in Wall Street and the merchant banks in the City of London. For the latter, unlike their continental counterparts, were still a force to be reckoned with in international finance both in their own right and through their multiple networks of influence, in the first place the Court of Directors of the Bank of England.

Such a presence was important because central banks became much more active in international financial and monetary affairs after the First World War. The first task was to rebuild the old monetary order, the second was to get it to work—until its final collapse in 1931. Central bankers played a major part in these processes, alongside government officials. The Bank of England was the leading protagonist, together with the Federal Reserve Bank of New York, during the first phase, the most active in terms of new initiatives; the two were joined by an ambitious Banque de France and a more assertive Reichsbank in the second phase. The role played by the Bank of England was not only a consequence of the pre-eminent position that Britain still retained in international politics and international finance and the responsibilities deriving from its great power status. It was also due to the personality of the Bank's longest serving governor, Montagu Norman.[33] Norman was the foremost central banker of the interwar years, if only by virtue of his length of time in office—he was governor from 1920 to 1944. But there was also his mission and style. The mission—the restoration of the international gold standard—is well known and has little to do with private banking. The style is well known too, but is far more relevant to our primary concern.

Montagu Norman was a most accomplished product of the nineteenth-century world of the London private banks. His father, Frederick Henry Norman, was a private banker—a partner in Martin & Co., a City private deposit bank. His maternal grandfather, Marks Wilks Collet, was also a private banker—a partner in Brown Shipley & Co., a City merchant bank—and a director and governor of the Bank of England. And his paternal grandfather, Henry Warde Norman, was a merchant in the City of London and one of the longest serving directors of the Bank of England (from 1821 to 1872), though

[32] Carosso, *Investment Banking in America*, pp. 255–62.

[33] There is a vast literature on the subject. See in particular H. Clay, *Lord Norman* (London, 1957); R. S. Sayers, *The Bank of England 1891–1944*, 3 vols (Cambridge, 1976); G. Peteri, 'Central Bank Diplomacy: Montagu Norman and Central Europe's Monetary Reconstruction after World War I', *Contemporary European History*, 1, 3 (1992), pp. 233–58; P. L. Cottrell, 'Norman, Strakosch and the Development of Central Banking: From Conception to Practice, 1919–1924', in P. L. Cottrell (ed.), *Rebuilding the Financial System in Central and Eastern Europe, 1918–1994* (Aldershot, 1997), pp. 29–73.

he was never governor. Montagu Norman himself started his career as a private banker, with Brown Shipley, which led to his being elected a director of the Bank of England in 1907, as Mark W. Collet's replacement. Norman's switch from private banking to central banking was complete by the time he became governor in 1920. He had actually left Brown Shipley in 1915, marked out for the possible post of 'permanent' governor, an option which had been contemplated for some time in the City and at the Bank. Yet his approach to international affairs remained very much that of a private banker. Central bank cooperation in the 1920s, with Montagu Norman as its linchpin, was in many respects a perpetuation of the old-fashioned world of *haute finance*, with its club like atmosphere and the emphasis on personal relationships.

The close collaboration between the Bank of England and prominent private banking houses in Britain and America, in particular in the schemes for the monetary reconstruction of central Europe, added to their weight in international finance. Moreover, several Bank directors close to Norman, and key players in the glamorous world of international financial diplomacy, were partners in the leading London merchant banks: Frank Tiarks, a partner in Schroders, assisted Norman in his negotiations with the Reichsbank in 1921; Robert Kindersley, a partner in Lazard Brothers, was a member of the First Committee of Experts on Reparations in 1924; Lord Revelstoke, Barings' senior partner, was a delegate to the conference on German reparations in Paris in 1928; Edward Grenfell, a partner in Morgan Grenfell, was in permanent contact with J. P. Morgan in New York. Other influential Bank directors came from a different background, as for example Charles Addis, who played a major role in the Bank's international relations, and was a former senior manager in London of the Hong Kong and Shanghai Banking Corporation. But the private banking element definitely predominated.

Such a prominence was a British peculiarity. Members of the Parisian *haute banque* were well represented at the Banque de France, making up nearly a third of the *régents*, including, in 1929, Ernest Mallet, Edouard de Rothschild, Felix Vernes, the Baron Hottinguer, and Jacques de Neuflize. Edouard de Rothschild was unquestionably a powerful voice. But the *gouverneur* traditionally came from the senior ranks of the Treasury and international affairs were in the hands of senior officials such as Charles Rist or Pierre Quesnay in the late 1920s.[34]

Private bankers' representation was even weaker in the Reichsbank, though leading names such as Max von Warburg and Simon Alfred von Oppenheim sat on its general council. Hjalmar Schacht, its President from 1923 to 1930,

[34] See for example E. Moreau, *Souvenirs d'un gouverneur de la Banque de France. Histoire de la stabilisation du franc (1926–1928)* (Paris, 1954); K. Mouré, *Managing the Franc Poincaré. Economic Understanding and Political Constraint in French Monetary Policy, 1928–1936* (Cambridge, 1991).

had been with the Dresdner Bank and his successor, Hans Luther, was a former Finance Minister and Reich Chancellor. At the time of Schacht's succession, Carl Melchior, a partner in Warburgs, appeared the candidate best suited to deal with foreign central bankers, but he was ruled out because he was Jewish.[35]

The influence of private bankers within the Bank of England is unlikely to have affected its policy which, despite the perceptive criticisms of Keynes and a few others, was rather consensual amongst British elites. It was a matter of style rather than content, and in many respects a legacy from the past. But it also reflected the long-lasting vitality of the City merchant banks, the most powerful group of private banks still active in Europe in the 1920s.

City Bankers

There is no doubt that City merchant bankers continued to play an essential role in international finance and thus remained a key component of the British banking system. Of course, the First World War put an end to London's unrivalled financial supremacy. The return to the Gold Standard in 1925 was a deliberate, and ultimately unsuccessful, attempt to restore the City's pre-war predominance: financial leadership had now to be, at least partly, shared with New York.[36] The City of London suffered from Britain's weakened financial position, in particular from the sale of part of the country's overseas assets in order to finance the war and from the constraints on its balance of payments throughout the 1920s. In other words, London lacked capital, which was in superabundance in New York. However, the challenge was only gradual, for if capital was henceforth to be in New York, experience and expertise remained in London. Nevertheless, New York did establish itself as the major centre for foreign capital issues in the 1920s: they amounted to \$969 million (£219 million) in 1924 as against £134 million in London. (The figures were respectively £275 million and £139 million in 1927; and £138 million and £94 million in 1929.)[37] New York also took advantage of the war to challenge London's supremacy in trade finance. The conditions for the development of a discount market, which hardly existed in New York, were laid by the Federal Reserve Act of 1913: national banks were permitted to create trade acceptances, which were eligible for discount at the newly established Federal Reserve Banks. The war and the ensuing shortage of sterling credits led to a surge of dollar

[35] H. James, *The Reichsbank and Public Finance in Germany 1924–1933. A Study of the Politics of Economics during the Great Depression* (Frankfurt, 1985), p. 158.

[36] See Y. Cassis, *Capitals of Capital. A History of International Financial Centres, 1780–2005* (Cambridge, 2005), pp. 152–67.

[37] Figures given in K. Burk, 'Money and Power: the Shift from Great Britain to the United States', in Cassis (ed.), *Finance and Financiers*, p. 364.

acceptances: they amounted to nearly half the commercial bills in London by the end of 1919 and they continued to expand in the 1920s so as to rival the bill on London by the end of the decade.[38]

American competition, however, did not sound the death knell for City merchant bankers. For one thing, they were able to retain a significant market share in their traditional issuing and accepting activities, and for another they started to launch into new fields of international and, especially, domestic finance. Crucially, they were able to maintain their key position within the English banking system. In terms of size, they were definitely dwarfed by the joint-stock banks. They had already been trailing by some distance since the turn of the century. The bank mergers of 1918 extended the gap to huge proportions: the resulting 'Big Five'—Midland, Lloyds, Barclays, Westminster, and National Provincial—now controlled some 90 per cent of the country's deposits. The Midland Bank emerged as the world's largest bank with total assets approaching £500 million by 1928. This compared with about £33 million for Barings and £27 million for Schroders, two of the country's leading houses. Size, however, had never played a major part in the merchant banks' financial clout. The English banking system remained highly specialized in the interwar years, and merchant banks were still able to maintain their hold on their traditional niche activities, the accepting and issuing businesses, though they were facing increasing competition from the clearing banks. Their share of acceptances of bills of exchange, for example, had fallen to about 50 per cent by 1923, a still respectable market share. The major houses, however, were able to recover their pre-war position, at current if not at constant prices. Kleinworts and Schroders resumed their leadership, with respectively £18.6 million and £13.9 million in 1925, followed by Hambros and Barings with about £10 million.[39]

In the issuing business, merchant banks suffered from the informal control on foreign lending exerted by the Bank of England until 1925, in the run-up to the return to gold. And even though international capital outflows took off again between 1925 and 1931, they never regained their pre-1914 level: from £162 million in 1911–12, representing some 80 per cent of the new issues made, foreign issues fell to £85 million in 1925–9, representing only 30 per cent of these years' new issues.[40] Despite an undoubted decline, there was still a fair amount of foreign issuing business for merchant bankers to handle in London, and the competition from the clearing banks remained limited. Old loyalties survived: Barings resumed their privileged relationships with

[38] Roberts, *Schroder*, pp. 213–14.

[39] Wake, *Kleinwort Benson*, p. 476; Roberts, *Schroders*, p. 188; Ziegler, *Sixth Great Power*, p. 378.

[40] Figures quoted in S. Pollard, *The Development of the British Economy*, 3rd edn 1914–80 (London, 1983), p. 119.

Argentina, and Rothschilds with Brazil, even though a few loans could not be prevented from going to New York, especially in the early 1920s when special permission had to be obtained from the Treasury.[41] European issues gained in importance, with an informal distribution among the leading houses: Morgan Grenfell, through their links with J. P. Morgan, tended to lead the syndicates in German and Austrian government loans, Rothschilds in the Hungarian loans, and Barings in the Czechoslovakian ones. Hambros retained their hold on the Scandinavian business, while Schroders were the clear leaders in German corporate and municipal issues. However, in a more competitive international climate, and given the increased scale of foreign loans, the leading London firms stepped up their cooperation. Barings, Rothschilds, and Schroders had particularly close ties, sweeping aside their old rivalry and jointly floating sixteen issues in the 1920s—an alliance known in the City as the Trinity.[42]

Another important departure was the merchant banks' willingness to compensate for the decline in overseas issues by turning their attention to domestic issues, a field they had almost completely neglected before the war. Various reasons have been invoked for this lack of interest, the most convincing being the size of the issues involved: the foreign issues that the merchant banks generally handled were large, often in excess of £1 million, and offered fees that it was not possible to obtain with domestic issues, which averaged much less. The situation changed after the war, with several industrial companies (Anglo-Persian, Shell, ICI, Unilever, Dunlop, Courtaulds, Vickers, Royal Mail Group, and so on) reaching truly giant sizes, often as a result of far-reaching mergers.[43] Seizing these new opportunities, however, was a gradual process, which was only starting in the 1920s.

All the leading houses tried their hand, some more successfully than others. Morgan Grenfell was possibly the first merchant bank to become involved in advising and financing industry—what has become known as corporate finance. In 1925 in particular, they acted on behalf of General Motors, which was intent upon expanding in Britain, first in its failed attempt to buy Austin Motors, and then in its successful purchase of Vauxhall Motors.[44] Baring Brothers, at the instigation of the Bank of England, was drawn in 1924 into the intricacies of the declining industries: they raised money (£5 million in total) and provided financial advice to the ailing giant shipbuilding and armaments company, Armstrong Whitworth (which was merged with Vickers in 1928), for seemingly very little return. Their £4 million issue for the Underground Electric Railway (jointly with Rothschilds, Schroders, and

[41] Ziegler, *Sixth Great Power*, pp. 350–1; Ferguson, *World Banker*, p. 989.

[42] Burk, *Morgan Grenfell*; Ziegler, *Sixth Great Power*; Ferguson, *World Banker*; Bramsen and Wain, *Hambros*; Roberts, *Schroders*.

[43] See L. Hannah, *The Rise of the Corporate Economy* (London, 1983); Y. Cassis, *Big Business. The European Experience in the Twentieth Century* (Oxford, 1997).

[44] Burk, *Morgan Grenfell*, pp. 91–3.

Speyers) in 1928 proved far less troublesome and their flotation of the brewing company Taylor Walker in 1927 was far more profitable.[45] Schroders' main incursion into industrial finance was the formation in 1926 of the Pressed Steel Company, with a capital of £1.6 million, in order to exploit in Britain the patent for the production of steel car bodies by hydraulic pressing, pioneered by the Budd Company in Philadelphia. William Morris was one of the major subscribers in the new company.[46] Kleinworts, with little experience of the issuing business, were more adventurous and encountered more trouble: their involvement with the Sperling Combine, an audacious attempt at rationalizing the British shipbuilding industry in the 1920s, turned into an unwilling long-term commitment; and they lost money by imprudently backing the company promoter Clarence Hatry, whose ambition to rationalize the British steel industry led to his spectacular downfall in 1929.[47] All this activity must, however, be put into perspective: in the 1920s, the merchant banks' business outlook remained decidedly international.

All in all, merchant banks managed to hold their own in the 1920s. Their position within the City's corporate structure remained virtually unchanged.[48] Their total number very slightly declined (58 in 1930 as against 63 in 1910, according to the *Banking Almanac*[49]), though a certain amount of turnover is hidden behind this relative stability. In the same way, a number of firms were still partly involved in commercial, as opposed to purely financial, activities, though the proportion is impossible to establish, given that a majority still described themselves as merchants—including such names as Rothschilds, Barings, Kleinworts, or Morgan Grenfell. As before 1914, however, members of the Accepting Houses Committee represented the upper stratum of merchant banking, an inner circle which continued to exert a disproportionate influence over British finance. In 1930, its membership had hardly changed since its foundation in 1914. Two members had merged in 1920: Frühling & Goschen and Cunliffe Brothers to form Goschen & Cunliffe; and two had disappeared: Horstman & Co., established as early as 1802, and König Brothers, established as late as 1899, though neither of them belonged to the front-ranking houses.

With no weighty newcomers, the old hierarchy remained strongly in place, with Barings, Hambros, Kleinworts, Morgan Grenfell, Rothschilds, and Schroders leading the pack. In which order were they ranked? The question is

[45] Ziegler, *Sixth Great Power*, pp. 342–6. [46] Roberts, *Schroders*, pp. 208–9.

[47] See S. Diaper, 'The Sperling Combine and the Shipbuilding Industry: Merchant Banking and Industrial Finance in the 1920s', in J. J. Van Helten and Y. Cassis (eds), *Capitalism in a Mature Economy. Financial Institutions, Capital Exports and British Industry, 1870–1939* (Aldershot, 1990), pp. 71–94; Wake, *Kleinwort Benson*, pp. 237–42.

[48] See P. Arnold, *The Bankers of London* (London, 1938).

[49] R. Roberts, 'What's in a Name? Merchants, Merchant Bankers, Accepting Houses, Issuing Houses, Industrial Bankers and Investment Bankers', *Business History*, 35, 3 (1993), p. 25.

difficult to answer. In many respects, one can discern a certain convergence between the top six. This was partly the result of the new position of the Rothschilds, no longer in a class of their own. Figures are unfortunately not available after 1918, and so a precise assessment of the position of the firm is still impossible. Schroders and, especially, Kleinworts remained very strong on acceptances—with respectively £13.8 and £20.3 million in 1928. Schroders, however, had a larger issuing business and a direct presence in New York, which was to prove a precious asset in the following decades.[50] In 1923, the partners established J. Henry Schroder Banking Corporation (known as Schrobanco), with a paid-up capital and surplus of $3.2 million, rising to $9.4 million in 1929. Schrobanco was primarily engaged in dollar trade finance, which provided 80 per cent of its revenues in the 1920s, as well as in foreign exchange operations, underwriting and securities activities, and short-term loans to clients, in other words, the traditional activities of a London merchant bank for which New York now offered ample opportunities. Adding the total assets of the New York bank to those of the London house, one reaches £34.4 million, about the same as Barings and Hambros.[51]

Hambros was some way behind the others before 1914 and enjoyed a spectacular growth in the 1920s, due to a large extent to its merger in October 1920 with the British Bank of Northern Commerce under the name of Hambros Bank of Northern Commerce Ltd.[52] The British Bank of Northern Commerce had only been founded eight years earlier, in 1912, and with its strong Scandinavian connections (three quarters of its capital was in Danish, Norwegian, and Swedish hands) was an excellent match for Hambros. Nevertheless, such a move was unique among City merchant bankers, who rarely merged with each other, let alone with a joint-stock bank. The merger did not signal the end of Hambros as a private bank. The new bank was admittedly a joint stock company, with £1 million paid-up capital. However, the partners in C. J. Hambro & Son took up half the shares on its foundation and secured an absolute majority in 1928, when its capital was increased to £1.4 million. The first chairman in 1920 was Everard Hambro, then aged 78; he was succeeded by his eldest son, Eric, on his death in 1925, who was himself succeeded by his younger brother, Olaf, on his retirement in 1932. Olaf was to remain chairman until 1961. The family control was further emphasized by the name of the bank, which was changed to Hambros Bank Ltd in August 1921.

Baring Brothers also had a successful decade and could be considered as the premier merchant bank in the City in the 1920s. This was a remarkable

[50] See Roberts, *Schroders*, pp. 214–28.

[51] Without the Schrobanco, Schroder's total assets stood at £27.4 million in 1928, as against £34 million for Hambros, £33.4 million for Barings and £14.6 million for Morgan Grenfell. Figures are not available for Rothschilds and Kleinworts. See Roberts, *Schroders*; Bramsen and Wain, *Hambros*; Ziegler, *Sixth Great Power*; Burk, *Morgan Grenfell*.

[52] See Bramsen and Wain, *Hambros*, pp. 370–97.

achievement after the near collapse of 1890. Barings was one of the largest merchant banks in terms of balance sheet total, with a significant presence in both acceptances and securities businesses. Baring Brothers was also an extremely profitable bank: between 1920 and 1929, its annual net profits averaged £613,600, as against £382,500 for Kleinworts,[53] £334,200 for Morgan Grenfell, and £285,400 for Schroders. Finally, there was the prestige of its senior partner, John Baring, 2nd Lord Revelstoke. He might have been old-fashioned in his Edwardian grandeur, autocratic, vain and a snob. Yet under his guidance, Barings regained its reputation. He had the good sense to call in outside help and in 1924 offered the Canadian-born Edward Peacock a partnership in the bank, with the promise that he would succeed him as senior partner. Peacock was to prove his worth. But until his death in April 1928, Lord Revelstoke remained the 'indispensable man of British financial life',[54] and this was an undoubted bonus for his house.

In contrast to the survival of merchant banks, the disappearance of private deposit banks accelerated after the war. Only a handful of firms had survived until then: Glyns in the City, Coutts, Childs, Drummonds, and Hoares in the West End, and a few issuing and non-issuing provincial banks, including the distinguished Beckett & Co. of Leeds and York. By the end of the decade, all but two—Glyns and Hoares—had disappeared or lost their independence: Coutts & Co., bankers to the Royal family, merged with the National Provincial Bank in 1919, but retained its name, management, and style of service; Beckett & Co. was taken over by the Westminster Bank in 1921; and Drummonds by the Royal Bank of Scotland in 1924. While Hoares independence can be considered an oddity, the exception that confirms the rule, Glyn's remained a bank of some standing in the City in the interwar years. Size had long ceased to be any kind of asset and matters did not improve with the advent of the 'Big Five'. Nevertheless, Glyn's strengthened their position by amalgamating with two private banks: in 1923 with Holt & Co., who mainly acted as Army Agents; and twelve months later with Child & Co., of No. 1 Fleet Street, possibly the oldest bank in London, which had belonged for more than a century to the Earls of Jersey. Like Coutts, Child & Co. retained a separate identity within the enlarged bank known henceforth as Glyn, Mills & Co.[55]

Throughout the interwar years, Glyns was led by General Sir Herbert Lawrence, a Mills by marriage—he married in 1892 Isabel Mary, eldest

[53] The figures for Kleinworts might be underestimated as they relate to distributed profits. However, they do not include the years 1920 and 1921, for which no data are available and which on the whole were not very profitable. In addition, Kleinworts' capital *decreased* from £5.2 million in 1920 to £2.7 million in 1929, suggesting that the difference between net profits and distributed profits must not have been very large.

[54] Ziegler, *Sixth Great Power*, p. 333.

[55] See R. Fulford, *Glyn's 1753–1953. Six Generations in Lombard Street* (London, 1953), pp. 232–3.

surviving daughter of Charles Henry Mills, 1st Lord Hillingdon. Lawrence had originally joined the partnership in 1907, but he left Lombard Street on the outbreak of war in 1914 and returned as managing partner of Glyn's in 1919, bringing it much enterprise and energy.[56] Though no longer the force it had been in the mid-nineteenth century, Glyn's retained some of its clout in both domestic and international finance. The partners continued to hold directorships in the many City institutions traditionally linked to the bank. As chairman of Vickers, Glyn's long-standing customers and one of Britain's largest companies, Herbert Lawrence was at the very heart of the restructuring of the British shipbuilding and armaments industry, presiding, in particular, over its merger with Armstrong Whitworth in 1927. As chairman of the Anglo-Austrian Bank, he was part of Montagu Norman's banking schemes for Central Europe. But Glyn's were also part of Norman's plans for British banking, in particular his dreams of creating a Big Six.[57] Plans of a merger with the Lancashire banks[58], however, fell by the wayside. Finally, the bank's capital was sold to the Royal Bank of Scotland in the summer 1939. The partners were mostly young men and with the approach of war it was feared that if some of them were to be killed, the payment of death duties on their family holdings would cause formidable difficulties. Thus disappeared the last private (deposit) bank in the City of London.

Paris and the Provinces

For a generation or so, most members of the Parisian *haute banque* had primarily been involved in managing wealth, whether their own or that of their exclusive clientele. To a large extent, this meant leaving the initiative to more dynamic operators, whether newcomers or the already established *banques d'affaires*. Hottinguer & Cie for example, one of Paris's oldest houses and Barings' close allies for three generations, seemed, in Lord Revelstoke's words, to have no 'nervous desire to compete with more modern conditions, or to be tainted by the "get-rich-quick" feeling which is so prevalent nowadays'.[59] The other members of the Protestant *haute banque*—Mallet, de Neuflize, Vernes—were in a similar position. Mirabaud, for their part,

[56] See R. P. T. Davenport-Hines, 'Lawrence, Sir Herbert Alexander (1861–1943): Banker and Industrialist', in Jeremy, *Dictionary*, vol. 3, pp. 667–74.

[57] Sayers, *Bank of England*, pp. 248–52.

[58] Several joint-stock banks in Lancashire had not been involved in the mergers wave leading to the formation of the 'Big Five', in particular the District Bank, the Lancashire and Yorkshire Bank, the Manchester and County Bank, the Bank of Liverpool and Martins (from 1928, Martins Bank), and Williams Deacon Bank.

[59] Quoted by Ziegler, *Sixth Great Power*, p. 337.

continued to make handsome profits through the Mines de Bor which they had promoted early in the century.

De Rothschild Frères, which had towered above the rest of the *haute banque* since the early nineteenth century, was still a financial power. However, with the third generation now in control, they were showing unmistakable signs of entrepreneurial decline. They were content to manage their industrial interests—in railways (Chemin de fer du Nord), mining (Le Nickel, Peñaroya), electricity, and oil—without taking much initiative. For Guy de Rothschild, who would take up the reins after the war, the house was in need of a 'bold innovator'.[60] Guy's father Edouard (1868–1949), head of the house since 1905, was, in Jean Bouvier's words, 'a man who was feared, who was consulted and who was needed. But the Rothschilds were no longer domineering.'[61] They certainly continued to oblige the French government: Guy de Rothschild recounts, for example, how in the 1920s his father lent Wilfrid Baumgartner, the then secretary to the Treasury, the money he needed to make an important payment which he could not honour at the due date, without asking any question.[62]

On the other hand, major decisions could now be made against their will. This was most notably the case with the franc's return to gold in 1928. Poincaré's return as Prime Minister in 1926 had restored confidence and halted the flight of capital which threatened a total collapse of the franc; the question was now the rate at which to stabilize it. Edouard de Rothschild, together with the steel magnate François de Wendel, both *régents* of the Banque de France, advocated at return to, or near, its pre-war level, which implied a high revaluation; while the *gouverneur* of the Banque de France, Emile Moreau, was in favour of a de facto devaluation at a fifth of its 1914 value. Edouard de Rothschild suited his actions to the words by lobbying the government, and even selling sterling and dollars, in the run up to the decision in order to strengthen the franc. But in the end, the governor's point of view prevailed, something which would have been unthinkable in Alphonse's days.[63]

The 1920s saw the advent of Lazard Frères as a private *banque d'affaires*. Earlier than other French private banks, and not unlike Morgan Grenfell in Britain, Lazard became closely associated with major industrial companies in both a financial and advisory capacity, in a fashion prefiguring modern corporate finance practices. Their most important involvement was with Citroën, France and probably Europe's largest car manufacturer in the late

[60] G. de Rothschild, *Contre bonne fortune . . .* (Paris, 1983), pp. 78, 83.
[61] J. Bouvier, *Les Rothschild* (2nd edn Brussels, 1983), p. 309.
[62] Rothschild, *Contre bonne fortune . . .* pp. 77–8.
[63] Bouvier, *Rothschild*, pp. 299–309. See also Moreau, *Souvenirs*.

1920s. Its founder, André Citroën, was the first to apply American methods of mass production to the French motor industry, not only in production (he introduced assembly lines as early as 1919), but also in distribution (he set the pace in car advertising and pioneered sole dealers and hire purchase). Lazard not only sponsored Citroën's fourfold capital increase (to reach 400 million francs) between 1927 and 1928 but also took a stake in the company and was represented on its board of directors. Lazard proceeded, in particular, to introduce modern accountancy techniques to the firm. They also suggested that a 25 per cent stake in the company should be sold to General Motors, though to no avail. Relationships, however, soured and Lazard and Citroën parted in 1930.[64]

Another newcomer, at least so far as banking is concerned, was Worms & Cie. The merchant house had been founded in 1848 when Hippolyte Worms was set up to import British coal into France. His fortune was made from the building of the Suez Canal, as the main coal supplier to those building the canal and later to the ships passing through it. Worms diversified into shipping, and later into oil (as Shell's managing agent in Egypt and Sudan), and finally decided to develop its own banking business in 1929. Hippolyte Worms, the founder's grandson, who made the move into banking, had been impressed by the English merchant banks and intended to develop the business on these lines. The bank hardly took any deposits, using its own capital and reserves. Indeed, one of the reasons for starting a bank was to finance its own commercial activities in coal merchanting, shipping, consignment, and forwarding, though it soon followed the traditional pattern of merchant banking development into trade finance.[65]

The fate of private country banks is not easy to ascertain. There is little doubt about their continuing decline, but precise statistical evidence is still lacking, whether about their number or their share of the country's banking business. There must have been well over 1,000 provincial private banks in 1929 (though only 276 French banks published a balance sheet in that year);[66] but their economic significance cannot have been anything but limited *on a national scale*. However, they continued to play a useful part at the local and regional levels, despite the fierce competition from the 'big' banks (Crédit Lyonnais, Société Générale, Comptoir d'escompte) and even more from the large regional banks (Crédit du Nord, Société Nancéenne de Crédit, and others). They were able to survive by concentrating on niche markets,

[64] A. Sabouret, *MM Lazard Frères et Cie: une saga de la fortune* (Paris, 1987), pp. 91–6; H. Bonin, 'Les banques face au cas Citroën, 1919–1930: Essai d'appréciation de la puissance bancaire', *Revue d'histoire moderne et contemporaine*, 32 (1985), pp. 74–98.

[65] See *Un centenaire 1848–1948. Worms & Cie* (Paris, 1948).

[66] H. Laufenburger, *Les banques françaises* (Paris, 1940), p. 43.

especially local small and medium-sized businesses, by taking full advantage of their knowledge of, and reputation among, these local communities.[67]

Tarneaud, for example, bankers in Limoges since 1809, proved their worth during the post-war depression in 1920–1 by providing ample credit but only to companies they knew well enough. With some 50 million francs deposits in 1930, Tarneaud was a small bank, though it had expanded in the 1920s, opening new outlets and taking over small local banks, and had fourteen branches by the end of the decade. More importantly, Tarneaud was the local market leader, with a lot of customers in traditional industrial and commercial activities. They held the accounts of most of the region's shoe manufacturers, those of a host of papermakers, cardboard manufacturers, wholesale grocers, and, of course, Limoges porcelain manufacturers. But they were also bankers to various small traders, especially in the clothing industry, wine, and hardware, as well as to builders and garage owners. Courtois, in Toulouse, were in a similar position with about 41 million francs deposits and fifteen outlets in 1930; and local customers mostly in food and drink, and leather and clothing, trade and industry. Significantly, they were hardly involved in the sunrise industries which moved to the area from 1914 onwards—electricity, electrometallurgy, engineering, aerospace, which relied on the big banks.

Even smaller banks managed to survive by specializing in still narrower 'niches'. One of them was Lenoir & Bernard, in Amiens, in the north of France. They faced competition from the big banks and powerful regional banks such as the Crédit du Nord, having a capital of only 200,000 francs. However, the bulk of their activity was in brokerage, especially placing securities among their customers, in addition to a vast strong room and some discounting. There was thus some life left in the declining world of French private country banks. So much so, that new banks could still be established and grow rapidly in a highly competitive environment. In Grenoble, Nicolet-Lafanechère was founded in January 1923, with a capital of 500,000 francs, by Ernest Lafanechère, a former manager in bank Charpeney, and Victor Nicolet, a local wealth holder. The latter not only provided the capital, but also a wealth of connections within the local business community. By 1929, its capital had increased to 5 million francs.

Reputation and information, even combined with the most entrepreneurial drive, could not entirely compensate for lack of resources. Here, local private bankers could rely on two sources of financing. One was to widen their capital basis by turning their bank into a limited company without, however,

[67] The following two paragraphs are based on H. Bonin, 'Grosse Histoire du Crédit du Nord', unpublished typescript, 1998. A shorter version has been published under the title *Histoire de banques. Crédit du Nord 1848–1998* (Paris, 1998).

relinquishing control; the other was to secure the backing of a large Parisian bank, which could refinance their bills. In fact, most local or even regional banks, whatever their legal form, remained in family hands. Take the case of Courtois, in Toulouse. On 18 August 1919, the brothers Armand and Louis Courtois, members of the fifth generation in the business, turned their firm into a limited company with a capital of seven million francs (increased to ten million in 1921). The Courtois took up two millions, with the remaining five distributed among their local bourgeois acquaintance—around a hundred people, all relations or friends of the family. Armand Courtois became chairman and Louis Courtois managing director, though they did rely on the services of a general manager. In addition, the Banque de l'Union Parisienne took up 10 per cent of its capital in 1920.

The question remains, however, whether the surviving local and regional private banks were able to meet the demands of small and medium-sized firms in France. The answer is probably no. Their decline since the beginning of the century left a gap which was not immediately filled by the new semi-public institutions, such as the popular banks and the Crédit National, specifically created for this reason.[68] The 1920s thus appear as a transitory period, leading to the final demise of the private country banks as an essential component of the French banking mechanism.

Inflation and Consolidation in Germany

In Germany, the leading private banks survived the traumas of hyperinflation, mostly through their gains on the foreign exchanges, and remained major players within the 'niche' they had secured before the war. Their traditional network of international relationships was to prove an invaluable asset after the war, both in government and industrial finance, as Germany became a massive importer of capital and turned to foreign capital markets: until at least 1926 or 1927, leading private banks competed successfully against the credit banks for the mobilization of foreign capital.[69] They also maintained their overall position within the German corporate economy: in 1929, they still held 36.7 per cent of the seats held by bankers on the supervisory boards of industrial companies, as against 52.7 per cent for representatives of the big banks and 10.6 per cent for those of provincial banks.[70] They were also well represented among the so-called 'big linkers', with their multiple overlapping

[68] See M. Lescure, *PME et croissance économique* (Paris, 1996).
[69] Wixforth and Ziegler, 'The Niche', p. 116.
[70] Wixforth and Ziegler, 'The Niche', p. 106.

directorships in the major German companies. In 1927, four of them were in the 'top ten',[71] led by Louis Hagen, with sixty-four supervisory board seats!

In Berlin, Bleichröder, though still a prestigious name, continued its irreversible decline; and by 1931, when a community of interest was arranged with the flourishing Dresden bank Gebrüder Arnhold, it had become 'a shadow of itself'.[72] Mendelssohn, on the other hand, the other big name in Berlin private banking, stayed at the top, successively converting from foreign government finance, especially Russian state loans, to international currency transactions and loans to the German government. One of the key elements of its strategy was the opening of a branch in Amsterdam, led by Fritz Mannheimer, 'probably the most gifted and certainly the most colourful of the international speculators of the 1920s'.[73]

In Cologne, the long-standing leading house, Sal. Oppenheim jr. & Cie, had to join forces with the City's rising force, A. Levy & Co. The two banks formed a 'community of interests' in 1922, with Louis Hagen becoming a partner in Sal. Oppenheim. Such moves were relatively rare between private banks, though a number of them had pooled their foreign exchange business during the inflation years.[74] A. Levy had been founded in 1858 by Abraham Levy, the son of a small moneylender and moneychanger who had worked for Oppenheim, as a cashier's attendant, in the 1840s. In 1873 Louis Levy, Abraham's grandson—who took on his wife's name of Hagen and converted to Catholicism—succeeded to the business and became one of Germany's most influential figures in industrial finance in the following decades. He made a fortune in steel, hard coal, cables, electricity, and engineering, specializing in mergers and acquisitions and gaining the reputation of an 'industrial marriage broker'.[75] Louis Hagen's stature grew during the war. He became President of the Cologne Chamber of Commerce in 1916, and after the war he was regarded as a key figure in the economic reorganization of the German territories under French occupation. The reasons behind this *rapprochement* are not known, though Louis Hagen must have brought dynamism and new business opportunities to the Oppenheim bank, while gaining for himself and his bank a respectability which had so far eluded him. For Sal. Oppenheim jr. & Cie the later part of the 1920s were boom years, with its balance sheet

[71] H. Wixforth and D. Ziegler, 'Deutsche Privatbanken und Privatbankiers im 20. Jahrhundert', *Geschichte und Gesellschaft*, 23, 2 (1997), p. 221.

[72] F. Stern, *Gold and Iron. Bismarck, Bleichröder and the Building of the German Empire* (New York, 1977), p. 547.

[73] H. James, *The German Slump. Politics and Economics 1924–1936* (Oxford, 1986), p. 145.

[74] K. Donaubauer, *Privatbankiers und Bankenkonzentration in Deutschland von der Mitte des 19. Jahrhunderts bis 1932* (Frankfurt, 1988), pp. 83–4. Examples of such links include: Gebr. Bethmann with Deichmann & Co. in Cologne; Mendelssohn & Co. in Berlin with Gebr. Sulzbach in Frankfurt; the joint creation of the foreign exchange affiliated company, Marx, Hertl & Co., in Berlin, by S. Bleichröder, Delbrück, Schickler & Co., Hardy & Co., and E. Friedmann & Co.

[75] Stürmer et al., *Striking the Balance*, pp. 322–3.

total more than doubling between 1924 and 1928, from 50 million to about 125 million marks (£6.25 million).

Another bank in the Rhineland, Hirschland & Co., of Essen, also enjoyed rapid growth in the 1920s. Acting as an intermediary between foreign banks, especially British and American, and German industry, Hirschland was able to arrange the provision of credit for a number of leading Ruhr companies, including Gutehoffnungshütte, Mannesmann, Thyssen, GBAG, RWE, Klöckner, Phoenix, the Vereinigte Stahlwerke, and above all, Krupp. As early as 1924, Kurt Martin Hirschland negotiated a $10 million loan with an American syndicate led by Goldman Sachs, of New York. Significantly, Hirschland provided its customers with cheaper finance, more rapidly, than the big banks.[76]

The most conspicuous house of the decade, however, was M. M. Warburg & Co., of Hamburg. More than any private bank in continental Europe, Warburg was able to take advantage of its American connections, established mainly through marriages in the pre-war years. A major link was the International Acceptance Bank, established in New York 1921 under the auspices of Paul Warburg, who became its first chairman. Its original shareholders reflected the Warburgs' wide network of international relationships and included, besides the Hamburg house, banks in Britain (in particular N. M. Rothschild) and in the former neutrals (the Netherlands, Sweden, and Switzerland). The International Acceptance Bank developed a substantial business in the financing of international trade, and by the time of its amalgamation with the Bank of Manhattan in 1928, its acceptances had reached $60 million (over £12 million).[77] M. M. Warburg served at its European agent and executed much of its European business.[78] Another step was taken in October 1924 with the foundation, mainly through Paul Warburg, of the American and Continental Corporation, with a capital of $10 million, in order to extend credit and further investment in German industry. In London, the Warburgs initiated the formation of the Industrial Finance and Investment Corporation, another vehicle for German portfolio investment, whose shareholders included the Rothschilds, Kleinworts, and Japhets among merchant banks, Sir Alfred Mond (the chairman of ICI), as well as the Prudential Assurance and the International Acceptance Bank. In 1928 Warburgs established, together with Mendelssohn and the Nederlandsche Handels-Maatschappij, an international investment trust in Amsterdam, the N.V. Nederlandsche Credieten Financiering-Maatschappij, with a capital of 12 million guilders.[79]

[76] Wixforth and Ziegler. 'The Niche', p. 114.
[77] Rosenbaum and Sherman, *Warburg*, pp. 126, 140.
[78] R. Chernow, *The Warburgs. A Family Saga* (London, 1993), p. 224.
[79] Rosenbaum and Sherman, *Warburg*, pp. 135–40.

Warburgs were thus in a unique position to facilitate the inflow of foreign, especially American, capital to Germany and to raise funds for industrial customers such as AEG (for which they placed 25 million of a 100 million Mark capital issue with Guggenheim Brothers, of New York, in 1920), Daimler-Benz, Fried. Krupp, HAPAG, Karstadt, or IG Farben; for local authorities (Hamburg, Westphalia); and for public institutions (in particular a rediscount credit of $5 million, later raised to $10 million, for the Gold Discount Bank, a subsidiary of the Reichsbank, arranged with the International Acceptance Bank in April 1924). The firm's expansion and its increasingly national stature led to the establishment of a presence in Berlin in 1927. At first, this only consisted of an apartment for the accommodation of partners and the entertainment of Berlin-based clients, but it was extended into a small office the following year, with an up and coming member of the family as manager, Siegmund Warburg. In 1929, Warburg's total balance sheet stood at 382 million Mark (£19.1 million), making it one of the largest German private banks, probably on a par with Mendelssohn, though still some way behind the largest City merchant banks.

Provincial private bankers hardly lost ground, at least in numbers. Estimates by the Central Association of Bankers (Centralverband Deutschen Bank- und Bankiersgewerbes) show an actual *increase*, from 1,800 in 1913 to 2,000 in 1929, with a peak of 2,500 in 1925 as a result of a proliferation of unlicensed, sometimes crooked houses during the inflation years. But even in the 'normal' years, there can be little doubt that these figures included a high proportion of non-banking houses, especially brokers and other money dealers. Statistics from the Reichsbank reveal a slight *decrease* during the same period, from 1,221 to 1,100 (with a peak at 1,406 in 1925). In the 1920s, the amalgamation movement in German banking mostly proceeded at the expense of the provincial joint-stock banks. They were already linked to the big banks through 'community of interests' in the pre-war years, but were taken over by the latter in the early 1920s: their number fell from 104 in 1913 to 60 in 1929. As a result, private banks strengthened their position within the world of commercial banking (i.e., not including savings banks, cooperative banks and other special banks which dominated the German banking system) in the late 1920s. After falling from 24 per cent in 1913 to 13 per cent in 1925, their share of the total assets held by commercial banks rose to 19 per cent in 1929. By contrast, the share of regional banks, which had remained stable at around 36 per cent between 1913 and 1925, fell to 11 per cent in 1929, mostly to the advantage of the big banks.[80]

As in the case of France, the question of the economic significance of the hundreds of surviving provincial private banks remains open. Recent

[80] G. Hardach, 'Banking in Germany, 1918–1939', in C. Feinstein (ed.), *Banking, Currency and Finance in Europe between the Wars* (Oxford, 1995), p. 280.

estimates by Harald Wixforth and Dieter Ziegler can help to shed some light on the matter. Taking a more restrictive definition of a private bank, they only consider those which served as dividend payment offices for joint-stock companies, and were therefore more closely linked to trade and industry. Not surprisingly, the total number of such banks (365 in 1927) was substantially smaller than those with an account at the Reichsbank. Their decline since the beginning of the century was also steeper (down from 522 in 1907). More importantly, this decline was unevenly spread across the country. The number of those in financial centres such as Berlin, Hamburg, or Frankfurt, which in the German context cannot really be considered as provincial banks, hardly fell at all (from a combined 140 for the three cities in 1906 to 137 in 1927). In the deeper provinces, by contrast, there was a near collapse: from sixty-three to thirty-four in the North West (Hanover and Schleswig-Holstein, Oldenburg, Bremen, and Braunschweig); from sixty-three to forty-four in Sachsen and Thüringen; and from twenty-six to four in the North East (Pommern, Posen, West and East Prussia), where an added factor was the loss of the latter province to Poland after the First World War.[81] Such a decline of the very banks which were most closely linked to business enterprises would suggest that, as in France, local and regional private banks played at best a marginal role in the German economy in the 1920s, where they faced increased competition from the savings banks: the latter's share of total assets of all German banks reached 31 per cent in 1929 as against a mere 6 per cent for private banks.[82] The real upheaval, however, would only take place in the 1930s.

The Former Neutrals

Private bankers in smaller European countries had fewer opportunities to be involved in large international financial transactions. Geneva private bankers must have been the recipient of foreign funds fleeing from the financial chaos in Central and East-central Europe, though the amount remains enshrined in total secrecy.

Belgian private bankers were very much in decline, the few remaining meaningful houses (Hallet, Lambert, Nagelmackers, Philippson) only playing a marginal role in the country's banking life. However, they retained a strong presence on the boards of the railways, industrial, financial, colonial, and other companies, with which they had been connected since before the war; and like many of their counterparts across Europe, they became increasingly engaged in private wealth management.[83]

[81] See the complete figures in Wixforth and Ziegler, 'Deutsche Privatbanken', Table 3, p. 216.
[82] Hardach, 'Banking in Germany', p. 274.
[83] Information kindly provided by Ginette Kurgan-van Hentenrijk.

In Sweden, the Stockholm Enskilda Bank remained something of an oddity: a large bank where family ownership was strong and family control almost total. In 1925, the bank's chairman was K. A. Wallenberg, the deputy chairman was his brother Marcus Wallenberg, the managing director was Jacob Wallenberg (Marcus's elder son), and the deputy managing director was Marcus Wallenberg Junior (Jacob's younger brother). Moreover, the bank acted in many respects as a private bank, deriving much of its profits from commission rather than interest earnings.[84]

The Dutch private bankers were the most active on the international scene, a reflection of both their persisting strength and Holland's pivotal role in international financial transactions. Pierson & Co., for example, known until 1917 as Boissevain & Co., was one of them. Among other activities, it closely collaborated with Mendelssohn & Co. and the Nederlandsche Handel-Maatschappij in domestic and foreign issues, and together they founded the Nederlandsche Accept-Maatschappij in 1924 to provide trade credit to Germany. Extending its activities to other Central and East-central European countries, Pierson also came to manage the currency affairs of the Hungarian National Bank following Allard Pierson's appointment as Consul-General for Hungary in 1922. By 1925, its balance sheet reached 100 million guilders (about £8 million).[85] In the end, it is Hope & Co., one of the oldest private banks in Europe, which best illustrates the persistence of the *haute banque* in the 1920s. Still a highly prestigious, if no longer a truly large house, Hope acted as co-issuer of the two major international loans to Germany, the Dawes Loan in 1924 and the Young Loan in 1929, while one of their partners, C. E. ter Meulen, was a founder member, and sometimes chairman, of the Financial Committee of the League of Nations.[86]

[84] Olsson, *At the Centre of Development*, pp. 161–4.

[85] J. Jonker, Mees Pierson. *The Link between Past and Future. 275 years of Tradition and Innovation in Dutch Banking* (Amsterdam, 1997), pp. 72–3.

[86] J. Jonker, Mees Pierson. *The Link between Past and Future*, pp. 59–60.

7

Decline and Renaissance, 1931–2015

Considering the depression of the 1930s as a crisis of the private banks would be rather narrow. The worst depression of the twentieth century is more seriously remembered for the dramatic fall in industrial production—down by 28 per cent in Europe between 1929 and 1932, and by as much as 39 per cent in Germany, the worst affected country; for the collapse of world trade, down by 61 per cent at current prices; and for its dramatic social consequences, in the first place mass unemployment, with rates rising to well over 20 per cent in most countries.[1] Even more than the First World War, the crisis of the 1930s can be seen as a turning point in the world economic order, with the final demise of Britain's worldwide role, the collapse of the Gold Standard, the failure of laissez-faire, and the onset of state intervention.

The economic crisis was of course closely intertwined with the banking crisis of the early 1930s, whose main feature was the troubles of the 'big banks', and the collapse of some of them. First came the failure, in summer 1930, of the two major Italian banks, the Banca Commerciale Italiana and the Credito Italiano. They were secretly rescued by the national bank and the Italian government, which proceeded to a complete overhaul of the Italian banking system, putting an end to mixed banking and nationalizing the country's three largest banks.[2] The collapse of the Credit-Anstalt of Vienna—and its rescue by the Austrian government—followed in May 1931.[3] Two months later, on 13 July 1931, the Danat Bank, one of the Berlin 'big banks', closed its doors, prompting a run on German banks, which had to ration payments. Two days later, the Dresdner Bank declared itself bankrupt. Once again, the government had to step in. Its rescue package included an imposed merger between the Danat Bank and the Dresdner Bank, a quasi-nationalization of the German big banks, and the purging of their management.[4]

[1] Figures from C. H. Feinstein, P. Temin, and G. Toniolo, *The European Economy Between the Wars* (Oxford, 1997).

[2] See G. Toniolo, *Industria e banca nella grande crisi 1929–1934* (Milan, 1978).

[3] A. Schubert, *The Credit-Anstalt Crisis of 1931* (Cambridge, 1991).

[4] See K. E. Born, *Die Deutsche Bankenkrise 1931* (Munich, 1967); H. James, 'The Causes of the German Banking Crisis of 1931', *Economic History Review*, 38 (1984); H. James, *The German*

The French leading banks fared better. The Banque Nationale de Crédit, the country's fourth largest bank, suspended payments in 1931 and was built up again the following year, with help from the state, under the name of Banque Nationale pour le Commerce et le Crédit (BNCI), while the Banque de l'Union Parisienne, the second largest investment bank, was on the brink of bankruptcy in 1932 but was saved by the joint intervention of the Banque de France and the main Parisian banks.[5] Even in Switzerland, already a safe haven for fleeing capital, only the two largest banks—Swiss Bank Corporation and Crédit Suisse—were able to avoid large reductions of capital. Among the country's 'big banks', the Banque d'Escompte Suisse, Geneva, collapsed in 1934, while another, the Swiss Volksbank, Berne, was only saved by the intervention of the Federal government.[6]

The Great Depression thus signalled the end of the expansion of the big banks, which had proceeded more or less unabated since the 1880s. They survived and even the weakest were saved—their very size together with a concern about the safety of deposits ensured that public authorities would not let them fail. In other words, they were already 'too big to fail'. But they became more heavily regulated. In all countries (with the exception of Britain, and France until 1941), banking legislation came into force between 1934 and 1936, introducing—or strengthening—banking supervision and leading in some countries, such as Italy and Belgium, to a separation between commercial banking and investment banking. The big banks' expansion was also halted. With the loss of confidence resulting from the depression, they lost ground to public and semi-public institutions. In Germany, the commercial banks' share of the country's total banking assets fell from 49 per cent in 1925 to only 15 per cent in 1938, while that of the savings banks rose from 19 to 45 per cent.[7] In France, the four largest banks (Crédit Lyonnais, Société Générale, Comptoir d'escompte, and Crédit Industriel et Commercial) controlled 30 per cent of the country's total deposits (including publicly-owned financial institutions) in 1913. Their share had fallen to only 17 per cent by 1937 while that of the savings banks and the Caisse des Dépôts et Consignations had risen to a staggering 67 per cent.[8] Even in Britain, where they escaped unscathed from the storm, the big banks lost ground to

Slump. Politics and Economics, 1924–1936 (Oxford, 1986); T. Balderston, 'The Banks and the Gold Standard in the German Financial Crisis of 1931', *Financial History Review*, 1, 1 (1994).

[5] H. Bonin, *La Banque nationale de crédit. Histoire de la quatrième banque de dépôts française en 1913–1932* (Paris, 2002), pp. 165–77; H. Bonin, *La Banque de l'union parisienne (1874/1904–1974). Histoire de la deuxième banque d'affaires française* (Paris, 2002).

[6] P. Ehrsam, 'Die Bankenkrise der 30er Jahre in der Schweiz', in Eidgenössische Bankenkommission (Hg.), *50 Jahre eidgenössische Bankenaufsicht* (Zurich, 1985), p. 87.

[7] G. Hardach, 'Banking in Germany, 1918–1939', in C. H. Feinstein (ed.), *Banking, Currency and Finance in Europe between the Wars* (Oxford, 1995).

[8] Figures from A. Gueslin, 'Banks and the State in France from the 1880s to the 1930s: The Impossible Advance of the Banks', in Y. Cassis (ed.), *Finance and Financiers in European History 1880–1960* (Cambridge, 1992).

mutual and cooperative financial institutions: while the total assets of the savings banks and building societies together represented 17 per cent of those of the clearing banks in 1920, the proportion had risen to 37 per cent by 1933.[9]

This was to be a temporary setback. By the 1960s, large commercial banks had re-established the dominant position they enjoyed in the late 1920s and they continued their forward march in the following decades through internal growth, mergers, and mega-mergers. However, by the 1980s, the top firms included banks originating from the world of savings banks, mortgage banks, cooperative banks, which had so far lived apart from the world of commercial banking. Prominent among them were the Crédit Agricole in France; Rabobank in the Netherlands; the Banca Nazionale del Lavoro in Italy; the Westdeutsche Landesbank (WestLB) and the Bayerische Hypotheken- und Wechsel-Bank (Hypo-Bank) in Germany; the Abbey National and the Halifax in Great Britain.

The private banks were not able to take advantage of the big banks' setback. For them, the depression of the 1930s spelt the beginning of the end. The thrust of their story is fairly simple. Private country banks, which had retained some significance in France and Germany, were (nearly) wiped out by the crisis and its consequences. In their case, there was to be no revival in the post-war years. The *haute banque*, on the other hand, was weakened by the crisis, the slump and the war years. But it survived. The London merchant banks, in particular, still had plenty of life left in them. However, as they regained power and influence from the 1960s onwards, few of them could still be regarded as private banks in the traditional sense of the word since new types of partnerships were emerging in the financial world.

Paradoxically, despite the consolidation movement in European banking, the total number of banks increased in all countries in the late twentieth century: in Germany, for example, after falling to 3,792 in 1960, the number of banks rose by 600, to 4,390 in 1988. In Britain, the number of banking institutions, including building societies, increased from 773 to 784 between 1983 and 1988, and in Switzerland from 593 to 630.[10] 'Specialized' banks and foreign banks have been mainly responsible for this resurgence and one of the fastest growing 'specialisms' since the 1980s has been 'private banking'. By then, however, private banking had taken on a new meaning. It no longer described a form of banking organization—the partnership—but a type of banking activity—wealth management on behalf of high net worth individuals. Significantly, the newcomers were mostly subsidiaries of foreign or domestic financial institutions. With the exception of a few partnerships with unlimited liability, private banking had become dissociated from private banks.

[9] M. Collins, *Money and Banking in the UK. A History* (London, 1988).

[10] R. S. Sayers (ed.), *Banking in Western Europe* (Oxford, 1962); Gardner and Molyneux, *Changes in Western European Banking*.

PRIVATE BANKS IN THE WORLD ECONOMIC CRISIS

For the London merchant banks, the German banking crisis of 1931 had a familiar ring to it. It was only seventeen years earlier, in August 1914, that failure by German firms to pay outstanding acceptance bills had brought some of the City's biggest names to their knees. Since the beginning of the depression, merchant banks had been badly affected by the collapse of world trade. For most houses, trade finance remained the single largest source of income, and the value of the foreign drawn bills on the London discount market had fallen from £365 million to £134 million between 1929 and 1933.[11] In the same way, their issuing business had been hampered by restrictions on capital exports imposed by the British government, with new overseas issues falling from £97 million to £46 million between 1930 and 1931.[12] However, the introduction of exchange controls by the German government in July 1931, as one of the measures designed to check the banking crisis, was a more severe blow: it meant that remittances to foreign creditors could no longer be paid.

Negotiations took place with the German government, involving, for the merchant banks, some of their representatives during the 1914 crisis—Frank Tiarks, of Schroders, R. H. Brand of Lazards. They resulted in the so-called Standstill agreement, signed in September 1931, which provided for the payment of interest on Germany's commercial debt in convertible currency, and for a freezing of debt repayment. A series of Standstill agreements followed yearly until the outbreak of war, each negotiated in more difficult conditions. Mechanisms were designed for repaying some of these acceptance credits in Reichsmark; facilities offered for liquidating them, though at a substantial loss, met with little success with British creditors. But there was no repayment of principal until the 1950s. The pressure on the most vulnerable houses increased in 1937 when the Bank of England instructed that 30 per cent of the outstanding Standstill bills should be withdrawn from the discount market, when repurchase fell to the firm that had accepted them. A further 40 per cent was required two years later.

The most vulnerable firms were of course those most heavily involved in German trade finance. In the first place, as in 1914, was Kleinworts, with £9.3 million frozen credits in 1936 (including £5.8 million acceptances), three times the partners' capital; and Schroders, with £4.9 million (including £3.7 million acceptances), was also well in excess of the partners' capital and reserves. Schroders sustained total losses amounting to £1.5 million in 1931; Kleinworts'

[11] Figures quoted in R. Roberts, *Schroders. Merchants and Bankers* (London, 1992). See also O. Accominotti, 'London Merchant Banks, the Central European Panic and the Sterling Crisis of 1931', *Journal of Economic History*, 72, 1 (2012).

[12] J. Atkin, 'Official Regulation of British Overseas Investment, 1914–1931', *Economic History Review*, 33, 2 (1970).

German losses were estimated to have reached £3.3 million by 1935.[13] According to a Bank of England report of 1936, four other members of the Accepting Houses Committee were technically insolvent: Huths, Japhets, Goschen & Cunliffe, and Arbuthnot Latham.[14] The two largest houses, Schroders and Kleinworts, survived by drawing on the private resources of their partners and through loans from the Westminster Bank. Houses such as Fredk. Huth & Co. and Goschen & Cunliffe, which had never completely recovered from the war, disappeared from the scene.

Other leading houses, however, recovered rapidly from 1932 onwards, especially those belonging to the 'old families of the banking aristocracy'—Barings, Morgan Grenfell, Hambros.[15] Hambros was probably the most remarkable success story of the 1930s, emerging from the crisis as the City's largest merchant bank. The bank was severely hit by the depression: in 1933, acceptances and total balance sheet were down by a third from their 1929 level. By 1937, the total balance sheet, £33 million, was again approaching its 1929 level, with acceptances at nearly £14 million, Hambros was well ahead of Schroders and Kleinworts, who would need another decade to extricate themselves from the traumas of their commitments in Central Europe.[16]

For the City merchant banks, recovery in the 1930s meant a shift from international to domestic finance, especially as far as the issuing business was concerned. The trend had already started in the 1920s, but it gained a new momentum as a result of Treasury restrictions on foreign issues on the one hand, and economic recovery in Britain on the other hand. New capital issues for foreign countries or companies declined sharply after 1931—to one fifth in 1935 of their annual value in the 1920s. But of course, they did not come to an abrupt end. Most houses were able to obtain the necessary permissions for a limited number of issues. Baring Brothers' participation in issues for overseas borrowers fell from nineteen between 1918 and 1928 to eleven from 1929 to 1939,[17] including, between 1934 and 1936, five large issues (ranging from £2.3 million to £4.5 million) of Argentine government sterling bonds, jointly organized with Morgan Grenfell.[18] In 1933, Hambros undertook the issue of a £1 million loan for Denmark.[19] From 1936 to 1938, Schroders conducted five issues for the Konversionkasse für Deutsche Auslandschulden (Debt

[13] Roberts, *Schroders*, pp. 262–6; J. Wake, *Kleinwort Benson. The History of Two Families in Banking* (Oxford, 1997), pp. 244–9.

[14] Quoted in Roberts, *Schroders*, p. 265.

[15] See Y. Cassis, 'Bankers in English Society in the Late Nineteenth Century', *Economic History Review*, 38, 2 (1985), pp. 210–29.

[16] B. Bramsen and K. Wain, *The Hambros, 1779-1979* (London, 1979), pp. 370–97.

[17] J. Orbell, *Baring Brothers & Co., Limited. A History to 1939* (London, 1985), p. 81.

[18] D. Kynaston, *Cazenove & Co. A History* (London, 1991), p. 148.

[19] Bramsen and Wain, *Hambros*, p. 394.

Conversion Office), which was responsible for settling with creditors as part of the Standstill agreements with Germany.[20]

To what extent did domestic issues compensate for the decline of foreign issues? A definite answer remains difficult to provide. More than in the 1920s, all leading houses entered the field. Barings was involved in transport, with four issues on behalf of the Underground Electric Railways Co. of London, and one in 1939 for the Southern Railway Company (£7.5 million to finance the electrification of its track); public utilities, with a 1935 issue for the Charing Cross Electricity Supply Company and another in 1939 for the North Metropolitan Power Station Company; shipping (P.&O., Royal Mail Group, British Tanker Co., the latter with Schroders), as well as brewing (Charrington & Co., with Rothschilds).[21]

Schroders sponsored issues for Stevenson, Clark and Associated Companies, a firm of coal factors, for the Lancashire Steel Corporation, and for the Pressed Steel Company;[22] Hambros for John Brown & Co., the heavy engineering group, and for the Consett Iron Co.[23] Even the Rothschilds, for whom government loans had almost been a preserve throughout the nineteenth century, had to follow the trend with, besides their joint ventures with Barings and Schroders, issues for the London National Property Company in 1930 and Woolworth's, the retail chain, in 1931.[24]

Morgan Grenfell, for their part, maintained the lead they had established in the 1920s, especially through their long-term involvement in the steel industry. Their most important client in the 1930s was the United Steel Company, for which they undertook several issues (£2.5 million debenture stock in 1934, £3.35 million shares in 1936, and £1.5 million 10-year notes in 1938). They also offered them advice in matters of reorganization, following the Hatry debacle in 1929, and merger and acquisitions.[25] Despite the alleged gap between the City and industry, the heavy industries thus provided merchant bankers with a solid customers' base.

Nevertheless, it is unlikely that this somewhat sporadic domestic activity could have made up for the loss of a much steadier foreign business. Schroders is a case in point. According to Richard Roberts' detailed analysis of its sources of income, unfortunately unavailable for most other houses, the revenue from issuing and underwriting in 1931–9 was £447,000, down from £2.1 million in 1919–30. These revenues represented 16 per cent of total income in 1932–9, as against 29 per cent in 1919–30.[26] Schroders might not have

[20] Roberts, *Schroders*, pp. 260, 269.
[21] Orbell, *Baring Brothers*, pp. 83–4.
[22] Roberts, *Schroders*, pp. 269–70.
[23] Bramsen and Wain, *Hambros*, p. 395.
[24] N. Ferguson, *The World's Banker. The History of the House of Rothschild* (London, 1998), p. 995.
[25] K. Burk, *Morgan Grenfell 1838–1988. The Biography of a Merchant Bank* (Oxford, 1988), pp. 160–6.
[26] Roberts, *Schroders*, pp. 270, 265, 185.

been a typical merchant bank in the 1930s, given its heavy losses from its interests in Central Europe. However, as Roberts points out, the £447,000 earned from issuing and underwriting were 'not far short of the £487,000 apparently earned by sector leader Morgan Grenfell in the same period'.[27] This early involvement in domestic industry must thus be put in perspective. But it certainly represented a useful period of apprenticeship. Merchant bankers established the contacts, gained the expertise, in short laid the foundations of what was to become their major field of activity after the war—corporate finance.

Could merchant bankers have done better? Possibly. For, as in the 1920s, the field remained free from competition by the big banks. Other, non-banking private houses—especially stockbrokers (such as Cazenove & Co., Greenwell & Co., or Cohen Laming Hoare) and issuing houses (such as Helbert, Wagg & Co. or Charterhouse Investment Trust)—did in fact better than the richer and more experienced merchant banks. Taking 1937—a not unusual year—as an example, David Kynaston found that London stockbrokers sponsored more issues than non-broker issuing houses (242 to 228) and were responsible for a nominal value 45 per cent higher.[28] And among non-broker houses, merchant bankers were definitely not in the lead. Only two firms sponsored or co-sponsored more than ten issues: the Investment Registry (with twelve) and Charterhouse Investment Trust. Of the merchant banks, Barings came first with only three issues.

The reason why merchant banks lagged behind could well be a lack of entrepreneurship, an inability to seize new market opportunities. But it might also have to do, as in the pre-war years, with the size of the issues. Merchant banks continued to deal with large issues: all three Barings' issues in 1937 were over £1 million, while only one of Helbert, Wagg's six issues was above £300,000.[29] Some effort was made to assist small and medium-sized enterprises. The creation in July 1935 of Leadenhall Securities Ltd, with £125,000 paid-up capital, as a fully owned subsidiary of Schroders, was such a move. It came as one of the few responses by the leading merchant banks to the so-called 'Macmillan Gap'—the difficulty encountered by small and medium-sized companies in raising capital, especially for amounts ranging from £50,000 to £200,000, revealed in the report of the Macmillan Committee published in 1931.[30] On the whole, however, merchant banks were primarily concerned with large-scale operations, and such opportunities were not unlimited in the 1930s.

[27] Roberts, *Schroders*, p. 270. The data on Morgan Grenfell are from Burk, *Morgan Grenfell*, pp. 268–9.

[28] Kynaston, *Cazenove*, p. 158.

[29] Kynaston, *Cazenove*.

[30] Committee on Finance and Industry, *Report*, Cmd 3897, 1931.

All in all, the depression took its toll on the City merchant banks. Their number fell from fifty-eight in 1930 to forty-five in 1940, including those describing themselves as merchants, of whom there were still twenty-two, as against thirty-one ten years earlier. In addition to Fredk. Huth and Goschen & Cunliffe (whose business was taken over by Guinness Mahon in 1941), other major disappearances included Arthur H. Brandt & Co., established in 1899 and a member of the Accepting Houses Committee, who wound up voluntarily; W. Ladenburg & Co., established in 1859; A. Ruffer & Sons, originally from Lyons, established in 1872; as well as the old merchanting firm Chalmers, Guthrie & Co., founded as early as 1793. Newcomers, especially issuing houses, hardly corresponded to the definition of a private bank, with their emphasis on raising capital (through issuing and underwriting) rather than on providing credit (through lending, discounting, or accepting).

For the German private banks, the 1930s were a watershed. Not only did their number fall dramatically (from 1,100 in 1929 to 709 in 1932 and 491 in 1938), but, collectively, their market share shrank from just over half a per cent to 0.15 per cent. German private banks, especially in the country's leading financial centres (Berlin, Hamburg, Frankfurt, Cologne) also lost some of their influence: their share of the seats held by bankers on companies' supervisory boards was still a respectable 40 per cent in 1928; by 1932, it had fallen to under 35 per cent.[31] And while there are no available estimates for the rest of the decade, one can safely assume a steep decline in this area. Significantly, whereas four of the top ten 'big linkers' (those with the highest number of outside directorships) in 1927 were private bankers, alongside four big banks' directors and two industrialists, there were only two in 1932 (Heinrich von Stein and Franz Koenigs), and a single one in 1938 (Kurt von Schröder).[32] Decline thus affected the 'haute banque' as much as the 'country banks'. Taking into account only private banks serving as payments offices, Wixforth and Ziegler found that the highest rate of disappearance took place in Berlin (80 per cent between 1927 and 1938), followed by Frankfurt and Hamburg (78 per cent), while it was 68 per cent in Rhineland-Westphalia and 58 per cent in Bavaria.[33]

How to explain this sudden collapse? Why were private banks unable to preserve the 'niche' they had managed to carve for themselves in the highly fragmented German banking business? The pressure from the credit banks was certainly no greater than in previous decades. However, the 'great' banks

[31] H. Wixforth and D. Ziegler, 'The Niche in the Universal Banking System: The Role and Significance of Private Bankers within German Industry', *Financial History Review*, 1, 2 (1994), p. 106.

[32] H. Wixforth and D. Ziegler, 'Deutsche Privatbanken und Privatbankiers im 20. Jahrhundert' in *Geschichte und Gesellschaft*, 23, 2 (1997), p. 221.

[33] Percentages calculated from Wixforth and Ziegler, 'Deutsche Privatbanken', p. 216. The average rate was 70 per cent (from 365 banks in 1927 to 108 in 1938).

benefited far more from government aid during the banking crisis of 1931, while private banks suffered from the reluctance of the Reichsbank to refinance them. More importantly, the political climate had radically changed, undermining the ground on which private banks had survived and prospered in the age of the corporate economy. Their role in international finance lost much of its significance from about 1937, with the autarkic economic policy of the Third Reich, while their role in industrial finance was hampered by the ban on Jewish bankers sitting on companies' supervisory boards. Private banks also suffered from increasing competition from the savings banks, which were favourably viewed, and increasingly controlled, by the Nazi regime. And of course, the regime's anti-Semitic policy led to the 'voluntary' liquidation of hundreds of small Jewish banks during the mid-1930s and the 'aryanization' of the largest ones in the late 1930s.[34]

For in many respects, the collapse of German private banks was the collapse of Jewish banks. The decline had already started in the 1920s: there were an estimated 1,225 Jewish private banks in 1923 as against 919 non-Jewish ones, and respectively 485 and 509 by 1930. But it accelerated from 1935: while there were still more than 400 Jewish private banks in that year, their number had dropped to 275 in mid-December 1937 and to 209 in March 1938, when the 'aryanization' measures started in earnest.[35] The elimination of Jewish private banks in Nazi Germany was thus a gradual process. On the whole, Jewish banks, especially the largest among them, were spared the most blatant forms of anti-Semitic attacks, which took place in spring 1933, following Hitler's seizure of power—acts of physical violence against the Jewish communities, boycotts of Jewish shops, with a national boycott of Jewish businesses organized on 1 April 1933.

Private banks escaped this fate mainly because of their international position. The leading houses had a wide network of relationships abroad, especially in the United States and the United Kingdom, and the Nazi regime was still careful not to upset the western powers where public opinion was shocked by such anti-Semitic brutalities. Moreover, private banks still played a crucial role in providing Germany with much needed foreign exchange. Although their share of the country's bank deposits had shrank to negligible proportions, their share of foreign credit transactions was far from insignificant—as much as 14.2 per cent for the five leading houses (Warburg, Mendelssohn, Oppenheim, Hirschland, and Arnhold/Bleichröder) in 1935.[36]

[34] These explanations are provided by Wixforth and Ziegler, 'The Niche', pp. 118–19.

[35] Figures quoted in C. Kopper, *Zwischen Markwirtschaft und Dirigismus. Bankenpolitik im 'Dritten Reich' 1933–1939*, (Bonn, 1995), pp. 220, 255–6.

[36] M. Stürmer, G. Teichmann, and W., Treue, *Striking the Balance. Sal. Oppenheim jr.& Cie. A Family and a Bank* (London, 1994), p. 354. These five banks alone accounted for 29.4 per cent of the balance sheet of Germany's 915 private banks in 1935.

Hjalmar Schacht, President of the Reichsbank from 1933 to 1939 and Economics Minister from 1934 to 1937, is usually credited with protecting Jewish banks against the abuses of party activists. Schacht was not really trusted by the Nazi dignitaries, but was seen as indispensable, not least by Hitler, in the early years of the new regime, because of his technical skills, his prestige as the architect of Germany's economic recovery, and the confidence he enjoyed from business leaders both in Germany and abroad. Until 1936, he remained in a remarkably strong and independent position, which he used to prevent, as much as possible, any economic discrimination against Jewish banks. He made sure, for example, that the leading private banks, all Jewish or of Jewish origins, remained members of the Reich Consortium for state loans, the last three leaving as late as 1938. This attitude fitted with Schacht's more liberal outlook in matters of economic policy and his aim to eventually bring Germany back into the world economy.

However, Schacht's defence of Jewish bankers' economic rights did not extend to their civic and political rights.[37] Significantly, he was not opposed to the Nuremberg Laws of 1935, which forbade marriages between Jews and non-Jews and deprived German Jews of their citizenship. As he confided to Max Warburg, they did not diminish the status of the Jews, but only assigned a different value to them, their purpose being to restore tranquillity to economic life.[38] In addition, while strongly defending the right of the leading Jewish private banks to compete on equal terms, Schacht was actively promoting a rationalization of the German banking system. This implied the liquidation of hundreds of small and weak private banks. As it happened, most of the private banks disappearing during this period were Jewish. This did not necessarily mean that they were the weakest, though some had been severely shaken by the banking crisis, including the famous Frankfurt house Lazard-Speyer-Ellissen.[39] But in the prevailing racist climate, several Jewish bankers preferred to transfer or sell their business to non-Jewish concerns.

For all Jewish private banks, working conditions were becoming increasingly difficult. Between June 1935 and June 1936, the position of the so-called 'non Aryan' private banks had clearly deteriorated compared with the 'Aryan' ones, with the former suffering a fall in both their aggregate balance sheet (10.7 per cent) and equity (12 per cent), and the latter enjoying overall growth.[40] One of the reasons was the shift of clients to 'Aryan' banks. M. M. Warburg & Co., one of Germany's largest private banks, lost 3,366 of its 5,241 clients—nearly two thirds—between 1931 and the end of 1933.[41] The same happened

[37] See Kopper, *Zwischen Marktwirtschaft und Dirigismus*, pp. 224–39.

[38] R. Chernow, *The Warburgs. A Family Saga* (London, 1993), p. 435.

[39] Kopper, *Zwischen Markwirtschaft und Dirigismus*, p. 246.

[40] Stürmer et al., *Striking the Balance*, p. 357.

[41] E. Rosenbaum and A. J. Sherman, *M.M. Warburg & Co. 1798–1938. Merchant Bankers of Hamburg* (London, 1979), p. 160.

at Sal. Oppenheim jr. & Cie, a target for Nazi officials because of its name and Jewish origins, even though the family had been christened two or three generations earlier: numerous customers transferred their account to J. H. Stein, a smaller rival in Cologne led by Kurt von Schröder, a Nazi sympathizer.[42]

The loss of seats on supervisory boards was a gradual process. Friedrich Carl and Waldemar von Oppenheim were forced to leave their seats on the board of such important engineering companies as Orenstein & Koppel and Felten & Guilleaume, following manoeuvres by Kurt von Schröder.[43] The partners in Warburgs lost eighteen of their 108 seats in 1933, including some of their historical and most prestigious corporate links, such as the shipping company Hapag and the Deutsch-Atlantische Telegraph-Gesellschaft. However, they only lost the bulk of their seats—eighty—between 1936 and 1938.[44] In fact, new business opportunities arose in the early years of the regime, with the formation of a 'Jewish economic sector': Jewish customers flocked to Jewish banks as they suffered discrimination from other banks, especially savings banks. Larger Jewish banks could also pick up clients from disappearing smaller provincial ones. Warburgs, for example, could ensure confidentiality to Jewish businessmen and aided them with foreign exchange and in negotiating the sale of Jewish businesses to 'Aryan' firms. In 1935, the number of their clients rose again, from 1,875 to 2,183, even though the volume of their credit business contracted.[45]

The departure of Schacht from the Ministry of Economics in September 1937, following Goering's increasing influence over economic and rearmament policy, marked a turning point in the fate of Jewish private banks. Goering was the driving force behind the intensification of the 'aryanization' process of Jewish enterprises, which started in earnest in 1938. Fears of offending western public opinion was no longer an issue and pressure mounted, including on the leading houses, as enterprises were defined as Jewish—and thus faced discrimination—if only one of their partners was Jewish. 'Aryanization' finally became compulsory following the 'Crystal Night' pogrom of 9 and 10 November 1938 and the declared aim that the Jews should be completely removed from the economy. Jewish private bankers were faced with two possibilities: they could either sell their business to another—'Aryan'—bank; or the bank could continue to trade but under an 'Aryan' name and ownership. For their part, 'Aryan' banks, whether private or joint-stock, could be tempted to take advantage of the situation—the

[42] Stürmer et al., *Striking the Balance*, p. 367.

[43] Kopper, *Zwischen Marktwirtschaft und Dirigismus*, p. 244.

[44] W. E. Mosse, *Jews in the German Economy. The German-Jewish Economic Elite 1820–1935* (Oxford, 1987), pp. 377–8.

[45] Chernow, *Warburgs*, p. 433.

bargaining position of Jewish bankers who were selling could hardly have been weaker. Some, though not all, did.[46]

Gebrüder Arnhold, of Dresden, the first of the five largest private banks to be 'aryanized', was taken over by the Dresdner Bank at a bargain price. One of the partners, Kurt Arnhold, was arrested at the end of 1937 in the middle of the negotiations, suggesting a possible link up between the Dresdner Bank and the Gestapo. Under such duress, Kurt Arnhold decided in February 1938 to sell immediately. The Dresdner Bank took full advantage of the situation, refused to honour its payment commitments and deprived the partners of a large part of the value of their business.[47] The Munich-based private bank Merck, Fink & Co. behaved in a similar fashion in its takeover of the Berlin business of J. Dreyfus & Co.,[48] one of the larger private banks. The purchase price of just under 2 million RM was a particularly harsh deal for the owners. Mendelssohn & Co., on the other hand, received fairer treatment from Hermann Abs and the Deutsche Bank when the Jewish partners asked them, in August 1938, to take over their business.[49]

M. M. Warburg & Co. chose another route. Rather than liquidating or selling the bank, they decided to carry on the business under 'Aryan' ownership and management. The bank was turned into a limited private company with a capital of 11.6 million RM.[50] The Warburg partners kept a 25 per cent stake (they had hoped for more), though without voting rights. Other sleeping partners included the Bank für Industrie-Obligationen, the Berliner Handels-Gesellschaft, Gutehoffnungshütte (the metal and engineering concern), Siemens, as well as a number of merchants and businessmen in Hamburg. The new partners, chosen by the Warburgs, were Rudolf Brinckmann, a non-Jewish manager who had been in the bank since 1920 and Paul Wirz, a Hamburg merchant. The bank's name was only changed to Brinckmann, Wirz & Co. in 1941.

S. Hirschland & Co., another of the 'Big Five' private banks, also chose to carry on as an 'aryanized' bank. Discussions took place in April 1938 between the senior partner, Georg Hirschland, and Karl Kimmick, of the Deutsche Bank. With the agreement of the family, the Deutsche Bank set up a

[46] The following paragraph is based on Kopper, *Zwischen Marktwirtschaft und Dirigismus*, pp. 254–75.

[47] On the takeover of Gebrüder Arnhold by the Dresdner Bank, see D. Ziegler, *Die Dresdner Bank und die deutschen Juden* (Munich, 2006), pp. 135–61.

[48] The business of the Frankfurt branch had previously been transferred to the 'Aryan' private bank B. Metzler seel. Sohn & Co.

[49] For details of the takeover of Mendelssohn by Deutsche Bank, see H. James, *The Deutsche Bank and the Nazi Economic War against the Jews* (Cambridge, 2001), pp. 70–7.

[50] This was a fair price, though it did not include any goodwill, which Jewish sellers were forbidden to receive. The owners were actually paid only 6.4 million RM as certain properties in Hamburg remained in the family's ownership. They also had to pay 850,000 RM in taxes and another million for approval of the 'aryanization'.

consortium to take over the bank's capital and looked for two suitable partners. On 5 October 1938, the business of Hirschland & Co. was transferred to a new limited liability company, Burkhardt & Co. Among the sleeping partners were the Deutsche Bank (with 2.5 million RM out of a 6.5 million RM capital and in actual control of the bank), the National-Bank, the Bank für Industrie Obligationen, Merck, Finck & Co., and two heavy industry concerns from the Ruhr. Otto Burkhardt, finance director of the textile company Christian Dirieg & Co. and Gottfried von Falkenhausen, manager of the Deutsche Bank's Essen branch, took over as partners with 500,000 RM investment each. Finally, Sal. Oppenheim Jr. & Co., which technically was not a 'Jewish bank', still had to change its name and traded from 20 May 1938 under the name of Pferdmenges & Co.

The banking crisis of 1930s took a different shape in France. Rather than a short and violent shock, it extended over several years, with waves of failures, especially among small local and regional banks. Between October 1929 and September 1937, 670 banks failed in France, 276 of which were joint-stock banks.[51] Put another way, nearly 400 private banks, including 150 brokers, failed during these years. Moreover, a good many of the 276 joint-stock banks worked with very little capital, mostly held by family members, and can thus be considered as private or quasi-private banks—though the proportion cannot be precisely assessed. The cause of this collapse did not lie with any fundamental flaw of the French banking system. It was rather a result of poor management and careless lending behaviour on the part of smallish banks all too ready to embrace the practice of universal banking. Local and regional banks had undoubtedly played a dynamic role in the French economy during the 1920s, especially through their support for industry. Unlike the big deposit banks, however, which remained highly liquid throughout the period, they overcommitted themselves during the years of prosperity, becoming highly vulnerable in times of crisis. Difficulties could be aggravated by the attitude of the local branch of the Banque de France: some of them dramatically tightened the conditions at which they were prepared to rediscount bills of exchange.

French country banks were severely weakened by the depression of the 1930s, but not entirely eliminated. Some managed to weather the storm, though not without suffering heavy losses. Between 1930 and 1933 Tarneaud, in Limoges, saw its balance sheet shrink by 20 per cent, Courtois, in Toulouse, by nearly 40 per cent. The latter had to face a run at the end of 1930, with Ff.16 million—a third of its sight deposits—being withdrawn in a few days. For both banks, salvation came from enjoying a basically sound position and from adopting a far more rigorous lending policy. Tarneaud, for example, considerably reduced the permanent facilities given to its customers, acknowledging,

[51] H. Laufenburger, *Les banques françaises* (Paris, 1940), p. 237.

somewhat belatedly, that 'the role of a bank is to limit itself to granting temporary accommodation not to take the place of a sleeping partner'.[52] Likewise Courtois selected its borrowers more carefully, having paid a high price for past mistakes: at the end of 1934, the bank faced Ff.10 million of bad and doubtful debts out of Ff.30 million of debit balance, Ff.4 to Ff.6 million being probably entirely lost. In addition, they did not accept any new business without prior checking that rediscounting would be possible at the Banque de France.[53]

Frauds and scandals are part and parcel of all crises and French private banks were no exception to the rule. One of the most resounding was the failure of the Banque Oustric in November 1930, which triggered off the collapse of several other banks. The bank had been founded in 1919 as a partnership by Albert Oustric, the son of a café proprietor in Carcassonne. Its activities were small-scale and rather dubious: Oustric started to dabble in the business of war damage, buying at a discount compensation entitlements from needy people preferring immediate cash to often late instalment payments, and placing the securities of more or less dubious companies. The bank was converted into a joint-stock company in 1921, but with Oustric still very much in control. The big time came in 1926, when Oustric succeeded in getting a listing on the Paris Bourse for Snia Viscosa, an Italian synthetic fibres company. This could only be done through friends in high places, as the required authorizations from both the Ministry of Foreign Affairs and the Ministry of Finance were very difficult to obtain due to the government's efforts to check capital flight.

Oustric's standing rose immediately, and considerably. Between 1926 and 1930, he gained control over a number of companies, mainly through the purchase of founders' shares. He was able to raise money by drawing bills on these various companies, which were then discounted at the Banque de France, the proceeds being used for lending and speculative purposes. Oustric took full advantage of the bull market of the late 1920s. At the peak of his success, he was admitted to the board of some of France's leading companies, including the Automobiles Peugeot, which were to lose over Ff.60 million between 1929 and 1931 as a result of their involvement in his affairs.[54] For Oustric became increasingly rash in his dealings, paying inflated prices to secure control over an ever growing number of businesses. The bubble burst with the fall of stock-market prices in 1930 and on 7 November, the Banque Oustric went into liquidation.

[52] Quoted by H. Bonin, 'Grosse Histoire du Crédit du Nord', unpublished typescript, 1998. A shorter version has been published under the title *Histoire de banques. Crédit du Nord 1848–1998* (Paris, 1998).

[53] Bonin, 'Grosse Histoire du Crédit du Nord'.

[54] R. Sédillot, *Peugeot. De la crinoline à la 404* (Paris, 1960), p. 124.

The Oustric affair is remembered as much for its political as for its economic impact. The political scandal related to the corruption of a number of ministers, in the first place Raoul Péret, who as Finance Minister authorized the Stock Exchange listing of Snia Viscosa in June 1926, days before leaving his post and against the recommendation of his advisers. He became legal adviser to the Banque Oustric the following year.

Several such scandals, including the Stavisky affair in 1934,[55] inflamed by the collusion between business and politics, were to poison the political climate in France in the years leading to the Popular Front. But they also had serious economic consequences. The Banque Oustric dragged other banks down with it: the Banque Besnard and the Banque Vasseur, closely linked to it, and above all the Banque Adam, a family-controlled regional bank in the North, with 167 branches, whose resources had been heavily drawn upon by Oustric. The collapse of the Banque Oustric marked the beginning of the banking crisis in France.

The *haute banque* proved more resilient. None of the ten to fifteen leading houses disappeared during this period, though not much is known about their business activities and the extent to which they suffered from the depression. Some did not escape unscathed. Lazard Frères, like Lazard Brothers in London, were threatened by the huge losses which engulfed the Brussels branch: they needed the support of the Banque de France and had to rely on the private resources of the members of the founding families to remain afloat.[56] Others, like Mirabaud, cruised fairly peacefully through these troubled years: while new profitable ventures were increasingly difficult to come by, the various enterprises to which the bank was linked did reasonably well. In the end, the hardest blow dealt to the *haute banque* was of a political rather than an economic nature. In 1936, the Popular Front government proceeded with its decision to reform the statutes of the Banque de France. Though the measures came short of a full nationalization, which did not take place until 1945, it did place the central bank under firmer state control. The 200 largest shareholders

[55] On 8 January 1934, the body of Alexandre Stavisky, a Ukrainian-born businessman with connections in political and media circles, was discovered in a chalet in Chamonix. A few days earlier, on 24 December 1933, the manager of the Crédit municipal de Bayonne, a semi-public local bank, had been arrested. He was involved with Stavisky in the issue, through his bank, of false bonds amounting to a total of 200 million francs, all with the tacit agreement of the deputy and mayor of Bayonne, Dominique-Joseph Garat. Another bank linked to Stavisky, the Crédit municipal d'Orléans, had also issued 70 million francs of such bonds. Thanks to his political connections, Stavisky had been able to place these bonds, which did not enjoy any state guarantee, with insurance companies. Moreover, despite being charged with fraud and forgery, Stavisky was not tried, thanks to support in high places involving the left of centre Radical Party, which was in power. On 6 February 1934, a demonstration against 'the thieves', organized by the extreme right parties, ended with sixteen deaths after a guard fired at the crowd, and led to the resignation of Edouard Daladier, the Radical Prime Minister, intensifying political tensions in France.

[56] A. Sabouret, *MM Lazard Frères et Cie. Une saga de la fortune* (Paris, 1987), pp. 86–8.

lost their privilege of electing the *conseil des régents* (the Bank's court of directors), where representatives of the *haute banque* had featured prominently for several generations. The *conseil des régents* itself was replaced by a twenty strong general council. Two of its members were elected by the general meeting; the others were appointed by the government and various interest groups, with the state clearly having the upper hand.[57]

The 1941 Banking Law, enacted by the Vichy regime, had a profound effect on French banking. So far the profession had been free and open to any potential entrant. From then on it became regulated and controlled. Banks had to be registered and were classified according to their type of activity. A clear distinction was introduced between deposit banks and *banques d'affaires* (investment banks). Specialized institutions were also defined according to either their operations or their clientele and included a number of finance companies, discount houses, bullion brokers, French banks operating mainly abroad, and banks under foreign control. In the process, small banks, including an array of private banks, were threatened with disappearance pure and simple. Two forces were in action: rationalization and anti-Semitism.

The guiding spirit behind the banking reform was Henri Ardant, France's leading banker under Vichy. Ardant was general manager, and, from 1941, chairman of the Société Générale, one of the country's big banks, and was appointed, in 1940, chairman of the *comité d'organisation* for banking.[58] In an attempt to rationalize the French banking system and get rid of what he called its 'most sordid' elements, Ardant intended to bar from registration banks which did not satisfy a minimum capital, fixed at respectively Ff.20 million for joint-stock banks and Ff.10 million for private banks.[59] This would have led to the elimination of 63 per cent of French banks. However, small banks still enjoyed protection in Vichy France. As a counterweight to the power of the big banks, they had been granted two of the six seats on the banking *comité d'organisation*: one was held by Jacques de Boissieu, owner of a small local bank bearing his name with a capital of only Ff.600,000; the other by René Varin-Bernier, a partner in a somewhat larger regional bank (capital Ff.20 million) also bearing his name. The Banque de France and the Treasury, which favoured a more liberal approach in this matter, also opposed Ardant's project. In the end, the minimum was lowered, at first to Ff.5 and Ff.2 million respectively, and eventually to a meaningless Ff.2 million for joint-stock banks, Ff.1 million for Parisian private banks and Ff.500,000 for provincial

[57] See J. Bouvier, *Un siècle de banque française* (Paris, 1973), pp. 178–92.

[58] The *Comités d'Organisation* were the corporatist institutions set up in each industry by the Vichy regime in order to replace both trade unions and employers' organizations and control economic activity.

[59] See C. Andrieu, *La banque sous l'occupation. Paradoxes de l'histoire d'une profession* (Paris, 1990), pp. 232–5.

private banks. As a result, the number of local banks (including a good many private banks) fell by 22 per cent between 1940 and 1944, from 262 to 205.

Another group of (mostly) private banks suffered from the selective measures of the *comité d'organisation*: those 'specialised according to the nature of their operations', many of them being more akin to finance houses than banks. Their number dropped by more than half, from sixty to twenty-nine between 1940 and 1946. One reason was the financial scandals which broke out before the war (Oustric, Stavisky etc.) and often involved such banks. Another was the high proportion of Jewish houses among them, 22 per cent (thirteen out of sixty), as against a national average of 6 per cent (thirty banks 'recognized as Jewish' by the *comité d'organisation* out of a total of 542).[60] As in Germany, rationalization and anti-Semitism went hand in hand. For Xavier Vallat, high commissioner for Jewish Questions, it was 'appropriate to eliminate from the Parisian market Jewish banks which unnecessarily overlapped with similar Aryan ones'.[61]

As in Germany and other occupied countries, French Jewish banks were liquidated or 'aryanized'.[62] About a hundred cases (including banks and other type of finance houses) were examined by the *commissariat général aux questions juives*.[63] Most of them were liquidated—including the two leading private houses, de Rothschild Frères and Lazard Frères, but they didn't suffer confiscations and re-emerged after the war.[64] Others were 'aryanized', though many cases were still pending in 1942. Interestingly, out of the thirty banks 'recognized as Jewish' by the *comité d'organisation* in 1940, twenty-three were officially registered as banks in 1945–6 yet ten of these twenty-three had been liquidated a couple of years earlier and had thus managed to ensure their maintenance during these dark years.[65]

RECONSTRUCTION AND REGULATION

Private banks were not wiped out by the great slump and the Second World War, but their number had continued to decrease. In some countries, especially in Germany, they had lost much of their significance following the disappearance of several of the most prestigious names. In others, such as

[60] Andrieu, *La banque sous l'occupation*, pp. 250–1.
[61] Quoted in Andrieu, *La banque sous l'occupation*, p. 251.
[62] See J.-M. Dreyfus, *Pillages sur ordonnances. Aryanisation et restitution des banques en France 1940–1953* (Paris, 2003).
[63] Andrieu, *La banque sous l'occupation*, pp. 274–7.
[64] Dreyfus, *Pillages sur ordonnances*, pp. 214–38.
[65] Andrieu, *La banque sous l'occupation*, p. 278.

Britain and, to a lesser extent, France, life returned more or less to normal. Real changes did not take place before the 1960s.

The fall in the number of banks was particularly striking in countries where private country banks had been able to survive well into the twentieth century. Figures concerning this type of bank remain uncertain and only broad estimates are available. In France, the number of *local banks*, most of them in private hands, even when registered as limited companies, fell from 364 in 1935 to 158 in 1954.[66] (These figures do not include members of the Parisian *haute banque*, brokers and discounters in Paris or the provinces, and privately owned *regional* banks). In Switzerland, the number of local banks, not all private, likewise decreased from 115 to 86 during the same years.[67] In Germany, the number of private banks dropped from 491 in 1942 to 213 in 1955—the Bundesbank's statistics do not isolate a group of local banks.[68]

Private country banks were thus still alive in continental Europe in the aftermath of the Second World War and remained closely linked to the local economy. In France, most local banks were very small. In 1954, 77 per cent (122 out of 158) had balance sheet totals of less than Ff.500,000 and, as before the war, some of them depended for their livelihood on 'little more than a glorified stockbroking business'.[69] Yet they continued to play a useful role in the financing of small firms. And even larger firms often found it convenient to keep an account with them as a means of securing valuable advice in connection with a particular transaction.[70]

Regional banks tended to be larger, with a network of branches extending beyond a single town or even a *département*. Among the twenty-two banks classified as such by the Banking Control Commission in 1954, several were still in private hands, alongside larger joint-stock regional banks such as the Crédit du Nord or the Société Marseillaise de Crédit. Best known among them were: Varin-Bernier (with a balance sheet total of Ff.9.1 billion) at Bar-le-Duc, in Lorraine; the Banque Hervet in the Loire Valley (Ff.4.4 billion); the Banque Courtois (Ff.2.26 billion) in Toulouse; Tarneaud Frères & Cie (Ff.2.32 billion) in Limoges; Nicolet-Lafanechère in Grenoble; and the Banque Laydernier in Annecy. In addition, some seemingly typical 'joint-stock' regional banks were in fact to a large extent 'private'. At the Banque de l'Isère, in Grenoble, for example, a third of the capital was in the hands of the *gérants* and the members of supervisory boards, with the rest divided between about a thousand local shareholders.

[66] Laufenburger, *Les banques françaises*, p. 22, for 1935, J. S. G. Wilson, *French Banking Structure and Credit Policy* (London, 1957) p. 2, for 1954.

[67] F. Ritzmann, *Die Schweizer Banken. Geschichte-Theorie-Statistik* (Bern, 1973), pp. 265–6.

[68] Deutsche Bundesbank, *Deutsches Geld- und Bankwesen in Zahlen, 1876–1975* (Frankfurt, 1976), pp. 118–19, 172–3.

[69] Wilson, *French Banking*, p. 41.

[70] Wilson, *French Banking*, p. 41.

The persistence of private country banks in France cannot be separated from that of the local and regional banks as a whole. As in previous periods, they still fulfilled a useful function, in the first place the financing of an array of small (sometimes very small) and medium-sized enterprises. In the early post-war years, their intimate knowledge of business conditions, based on their long-term relationships with a loyal clientele, enabled them to take greater risks than other banks were prepared to contemplate, and carry local firms through very uncertain times. In banks such as Tarneaud, Laydernier, and Nicolet-Lafanechère, overdrafts had climbed dangerously, reaching about a third of total assets by 1946 and thus threatening their liquidity. But the risks were well spread around a hard core of safe customers. Moreover, they could rely on the support of a larger partner (usually the Banque de l'Union Parisienne) and they were safe in their knowledge that their bills could be rediscounted at the Banque de France.[71]

Nevertheless, the days of the private country bankers were numbered. Such predictions had been made about English banks in the 1850s. The end came a century later in continental Europe, with the number of private banks falling sharply in the 1960s and 1970s, and local private banks becoming increasingly integrated into larger banking groups.

In the few centres where it was still to be found, the *haute banque* was in better shape and its prospects brighter in the short to medium term. Its stronghold remained the City of London, where the merchant banks formed the most impressive force in European private banking. In Paris, whatever the setbacks caused by a decade of economic and political turmoil, the *haute banque* still enjoyed wealth, prestige, and influence. A third financial centre where old-established houses were still thriving was Geneva: from an early stage, its bankers had specialized in what was to become the very essence of private banking, the management of private wealth. As a group retaining a degree of economic and social significance, the *haute banque* only survived in these three cities, though prestigious names could also be found elsewhere, including in Germany.

The London merchant banks fared reasonably well in wartime conditions—some better than others. While Morgan Grenfell's net profits averaged an decent £191,700 between 1940 and 1945, thanks to the revival of private transactions from 1942 onwards,[72] those of Schroders were a meagre £26,000, as a result of the collapse of its acceptance business and the burden of the Standstill debts.[73] In any case, the number of firms hardly fell during the 1940s—from forty-five in 1940 to forty in 1950[74]—and all the leading houses were still around in their traditional private family form. The wave of conversion into private limited companies which seized the industry in the early

[71] Bonin, 'Grosse histoire'.

[72] Burk, *Morgan Grenfell*, pp. 268–9.

[73] Roberts, *Schroders*, p. 536.

[74] R. Roberts, 'What's in a Name? Merchants, Merchant Bankers, Accepting Houses, Issuing Houses, Industrial Bankers and Investment Bankers', *Business History*, 35, 3 (1993), p. 25.

post-war years, with eight major banks converting between 1945 and 1950, did not alter their fundamental nature: for the next two or three decades, merchant banks undoubtedly remained private banks.

The economic environment in which merchant bankers operated in the post-war years was less congenial to the conduct of their international financial operations than at any time in their history. London was no longer the world's main financial centre nor was it vying for this position: until the mid-1960s, New York's financial predominance remained undisputed.[75] The status of the pound reflected, and partly explained, this reversal of fortune. The dollar had become the main trading currency and the cornerstone of the international monetary system. The pound's international role outside the sterling area suffered from not being fully convertible on current account until 1958 (though increasingly facilities existed from the early 1950s) and from its recurrent crises between the two devaluations of 1949 and 1967. Nevertheless, the merchant banks were successful in expanding, and for some in rebuilding, their business. The volume of their operations quickly surpassed its pre-war years' level, at both current and constant prices. In terms of size, however, they were only minnows. In 1955, the total assets of the Midland Bank (£1,540 million) were eighteen times larger than those of the largest merchant bank, Hambros (£85 million), and nearly four times as large as those of all the members of the Accepting Houses Committee put together (£425 million). More than ever before, merchant banks had to rely on a few specialities, on 'niche' markets where they enjoyed a competitive advantage. The accepting and issuing businesses still offered clear possibilities. More importantly, they provided the basis (in terms of skills, experience, networks of relationships) on which merchant banks could build in order to offer new financial services, especially in corporate finance and in the Euromarkets.

Acceptance credit resumed after the war, in the wake of the strong growth of international trade and British exports. For most merchant banks it remained the principal activity well into the 1960s, if not the 1970s. This was certainly the case at Hambros, the market leader with £21 million acceptances outstanding in 1955.[76] Acceptances (£8.7 million in 1955) formed the 'bedrock of Kleinworts' operations'.[77] At Schroders (£7.2 million in 1955), they were the single largest source of revenues, accounting for 30 per cent in the years 1946–53 and for 25 per cent between 1954 and 1958, proportions similar to the 1930s.[78] Schroders and Kleinworts had traditionally been strong on acceptances, but even at Morgan Grenfell, where foreign and later domestic issues had been predominant, acceptances reached £5.3 million in 1955.

[75] Y. Cassis, *Capitals of Capital. A History of International Financial Centres, 1780–2005* (Cambridge, 2006), pp. 204–13.

[76] Bramsen and Wain, *Hambros*, p. 436.

[77] Wake, *Kleinwort Benson*, pp. 342, 476.

[78] Roberts, *Schroders*, p. 326.

However, this was not how merchant banks were perceived by the public. In the press, in particular, they were most frequently mentioned 'in connexion with takeovers, share issues, and the affairs of British companies generally, since they have become increasingly important in this field with the decline of their overseas business'.[79] This involvement in corporate finance had started in the 1920s, but, from the 1950s, it was no longer only a matter of issuing securities on behalf of industrial companies, but also of providing them with advice, especially in connection with mergers and acquisitions. This was the business all firms were keen to expand, and in due course all the leading houses—Morgan Grenfell, Hambros, Lazards, Barings, Rothschilds, Schroders, Kleinworts—built a strong list of corporate clients. Morgan Grenfell, for example, had become the major 'steel house' in the City. After the Conservatives' return to power in 1951, they lead the consortium of eight issuing houses entrusted by the government and the Bank of England with the denationalization of the iron and steel industry, which had been somewhat reluctantly nationalized by Labour two years earlier.[80] Hambros, for its part, took charge of the denationalization of the Consett Iron Company. The bank also dealt with small industrial issues, from 1951, mainly from its subsidiary, Bentworth Trust Limited.[81] Schroders remained involved with the Pressed Steel Company, and through it developed close relations with the British car industry with, in particular, issues on behalf of Rover (in 1952 and 1960) and Standard Motors (five between 1945 and 1960).[82]

The leading player, however, was a newcomer, S. G. Warburg & Co.[83] The bank had been established in 1934 as the New Trading Company and changed its name to S. G. Warburg & Co. in 1946. Its founder, Siegmund Warburg (1902–82), is often considered the greatest banker of the post-war era. Such judgements are meaningless, but his achievements were, nonetheless, extremely impressive. Siegmund Warburg was a scion of the famous Hamburg banking dynasty, though he did not belong to the same branch of the family as his older cousins Max (who controlled the bank in Hamburg), and Paul and Felix (who became partners in Kuhn Loeb in New York). Siegmund did not grow up in Hamburg but in the Swabian Alps where his father had settled as a gentleman farmer due to ill health. However, he was entitled to a partnership and entered the family bank in 1920. After a few years as a trainee in London

[79] P. Ferris, *The City* (London, 1960), p. 85.

[80] See K. Burk, *The First Privatisation. The Politicians, the City and the Denationalisation of Steel* (London, 1988). The other members of the consortium were Barings, Rothschilds, Schroders, Lazards, Hambros, Helbert Wagg, and Robert Benson Lonsdale.

[81] Bramsen and Wain, *Hambros*, pp. 426–8.

[82] Roberts, *Schroders*, pp. 342–5.

[83] On Siegmund Warburg, see N. Ferguson, *High Financier. The Lives and Time of Siegmund Warburg* (London, 2010). See also J. Attali, *Un homme d'influence. Sir Siegmund G. Warburg (1902–1982). L'inspirateur du capitalisme moderne* (Paris, 1985).

(with N. M. Rothschild & Son), Boston (with the accounting firm Lybrand Ross Brothers & Montgomery), and New York (Kuhn Loeb and the International Acceptance Bank), he became a partner in M. M. Warburg & Co. in 1930, aged twenty-eight. From 1931, he managed the bank's newly opened branch in Berlin. Despite some tensions within the family, his career appeared perfectly mapped out until the Nazis came to power, and, in 1934, Siegmund Warburg moved to London.

Siegmund Warburg became joint managing director (with Harry Lucas, an Old Etonian, also Jewish, and former manager of the National Discount Company), of the New Trading Company, taking up 10 per cent of its £120,000 capital, with half going to the Dutch International Corporation (founded earlier in the year by M. M. Warburg & Co. and the Berliner Handels-Gesellschaft) and a quarter to Harry Lucas. There is no doubt, however, that the London firm was built up by Siegmund Warburg, in association with a tightly-knit group of three other Central European Jewish immigrants, known as the 'uncles', who were to play a crucial role in the firm's post-war development: Eric Korner, Ernest Thalmann and, especially, Henry Grunfeld.[84] By the late 1930s, the New Trading Company had become 'an established rather than a major force'[85] in the City, involved in small-scale financial dealings, sometimes passed to them by the Rothschilds, as well as in helping Jewish families to leave Germany and transfer their money abroad.

S. G. Warburg & Co., as it was renamed in January 1946, really took off after the war, through its deals in industrial finance rather than in banking proper. However, it did not reach a first rank position before the late 1950s. On the investment side, Warburgs acquired a variety of companies. In 1946 it organized the sale of Brandeis-Goldschmidt, a leading metal trading house, to the Rio Tinto Company and a few other investors, including S. G. Warburg & Co., and a few years later bought out the entire company. Following the death of its head, Paul Kohn-Speyer, Siegmund's relative by marriage, the firm needed to be rebuilt and Warburgs, this time in the person of Henry Grunfeld, successfully applied to do so: Brandeis-Goldschmidt was to prove a major moneymaker for the bank.[86] In 1954, Warburgs set up a holding company, Mercury Securities Limited, whose portfolio of investments included an advertising company, a firm of rubber merchants, a firm of insurance brokers, and a property-development company.

On the banking side, Warburgs mostly lent to local authorities and medium-sized British companies. A first major opportunity occurred in 1957, with the acquisition of Seligman Brothers, a member of the Accepting House Committee,

[84] See Ferguson, *High Financier*, pp. 88–90, 100–5.

[85] D. Kynaston, *The City of London*. Vol. III: *Illusions of Gold 1914–1945* (London, 1999), p. 341.

[86] Chernow, *Warburgs*, p. 557.

which secured S. G. Warburg & Co. an entry into the inner circle of London's *haute banque*. Another opportunity, Siegmund's association with Kuhn Loeb, did not entirely bear fruit. In 1951, Siegmund Warburg was offered a partnership in the New York firm, with the possibility of soon becoming senior partner, providing he moved to New York and made it his principal activity. But Siegmund did not wish to abandon his London bank. Nevertheless, he became an associate director of Kuhn Loeb in 1952, and a full director and partner in 1956, dividing his time between London and New York. Kuhn Loeb was a highly prestigious firm but suffering from entrepreneurial sclerosis, and Siegmund was seen as the man capable of restoring it to its former grandeur. In the long run, however, increasing tension between Siegmund and his American partners, especially his relative Frederick M. Warburg, led to his resigning his partnership in 1964.[87]

However, it was Kuhn Loeb, which in 1957 provided Warburg with its connection with the American aluminium company, Reynolds Metals, and hence with this master stroke, a victory in the 'Aluminium War', which propelled him into a top position in the City.

The 'Great Aluminium War', as Fleet Street called it, is considered as one of the defining moments in recent City history, a turning point in both business practice and business culture, which radically transformed the field of corporate finance by popularizing the hostile takeover bid. That the main contenders should still have been private bankers is clear evidence of their enduring role in British, and, indeed, international finance. The 'war' was about the control of British Aluminium, an ailing company whose share price had more than halved in two years and was clearly ripe for takeover.[88] On one side, were the predators: the American company Reynolds Metals and the British company Tube Investment. Reynolds intended to expand in Europe by acquiring British Aluminium and was advised by Siegmund Warburg. Warburg strongly recommended that in order to be successful, the bid should be jointly made with a British company. Reynolds thus teamed up with Tube Investment, a Midland engineering company advised by Lionel Fraser, chairman of Helbert Wagg, and by Schroders; the agreement was that in case of victory, Tube Investment would hold a majority stake of 51 per cent.

On the other side was the prey, British Aluminium, advised by Hambros and Lazards, whose defence plan consisted in ceding a 33 per cent stake to the giant Aluminium Company of America (Alcoa), presenting the deal as some sort of partnership with, rather than a takeover by, an American company. Reynolds and Tube Investment quickly built up a 10 per cent stake in British

[87] Ferguson, *High Financier*, pp. 176–83.

[88] Accounts of the 'Aluminium War' can be found in all the company histories of the merchant banks involved, especially those of Warburg and Schroder Wagg. A good recent discussion is D. Kynaston, 'A City at War with Itself', *Financial Times*, 7–8 January 1989.

Aluminium and, in November 1958, offered, through their bankers, to buy the company at 78s a share. Their offer was rejected, without being submitted to the shareholders, and, on 28 November, Lord Portal, chairman of British Aluminium, officially announced that Alcoa had agreed to purchase a third of British Aluminium's capital at 60s a share. On the same day, the Reynolds/Tube Investment offer was made public: Siegmund Warburg had decided to appeal directly to the investing public, against the wish of the incumbent board.

The war had begun and was to be fully covered by a press which, on the whole, sided with the investors. Passions ran high, with claims that British Aluminium must be kept British, and there were bitter exchanges between the two camps. On 1 January 1959, the governor of the Bank of England, Cameron Cobbold, even attempted a peace initiative. Against Warburg and his allies, Hambros and Lazards organized a powerful consortium of fourteen leading City houses, including the merchant banks, Morgan Grenfell, Brown Shipley, Samuel Montagu, Guinness Mahon, and the stockbrokers, Cazenove, and Rowe & Pitman. They offered to buy British Aluminium's shares at 82s. The Warburg camp increased its offer to 85s. In the end, the battle was won in the market: on 6 January 1959, Reynolds and Tube Investment announced that they had gained a majority control of British Aluminium.

Much has been made of the significance of this battle, in words reminiscent of the old struggle between James de Rothschild and the Pereire brothers. Its outcome has been seen as a victory of the dynamic outsider against a conservative establishment, the triumph of a new, more professional, if also more ruthless, business approach over an old-fashioned, amateurish, and cliquish way of dealing. There is of course some truth in this: Siegmund Warburg, the German Jewish immigrant, and Lionel Fraser, the self-made butler's son, against Olaf Hambro and Lord Kindersley, of Lazards, who epitomized the old City establishment. And yet, as in the case of the Pereire against the Rothschilds, the division between the two camps was not always clear-cut. Warburg, for example, knew that Barings, Rothschilds, and Kleinworts, three old-established houses, had sided with him.[89] In order to succeed, outsiders have to break the mould, and Warburg certainly did so, but rather by shaking the culture and work ethics of the City, than by vastly improving on its business methods. Siegmund Warburg did not invent the takeover bid, but he was the first merchant banker to get involved in a battle, something that the City establishment, including the Bank of England, did not consider to be acceptable.

Warburg's victory can certainly be attributed to his determination, the professionalism, of his team, and the mistakes of the opposition.[90] Yet this is not enough to explain why the formidable consortium assembled by Hambros

[89] Chernow, *Warburgs*, p. 650.
[90] On Siegmund Warburg's strategy and tactics, see Ferguson, *High Financier*, pp. 183–200.

and Lazards, with ample resources at its disposal, was unable to secure victory. David Kynaston has recently provided a convincing explanation: 'Almost certainly, the reason was the instinctive reluctance of Hambros and Lazards, supported by their brokers, to enter the market while peace negotiations were still in progress under the auspices of the governor of the Bank. Warburg, however, felt no such constraint and in so doing rewrote the rules of the game. It is hard to believe that in a comparable situation today, the banks and their advisers would stand aloof from the battlefield.'[91] It was indeed more a matter of the rules of the game than the quality of the players. For all the leading merchant banks had already started to build highly professional teams which adapted fairly easily to the new rules and maintained their hold over corporate finance in the following decades. For Siegmund Warburg, now installed and accepted as one of the City luminaries, and for his bank, it was the beginning of a glorious era.

The other major development of the period that affected merchant banks, and the City as a whole, was the emergence of the Euromarkets—for Eurodollars, then for Eurobonds, and Eurocredits. Eurodollars are dollars deposited outside the United States, free of American regulations. Their origins date back to the early 1950s when, for various reasons, dollars started to accumulate in European banks, especially in London. The cold war played a role in this process: the Soviet Union and Eastern European countries preferred to deposit their dollars in Europe rather than in the United States for fear of their being blocked in case of international tension. The first such deposit is traditionally considered as having been made in Paris, at the Banque Commerciale pour l'Europe du Nord, a Russian bank whose telegraphic address was Eurobank, hence the appellation Eurodollar. The flow of dollars to Europe, however, was primarily a result of United States overseas investment, mainly by multinational companies but also in foreign and military aid, as well as its growing payment deficit. Banking regulations also played their part, in particular the so-called Regulation Q, which dated back to the Banking Act of 1933 and enabled the Federal Reserve System to put a ceiling on the rate of interest which banks paid on domestic bank deposits. As British banks were able to offer a higher rate, funds were attracted to Britain.[92]

The very first transaction in Eurodollars has been attributed to the Midland, one of Britain's 'Big Five' clearing banks, through an arbitrage on interest

[91] Kynaston, 'A City at War with Itself'.

[92] See C. Schenk, 'The Origins of the Eurodollar Market in London, 1955–1963', *Explorations in Economic History*, 35 (1998); S. Battilossi, 'Introduction: International Banking and the American Challenge in Historical Perspective', in S. Battilossi and Cassis (eds), *European Banks and the American Challenge. Competition and Cooperation in International Banking Under Bretton Woods* (Oxford, 2002), pp. 1–35.

rates.[93] However, the innovation would soon be taken up again for other purposes. The ban on using sterling instruments to finance third-country trade, imposed by the British government to counter downward pressure on the pound that intensified in 1957, led the City's banks—which did not want to lose their clients—to use these dollars instead. The initiative was taken by the merchant banks, in particular Kleinworts, Samuel Montagu, and Warburgs, and by the overseas banks, first and foremost the Bank of London and South America, at the instigation of its chairman, Sir George Bolton.[94]

With the European currencies returning to external convertibility in December 1958 and, from the early 1960s, the gradual relaxing of controls on capital flows, the Eurodollar market expanded rapidly. It was supplied mainly by American multinationals and by European central banks, either directly or through the Bank for International Settlements. It provided credit on a worldwide scale in hitherto unprecedented proportions. This credit mainly provided interbank deposits and financed international trade and other short-term loans—transactions involving extremely large sums. From approximately $1.5 billion when it started in 1958, this market reached $25 billion ten years later and $130 billion in 1973.[95]

The Eurodollar market quickly gave rise to the Eurobond market.[96] The idea of using funds deposited in this way not only for bank loans but also for issuing dollar-denominated bonds, in London rather than in New York, did not take long to form in City bankers' minds. Foreign issues in the United States aroused little interest in the American public and yielded a far better return to American banks than to European ones, even though it was the latter that mainly took charge of placing securities with their clients. The time thus seemed right to re-launch these issues—one of the City's historical specialities—and the Bank of England gave its consent in July 1962. The first banker to conceive the idea of a dollar issue in London rather than in New York is usually considered to be Siegmund Warburg—though 'the idea [had] evolved over time with the participation of dozens of individuals'.[97]

[93] In June 1955, the Midland Bank offered an interest rate of 1⅞% on 30 days deposits denominated in dollars, whereas the maximum payable in the United States was 1%. The bank needed to increase its sterling deposits and put these funds to domestic uses, selling the dollars for pounds sterling cash and repurchasing them forward, all at a rate below the Bank of England's discount rate. See Schenk, 'Origins of the Eurodollar Market'.

[94] R. Fry (ed.), *A Banker's World. The Revival of the City 1957–1970. The Speeches and Writings of Sir George Bolton* (London, 1970).

[95] OCDE, *International Capital Markets Statistics, 1950–1995* (Paris, 1996).

[96] See I. M. Kerr, *A History of the Eurobond Market. The First 21 Years* (London, 1984); 'Witness Seminar on the Origins and Early Development of the Eurobond Market', introduced and edited by Kathleen Burk, *Contemporary European History*, 1, 1 (1992), pp. 65–87; Ferguson, *High Financier*, pp. 216–21.

[97] M. von Clemm, of Crédit Suisse First Boston, to K. Burk, quoted in Burk, 'Witness Seminar', p. 67.

Siegmund Warburg first envisaged, early in 1962, the issue of a dollar loan for the European Coal and Steel Community in London, but gave up the idea and turned his attention to the steel company, Finsider. It was a subsidiary of the Italian state-owned holding I.R.I., but in order to avoid Italian taxation, the borrower was officially Autostrade Italiana, which benefited from a special dispensation. An agreement was reached on 14 January 1963, and after six months organizing the paperwork and obtaining the legal and administrative authorizations, a loan of $15 million was finally issued on 1 July 1963 over six years, at 5.5 per cent. It was issued in the Netherlands, by a consortium of four banks, led by S. G. Warburg and including the Deutsche Bank, the Banque de Bruxelles, and the Rotterdamsche Bank. This was not, however, the very first Eurobond issue. A few weeks earlier, in mid-May, the merchant bank, Samuel Montagu, had already succeeded in placing a loan of $20 million at 5 per cent on behalf of the Belgian government. This, bought at par by a banking consortium, was not allotted to the public, which explains why it did not attract as much attention.

In any case, Eurobonds quickly proved very popular, especially as they were in bearer form and without deduction of any withholding tax. And with the introduction later in 1963 of the Interest Equalization Tax by the American authorities, a tax on purchases of foreign securities by US residents to check the outflow of capital, American multinationals increasingly borrowed outside the United States. The Eurobond market grew to $4.8 billion between 1963 and 1967, to $17.5 billion for the years 1968–72, to $47 billion in 1973–7, and to $165.6 billion over 1978–83.

The emergence and development of Euromarkets signalled the rebirth of the City of London—a story that cannot be followed in detail here. The City soon established itself as the home of this new market, taking advantage of its long experience of international finance and its large pool of skilled personnel, together with the positive attitude of the Bank of England, in contrast to its more cautious European counterparts, especially in France and Germany. The choice of the British monetary authorities meant differentiating between domestic financial activities denominated in sterling, which were tightly regulated, and international activities in foreign currencies on behalf of non-residents, who enjoyed far greater freedom.

The merchant banks clearly played a major role in the emergence of the Euromarkets and benefited from their early expansion. Their deposits registered a 20 per cent a year increase between 1959 and 1965, as against only 5 per cent for the clearing banks,[98] as a result of the expansion of the interbank market, which grew hand in hand with the Euro-currency market. The proportion of non-sterling deposits on the aggregate balance sheets of

[98] S. Pollard, *The Development of the British Economy. Third Edition 1914–1980* (London, 1983), p. 389.

members of the Accepting Houses Committee grew from 45 per cent in 1962 to 54 per cent in 1973.[99]

However, unlike corporate finance which remained a 'niche' for merchant banks, the Euromarkets had to be shared with others, especially foreign banks, mainly American, which invaded the City from the late 1950s onwards: their number nearly doubled between 1957 and 1969 to reach 150, with their deposits rising from £263 million to £12.5 billion, again largely in foreign currencies.[100] The merchant banks managed to hold their own, though not in a manner comparable to their share of the accepting and issuing markets before 1914. Their share of the foreign currencies and US dollar deposits held by non-residents rose from 10.8 per cent in 1958 to 18.6 per cent in 1962, which put them behind the American banks in London (27 per cent up from 16.6 in 1956) and the British overseas banks (23 per cent, down from 33.3 per cent). During the rest of the 1960s, however, they lost ground against the American banks, whose share of total liabilities of UK banks in foreign banks reached 53.9 per cent in 1969, against 7.6 per cent for the accepting houses and 16.5 per cent for the British overseas banks.[101] In the Eurobond market, only three merchant banks—Warburgs, Rothschilds, and Hambros—appeared in the list of the top twenty lead banks or joint-lead banks of issue syndicates between 1963 and 1972.[102]

The late 1950s and early 1960s were a period of consolidation for the London merchant banks. With new business opportunities and increased competition, several firms sought to strengthen their position through merger. In 1957, Warburg merged with Seligman, and Hambros acquired the old-established bullion brokers Mocatta & Goldsmid to expand their foreign exchange business. In 1959, Philip Hill absorbed Higginson and Erlangers, while in 1960, Lazard took over de Stein, Schroders bought Helbert Wagg, and Kleinworts merged with Robert Benson Lonsdale. And in 1965, the recently formed Hill Higginson Erlanger merged with M. Samuel & Co. to form Hill Samuel, the largest merchant bank in the City. The trend was clearly towards alliances between houses whose strength was mainly in the issuing and securities business (Warburg, Philip Hill, Robert Benson Lonsdale, Helbert

[99] Bank of England, *Statistical Abstract*, quoted in Roberts, *Schroders*, p. 442.

[100] Figures given in R. Michie, *The City of London. Continuity and Change, 1859–1990* (Basingstoke and London, 1992), p. 92. On the 'invasion' of the City by American banks see R. Sylla, 'United States Banks and Europe: Strategy and Attitudes', in Battilossi and Cassis, *European Banks and the American Challenge.*

[101] S. Battilossi, 'Banks, Multinationals and Financial Innovation in International Banking: The Euro-Dollar Challenge, 1958–1971', Paper given at the Fondazione ASSI/Instituo di Storia Economica, Università L. Bocconi Seminar, Milan, 5.6.1998.

[102] Kerr, *History of the Eurobond Market.*

Wagg), and houses primarily engaged in banking (Kleinwort, Seligman, to a certain extent Schroders).

On the whole, stronger banks came out of these mergers—though the formation of Hill Samuel proved a failure, mainly because of clashes of personalities. The 1960s undoubtedly marked a revival, almost a new golden age for merchant banks. With their business developing along the three areas of wholesale banking, corporate finance, and investment management, in addition to their traditional role as accepting houses, they enjoyed an aura unequalled in any other sector of British banking. The question is whether this success could be sustained in the long term, and whether it could remain compatible with their private bank structure.

The Parisian *haute banque* survived the war, though some of the houses had to be rebuilt almost from scratch. Guy de Rothschild recalls that when he returned to Paris in 1944, 'there were only half a dozen clerks . . . a handful of customers, derisory deposits, a few securities and not enough money in the till to [manage] a financial institution'.[103] However, the family still owned substantial assets, which were recovered after the war and formed the basis of the bank's reconstruction. Business had to resume in new conditions. To the nationalization of railway companies in 1937 were added, in 1945 and 1946, those of the Banque de France (whose statutes had already been altered in 1936), the clearing banks, insurance companies, as well as coal, electricity, and gas, all fields in which Parisian private bankers had traditionally held directorships. In addition, the Banking Law of 1945 required all banks to register either as deposit banks or as *banques d'affaires*. Members of the *haute banque*, who had usually been doing a mixture of the two, had now to choose and, to a certain extent, adjust their business accordingly.

The majority opted to register as *banques de dépôts*. The more important amongst them were the old members of the *banque protestante*: Vernes & Cie, the largest with a total balance sheet of about Ff.11 billion in 1954; de Neuflize, Schlumberger & Cie (Ff.10.51 billion), the product of the merger in 1945 between the old-established house de Neuflize & Cie and Schlumberger & Cie, formed in 1919, though its founder, Maurice Schlumberger, belonged to an old Protestant family from Alsace with industrial connections and was related by marriage to the de Neuflize; Mallet Frères & Cie (Ff.4.54 billion), the capital's oldest bank; and Hottinguer & Cie (Ff.3.12 billion). Major private deposit banks also included Lehideux & Cie (Ff.5.27 billion) and Demachy & Cie (Ff.3.99 billion).[104] They were thus small banks, even by comparison with their provincial counterparts, though their off-balance activities must be expected to have been significantly larger, as the management of private investment portfolios remained, for all banks, the bedrock of their business.

[103] G. de Rothschild, *Contre bonne fortune* . . . (Paris, 1983), p. 197.
[104] Wilson, *French Banking*, p. 139.

However, all developed, in one way or another, their commercial banking activities. Mallet & Cie, for example, granted credit in all the usual ways, including documentary credit and acceptances. If a particular credit was too large to be handled by Mallet alone, it was common practice to work with other private bankers in a credit consortium. Vernes was concerned mostly with the finance of imports and exports, especially with New York, mainly on the basis of documentary credits. Demachy & Cie had many industrial customers, in the first place the de Wendel, with their large metallurgical interests, who were related to the founding families and held a capital interest in the bank. And within the limits imposed by their registration as deposit banks, most banks were also engaged in the investment field, through a number of *participations*, especially Vernes and de Neuflize Schlumberger.[105]

The most important members of the *haute banque* who opted for registration as a *banques d'affaires* were de Rothschild Frères, Worms & Cie, Lazard Frères & Cie, and Mirabaud & Cie, the latter being taken over by the Banque de l'Union Parisienne in 1953. The largest of them in the mid-1950s was possibly Worms & Cie,[106] though this is difficult to establish in the absence of either published balance sheets or archive-based histories of these firms. Unlike the London merchant banks, these firms did not possess an obvious 'niche market' to retain or to conquer. As far as international financial operations were concerned, Paris offered far fewer opportunities than even a highly-regulated London. The first Eurodollars might have been deposited in a bank in Paris but the market did not develop there, mainly because of the far greater degree of sophistication of London as a financial centre, as well as the far more positive attitude of the British monetary authorities. The nascent field of corporate finance was also growing more slowly than in Britain. In addition, private banks faced competition from the larger *banques d'affaires*, organized as limited liability companies, which had *not* been nationalized in 1945, in the first place the Banque de Paris et des Pays-Bas. Strategies thus varied, as exemplified by the contrasting experiences of de Rothschild Frères and Lazard Frères & Cie.

A new generation took the helm at Rothschilds at the end of the Second World War, headed by Guy, aged only 35 in 1944, with his two younger cousins Alain and Elie. Guy was determined to instil a new dynamism into the family affairs after the rather lethargic inter-war years under his father Edouard. The strategy was to develop the banking business and to bring together the huge assets owned by the Rothschild family in order to build, by the interplay of controlling stakes, an integrated Rothschild banking group. The cornerstone of this group was to be the old Compagnie des chemins de fer du Nord, the flagship of the Rothschild empire. Guy first set about

[105] Wilson, *French Banking*, pp. 135–43.

[106] Wilson, *French* Banking, p. 144.

re-launching the bank by making the many companies in which the family held important, often majority stakes, bring their balances back to the bank. All the members of the family also deposited their cash and securities with the bank, and by 1947, total deposits reached some Ff.700 million. A decisive step was taken in 1953 with the creation of the Société d'Investissement du Nord (S.I. Nord), which took over assets belonging partly to the Rothschild family and partly to the Compagnie des chemins de fer du Nord.[107] The new S.I. Nord, akin to an investment trust (the first private company of this kind in France), had a capital of Ff.4 billion and held substantial stakes in such companies as Royal Dutch Shell, De Beers, Le Nickel, Peñarroya, and many others, its entire portfolio being valued at Ff.16.5 billion in 1959.[108] As Guy de Rothschild put it: 'For Messieurs de Rothschild Frères, the first stage had passed, the old house had regained a position on the Paris financial market.'[109]

A new step in the consolidation of the Rothschilds' interests took place in 1966 with the absorption of the S.I. Nord by the Compagnie du Nord. A single holding company now brought together the expanded Rothschild *participations* in oil (ANTAR), shipping (SAGA, CGEF), nonferrous metals (Le Nickel, Peñarroya, Mokta), tourism (PLM), building and construction (SNC). The whole investment portfolio was worth some NF800 million in 1968,[110] that is, about half that of Paribas and 60 per cent that of Suez. In the meantime, the banking house itself, de Rothschild Frères, was growing far more slowly. By the mid-1960s, it was felt by the partners to be too small to achieve economies of scale and support the development of the entire group. Expanding meant increasing the volume of deposits. So in 1967, the French Rothschilds took the historical decision of going public: from 1 January 1968, de Rothschild Frères became the Banque Rothschild, with new modern premises erected on the old site of 21, rue Lafitte. Its capital was raised from NF20 to NF50 million, 73 per cent of which being taken up by the Compagnie du Nord, the rest by the three partners. The Banque Rothschild thus became the banking arm of the Rothschild-Compagnie du Nord group. The new bank became a deposit bank and opened branches in Paris and a number of major provincial cities.

Lazard Frères & Cie remained a more firmly focused *banque d'affaires*. The bank had undoubtedly taken off in the 1920s but in no way had the partners and their families accumulated assets approaching those of the Rothschilds. In order to rebuild their bank, Lazard had to rely more on human than on financial capital. Recruiting new financial talent has always been their

[107] The railway company, controlled by the Rothschilds since its foundation in 1845, had been nationalized in 1937 but had kept a number of assets and remained a publicly-quoted company, with a wide investment portfolio (including 270,000 shares in the national railway company, the SNCF).

[108] J. Bouvier, *Les Rothschild*, 2nd edn (Bruxelles, 1983), pp. 323–4.

[109] Rothschild, *Contre bonne fortune*, p. 203.

[110] The 'new' franc (NF), introduced in 1960, was worth 100 'old' francs.

speciality, something that even Guy de Rothschild admitted in his memoirs, as Lazards eventually overtook Rothschilds to became the premier private bank in France: 'I have always admired this success without ever being able to imitate it'.[111] Not that the Rothschilds were unable to attract top people. Georges Pompidou, to give but the best known example, the future Prime Minister and President of the Republic, joined the bank in 1953 soon to become chief executive. A significant difference, however, was that at Lazards, outsiders were offered a partnership, even with a minute fraction of the bank's capital. Another difference was Lazards' presence in New York. As we have seen, Lazard Frères New York had been established as early as 1880. In the 1940s, it was a highly respected Wall Street investment bank, with a mix of business (bond underwriting, investment trusts management, gold trading, retail stockbroking) and branches in Boston, Chicago, and Philadelphia, though 'it wasn't a major money-making proposition'.[112] Its fortunes were radically transformed by the arrival in 1940 of one of the Paris partners, André Meyer.

André Meyer has been described by David Rockefeller as 'the most creative financial genius of our time in the investment banking field'[113] and several other opinions have concurred. Three years after his arrival in New York, he took control of Lazard Frères, ousting the incumbent, second generation senior partner Frank Altschul. By 1945, all the old partners had been dismissed and by 1948 the three branches outside New York closed. Meyer's objectives were threefold: first, Lazard Frères should be associated with first class international issues; secondly, it should build a small, but highly selective private clientele; and thirdly, for speculative purposes, it should take a stake in undervalued companies with potential for internal or external growth. It is through this third activity that Lazards made huge amounts of money in the 1950s. From the 1960s, Meyer increasingly turned his attention to corporate finance, making Lazard Frères the clear leader in takeover bids, capable of commanding enormous fees through their advice to top companies, such as R.C.A. (in their acquisition of Hertz and Random House), MacDonnell (in their acquisition of Douglas Aircraft), and above all, the International Telephone & Telegraph Company (ITT). During the 1960s, ITT, under Harold Geneen, launched an acquisition spree, becoming by 1971 the ninth largest industrial company in the United States, with 75 per cent of its $8.8 billion revenues derived from acquired companies. Lazard Frères had been associated with all its major deals. Between 1964 and 1968, Lazards earned some $10 million in merger and acquisition fees, with ITT contributing 28 per cent of the total.

[111] Rothschild, *Contre bonne fortune*, p. 210.

[112] C. Reich, *Financier. The Biography of André Meyer. A Story of Money, Power, and the Reshaping of American Business* (New York, 1983), p. 38.

[113] Reich, *Financier. The Biography of André Meyer*, p. 19.

To the extent that the Paris and New York firms were separate, the business of Lazard Frères New York cannot retain too much of our attention here. There was, however, some synergy. Pierre David-Weill, the last descendant of the founding families, was equal partner with André Meyer in New York: each owned 25 per cent of the firm, though it was agreed from the start between the two men that Meyer would be in charge in New York. We do not know to what extent the Paris house shared in the profits made in New York, but some benefit must have accrued. The New York house and André Meyer also played an invaluable role as a source of both business and political contacts for Lazard Frères & Cie in Paris, from which many a deal would originate. But they also exerted a more general influence on their strategic choices.

André Meyer remained a partner in Paris and even though his visits to the French capital were infrequent, his presence was strongly felt. In many respects, the two firms developed along similar lines. In Paris, as in New York, the firm was kept small and priority was given to activities based on fees, in the first place corporate finance, rather than banking activities based on interest differentials, though the latter were not entirely neglected. Just after the war, the firm was able to recover some of its old clients, such as Peugeot, de Wendel, Michelin, and introduced to the Paris Bourse the stock of major companies such as Fiat, Prisunic, the Lainière de Roubaix, Pechiney, International Nickel. In 1963, they founded Locatel, a TV rental company, whose market capitalization rose from 8 to 240 million francs in fifteen years, at which point they decided to sell their 60 per cent stake. In 1967, the business was reorganized by separating the banking house from its various *participations*. The latter were structured around two property companies (Rue impériale and Immobilière Marseillaise) and an investment company, Eurafrance. The big time came in 1968, with the resounding takeover bid by the glassmaker BSN for its larger competitor and pillar of the French business establishment, Saint-Gobain. Such moves were still exceptional in France and BSN, advised by Lazard, eventually failed to acquire a sufficient number of shares. Lazard Frères, however, received a commission of NF5 million and, more importantly, made a name for themselves in the field of corporate finance. They would really take off in the following decades.

The position of the *haute banque* was different in Germany. As we have seen, the term had never really suited the country's leading private banks. The blow dealt to Jewish banks by the Nazi regime, the disappearance of Berlin as a financial centre, and the inward orientation of German banking in the two decades following the war—all this meant that the few remaining prestigious names had lost much of their significance in both German and international finance.

Most of the great Jewish banks did not re-emerge after the war. The leading bank in Weimar days, M. M. Warburg & Co., was able to preserve its identity after its 'aryanization' under the name of Brinckmann, Wirtz & Co. The firm remained one of the country's major private banks, with well over a hundred employees in 1947, and soon benefited from the German 'economic miracle' and the Warburgs' international connections. However, the relationships between the new partners, especially Rudolf Brinckmann (Paul Wirtz died in 1946), and the Warburg family proved difficult. Brinckmann asked Eric Warburg, on his return to Hamburg in 1945 as an officer in the American army, whether the Warburg partners intended to return and retake control of the bank, but no decision could be made at the time. A restitution deal was agreed four years later in 1949: the Warburgs were given a 25 per cent stake in the bank and 80,000 deutsche marks in reparations, with an option to increase their stake to a controlling 50 per cent within five years. However, no change of name was demanded by their representative in the negotiations, Eric Warburg. This was to lead to a protracted battle between Rudolf Brinckmann and the Warburgs, as the question of the name was of paramount importance to all members of the dynasty. In 1953, mainly as a result of family disagreements, the Warburgs did not exercise their option to take a controlling stake in the bank. This did not deter Eric Warburg, Max's only son, from becoming a partner in Hamburg in 1956. In January 1970, Rudolf Brinckmann finally agreed to change the firm's name to Warburg-Brinckmann, Wirtz & Co. It was then the third largest private bank in Germany.[114]

Another major private bank, Sal. Oppenheim jr. & Cie. in Cologne, reverted much earlier—in March 1946—to its original name. The case, however, was simpler, as no transfer of ownership had taken place and the Oppenheim partners had been able to remain in Germany for most of the war. In 1945, Waldemar and Carl Friedrich von Oppenheim were back in charge alongside Robert Pferdmenges. The firm undoubtedly benefited from being granted a licence to act as a foreign trade bank by the Bank deutscher Länder (the forerunner of the Bundesbank) in 1948. In the words of the bank's historians, this was 'a licence to print money', as all other banks had to use its services—a privilege which lasted for two crucial years, when German industry was returning to the world markets.[115] The status of Sal. Oppenheim Jr. & Co. was also enhanced by Robert Pferdmenges distinguished political career: he was a founder-member of the CDU in the Rhineland, an adviser and friend of Konrad Adenauer, and deputy at the Bundestag from 1949 to 1962. Pferdmenges was also supervisory board chairman of Thyssen AG, the giant metallurgical concern. In 1958, the bank's partners together held eighty-two seats on supervisory boards and advisory councils, including twenty-two for Robert Pferdmenges and twenty-nine for Carl Friedrich von Oppenheim.[116] With its strong involvement in the Colonia insurance group, in which it held a

[114] See Chernow, *Warburgs*, pp. 535, 568–71, 582–8, 663–7.
[115] Stürmer et al., *Striking the Balance*, p. 447.
[116] Stürmer et al., *Striking the Balance*, p. 436.

controlling stake, Oppenheim had emerged as the leading private bank in post-war Germany.

FROM PRIVATE BANKS TO PRIVATE BANKING

Private banks ceased to exist in any meaningful way during the 1960s. By the end of the decade, hardly any banking house of any substance could still be considered a private bank. The change took place with the conversion of most merchant banks and investment banks into public companies. The trend had in fact started earlier: Baring Brothers was registered as a limited company after its near collapse in 1890; Hambros and Morgan Grenfell in 1934; Schroders in 1959. However, they had remained in family hands. Significantly, the same phenomenon took place with the investment banks in Wall Street. J. P. Morgan, a commercial bank following the Glass Steagall Act of 1933, had done so as early as 1940—commercial banking required higher capital levels. Morgan Stanley, the investment bank offspring of the House of Morgan, founded in 1935, followed thirty years later, in 1970, with partial incorporation, and in 1975 with full limited liability. Most leading investment banks had converted earlier—Merrill Lynch, for example, in 1959, Dillon Read in 1964.[117]

What changed in the 1960s, in both Britain and the United States, was the opening of both ownership and control, on a large scale, to outside interests—not only outside the family, but also outside the traditional networks of relationships. This, ultimately, meant the end of the private bank character of these venerable institutions. The conversion into a limited company and, especially, into a public company, had a number of advantages. It could offer tax advantages to partners, it removed the risk of large capital withdrawals following the death of a partner, it enabled the firm to offer better incentives to valued executives and employees who could be lured by competitors, and it provided the firm with wider resources as they engaged in new activities, especially trading and principal investment, requiring ample financial capital, and had to incur the costs of new technology.[118]

[117] Chernow, *House of Morgan*, pp. 469, 586, 600; E. Perkins, *Wall Street to Main Street. Charles Merrill and the Middle-Class Investors* (Cambridge, 1999), p. 200; V. Carosso, *Investment Banking in America. A History* (Cambridge, Mass., 1970), pp. 505–7.

[118] See A. D. Morrison and W. J. Wilhelm, Jr, *Investment Banking. Institutions, Politics, and Law* (Oxford 2007), pp. 89–92, 267–92. Morrison and Wilhelm link investment banks' forms of organization to the type of skills required to perform their activities: partnerships are best adapted to 'tacit knowledge' characteristic of traditional investment banking, joint-stock companies to 'technical expertise', increasingly predominant in modern investment banking.

This did not prevent virtually all the leading merchant banks from being taken over by large, mainly foreign, banks. After the first mergers at the end of the 1980s (Morgan Grenfell, weakened by losses sustained during the stock-market crash of 1987, was taken over by Deutsche Bank in 1989), it was Baring Brothers' bankruptcy in February 1995[119] that sparked off a wide-spread buyout trend. In the same year, SG Warburg, weakened by losses and an abortive merger plan with Morgan Stanley, was bought out by the Swiss Bank Corporation, whereas Kleinwort, considering itself too small to remain both competitive and independent, preferred to become allied with Dresdner Bank. Schroders and Robert Fleming would do likewise by joining up with Citigroup and Chase Manhattan, respectively, in 2000. Ten years later, only N. M. Rothschild and Lazard Brothers were still independent. As for American investment banks, they ultimately have not done much better. Most have succumbed to universal banks after the repeal of the Glass Steagall Act in 1999 and the ravages of the subprime crisis in 2007–8. Bear Stearns was bought by JP Morgan, Merrill Lynch by Bank of America and, of course, Lehman Brothers collapsed. Only two, Goldman Sachs and Morgan Stanley, have survived as independent entities—and have in fact converted into bank holding companies.

A handful of private banks have survived in all European countries. However, only in Switzerland, and especially in Geneva, have private bankers managed, for reasons of both tradition and location, to retain a competitive edge enabling them to be considered as global players in the field of wealth management, primarily on behalf of high net worth individuals. The *haute banque* survived with the old Protestant banks, founded at the turn of the nineteenth century: Pictet & Cie, Lombard, Odier & Cie, Darier, Hentsch & Cie (the latter two merged in 2002), Bordier & Cie, and Mirabaud & Cie—with Pictet and Lombard Odier clearly in the lead. But there have been successful newcomers, mostly of Jewish origin: the Banque Privée Edmond de Rothschild, established in Paris in 1953 and in Geneva in 1965, the Republic National Bank, founded in 1966 by Edmond Safra, and the Union Bancaire Privée, founded in 1969 by Edgar de Picciotto. However, even in Geneva, cracks have started to appear. Republic National Bank of New York was sold to HSBC in 1999. And in 2013, Pictet and Lombard Odier, who claimed to embody the real values of private banks as their partners had unlimited liability, turned themselves into private limited companies.

[119] Like other merchant banks, and in the image of the American investment banks, the City's venerable banking house had gone into transactions on its own account in order to offset its shrinking margins. Things took a nasty turn when losses caused by speculating on derivatives on the part of its rogue trader in Singapore, Nick Leeson, exceeded £800 million—in other words, the bank's entire capital. It was bought up for the symbolic sum of one pound by the Dutch bank ING.

It might thus appear paradoxical to talk of a renaissance of private banks at the very time that its last survivors were disappearing, one after the other. The renewal of private banking since the 1980s has had little to do with the firms traditionally known as private banks (i.e., partnerships or at least houses under family ownership and control). It has rather been the remarkable growth of a banking activity (wealth management on behalf of high net worth individuals), which has come to be known as *private banking*, irrespective of the type of bank offering such services. At the end of 1997, the target market for private banks was estimated at around $17 trillion and expected to keep on growing at two to three times the pace of the overall banking market for years to come; it had grown to $152 trillion by 2013.[120] The development of private banking as a banking activity is outside our subject, especially as it has come to be mainly undertaken by large universal banks such as UBS, Crédit Suisse, HSBC, Deutsche Bank, JPMorgan Chase, Citibank, or ABN Amro, well ahead of 'traditional' private banks such as Pictet or Lombard Odier in Geneva, or 'former' private (investment) banks, such as Morgan Stanley or Goldman Sachs, which have recently been attracted by a business perceived as low risk and providing a steady income stream.[121] From this perspective, the financial debacle of 2008 had fairly limited impact on private banking.

Private banking has thus become increasingly divorced from the old-established private banks. There are, however, good reasons to plead in favour of a renewal of private banking in the late twentieth century. Private portfolio management has always featured amongst the activities of the *haute banque*, and private bankers have traditionally dealt with wealthy customers. It is also significant that the name of famous private banks has often been retained by their new owners and considered as a useful asset in this particular market. Likewise, descendants of old banking dynasties, and more generally of upper-class families (originally banking families which, according to Stendhal, constituted the aristocracy of the bourgeoisie), have held senior positions in private banking, where they have been in demand for a certain cachet, as well as for their network of relationships in these circles. Throughout the twentieth century, these have been the attributes on which private bankers have relied to gain a competitive edge in their business activities.

At another level, remnants of the partnership form of organization have persisted in the world of investment banking. The appellation 'partner', for example, was often preferred to that of 'director' in the newly converted firms: at Morgan Stanley, for example, where the number of partners increased from more than twenty in the early 1960s to nearly forty by the mid-1970s.[122] At Schroders, the number of directors increased from twenty to thirty-three

[120] *Financial Times*, 26 November 1997; 9 June 2014.
[121] *Financial Times*, 6 July 2014. [122] Chernow, *House of Morgan*, pp. 580, 598.

between 1962 and 1973.[123] Other firms, most notably Goldman Sachs, remained a private partnership until the very end of the twentieth century, by which time it had 174 partners. Even after going public in 1999, the firm retained a type of partnership structure—though closer to the modern corporation than to the private bank of old.[124] In new fields of financial activities, such as hedge funds and private equity, firms were set up by independent financiers, often with a partnership form of organization.

These remnants of the partnership model were increasingly present in the governance of the world's leading banks, especially those operating in the two global financial centres, London and New York. They all became universal banks and had to accommodate investment bankers in their ranks. Significantly, these investment bankers retained some of the characteristics, and also some of the prerogatives, of the old private investment bankers—in terms of status and, especially, level of remuneration, traditionally higher than in other sectors, but which has reached unprecedented levels in the new era of global finance.[125] Salaried managers and traders, who did not own their company, were able to enjoy some of the privileges of the partners of a private bank, in particular in terms of level of remuneration, without having to bear the concomitant responsibilities, in particular loyalty to the firm and risking one's own capital. Such remnants, however, were very remote from the values of the old private bankers.

[123] Roberts, *Schroders*, p. 426.

[124] C. D. Ellis, *The Partnership. The Making of Goldman Sachs* (London, 2008).

[125] According to a recent study on the United States, wages in the financial sector, compared to the rest of the private sector, exhibit a U-shape pattern between 1909 and 2006, with a sharp decline from the 1930s to the 1950s and a moderate one from the 1950s to the 1980s; see T. Philippon and A. Reshef, 'Wages and Human Capital in the U.S. Financial Industry', *NBER Working Paper* No. 14644, January 2009.

Conclusion

One conclusion of this very long-term history of private banks is the continuing relevance of the partnership form of organization in the world of banking and finance. This might appear obvious for the medieval and early modern periods, when joint-stock and public companies were the exception rather than the rule—though one should not forget the early development of such institutions as the Cassa San Giorgio in fifteenth-century Genova, or the Wissel Bank in seventeenth-century Amsterdam. Yet private bankers were clearly in command of banking and financial activities and did not really loosen their grip before the mid-nineteenth century. From the 1870s, they became increasingly marginalized but continued to take centre stage in the core activities of international finance, and the accepting and issuing businesses. Admittedly, the Parisian *haute banque* or the German private banks lost ground to the newly established joint-stock banks, but that was largely compensated for by the dominant position of the merchant banks in the City of London, the undisputed financial centre of the world.

This key role of European private bankers in international finance was reinforced, especially in the 1920s, by the status of the Wall Street investment banks, above all, the House of Morgan, which remained a partnership until 1934, when it decided to become a commercial bank in the wake of the Glass Steagall Act. The strategic role of private bankers continued after the Second World War, mainly in domestic finance, as merchant banks in London and investment banks in New York dominated the field of corporate finance, introducing innovative practices such as hostile takeover bids. Their role was also key in international finance, through their decisive contribution to the advent of the Euromarkets—though they eventually had to concede leadership to the big banks. Private banks virtually disappeared in the last quarter of the twentieth century. With the conversion of most London merchant banks into public limited companies, only marginal 'niche' players retained a partnership form of organization, with or without limited liability, foremost amongst them the Geneva private bankers.

And yet private banking survived and even enjoyed a renaissance from the 1980s. One aspect of this revival was the metamorphosis of private banking from a mode of organization—the partnership—into a type of activity—wealth management for high net worth individuals. Thus defined, private banking has become one of the fastest growing banking businesses, not least as a result of the rise of inequalities—wealth management providing a more reliable, though less glamorous, source of income than investment banking, especially after the financial debacle of 2007–8. However, with the bulk of private banking being undertaken by large universal banks, the continuity between private banks and private banking appears somewhat tenuous. Indeed, in the more recent sense of the word, the adjective 'private' more accurately describes banks' customers (who enjoy a more personalized service) than bankers (who are no longer owner-managers).

Nevertheless, some continuity can be observed in the 'exclusive' character of private banking, the key role of upper and upper middle-class individuals, not least through their networks within the world of the very wealthy. In many respects, the world of the *haute banque* has been perpetuated in modern day private banking, even when practised by incorporated banks. However, this 'exclusive' character has inevitably started to be diluted with the large banks' wealth management departments increasingly targeting very well-off or simply well-off customers.

It is in this light that the relationships between private banks and joint-stock banks—the old rivalry of the nineteenth century—should be examined. Not only have the two types of banks never really been antagonistic, not only have they always been complementary, but it can plausibly be argued that the joint-stock banks have been the servants of the private banks and private bankers. Early public banks such as the Cassa San Giorgio or the Wissel Bank were not competing against private merchants and bankers. On the contrary, by stabilizing the financial system, especially foreign exchanges, they facilitated the mercantile-cum-banking activities of the private banks. In the nineteenth century, joint-stock banks were founded by private bankers in order to extend the range and scope of their activities. In the City of London's golden age, between 1870 and 1914, the merchant bankers' dominance of the accepting and issuing businesses was made possible by a hierarchical division of labour by which the huge deposits of the clearing banks provided the cash credit required to perform these operations.

Joint-stock banks also offered a home for private bankers. In the late nineteenth and early twentieth century, the boards of directors of the leading joint stock-banks included a fair proportion of private bankers—whether the partner of one of the founding firms, the ex-partner of an acquired firm, or simply a business 'notable'. This proportion diminished after the First World War, and even more after the Second. However, at the turn of the twenty-first century, the status of star investment bankers in large universal banks was in several respects akin to that of the partners of the private banks of old—in terms of status and level of remuneration, though, without having to bear the concomitant responsibilities, in particular loyalty to the firm and risking one's own capital.

How to explain the resilience of private banks? A first explanation can be found in their type of activity. Private banks have always flourished in fairly narrow segments within the world of banking and finance, long before the emergence of joint-stock banks. Until the mid-nineteenth century, banking was still in its infancy. Banks were few in number, their level of assets and liabilities was low, a bank account was the privilege of a small elite, and the business of banking was mainly subordinate to the needs of trade and commerce. The rise of banking, as an economic pursuit in its own right, and as an engine as well as a product of modern economic growth has been mainly concomitant with the rise of the joint-stock banks.

Whether in their golden age, in times of decline, or in eras of revival, private banks have performed the same type of function. They have been involved in rather specialized 'niche' type of activities, free from competition from joint-stock banks. They have usually dealt with fairly exclusive customers, for example high net worth individuals, to use today's terminology, or foreign governments. The volume of their business has tended to be comparatively low (if measured by the number of customers or branches), but their profit margins relatively high. There have been some digressions from this pattern: private country banks in particular, which flourished in the nineteenth century in countries such as France and Germany, were clearly catering for 'ordinary' customers. And some of the 'specialized' areas dominated by private bankers could be very large indeed, for example the international issuing business in the City of London before the First World War. But they are the exceptions that confirm the rule: throughout their history, private banks have been specialist, rather than generalist, financial institutions.

A second explanation has to do with the position of private banks in the economy and in society. Private banking has always been essentially a matter of networks. First and foremost family networks, as private banks have tended to be family firms. Religious networks have been another major constituent, often superimposed on family ones, as exemplified by national or international banking dynasties—the Rothschilds being the most famous though by no means the only such example. The largest networks were formed by the Protestant and Jewish religious minorities, the former dominant in the eighteenth century, the latter in the nineteenth, with other denominations, not least the Quakers, also leaving their mark. Religious networks have certainly weakened, though they have not entirely disappeared and still play a role in terms of cultural identity. Moreover, elements of their modus operandi can be found in other types of network relationships—political, ethnic, 'old boys', and others. Finally, social networks have also been part of the fabric of private banking, here again often in conjunction with family and religious factors. The gradual integration of private bankers into the upper classes from the mid-nineteenth century and their ever closer links with the political elites have been both a cause and a consequence of their moving their business upmarket—a position best described by the notion of *haute banque*, which has kept its resonance to this day.

And a third explanation is related to the role of private bankers within the banking profession, in particular leadership and innovative capacity. Private bankers have been at the root of most financial innovation—whether the use of bills of exchange in fourteenth-century Italy, the issue of banknotes in seventeenth-century England, the emergence of the 'new' bank in nineteenth-century Europe, or the advent of the Euromarkets in twentieth-century London. This is perhaps not very surprising: small, lean firms have historically proved more innovative and more enterprising than large, bureaucratic ones. Interestingly, in the late twentieth century, the innovative drive of the big banks, in particular in the design of derivative products, came from investment bankers whose professional status was reminiscent of that of a private banker. And in the broader field of finance, the same can be said of hedge funds, where managing partners usually invest their own funds alongside those of their partners.

The possibility or even the desirability that investment banks should return to a partnership form of organization has been floated in some quarters—as a way to avoid the excesses that lead to the financial debacle of 2008. This hardly seems a realistic option for twenty-first-century banking, except for some firms in specialized niche activities. A more practical solution to combat recklessness and raise ethical standards would be to restore a clear distinction between the status and prerogatives of a joint-stock bank's executive—a salaried manager—and those of a private banker—an owner-manager.

Index

c.1300–1700, structural framework development 4, 7–38
  Amsterdam's supremacy 18–24
  Antwerp, rise of fall of 15–17
  emergence of private banking 7–11
  Hamburg and Frankfurt 25–9
  Italian private bankers 11–15
  London, early private bankers 5, 6, 29–38
1793–1815, war and economic transformation 79–112
  Amsterdam (1795–1815) 80–1
  British mercantile finance 88–9
  British overseas trade 84–9
  British war finance 89–94
  financing the war in Europe 95–8
  Frankfurt 83
  Hamburg 81–3, 84–5
  and the London money market 98–103
  private banks in revolutionary France 109–12
  wartime inflation and country banks 103–9
1815–1870, golden age 113–64
  banking reforms in England and Wales 144–55
  financing railways construction 136–43
  financing the recovery of international trade 120–5
  formation of the Parisian *haute banque* 128–33
  German universal banks 161–4
  industrialization in the Rhineland 134–6
  joint-stock banks emergence 143–55
  lasting influence of private bankers 207–15
  London financing of the European political settlement (post 1815) 113–16
  mixed banking, birth of 155–6
  'new bank' in France 156–61
  rise of the London merchant banks 126–7
  sovereign loans 116–20
1870–1914, onset of the corporate economy 166–215
  Berlin, Frankfurt, Hamburg, and Cologne 187–93
  lesser financial centres 193–9
  London 166–79
  Parisian *haute banque* 165, 180–7
  private bankers in the regions 199–207
1914–1918, First World War 217–24
  finance 218–24
1920–1931, Indian summer 224–45
  former neutrals 244–5
  inflation and consolidation in Germany 240–4
  London 230–6
  Paris and the provinces 236–40
  status and power 225–30
1931–2015, decline and renaissance 247–84
  banking crisis (early 1930s) 247–8
  corporate finance 253
  France, and the Great Depression 259–63
  German private banks (1930s) 254–9
  Great Aluminium War 269 n. 88, 269–70
  Great Depression 248–9
  Jewish bankers in Nazi Germany 255–9
  London post-1945 265–71
  mergers and buyouts (1980s) 282
  Paris *haute banque* 275–9
  private banks in the world economic crisis 250–63
  from private banks to private banking 281–4
  reconstruction and regulation 263–81

Abbema, Balthazar-Elie 74
Abbey National 249
Abbott, Robert 32
Aberdeen Banking Company 61
Accepting Houses Committee (founded August 1914) 220, 233, 251, 266, 179
Acciaiuli merchant banks 13, 14
Ackrill, Margaret 169–70
Addis, Charles 218, 229
Adenauer, Konrad 280
Ador, Jean 111
Ador, Vernes & Dassier 111
Alexander, James 61
Alexander & Co. 101
Alfred Salomon Cahen & Cie 226
Altschul, Frank 278
Aluminium Company of America (ALcoa) 269–70
American Civil War (1861–5) 127
American and Continental Corporation 242
American railways 172, 175, 177
American War of Independence (1776–83) 69
Amro, A. B. N. 212
Amsterdam 3, 4, 5, 10, 11

Amsterdam (*cont.*)
  *c.*1300–1700 18–24
  1795–1815 80–1
  1870–1914 195–6
  Beurs 19
  bills of exchange 2
  foreign loans 65–8
  kassiers (cashiers), and private banking 21–2
  licensed brokers 19
  merchant bankers 64–9
  population increase 19
  printed market price data 13
  Stock Exchange 195
Amsterdam Wisselbank (1609) 10
André, Ernest 157
Angerstein, John Julius 89, 92
Anglo-Austrian Bank 209, 236
Anglo-French free-trade treaty (1786) 79
Anglo-Netherlands textiles 16
Anglo-Sardinian Loan (1851) 127
Anglo-Scottish banking crisis of 1772 66, 67
Antwerp 4, 10, 11, 18
  bills of exchange 2
  Bourse 19
  exchange rates 16
  rise and fall of (*c.*1300–1700) 15–17
Ardant, Henri 262
Argentina 178
  and British capital 175–6
Arms Bank, Glasgow 61, 62
Armstrong Whitworth 232, 236
Arnhold, Kurt 258
Ashkenazi Jews, Hamburg 26
Asti bank, Genoa 8, 11
Astor, John Jacob 125
Augsburg 16, 206–7
Austin Motors 232
Austria:
  debt 81
  Imperial loan (1778) 76–7
  Imperial loan (1779) 93
  Imperial loan (1794) 91, 92, 95
  lottery loans 118
  state loans 197–8
Austro-Hungarian railway networks 158
Ayr Banking Co. 60, 61, 62, 66
  failure (1772–3) 45

Backwell, Thomas 47
Bagehot, Walter 211
Baltic trade 18, 24
  and British exports 84
Bamberger, Ludwig 194, 208
Banca Commerciale Italiana 247
Banca Nazionale del Lavoro 249
bank accounts, origin of 10
Bank Charter Act (1844) 149
Bank for International Settlement 272
Bank für Industrie-Obligationen 258
banknotes as paper money, London 34
  Bank Charter Act (1844) 149
  note issues 105, 106
Bank of America 282
Bank of Egypt 209
Bank of England 4, 47, 64, 93, 99
  1773 crisis 53, 60
  1825–6 crisis 124, 145–7
  Ayr Bank crisis 45
  and banking reforms 145
  Baring Brothers rescue (1890) 176–7
  and bill brokers 153
  charters (1833/44) 149, 151
  control on foreign lending 231
  Court of Directors 36
  financial crisis (August 1914) 219, 220
  founding (1694) 36–7, 38
  and international financial stability
    (1920–31) 228–9, 230
  'long' bills 101, 102
  managing the public debt 42
  monopoly over joint-stock banking 51
  note issue 105, 106
  opposition to metropolitan joint-stock
    banking 152
  paper currency circulation (1753–92) 53–4
  policies (1793–1815) 88
  shuttings rule (1858) 154
  Standstill bills 250
Bank of Ireland 64, 145, 147
Bank of Manchester 147, 152
Bank of Manhattan 242
Bank of New York 125
Bank of Palermo 20
Bank of Prussia 161, 162
Bank of Scotland (founded 1695) 60, 61, 64
'Bankers' Annuities', National Debt, British 35
Banking Act (1826) 147, 149
Banque Adam 261
Banque Besnard 261
Banque Commerciale pour l'Europe du Nord 271
Banque d'Escompte Suisse, Geneva 248
Banque de Belgique 137, 156
Banque de Bruxelles 208
Banque de Crédit et de Dépôt des
    Pays-Bas 208
Banque de France 110, 114, 130, 158, 215,
    226, 228, 229
  banking directory 201
  branching network 160–1, 202
  statute reforms (1936) 261–2
  and the war indemnity payments
    (1870) 180, 181

Banque de l'Isère 264
Banque de l'Union Parisienne 185, 209, 211, 213, 240, 248, 276
Banque de Paris 181, 208, 213
Banque de Paris et des Pays-Bas 181, 185, 186, 192, 194, 208, 276
Banque Internationale, Luxembourg 163
Banque Lambert 194
Banque Nationale de Crédit 248
Banque Nationale pour le Commerce et le Crédit (BNCI) 248
Banque Oustric debacle 260–1
Banque Priveé Edmond de Rothschild 282
Banque Thomas 204, 205
Banque Vasseur 261
Barclay, David I 46
Barclay, David II 46
Barclay, James 46
Barclay, John 46
Barclay, Bevan, Tritton & Co. 167, 169
Barclays Bank 44, 46, 47, 209, 211, 231
  as Limited Company 167, 169–70
Bardi merchant banks 13, 14
Barent Cohen, Hannah 87
Baring, Alexander, 1st Lord Revelstoke 96–8, 114, 116, 125
Baring, Edward Charles 176, 1st Lord Revelstoke
Baring, George 97
Baring, John, 2nd Lord Revelstoke 177, 224, 229, 235, 236
Baring, Sir Francis 87, 87 n. 28, 124, 177
Baring, Thomas II 125
Baring Brothers 5, 66, 87 n. 28, 90–1, 94, 95, 96, 173, 175–7, 178, 192, 219, 231–2, 232–3, 234 n. 51, 234–5, 251, 252, 281
  acceptance credits 123, 126
  assets (1928) 231
  bankruptcy (1955) 282
  financing railway construction 139
  First World War 220, 222
  rescue (1890) 170
  restructuring post 1827 125
  South American involvement 119–20
  sovereign loans to France (1817/18) 114–16
  trade finance post-1815 124–5
Baring & Co., Exeter 87 n. 28
Barnetts, Hoare & Co. 153, 168
Bartholony, François 140, 158
Basle, Council of (1431) 14
Basler Bankverein 208–9
Batavian Republic 80–1
Bates, Joshua 125
Batum Oil Refining and Trading Company 183
Bavarian Natonal Bank 144
Bayerische Hypotheken- und Wechsel-Bank (Hypo-Bank) 161, 249
Bear Stearns 282
Beaujon, Nicolas 71
Becker & Fuld 195
Beckett & Co. 200, 235
beet-sugar processing 130
Behrens, L. & Co. 187
Belgium 244
  Birth of mixed banking 155–6
  haute banque (1870–1914) 193–4
  'Iron Rhine' project 137–8
  and 'mixed banking' 156
Benfield, Paul 91, 93
Benoît Fould 134, 139, 157, 163
Berenberg Joh., Gossler & Co. 82
Bergisch-Märkische Bank 206
Berlin 241
  1870–1914 187, 188–9
Berlin decrees 79
Berliner Handels-Gesellschaft 162, 163, 258
Bernard, Samuel 71
Besançon 13
Bethman, Simon Moritz von 76
Bethmann, Gebrüder of Frankfurt 76–7, 83, 128, 187
Bethmann, Johann Philipp von 76
Beurze family 12
Bicci, Giovanni di 14
bill brokers 101–3, 105, 153–4
bill discounting 17, 21, 22, 25, 38, 53
bill transfer, by endorsement 21
bills of exchange 2, 3, 11–12, 14, 22, 53, 65
  on London 29, 30–1, 122–3, 126
  origins 10
  serial endorsement 16–17, 25
Bingham, William 96
Bischoffsheim, Goldschmidt & Cie 194
Bischoffhseim, Jonathan Raphael 137, 194
Bischoffsheim, Louis 158
Bischoffhseim, Ludwig-Raphael 194
Bismarck, Otto von 180, 188
Blackwell, Edward 34, 35
Blackwell's bank 33, 34
Blanc, Jean-Antoine 111
Bleichröder, Gerson von 188
Bleichröders 187, 188–9, 191, 192, 198, 241
Blount, Edward 140, 140 n. 82
Blyth, Greene, Jourdain & Co. 179
Bodeck, Johann von 28
Boden Creditanstalt 198
Boissieu, Jacques de 262
Bokanowski, Maurice 226
Boléo Compagnie 183
Bolton, Sir George 272

Bonnet bank 206–7
Bontems & fils 73
Bordier & Cie 282
Bouman, Johannes 73
Bouvier, Jean 181, 237
Bowman, William 48, 49
Boyd, Benfield & Co. 91, 95, 98
Boyd, Walter 91–4
Bradford Banking Co. 59, 147
branch banking, beginnings of 58–9
  Scotland 63
Brand, R. H. 250
Brandies-Goldschmidt 268
Brandt, Arthur H. & Co. 173, 254
Brandts 85, 123, 179, 220
Brandts, Jan Jacob 73
Brasilianische Bank für Deutschland 192
Brazil, and sovereign debt 119, 120
Brickwood & Co. 108
Brinckmann, Rudolf 258, 280
Brinckmann, Wirtz & Co. 279–80
Britain:
  1810 crisis 108
  1825–6 crisis 124, 143, 145–7
  1857 crisis 151
  1866 crisis 151
  Anglo-Scottish banking crisis of 1772 66, 67
  Bank Charter Act (1844) 149
  bank numbers (1988) 249
  'Bankers' Annuities', National Debt 35
  Banking Act (1826) 147, 148
  banking code (1844) 150, 150 n. 118
  banking reforms in England and Wales 144–55
  blockade (1795–1815) 80
  colonial commerce 43, 44
  Dutch trade connections 40–1
  government action in financial crisis (August 1914) 219, 220
  Great Depression 248–9
  financing railway construction 140–3
  financing the war in Europe (1793–1815) 89–94, 95–8
  financing wars 70 n. 80
  inflation (1793–1815) 103–9
  international trade post-1815 120, 126–7
  Irish Act (1821) 145
  loans to Russia (1914–17) 222
  mercantile finance 88–9
  mergers and amalgamations (1918) 231
  national debt 89, 95
  navigation Acts 24
  Navy bills 99
  overseas investment (1870–1914) 172
  overseas trade (1700–80) 42–3
  overseas trade (1793–1815) 84–9
  Peninsula army, financing 96
  private banks and national corporate structures 214–15
  public debt and foreign loans 65, 66
  'revolution' in government finance 42, 42 n. 12
  small notes, forbidden by Acts of parliament 54
  steel industry denationalization 267
  and US capital market (1914–18) 221–2
  war bonds and Treasury bills 221
British Aluminium 269–70
Brooks, Samuel 141
Brooks & Dixon 152
Brown Shipley & Co. 179
Bruce, James 101
Bruges, and exchange banking 4, 12, 16
  Place de la Bourse 12
Brussels private banking (1870–1914) 193–4
BSN Company 279
Budd Company, Philadelphia 233
Buenos Aires Supply and Drainage Company 176
bullion and coin 9, 11, 17, 33
  Amsterdam market 23
  French holdings 42
Burgess, Henry 56, 98
Burkhardt, Otto 259
Burton & Falkiner 63

Caillaux, Joseph 202
Caisse d'Épargne et de Prévoyance de Paris 130
Caisse d'Escompte (1776–93) 69, 74
Caisse de Comptes Courants 110
Caisse des Emprunts (1702–15) 69
Caisse Lécuyer 131
Caisse Legendre (1909–15) 69
caisses patriotiques ('patriotic banks') 109
call money 153–4
Calonne, Controller-General 73
Calvinists:
  Frankfurt 28
  Hamburg 25, 27
Cambio, Vieri de 14
Cameron, Rondo 200
Camondo I. & Cie 186
Camphausen, Ludolf 161
capital and credit, public/private markets 39–77
  Amsterdam's merchant bankers 64–9
  banking crises in British country banking (1793) 59–61
  British country banking, emergence 51–9
  creditworthiness 14, 30

Frankfurt 75–7
London private banks, eighteenth century 43–51
New York markets 227, 228, 230–1, 266
Paris as financial centre (1688–1793) 69–75
Scottish provincial banks 61–3
trade and financial networks 40–2
Capponi bank 15
Cassa San Giorgio, Genoa 286
Cassel, Ernest 127, 173
Cassel, Germain 194
Cassel, Léon 194
Cassel, Ernst 175
Castle Bank, Bristol 145
Central Association of Bankers, Germany 205, 243
Central Banks 228–30
Chalmers, Guthrie & Co. 254
Champagne fairs 11, 27
Chandler, Alfred 173
Chapman, S. D. 86, 88, 123
Charing Cross Electric Supply Company 252
Charpenay & Cie., Grenoble 203
Chartered Bank of Vienna 143
Chase Manhattan 282
cheques ('drawn notes') 30–1
origins 8, 10
and valorem duty 152
Child & Co. 235
Child's Bank 35, 38
Citigroup 282
Citroën 237–8
Citroën, André 237–8
City Bank, London 167
City of Glasgow Bank 168
Clayton, Robert 32
Cobbold, Cameron 270
Cohen, Levi Barent 86
Collet, Mark W. 229
Cologne 241–2
1870–1914 191
'railway private bankers' 138
Colonia Insurance Group 191, 280–1
commanditaires 204
commandite partnerships 162
Commerz- und Disconto Bank 189, 208
Commonwealth coinage, Britain 34
Compagnie d'Assurances Génèrales 130
Compagnie des Indes Orientales (East India Company) 71–2
Compagnie du Nord 277
Compagnie des Quatre Canaux 156
Compagnie Française des Mines de Bor 185
Compagnie Royale d'Assurance Maritimes 130
Comptoir d'escompte 158–9, 181, 203
Concordia Lebensversicherung 191
Congo 194
Congress of Vienna (1814–15) 83, 116
Consett Iron Company 252, 267
Consols 71, 92
1817 117
1825 119
'contango' operations 99
Constance, Councils of (1414–18) 14
Constantinople 8
Continental Blockade, Napoleonic 79, 83, 85
copper industry, Cornwall 54
Cordelois, De Vrijier & Mees 68
Cornish Miners' Bank, Truro 52 n. 39
cotton industry, British 106, 106 n. 87
exports (1793–1815) 85–7
Counter-Reformation 9
country banking, British 4, 47, 80
1870–1914 199–200
bill brokers 102
clearing operations 107
crises in 59–61
decline 148–51
emergence of 51–9
expansion (1793–1815) 104–5
and the legal profession 56
liquidity (1793–1815) 100, 101
and local industry and mining 54–5
note-exchange arrangements 107
note issue 105–7, 106 n. 87
provincial–metropolitan links (1793–1815) 100–1
suspension of cash payments (1797) 105, 108
Yorkshire 59
and the woollen trade 58
see also individual banks and houses
Court Banker functions, France 71
Courtois, Armand 240
Courtois, Louis 240
Courtois, Toulouse 203, 239, 240, 259–60, 264
Coutts, John 61
Coutts & Co. 167, 169, 235
Crédit Agricole 249
credit banks, Germany (1880s) 191–2
Crédit du Nord 205, 239, 264
Crédit Foncier 157
Crédit Industriel et Commercial 181
Crédit Lyonnais 152, 159, 199, 203
and war indemnity loans (1870) 181
Crédit Mobilier 5, 139, 143, 144, 157–8, 163
Crédit Suisse 196, 248
Credit-Anstalt, Vienna 197, 198, 247
Credito Italiano 247
creditworthiness 14, 30

Cromwell, Oliver 33, 34, 41
Crystal Night, Nazi Germany (November 1938) 257
Cunliffe, Brooks & Co. 141, 154
Currie, Bertram 170, 176
Currie & Co. 153, 170
Curtis Campbell & Co. 179

Daladier, Edouard 261 n. 55
Danat Bank, Berlin 247
Darier bank 282
Därmstädter Bank 163, 187, 189
Dassier, Auguste 111, 131
David, Feidel 76, 77
David-Weill, Pierre 279
Davillier family 129
Davis, R. 84
Davison-Bland & Co., Newcastle 52 n. 39
Dawes Loan to Germany (1924) 227, 245
Dawes Plan (1924) 227
d'Eichthal bank 131
d'Eichthal, Adolphe 128 n. 50, 138
De Beers Consolidated Mines 174, 175
de Habers 128
de Kock, Jean-Konrad 74
de Neutflize et Cie 182
de Neuflize, Schlumberger & Cie 275, 276
de Smeth 81
de Stein 274
Deichmann, Ludwig 163
Delbrück, Adelbert 191, 207–8, 212
Delbrück, Ludwig 215
Delbrück, Leo & Co. 207–8, 212
Delbrück, Schickler & Co. 188
Delessert, Etienne 73, 111
Delessert bank 128, 130, 131
Delvider, Henri & Cie 204, 205
Demachy & Cie 275
Demachy et F. Seillière 182
deposit banking 8–9, 14
Dessauer Bank 161
Deutsche Bank 187, 191–2, 194, 207–8, 211, 212, 218, 225, 258–9
  links with other banks 206
Deutsche Überseesiche Bank 192
Deutsche-Asiatische Bank 190, 192
diamond trade 97
Dillon Read 227–8, 281
Disconto-Gesellschaft 162, 163, 187, 189, 191, 192, 198
discounting (bills of exchange) 17, 21, 22, 25, 38, 53
Donon, Armand 159
Dorner, Martin 95
double-entry accounting 14
Down bank 47
Dresdner Bank 187, 189, 208, 247, 282, 258
Dreyfus J. & Co. 186, 189, 258
Du Fays 87
Dubois, Léopold 212
Dufour, Arlès 159
Dufour, Louis 111
Dumouriez, General Charles 74
Dundee Banking Co. 60

East Anglia, country banking 58–9
East India Company 33, 34, 38, 42, 48, 93, 122
East India Company, Dutch (Veenigde Oostindische Compagnie/VOC) 22–4
Edict of Nantes (1598) 41
Edinburgh, emergence of private banking 61
Edward III 14
Edward Johnston & Co. 179
Elford, Sir William 145
Emile Erlanger & Co. 127, 179, 274
Enskilda Bank, Stockholm 198–9, 223, 245
Equitable Life Assurance 45
Erlanger & Co. 189
Errera, Jacques 208
escompteurs 4
Esdailes bank 47, 100
Eurobond market 271, 272–3
Eurocredits 271
Eurodollars 271–2, 271 n. 93, 276
Euromarkets, emergence of 6, 271–4
Exchange Bank, Hamburg 27
exchange fairs 13
exchange rates 9, 20
  Amsterdam price current 20
Exchequer bills, British 99, 101
  driving the 1793 crisis 60

Fairholme, Adam 61
Fairholme, Thomas 61
Farrer, Gaspard 219
Federal Reserve Bank, New York 228
Ferguson, Niall 124, 174
Fermiers Généraux (tax farmers) 70
financial journalism, birth of 13
Finsider Company 273
First World War 5, 217–24
  financing 218–24
'Five Bells', Lombard Street, London 51
Fleming, Robert & Co. 173, 282
Florence, merchant bankers 4, 11, 13–15
florin banco 20, 21–2
florin current 21–2
'Flying Horse', London 32, 33
Fordyce, Alexander 45, 66
Forster country agency 47
Fould, B. L. & Fould-Oppenheimer 128 n. 50, 134–5

France 4
  1793–1815 109–12
  1825 financial crisis 157
  1848 revolution effects 158, 160
  Banking Act (1941) 200
  Banking Law (1945) 275
  banque d'affaires/banques de dépôts 275–6
  Boubon restoration (1815) 113–16
  corporate investment banks 156–61
  corporate/local private bank relations (1870–1914) 203
  First World War finance (1914–18) 222, 223
  franc as international currency 128–9
  franc revaluation (1920s) 237
  franc speculation (1924–6) 226
  Great Depression 248, 259–63
  haute banque/joint-stock bank competition (1870s) 181–2
  hyperinflation (1795) 109, 110
  industrial expansion post-1815 129
  influence of private bankers 215
  investors confidence in *rentes* (post-1815) 115–16
  national debt (1915) 113–14
  national debt (1919–21) 225–6
  Paris and the provinces (1920–31) 236–40
  provincial private banking decline 159–61
  public debt and foreign loans 65
  railway construction and corporate banks 157–8
  regional private banks (1870–1914) 200–5
  Royal Treasury 71
  Russian investments (1888–1914) 183
  sale of Louisiana to the American federal government 97–8
  state finance, eighteenth century 69–70
  taxation system 69–70
  under-banked theories 201
  Vichy regime banking laws (1941) 262
  war bonds and Treasury bills 222
  war indemnity payments to Prussia (1870) 180–1
  war indemnity payments to the Allied coalition (1815) 114–16
Franco-Prussian War (1870) 171, 180–1, 197
Frankfurt 3, 5, 75–7, 127, 128, 138, 163
  *c.*1300–1700 25–9
  1793–1815 83
  1870–1914 189–90
  Börse (established 1615) 28
  fairs price current 28
  foreign exchange transactions 28
  Jewish community 28–9
  printed market price data 13
  Wessil (1402) 20
Frankfurter Bankverein 209
Fraser, Lionel 269, 270
Freame, John 46
Freame & Barclay 37
Freame & Gould 46
Fredk. Huth & Co. 85, 179, 219–20, 251, 254
French Revolution 74, 80
Frescobaldi merchant bank 13
Friedr. Schmid & Co. 206–7
Frühling & Goschen 179, 220
Fugger merchant bankers 15
Fulchiron, Lyons 73
Futter, Henry 34

Gans & Cie 186
Garat, Dominique-Joseph 261 n. 55
Gebrüder Arnhold 188, 241, 258
Geneen, Harold 278
General Motors 232, 238
Geneva 244, 282, 286
  1870–1914 196–7
  bankers in Paris 72–3, 72–3 n. 87
  survival of private banks 282
Genoa 11
  bills of exchange 2
  inter-account movements 7–8
Germany:
  1870–1914 187–93
  bank numbers (1988) 249
  banking crisis (1931) 250–1
  company law (1870) 210
  credit banks (1880s) 191–2
  'Crystal Night' (November 1938) 257
  Dawes Loan (1924) 227
  First World War finance (1914–18) 222–3
  First World War reparations 225–6
  Gestapo 258
  government exchange controls (1931) 250
  Great Depression 248
  inflation and consolidation (1920–31) 240–4
  influence of private bankers 215
  Jewish bankers 1930s 255–9
  Jewish economic sector 257
  Nuremberg Laws (1935) 256
  post-1945 279–81
  regional private banks (1870–1914) 205–7
  two-tier boards (*Vorstand/ Aufsichtsrat*) 210–11, 212
  universal banks 161–4
  and US capital markets (1914–18) 223
  war bonds and Treasury bills 222
  see also individual cities
Gibbs, A. & Sons 121
Gibbs, Lyle 88
Gill, Francis 123
Gilliat J. K. & Co. 179

Girardot bank 73
Gladstone, William 159, 170
Glasgow, private banking 61–2
  Ship Banks 62
Glyn, George Carr 142–3
Glyn, Richard Car 46
Glyn, Sir Richard 44, 45, 46
Glyn, Mills & Co. 92, 100, 209, 235–6
Glyn, Mills, Currie & Co. 167, 169, 170–1
Glyns bank, London 50, 66, 153
Godfrey, Michael 36
Godschall Johnson & Co. 89, 92
Goering, Hermann 257
Gold Standard 6, 225, 230
  collapse of 247
Gold Standard Defence Association 170
Goldman Sachs, New York 178, 242, 282, 283, 284
Goldschmidt, B. A. & Co. 94, 119
Goldsmid, Abraham 90, 91, 93, 101
Goldsmid, Benjamin 90, 101
Goldsmid & Eliason 87
goldsmith banking 33–5, 37–8
  note circulation 37
Goldsmith's Company, London 33, 35, 44
Goodenough, Frederick 211
Goschen, George Joachim 168
Goschen & Cunliffe 233, 251, 254
Gossler, Johann Heinrich 82
Goud, Priscilla 46
Goutard J. F. & Söhne 77
Grand Junction Railway 141
Great North of England Railway 140
Grenfell, Edward 229
Grenus, Jean-Claude 73
Grove, Leslie 52 n. 40
Grunfeld, Henry 268
Gurnell Hoare & Co., London 66
Gurney, Bartlett 46
Gurney, Henry 46
Gurney, John 46, 101, 102
Gurney, John II 47
Gurney, Richard 46
Gurney, Samuel 101
Gurney bank 46, 54, 56, 101, 107, 140, 169
Gurney family 58–9
Gutehoffnungshütte 258
Gutmann, Eugen 208

Haber, Maurice 128 n. 50
Haber, Moritz von 163
Habsburg bankruptcy (1811) 81
Hagen, Louis 215, 241
Halifax Building Society 249
Halifax Swain Bank 59
Haller & Cie 73
Hallifax, Thomas 44, 45
Hambro, Carl Joachim 127
Hambro, Eric 234
Hambro, Everard 178, 234
Hambro, Olaf 234, 270
Hambros 127, 173, 178, 220, 231, 232, 234, 234 n. 51, 251, 252, 274, 281
  assets (1955) 266
  'Great Aluminium War' 269–71
Hambros Bank of Northern Commerce Ltd 234
Hamburg 5, 10, 24, 25–7, 242–3
  *c.*1300–1700 25–9
  1793–1815 81–3, 84–5
  1870–1914 190–1
  Ashkenazi Jews 26
  Börse 25
  commodity price current 25
  Dutch immigrants 25–6
  exchange rate current 27
  Iberian trades 85
  Lutherans 25, 27
  printed market price data 13
  Senate 26
  Sephardic Jewish community 25, 26
Hanbury, Osgood 49
Hanbury, Taylor, Lloyd & Bowman 44, 47, 49
Hanburys 153
Handelsbanken 223
Hankey, Henry 37
Hannah, Leslie 170
Hanseatic ports 25
Hansemann, David 159, 161–2
Hardy & Co. 188
Harman & Co. 87
Hasselaer, Pieter 23
Hatry, Clarence 233
Hatry bank debacle (1929) 252
haute banque see under Belgium; Paris *haute banque*
Heath, Charles 88
Heath, John 88
Heath & Co. 87–8
Heaths, Genoese house 95
Heine et Cie 182
Helbert Wagg 274
Hentsch, Henri 111
Hentsch & Cie 196, 282
Hermanssen, Herman 27
Herries, John 96
Herries, Farquhar & Co. 169
Hertling, Count von 224
Hervet bank 264
Heywood, Kennards & Co. 152
Hibernia Company 188
Hicks-Beach, Sir Michael 178
Higginson, John 183

Higginson, Lee 223, 227, 274
Hill Samuel 274, 275
Hirschland, Georg 258
Hirschland, Kurt Martin 242
Hirschland, S. 188, 258–9
Hirschland & Co. 242
Hitler, Adolf 256
Hoare, Richard 35, 37
Hoare's bank 38, 66
Höchstetter merchant bankers 15
Hoffaktor/Hofjude 76
Hogguers 80, 81
Holland, Swinton C. 116, 125
Holt & Co. 235
Homberg, Octave 226
Hong Kong and Shanghai Banking Corporation (HSBC) 218, 229
Hoop, Adrian van der 114
Hope, Henry 66, 68, 81
Hope, John 66
Hope, Thomas 66, 68
Hope & Co. 66–8, 80, 81, 91, 96–8, 118, 124, 177, 195, 245
  Quaker links 66
  sovereign loans to France (1817/18) 114–16
Horneca, Hogguer & Co., Amsterdam 73
Horstman & Co. 233
Hottinguer, Baron 229
Hottinguer, Jean-Conrad 111
Hottinguer, Jean-Henri 131
Hottinguer, Rudolphe 177
Hottinguer & Cie 128, 177, 182, 185, 236, 275
  financing railway construction 139
Houblon, John 36
Howell, James 35
Huddersfield Banking Co. 147
Huguenot exodus from France 41–2
Hungary 197
Huth Jackson, Frederick 220
Huth, Johann 85

Imhof merchant bankers 15
Imperial Ottoman Bank 186
income tax introduction, Britain 89
Industrial Revolution, and the emergence of banking facilities 57–9
industrialization (early), and banking 54–5
information and data collection 12–13
Ingram Kennet & Co., Halifax 59
Inquisition 26
  and refugee movement in Europe 19, 41
insurance 64, 130–1
  Rotterdam 68
interest rates and payments 14
  legal maximum 37
International Acceptance Bank 242, 243
International Telephone & Telegraph Company (ITT) 278
international trade, post-1815 120–5
Irish banking, beginnings 63
  Irish Act (1821) 145

Japanese government, sterling loans 190
Jefferson, Thomas 98
Jewish bankers:
  'Crystal Night' (November 1938), Nazi Germany 257
  economic sector, Nazi Germany 257
  expulsion from Flanders (1585) 21
  France (1940–4) 263
  Frankfurt 28–9
  merchants as Hoffaktoren 76
  Nazi Germany 255–9
  and the Nuremberg Laws (1935) 256
  private banking houses 6
  toleration in Napoleonic Europe 83
John Brown & Co. 252
joint-stock banks 1, 2, 3, 5, 63, 64, 30, 113, 142
  Bank of England opposition to 152
  discount companies limited liability 154
  emergence of 143–55
  London 151–5, 168
  Paris *haute banque* competition (1870s) 158–9, 181–2
  Prussia 136–7, 161–2
Joly de Fleury, Jean-François 71
Jones, Lloyd & Co. 44, 47, 49, 152
Jones, Sarah 49
Jonker, Joost 195
Joplin, Thomas 146, 147–8
Josse Allard 194

Kalkenhausen, Gottfried von 259
Kaskel, Felix von 208
Kaskel, Karl von 208
kassiers (cashiers), Amsterdam 21–2
Kaufmann, Eugen 182, 185, 204
Kerensky, Alexander 222
Keynes, John Maynard 225, 230
Kidder, Peabody & Co. 227
Kimmick, Karl 258
Kindersley, Lord Robert 229, 270
Kington & Radnorshire Bank 104 n. 75
Kleinwort, Alexander 127
Kleinworts 127, 173, 174, 178–9, 231, 233, 234, 235, 266, 272, 274, 282
  First World War 220–1
  German banking crisis (1931) 250–1
Kölnische Privat-Bank 161
Kölnische Rückversicherung 191
König Brothers 173, 233
Korner, Eric 268

Kuhn, Loeb & Co., New York 190, 227, 269
Kurgan, Ginette 156
Kutter, Gustav 208
Kynaston, David 253, 271

La Touche & Kane 63
Laborde, Jean-Joseph de 71
Labouchère, Pierre César 96, 97, 125
Ladenburg, W. & Co. 254
Lafanechère, Ernest 239
Laffitte, Blount & Cie 131–2
Laffitte, Charles 140, 140 n. 82
Laffitte, Jacques 114, 115, 143, 156
Lambert, Léon 194
Lambert, Samuel 194
Lancashire & Yorkshire Railway 141–2
Lancashire banks 236, 236 n. 58
Lancashire cotton industry 106, 106 n. 87
  British exports (1793–1815) 85–7
Lancashire Steel Corporation 252
Länderbank 198
Landes, David S. 64
Lasteyrie, Charles de 226
Law, John 69
Lawrence, General Sir Herbert 235–6
Laydernier Banque, Annecy 203–4, 264, 265
Lazard, Alexandre 186
Lazard, Elie 186
Lazard, Michel 226
Lazard, Raymonde Philippe 226
Lazard, Simon 186
Lazard, Speyer-Elissen 187, 256
Lazard Frères & Cie 127, 173, 186–7, 203, 225, 226, 237–8, 261, 263, 274, 276, 277–9, 282
  German banking crisis (1931) 250
  'Great Aluminium War' 269–71
  New York 278
Le Nickel Co. 183, 184
Leach, Pollard & Hardcastle, Bradford 59
Lead Co. 46
Leadenhall Securities Limited 253
League of Armed Neutrality (1780–3) 82
Lecouteulx de Cauteleu 71, 110
Leeds Commercial Bank 59
Leeson, Nick 282
Lehideux & Cie 275
Lehman Brothers 178, 282
Leipzig fairs 23, 25, 29
Leipziger Bank 161
Lenoir & Bernard 239
Leopold, King 188, 194
Levy, Abraham 241
Lidderdale, William 176
life annuities, Paris 72–3, 72–3 n. 87
Lille 204–5
Limoges 239
Lippmann, Rosenthal & Co. 195
Littledale of Rotterdam 66
Liverpool, Lord 146
Liverpool & Manchester railway 141
Livery Companies, London 33
Lloyd, Lewis 49
Lloyd, Sampson II 49
Lloyd, Sampson Samuel 213
Lloyds Bank 104, 168, 169, 209, 213, 231
Lombard, Odier & Cie 196, 282, 283
Lombard Street, London 12, 44
London:
  *c.*1300–1700 5, 6, 29–38
  1700–80 43–51
  1815–70 121–5, 126–7
  1870–1914 166–79
  1920–31 230–6
  Post-1945 265–71
  1960s/70s 274–5
  agency system 101
  amalgamations and mergers 167–9
  Bank of England founded (1694) 36–7, 38
  bankruptcies (1781–1783) 44
  banknotes as paper money 34
  banking partnerships and equity shares 50
  Baring Brothers rescue (1890) 176–7
  bills of exchange ('bills on London') 2, 30–1, 122–3, 171, 218
  capital market 175
  cashiers and loan brokers 31
  Civil War (1642–51) 33
  Deposit private banks 44–51, 166–71, 235–6
  development as a financial centre 10–11, 56
  emergence of deposit banking 50
  Euromarkets 273–4
  financing domestic industry (1920–31) 232–3
  financing the European political settlement (post-1815) 113–16
  German and Austrian firms (1914) 219
  and the German banking crisis (1931) 250–1
  goldsmith banking 33–5
  joint-stock banks 151–5, 168
  Joint Stock Discount 154, 155
  land bank proposals 36
  merchant banks 5, 6, 29–30, 39, 43–51, 56, 89–94, 95, 96, 120–1, 122, 126–7, 132, 133, 139, 165–6, 171–3, 176, 179, 181–2, 184, 186, 214, 218–22, 227–35, 243, 249, 250, 251, 252–4, 265–7, 271, 272, 273–5, 276, 281, 282, 285
  mergers and amalgamations (1860s) 153
  money markets 98–103, 153–5

and Nonconformists and Quakers 50
Paris compared 132
pawnshop businesses 33
post-Restoration period 34
provincial connections 46–9
scriveners 31–2, 32–5
stock market, and the embryonic London money market 99–100
the 'Trinity' (1920s) 232
war finance (1914–18) 218–22
worldwide branch house networks 121–2
London & Birmingham Railway 142
London City and Midland Bank 168, 172
London Clearing House (est. 1773) 50–1, 152, 166, 185
London National Property Co. 252
London Stock Exchange 94, 171
1802 90
closure (August 1914) 219
and the embryonic London money market 99–100
London & Westminster Bank 151, 152, 167, 168
Loucheur, Louis 224
'Loyalty' loans, Britain 93
Loyd, Entwistle 141
Loyd, Jones & Co. 165
Loyd, Lewis 49
Loyd, Samuel Jones, Lord Overstone 49
Lubbocks bank 153
Lucas, Harry 268
Luther, Hans 230
Lutherans in Hamburg 25, 27
Lyons 13, 15

M.A.N. Co. 207
'Macmillan Gap' 253
Magnus, Victor von 208
Magon de la Balue, Jean-Baptiste 71
Mallet, Charles 157
Mallet, Ernest 229
Mallet, Isaac 111
Mallet Frères & Cie 109, 110, 111, 128, 129, 131, 182, 184, 275, 276
international reach 133
Manchester & Liverpool District Bank 141, 147
Mangles, Charles 142
Mansfield, James 61
Marcus, Moses 82–3
market price data 12–13
Marquet de Bourgade, Jacques 71
Martin, Pernette Elisabeth 73 n. 87
Martin, Thomas 44
Martin & Co. 228
Martin Dorner 80
Martins bank 37, 44
Masterman, and country agencies 47, 100
Matzler B.seel. Söhn & Co. 77, 188
Medici, Cosimo di 14
Medici, Lorenzo 'the Magnificent' 15
Medici Bank 13, 14–15
and the papacy 14, 15
Mees & Zooner 195–6
Melchior, Carl 230
Mendelssohn, Franz von 189
Menselssohn, Robert von 189
Mendelssohn & Co. 187, 189, 191, 192, 198, 226, 241, 243, 245, 258
Merchant Adventurers Company, London 29
merchant banks, London 5, 6, 29–30, 39, 43–51, 56, 120–1, 122, 132, 133, 139, 165–6, 171–3, 176, 179, 181–2, 184, 186, 214, 218–22, 227–35, 243, 249, 250, 251, 252–4, 265–7, 271, 272, 273–5, 276, 281, 282, 285
rise of 126–7
war finance (1793–1815) 89–94, 95, 96
Merck, Finck & Cie 188, 258
Mercury Securities Limited 268
Merrill Lynch 281, 282
Metternich, Prince 118
Mevissen 162, 163
Mexico:
'piastre affair' 119
silver shipments 98
Meyer, André 278–9
Michelet, Rose Mary 88
Middleton, Lord 45
Midland Bank:
assets (1928) 231
assets (1955) 266
Eurodollar market 271–2, 272 n. 93
Milan decrees (1807) 79
Mildmay, Humphrey St. John 125
Mills, Algernon 170
Mills, Charles 45, 46
Mills, Isabel Mary 235–6
Milton, John 31
Mines de Bor 237
Mirabaud & Cie 182, 184–5, 236–7, 261, 276, 282
Mirabaud, Paccard & Cie 131
'Mississippi bubble' (1720) 69
Mitton, Henry 46
Mocatta & Goldsmid 274
Mollier, J.-Y. 132
Mond, Sir Alfred 242
Montague, Charles 36
Montmartel, Jean Paris de 71
Moreau, Emile 237
Morgan, Harjes 227

Morgan, James 89
Morgan, Junius Spencer 127, 175, 177–8
Morgan, John Pierpont 177, 221, 223, 226, 227, 232, 281, 282
Morgan, W. & J. 89
Morgan Grenfell 221–2, 227, 232, 235, 237, 251, 252, 253, 265, 266, 267, 281
Morgan Stanley 281, 282, 283
Morris, John 32
Morris, William 233
mortgage loans 32, 33, 35, 36, 37, 38, 137, 157
Moss, John 141
Muilman bank 81
Müller, Gustav 208
Municipal Loan Bank, Amsterdam 19

Nagelmackers Fils & Cie 194
Naples, Kingdom of, loans (1821–4) 129
Napoleon 113–14
  Continental Blockade 79–80, 88
Napoleonic France 5
National Provincial Bank 148, 231, 235
Navigation Acts, British 24
Necker, Jacques, General Controller of Finance 69, 72, 73
Nederlandsche Bank 155
Nederlandsche Handel-Maatschappij 245
Netherlands 18, 245
  1870–1914 195–6
  as centre for world trade, eighteenth century 64
  Dutch bankers in Paris 72, 73–4
  Dutch Lutherans in Hamburg 25, 27
  English trade connections 40–1
  political instability, late eighteenth century 68
  revolt (1572) 17
  West Indian Company 66
Neuflize, Jacques de 229
Neumann, Luebeck & Co. 173
New Trading Company 267, 268
New York, as hub of international finance 227, 228, 230–1, 266
New York Stock Exchange 171
Nicholson, Lucas 59
Nicolet, Victor 239
Nicolet-Lafanechère, Grenoble 239, 264, 265
Nonconformists, and London 'City' banks 50
Nord Railway Company 139
Norddeutsche Bank 192
Norfolk & Norwich Banking Co. 46, 101–2, 147
Norman, Henry Warde 228
Norman, Montagu 228–9
North Metropolitan Power Station Company 252
Nuremberg 16
Nuremberg Laws (1935), Germany 256

October Revolution (1971), Russia 222
Odier & Cie 282
Ogilvie, Gillanders & Co. 179
Oldenburgische Spar- und Leih-Bank 161
Opdenbergh, François 156
Oppenheim, Carl Friedrich von 280
Oppenheim, Eduard von 215
Oppenheim, Friedrich Carl 257
Oppenheim, Helene 134
Oppenheimer, Salomon jr. 135
Oppenheim, Simon Alfred von 229
Oppenheim, Waldemar von 257, 280
Oppenheimer, Joseph Süß 76
Oppenheims 128, 134–5, 136, 137, 138, 161–3. See also Sal. Oppenheim jr. & Cie
Oustric, Albert 260–1
Ouvrard, Gabriel-Julien 98, 114, 115, 119
Overend, Gurney & Co. 153
  demise of 155, 168
Overend, John 101

Paccard, Barthélemy 111
Paccard, Dufour et Cie 158
papacy, and the Medici bank 14, 15
Paris:
  1688–1793 69–75
  as capital market 129
  as financial centre 185–6
  notaries 74–5
  and the provinces (1920–31) 236–40
  Stock Exchange 171
Paris *haut banque* 132
  1870–1914 180–7
  1930s 261
  Post-1945 275–9
  Catholic houses compared with Jewish/Protestant houses 133
  decline 159–61
  financing railway construction 138–40
  formation 128–33
  joint-stock bank competition (1870s) 181–2
  and joint-stock banks 158–9
  London compared 132
Parish, David 118
Parish, John & Co. 82, 95
Parma, Duke of 17
Parr's Bank 209
Pascatore, Jean-Pierre 131
Paterson, William 36
pawnshop businesses, London 33
Payne, Edward 48
Payne, John 48

Payne, René 48
Peabody, George & Co. 127
Peace of Westphalia (1648) 27
Peacock, Edward 236
Pease, Henry 142
Pease, Joseph 140
Peel, Robert 146
Peñarroya Company 183, 184
Pereire, Emile 138, 143, 157–8, 270
Pereire, Isaac 143, 157, 270
Pereires 143
Péret, Raoul 261
Périer, Casimir 130
Périer, Claude 128, 129–30
Périer, Scipion 130
Périer Frères 129–30, 131, 143, 157
Perrégaux, Jean-Frédéric 111
Perrégaux, Laffitte & Cie 110, 111, 128
Perth Banking Co. 60
Peruzzi Company 14
Perzuzzi merchant banks 13
Peter Thellusson & Sons 89
Peugeot Company 260
Pferdmenges, Robert 280
Philip Hill 274
Philippson, Franz 194
Phillips, John Spencer 213
Phoenix AG 191
Piacenza bank, Genoa 8
Picciotto, Edgar de 282
Pictet, Guillaume 197
Pictet & Cie 196, 223, 282, 283
Pierson, Allard 245
Pierson & Co. 245
Pillet-Will, Frédérick 131
Pisa 12
Pitt, William 91, 92, 93, 94
Plessis, Alain 133, 184, 200, 202
Poincaré, Raymond 226, 237
Pole, Thornton & Co. 145
Pollard, William 59
Pompidou, Georges 278
Portugal:
  Inquisition 41
  Napoleonic wars 97
Post, Hermann Otto von 123
Postsparkassen 198
Pouyer-Quertier 180
Praed & Co., Truro 54
Prague 16
Pressed Steel Company 233, 252, 267
Pressnell, Leslie S. 52, 55, 105
price currents 12–13, 28
  Amsterdam 19–20
  commodity 16, 25
  Frankfurt fairs 28
private banking:
  emergence of 7–11
  and family connections 1–3
  foreign exchange 2
  Italy 11–15
  legal distinctions and terminology 1–2
  portfolio management 185
Protestant expulsions from Flanders (1585) 21
Prussia:
  commandite partnership 162
  financing railways contraction 136–43
  and joint-stock banks 161–2
  revolutions (1847–8) 135, 137
  and Rhineland industrialization
    (1815–70) 134–6

Quakers:
  bankers and railway contruction 140
  and London 'City' banks 50
Quesnay, Pierre 229

Rabobank 249
Railway Clearing House 142
Raphael, E. N. 186
Rath, Adolph vom 208
Rathbone Brothers 179
Rathenau, Walther 224
Raymond and Theodor de Smeth 80
RCA Company 278
Reformation 9
Reichsbank 228, 229–30, 243
Reid, Irving & Co. 119
religious persecution and refugees *see*
    Huguenots; Jews; Protestants; Quakers
renten 24
rentes perpétuelles (perpetual bonds) 71
rentes viagères (life annuities) 71, 72–3 n. 87
Réunion Financière 158
Reynolds Metals 269–70
Reynst, Hendrik 23
Rhenish Railway Company 137, 161
Rhodes, Cecil 174
Ricardo, David 94
Ricardo, J. & S. 119
Richardson, Thomas 101–2
Richtenberger, Lazare 194
Riley, J. C. 66
Rilliet & Cie 73
Rindskopf, Nehm Beer 87
Rio Tinto Company 175, 268
Rist, Charles 229
Robarts 94, 100, 153
  country agency 47
Robarts, Curtis & Co. 89–90, 92, 93
Robert Benson Lonsdale 274
Robert Fleming & Co. 173, 282

Roberts, Richard 252–3
Robertson, Daniel 148
Robinson, F. J. 146
Rockefeller, David 278
Roman Catholic Church, and bills of exchange 11
Rothschild, Albert de 197, 198
Rothschild, Alfred 221
Rothschild, Alphonse de 158, 180–1, 184
Rothschild, Amschel Mayer 189–90
Rothschild, Carl 118
Rothschild, Edmond de 282
Rothschild, Edouard de 229, 276
Rothschild, Gustave 184
Rothschild, Guy de 237, 275, 276–7, 278
Rothschild, James de 112, 117, 118, 124, 128, 130, 131, 138, 158, 270
Rothschild, Leo 221
Rothschild, Lionel 181
Rothschild, Louis de 197, 198
Rothschild, Mayer Amschel 77, 83, 96
Rothschild, Mayer Carl 190
Rothschild, Nathan Meyer 86–7
Rothschild, Nathaniel, Lord 96, 117–18, 123, 170, 174, 175, 218, 221
Rothschild, N.M. & Co. 173–5, 178, 192, 232, 234, 274, 282
  acceptance credits 123
  Barings rescue 176
  bullion movements 124
  capital assets 173–4
  commercial affairs 1820s 123–4
  decline (post-1918) 221
  government bond issues 175
  Prussian loans 1818/22 117–18
  and South American sovereign borrowing 119
  sovereign loans 117–19
Rothschild, Salomon 87
Rothschild, Wilhelm Carl 190
Rothschild Frères 112, 128, 208, 237, 263, 276–7
  1870–1914 182–4
  1914–18 223
  Banque Rothschild 277
  capital assets 182, 184
  financing railway construction 139
  non-ferrous metals interests 183, 184
  Russian loans 183
  Russian oil intersts 183–4
  sovereign loans 129
  and war indemnity loans 180–1
Rothschild & Söhne (Frankfurt) 187, 189–90, 197–8
Rothschilds 5, 115, 173, 287
Rotterdam 195–6
  kassiers 68–9
Rougement & Behrens 85
Rover Company 267
Royal Bank of Scotland (est. 1727) 60, 61, 64, 235, 236
Royal Mint, London 33
Rückers 123
Rüffer A. & Sons 173, 254
Rüppell & Harnier 83
Russia:
  British loans (1914–17) 222
  Kerensky provisional government 222
  October Revolution (1971) 222
  state finance (1822) 118

Safra, Edmond 282
Sal. Oppenheim jr. & Cie 188, 191, 222, 241–2, 257, 259, 280–1
Saloman, E. P. 91, 93
Salomons 87, 118
Salt, Thomas 213
Samuel & Co. 179
Samuel Montagu & Co. 173, 179, 272, 273
Sanderson country agency 47
savings bank, Paris 130–1
Schaaffhausen and Company 161
Schacht, Hjalmar 229–30, 256, 257
Schellinger, Hillebrand 23
Schickler brothers 212
Schlumberger, Maurice 275
Schoeller bank 197
Schröder, Bernard Heinrich II 84
Schröder, Christian Matthias 84
Schröder C. M. & Co. 84–5
Schröder, Johann Friedrich 84
Schröder, Johann Heinrich 85, 123
Schröder, Kurt von 257
Schroders 122–3, 178–9, 124, 173, 232, 233, 235, 252–3, 265, 266, 274, 281, 282
  acceptance credits and securities flotations 126
  assets (1928) 231
  and the First World War 220
  German banking crisis (1931) 250–1
  Schrobanco, New York 234, 234 n. 51
Schuster, Felix 200, 214
Schuster-Burkhardt, Jakob Johann 212–13
Schwarz, Max 207
Schwarzenburg, Joseph Prince 143
Scotland:
  branch networks 64
  provincial banks 61–3
scriveners 31–2, 32–5
Seillière, Baron 157
Seligman Brothers 127, 179, 186, 268, 274
Seligman-d'Eichthals 128

Sephardic Jews 19
Hamburg 25, 26
London 41
Seven Years War (1756–63) 65, 67, 69
Seydlitz & Merckens 135
Ship Bank, Glasgow 62
Sieghart, Rudolf 198
Siemens, Georg von 212
Siemens Company 258
Siena 8, 11
silk trade 44, 45
London 48
Sillem, Hieronymous 114
silver mining, central Europe 15–16
Skandinaviskabanken 223
Smith, Abel 48, 49
Smith, Francis Abel 214
Smith, Robert 48
Smith, Samuel I 48
Smith, Samuel George 169
Smith, Thomas 167
Smith, Thomas I 47–8
Smith & Holt 102
Smith Bank, Nottingham 56, 57
Smith, Bevan & Bening bank 46–7
Smith, Payne & Smiths 44, 47–9, 51, 90, 91, 93, 94, 167, 169, 213
and Exchequer bills 99
Smithfield market, London 31
Snia Viscosa 260, 261
Société Comanditaire de l'Industrie 156–7
Société de dépôts 159
Société d'Investissement du Nord (S.I. Nord) 277
Société Française d'Etudes et d'Enterprises 184–5
Société Générale, Paris 152, 158, 159, 181, 262
Société Générale de Belgique 156, 157, 185, 209, 213
Société Générale de Crédit industriel et commercial 159
Société Marseillaise de Crédit 264
Société Nancéenne de Crédit 205
Souchets, Frankfurt 87
South African gold and diamond mining 172, 174
South American republics, and sovereign loans 118–20
South East Banking Co. 142
'South Sea Bubble' (1720) 38
Spain:
during the Napoleonic wars 98
loan (1823) 129
Sperling Combine 233
Speyer Brothers 127, 179
Stadnistki, Pierre 73
stamp duty (1808–9) 105
Standard Motors 267
Standstill Agreements with Germany (from 1931) 250, 251, 265
Stattigkeit (1616) 28–9
Stavisky Affair (1934) 261, 261 n. 55
Stein, J. H. 188
Steinthal, Max 212, 218
sterling 121
depreciation, Napoleonic Wars 103
Stern, Jacob S. H. 187
Stern Brothers 127, 173
Stockholm Enskilda Bank 223, 245
Stockton & Darlington railway 140, 142
Strozzi merchant bank 13, 15
Stuckey, Vincent 147, 149
subprime crisis (2007–8) 282
Sweden 245
1914–18 223–4
1870–1914 198–9
foreign loans 67
public debt and foreign banks 66
Sweetaple, Sir John 37
Swiss Bank Corporation 197, 209, 211, 212–13, 248, 282
Swiss Volksbank, Berne 248
Switzerland:
1870–14 196–7
1914–18 223
bank numbers (1988) 249
Syndicate of Swiss Banks 223

Talabot, Paulin 140, 158
Tarneaud Freres, Limoges 203, 239, 259–60, 264, 265
tax-havens, and offshore financial centres 192
Taylor, John 49
Taylor & Lloyd bank, Birmingham 49
Taylor Walker 233
Ternaux, William 130
Terray, Controller-General 71, 73
Texeira family 19, 26
Thalmann, Ernest 268
Thiers, Auguste 180
Thirty Years War (1618–48), effects on banking 29
Thomas, Emile 204
Thompson, A. G. & A. 60
Thomson, Penelope 45
Thornton, Henry 39
Thurneyssen, Auguste 138
Thyssen AG 280
Tiarks, Frank 229, 250
Tipping, Thomas & John, Manchester 57

Torras, Jacques 111
Toulouse 239, 240
Treaty of Amiens (1802) 81
Trente demoiselle de Genève, life annuities 72–3, 72–3 n. 87
Tube Investments Company 269
Turgot, Controller-General of Finances 69, 72
Twentsche Bank 195
two-tier boards (*Vorstand/Aufsichtsrat*), Germany 210–11, 212

Underground Electric Railway Company 232–3, 252
Union Bank of London 152, 169, 200, 213
Union de Crédit 162
Union Financière 197, 223
Unionbank of Vienna 226
unitary boards (Britain/France) 210–11
United Steel Company 252
United States of America (US) 125
  Banking Act (1933) 271
  and British exports 84
  Civil War debt 177
  Federal Reserve Act (1913) 230
  Glass Steagall Act (1933) 281, 282, 285
  Louisiana, purchase of 97–8
  Regulation Q 271
  see also New York
Urbieta, Juan 85
Usury Acts 31
usury laws 17, 101
  Britain 31, 99

Vallat, Xavier 263
Van der Wee, Hermann 22
Van Eeghen & Co. 195
Vandenyver, Jean-Baptiste 74, 109
Varin-Bernier, Paul 204
Varin-Bernier, René 262
Varin-Bernier bank 204, 264
Vauxhall Motors 232
Venice 4
  bank accounts 8–9
  and 'bank money' 8
  minimum capitalization requirement 9
Vere, Joseph 44–5
Vere, Glyn & Halifax bank 44–6
Vereinigte Königs- und Laurahütte 188
Vereinigte Stahlwerke 227, 228
Verley, Decroix & Cie 204–5
Vernes, Charles 111
Vernes, Felix 229
Vernes & Cie 129, 182, 275, 276
Veuve Nettine et Fils 91
Vichy regime banking law (1941) 262
Vickers Company 236
Vienna, private banks (1870–1914) 197–8
von der Heydt-Kersten u. Söhne 138
von Erlanger u. Söhne 163
von Speyr & Co. 213
von Taussig, Theodor 198
Voûte, Robert 66, 68
Vyner, Sir Robert 34–5
Vyner, Thomas 33–4

wage payments in trade tokens 54
Wallenberg, Jacob 245
Wallenberg, Knut Agathon 199, 223–4, 245
Wallenberg, Marcus 199, 224
Wallenberg, Marcus jr. 245
Wallenberg, Oskar 198–9
Wallich, Hermann 212
Warburg, Eric 280
Warburg, Felix 190
Warburg, Frederick M. 269
Warburg, Fritz 190
Warburg, Gerson 82–3
Warburg, Jacob Samuel 26
Warburg, Juspa-Joseph 26
Warburg, Max 190, 224, 225, 229, 256
Warburg, Paul 190–1, 242
Warburg, Siegmund 243, 267–71, 272–3
Warburg, M. M. & Co. 82–3, 188, 190–1, 225, 242–3, 256, 257, 258, 258 n. 50, 279
Warburg, S. G. & Co. 267–71, 272, 273, 274, 282
Warschauer & Co. 187, 189
wealth management 1–2, 6, 282–4
Wechselzahlung, Frankfurt 20
Weill, Alexandre 186
Wellington, Duke of 115
Welser merchant bankers 15
Wendel, François de 237
Wendelstadt, Viktor 163
Wertheim & Gomperz 195
Westdeutsche Landesbank (WestLB) 249
Westinghouse, George 170
Westminster Bank 165, 200, 231, 235, 251
'White Horse', Lombard Street, London 44
Whitehall, Gilbert 35, 47
Wiener Bankverein 198
William I of England 42
William I of the Netherlands 155
Willmer & Co. 77
Wilson, Marriot & Co., Kendal 140
Wilson, T. & Co. 119
Wirz, Paul 258
Wisselbank (Exchange Bank), Amsterdam 19, 20–1, 22, 23, 36, 42, 64, 286

Wixforth, Harald 192, 243, 254
Wolff, Robert 226
woollen trade, British 40, 86
  and country banking in West Yorkshire 59
Woolworths Company 252
Worms, Hippolyte 238
Worms & Cie 238, 276
Württemberg, Karl Alexander, Duke of 76
Yorkshire Banking Co. 141–2
Yorkshire country banking 59
Young Loan (1929) 245

Ziegler, Dieter 192, 243, 254
Zollverein custom union 134
Zürich Bank 196
Zurich, private banking (1870–1914) 196
Zwicker, Hermann 208

www.ingramcontent.com/pod-product-compliance
Ingram Content Group UK Ltd.
Pitfield, Milton Keynes, MK11 3LW, UK
UKHW020849150926
475595UK00003B/81

* 9 7 8 0 1 9 8 7 3 5 7 5 5 *